DEPT.H

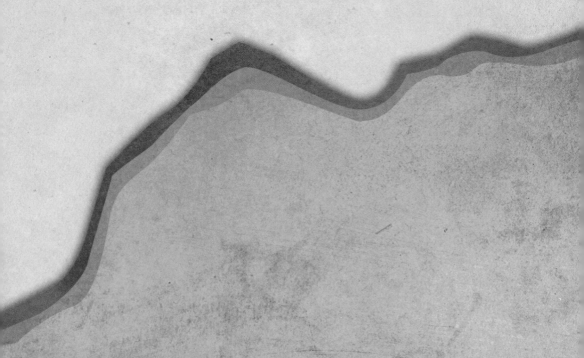

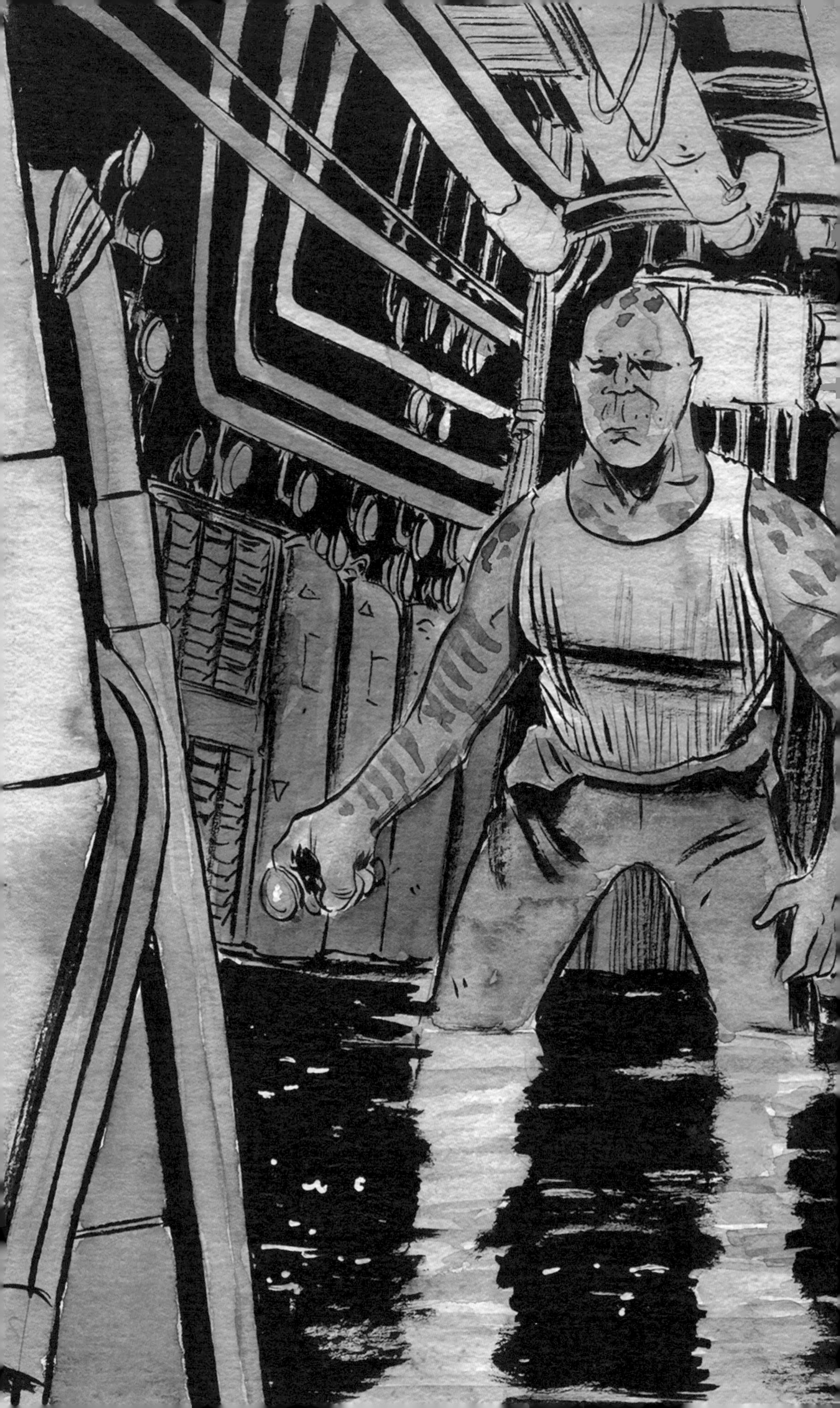

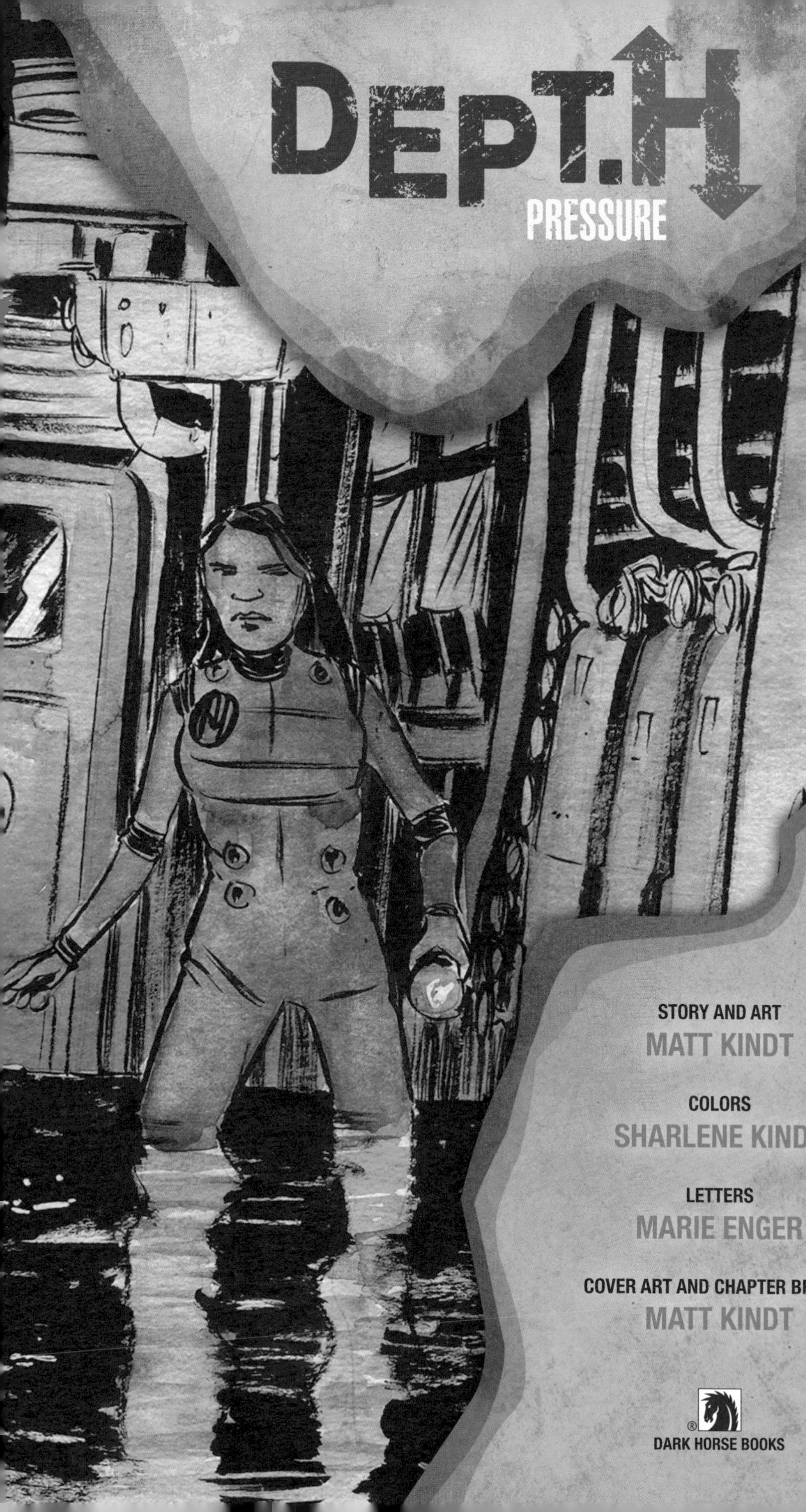

DEPT.H

PRESSURE

STORY AND ART
MATT KINDT

COLORS
SHARLENE KINDT

LETTERS
MARIE ENGER

COVER ART AND CHAPTER BREAKS
MATT KINDT

DARK HORSE BOOKS

PRESIDENT AND PUBLISHER
MIKE RICHARDSON

EDITOR
DANIEL CHABON

ASSISTANT EDITOR
CARDNER CLARK

DESIGNER
ETHAN KIMBERLING

DIGITAL ART TECHNICIAN
ALLYSON HALLER

Neil Hankerson, Executive Vice President • Tom Weddle, Chief Financial Officer
Randy Stradley, Vice President of Publishing • Michael Martens, Vice President
of Book Trade Sales • Matt Parkinson, Vice President of Marketing • David
Scroggy, Vice President of Product Development • Dale LaFountain, Vice Pres-
ident of Information Technology • Cara Niece, Vice President of Production and
Scheduling • Nick McWhorter, Vice President of Media Licensing • Ken Lizzi,
General Counsel • Dave Marshall, Editor in Chief • Davey Estrada, Editorial
Director • Scott Allie, Executive Senior Editor • Chris Warner, Senior Books
Editor • Cary Grazzini, Director of Specialty Projects • Lia Ribacchi, Art Direc-
tor • Vanessa Todd, Director of Print Purchasing • Matt Dryer, Director of Dig-
ital Art and Prepress • Mark Bernardi, Director of Digital Publishing • Sarah
Robertson, Director of Product Sales • Michael Gombos, Director of Interna-
tional Publishing and Licensing

Published by Dark Horse Books
A division of Dark Horse Comics, Inc.
10956 SE Main Street
Milwaukie, OR 97222

First edition: January 2017
ISBN 978-1-61655-989-2

10 9 8 7 6 5 4 3 2 1
Printed in China

International Licensing: (503) 905-2377
Comic Shop Locator Service: (888) 266-4226

Names: Kindt, Matt, author, artist. I Kindt, Sharlene, colorist. I Enger,
  Marie, letterer.
Title: Dept. H / story and art, Matt Kindt ; colors, Sharlene Kindt ;
  letters, Marie Enger ; cover art and chapter breaks Matt Kindt.
Description: First edition. I Milwaukie, OR : Dark Horse Books, 2017-
  Contents: v. 1. Pressure.
Identifiers: LCCN 2016034697 I ISBN 9781616559892 (v. 1 : hardback)
Subjects: LCSH: Comic books, strips, etc. I BISAC: COMICS & GRAPHIC NOVELS /
  Crime & Mystery.
Classification: LCC PN6727.K54 D47 2017 I DDC 741.5/973--dc23
LC record available at https://lccn.loc.gov/2016034697

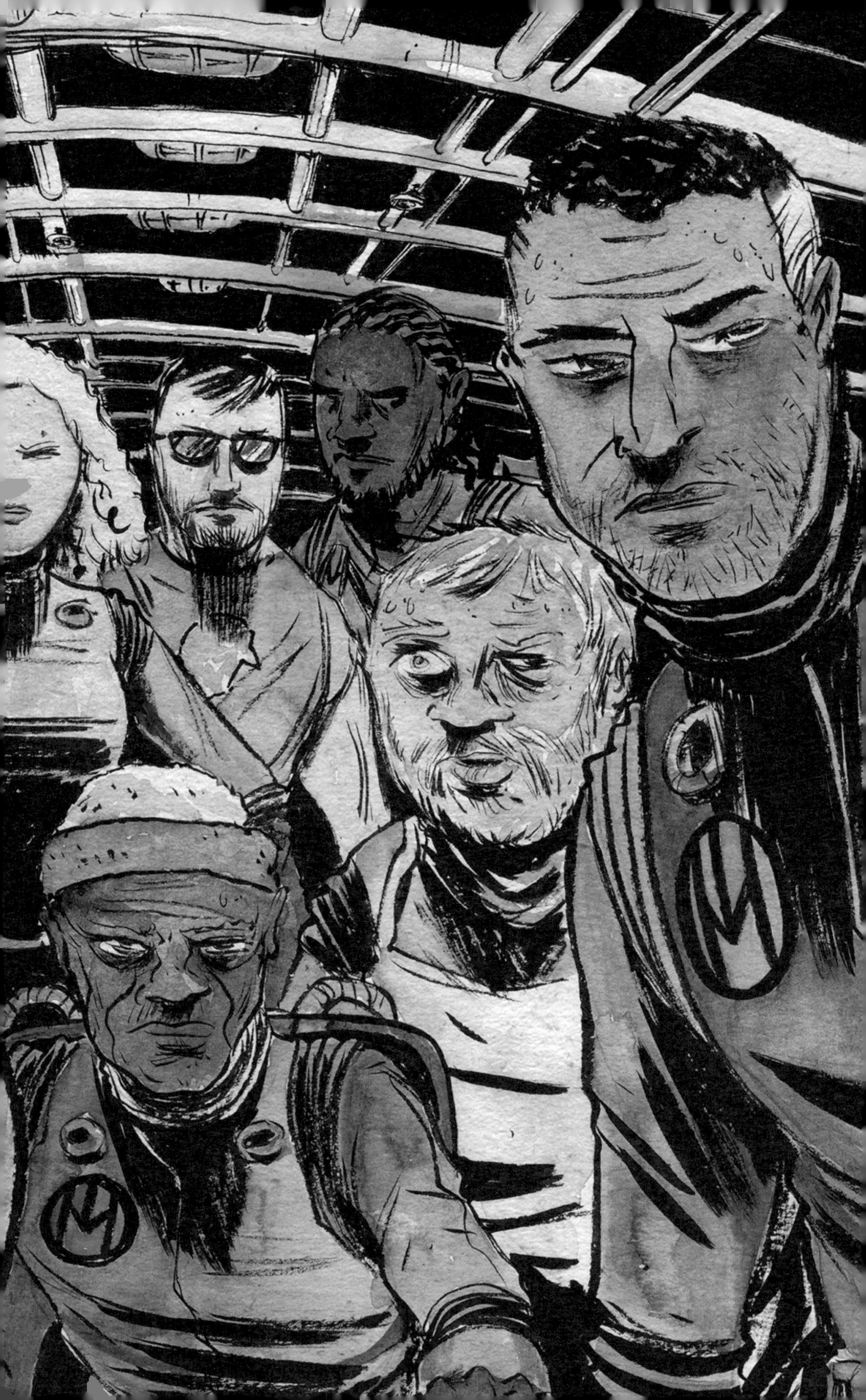

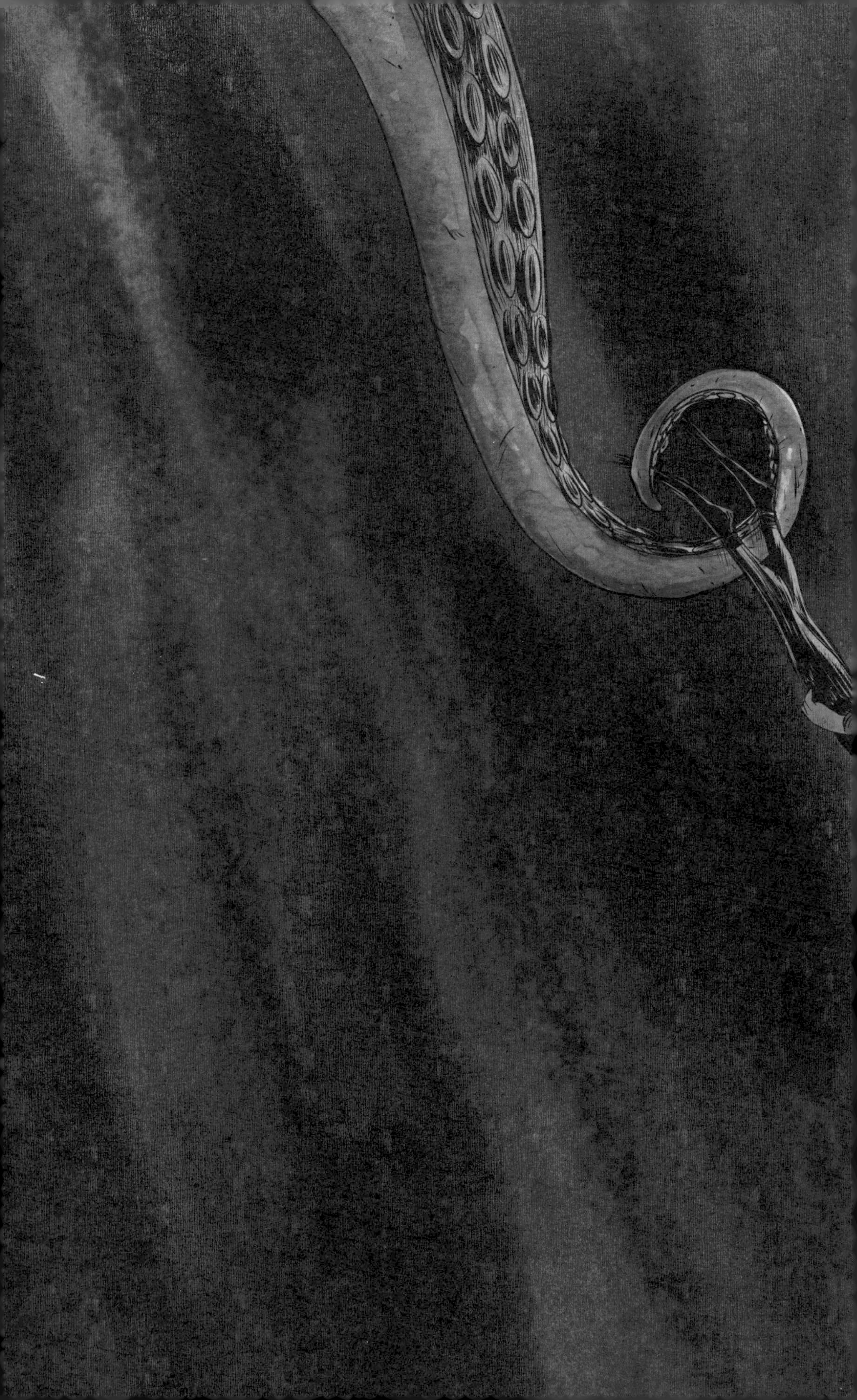

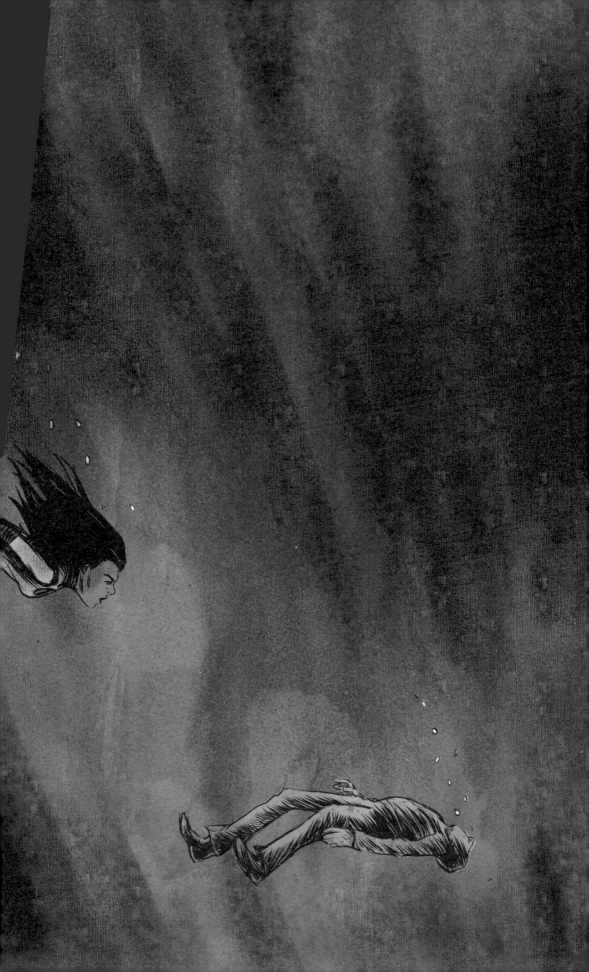

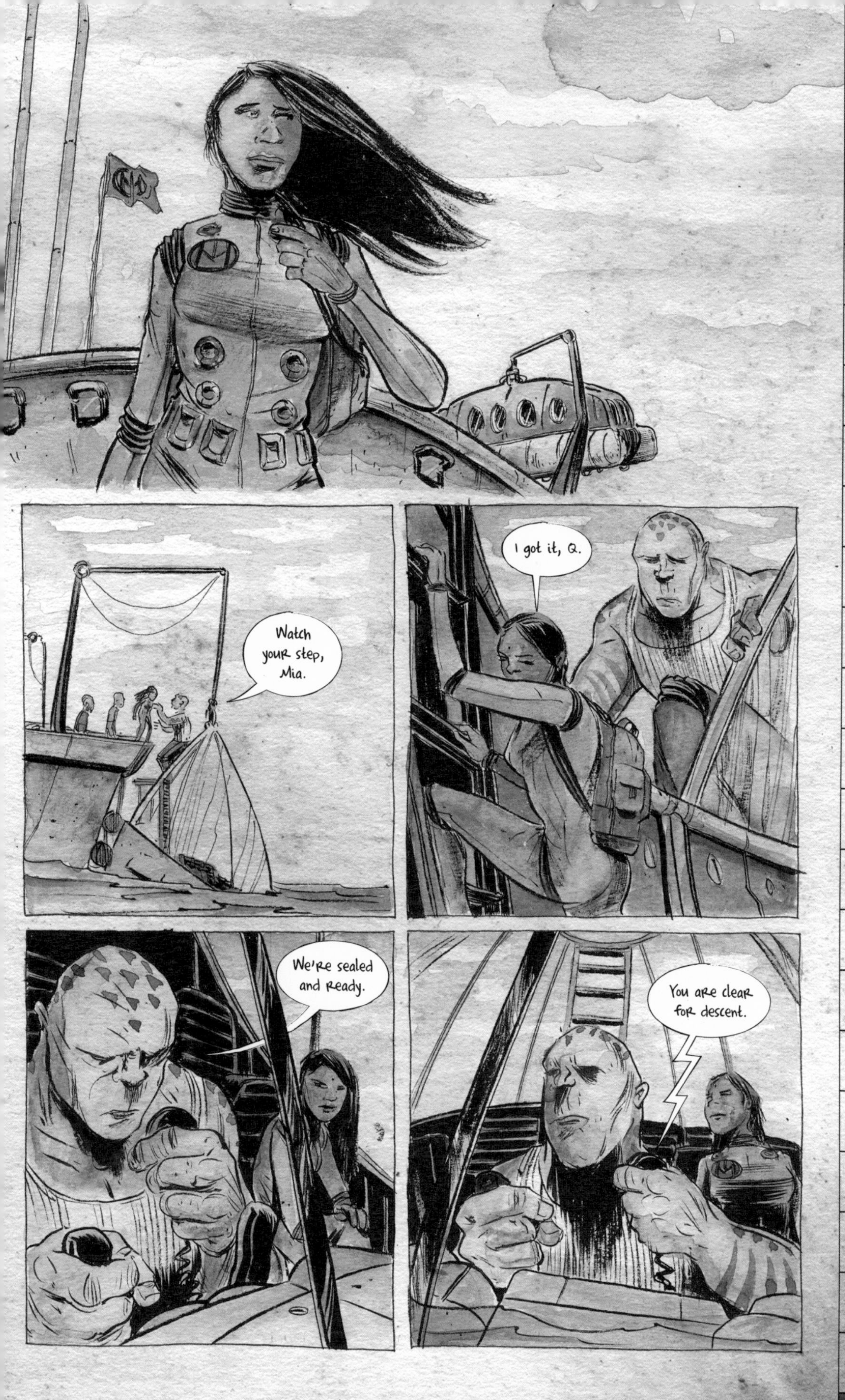
Watch your step, Mia.
I got it, Q.
We're sealed and ready.
You are clear for descent.

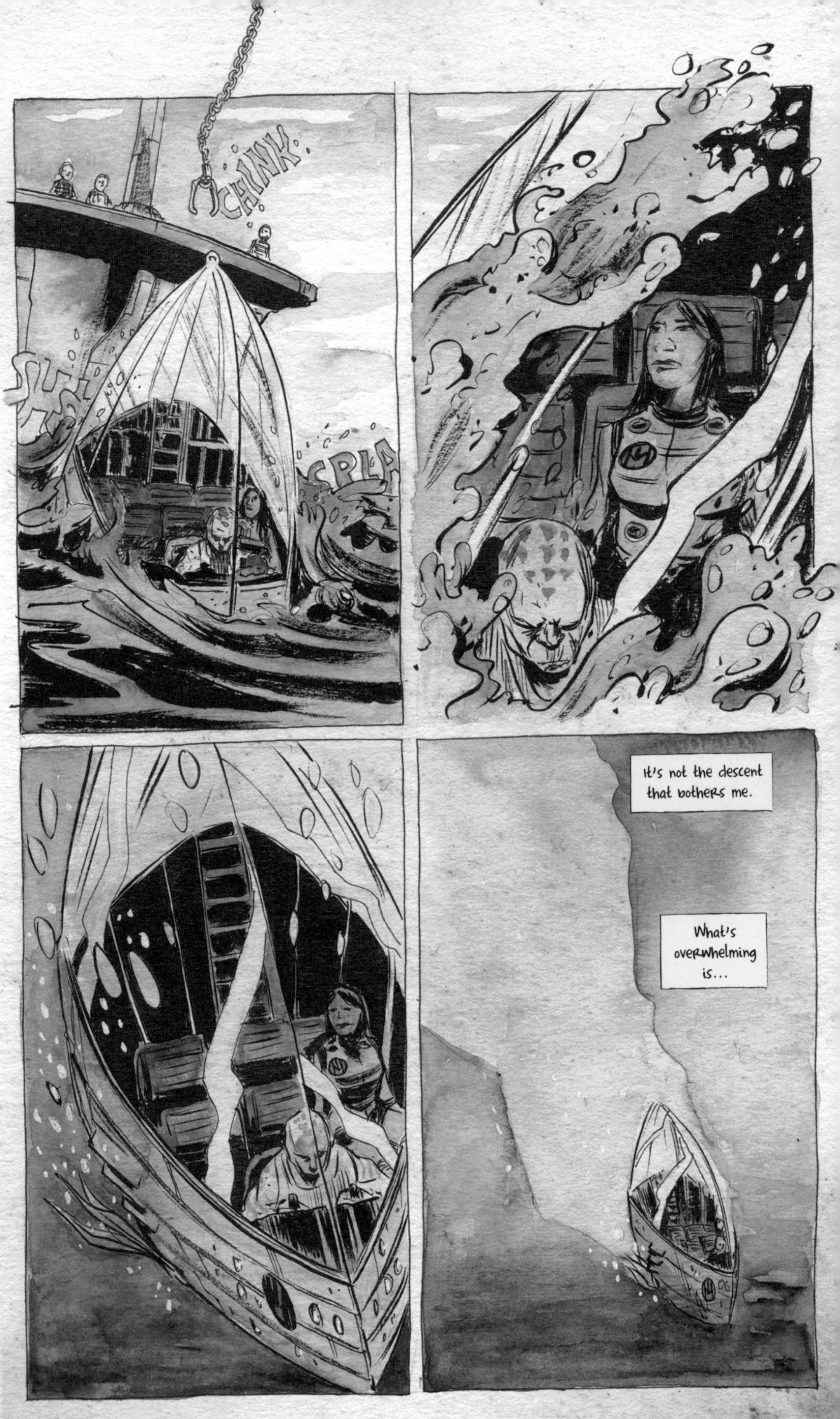
CHINK
SPLA
It's not the descent that bothers me.
What's overwhelming is...

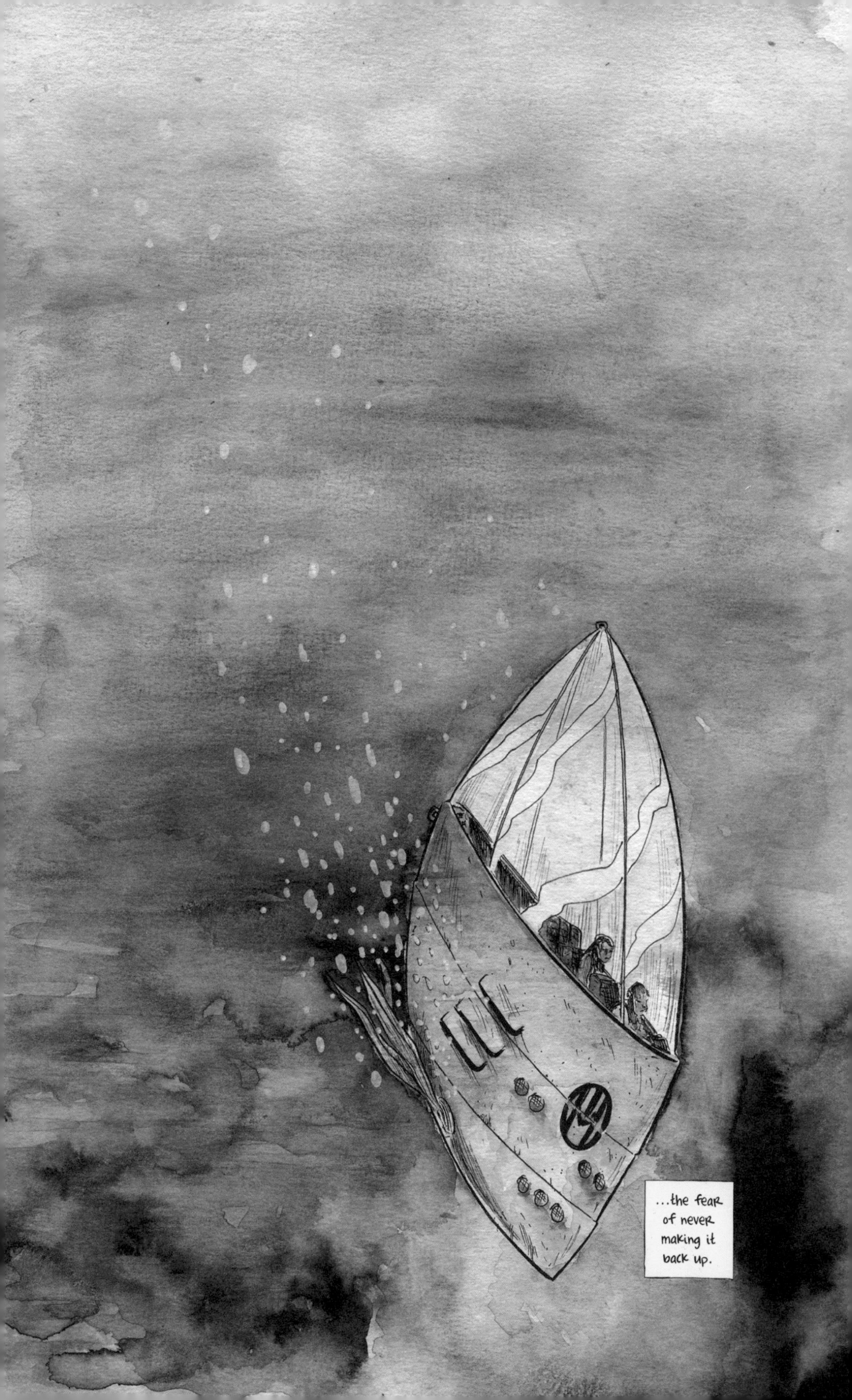
...the fear of never making it back up.

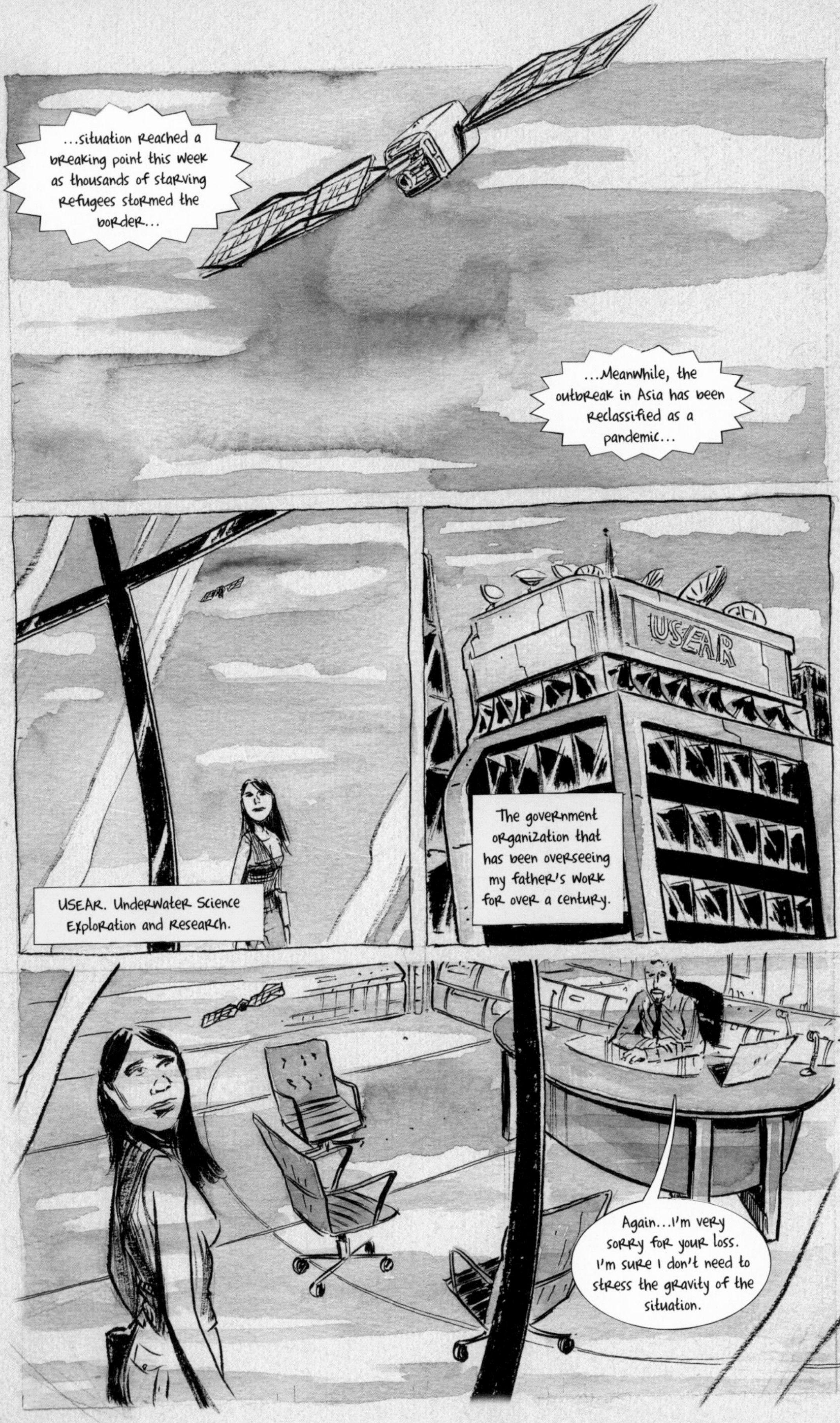
...situation reached a breaking point this week as thousands of starving refugees stormed the border...
...Meanwhile, the outbreak in Asia has been reclassified as a pandemic...
USEAR. Underwater Science Exploration and Research.
USEAR
The government organization that has been overseeing my father's work for over a century.
Again...I'm very sorry for your loss. I'm sure I don't need to stress the gravity of the situation.

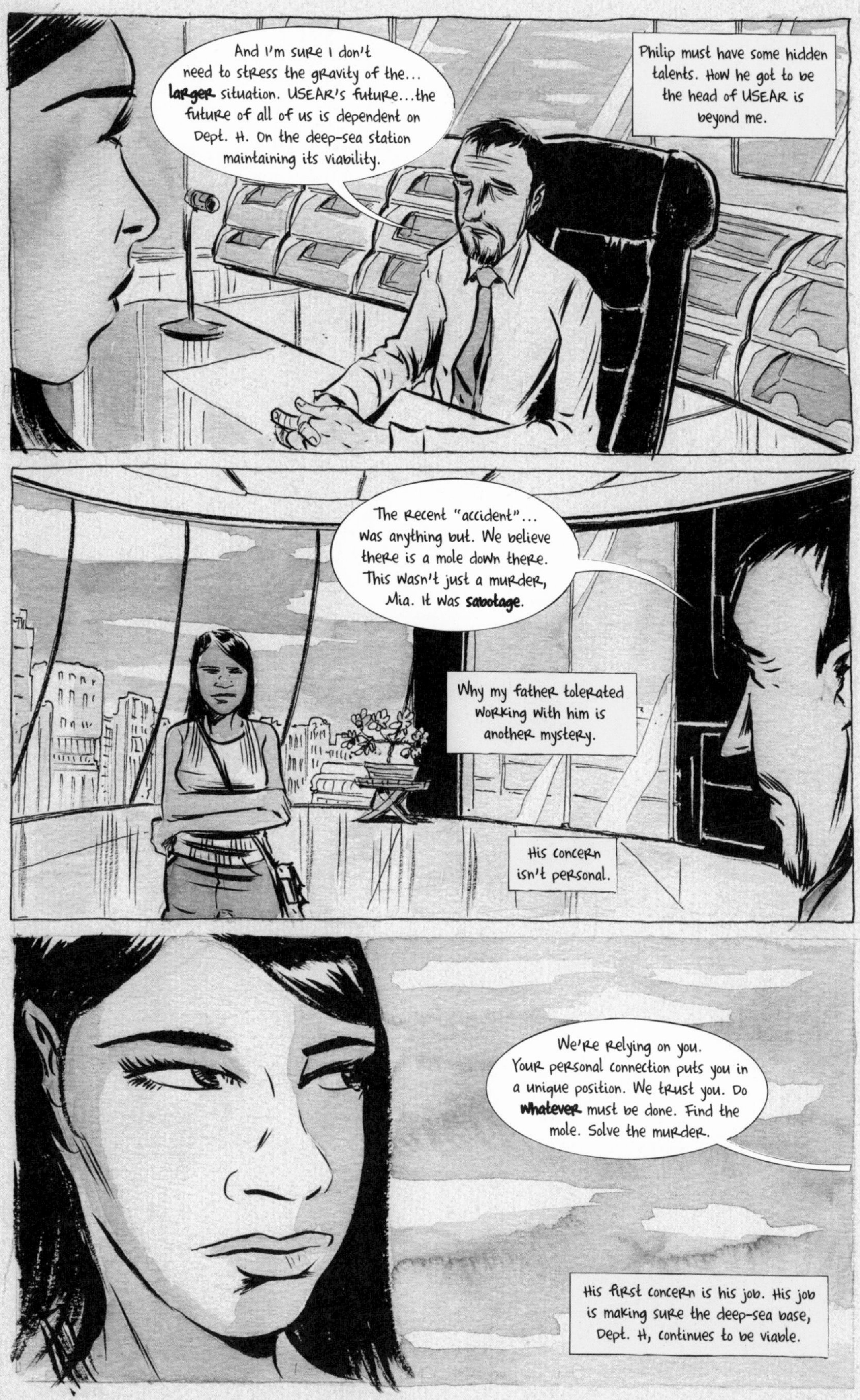
And I'm sure I don't need to stress the gravity of the... larger situation. USEAR's future...the future of all of us is dependent on Dept. H. On the deep-sea station maintaining its viability.
Philip must have some hidden talents. How he got to be the head of USEAR is beyond me.
The recent "accident"... was anything but. We believe there is a mole down there. This wasn't just a murder, Mia. It was sabotage.
Why my father tolerated working with him is another mystery.
His concern isn't personal.
We're relying on you. Your personal connection puts you in a unique position. We trust you. Do whatever must be done. Find the mole. Solve the murder.
His first concern is his job. His job is making sure the deep-sea base, Dept. H, continues to be viable.

"Treat everyone as a suspect."

It teeks a while ta get down there. We've got to rechahge the tanks and eleectreek.

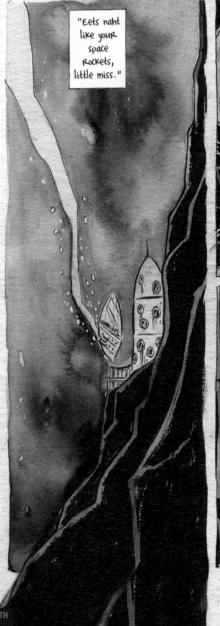

"Eets naht like your space rockets, little miss."

Outer space is a breeze compared tah what yer ganna geet down heyah.

Ah seen it break strongha men than me.

Don't worry about me, Q.

Dept. H is a specialized branch of USEAR.

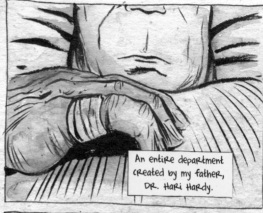

An entire department created by my father, DR. HARI HARDY.

But Dept. H has always been more than that.

A symbol of progress.

SSRACH SCRTCH

Oh. Ah ain't worried.

Optimism.

Hope.

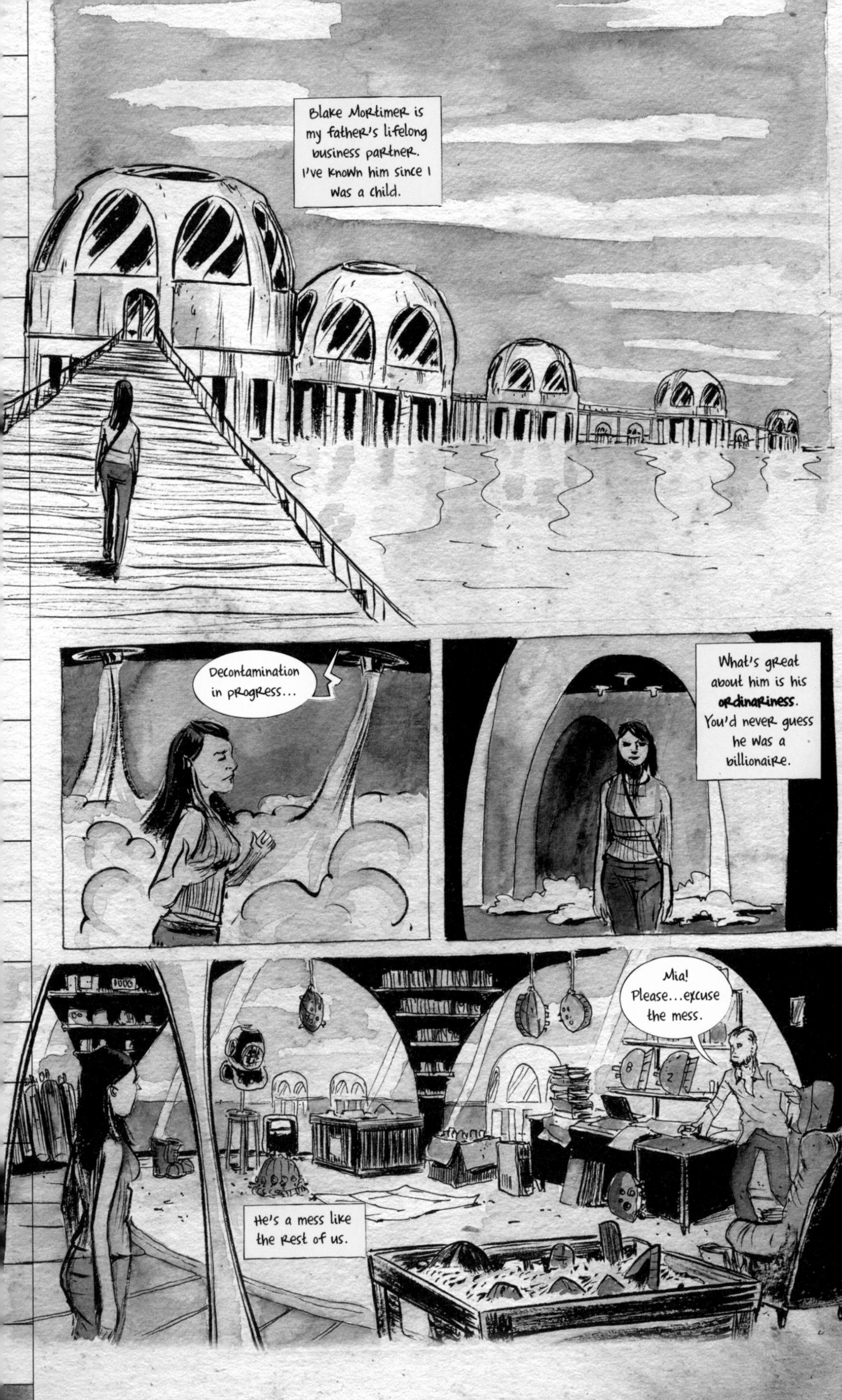
Blake Mortimer is my father's lifelong business partner. I've known him since I was a child.
Decontamination in progress...
What's great about him is his **ordinariness**. You'd never guess he was a billionaire.
Mia! Please...excuse the mess.
He's a mess like the rest of us.

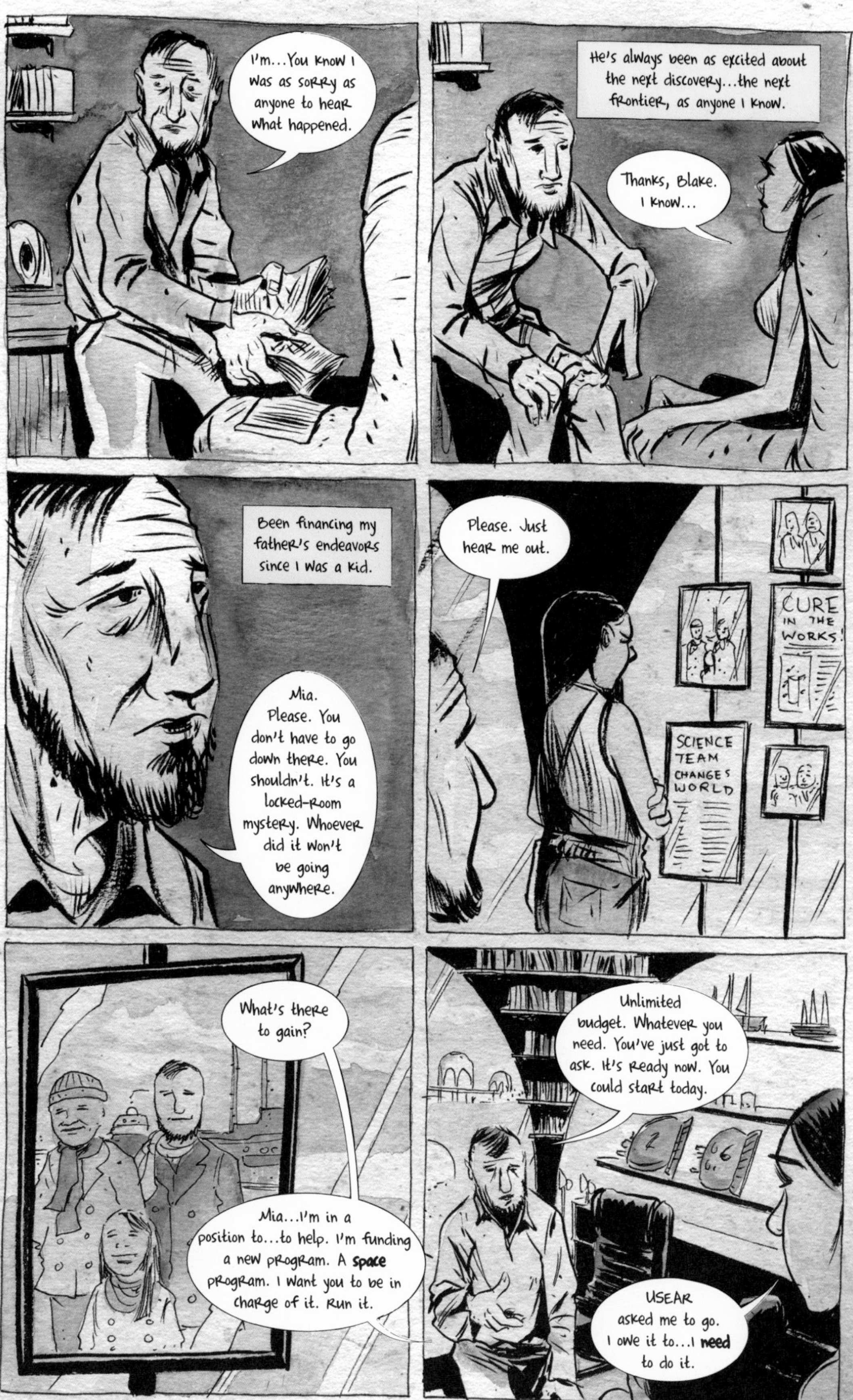
I'm...You know I was as sorry as anyone to hear what happened.
He's always been as excited about the next discovery...the next frontier, as anyone I know.
Thanks, Blake. I know...
Been financing my father's endeavors since I was a kid.
Mia. Please. You don't have to go down there. You shouldn't. It's a locked-room mystery. Whoever did it won't be going anywhere.
Please. Just hear me out.
CURE IN THE WORKS!
SCIENCE TEAM CHANGES WORLD
What's there to gain?
Mia...I'm in a position to...to help. I'm funding a new program. A **space** program. I want you to be in charge of it. Run it.
Unlimited budget. Whatever you need. You've just got to ask. It's ready now. You could start today.
USEAR asked me to go. I owe it to...I **need** to do it.

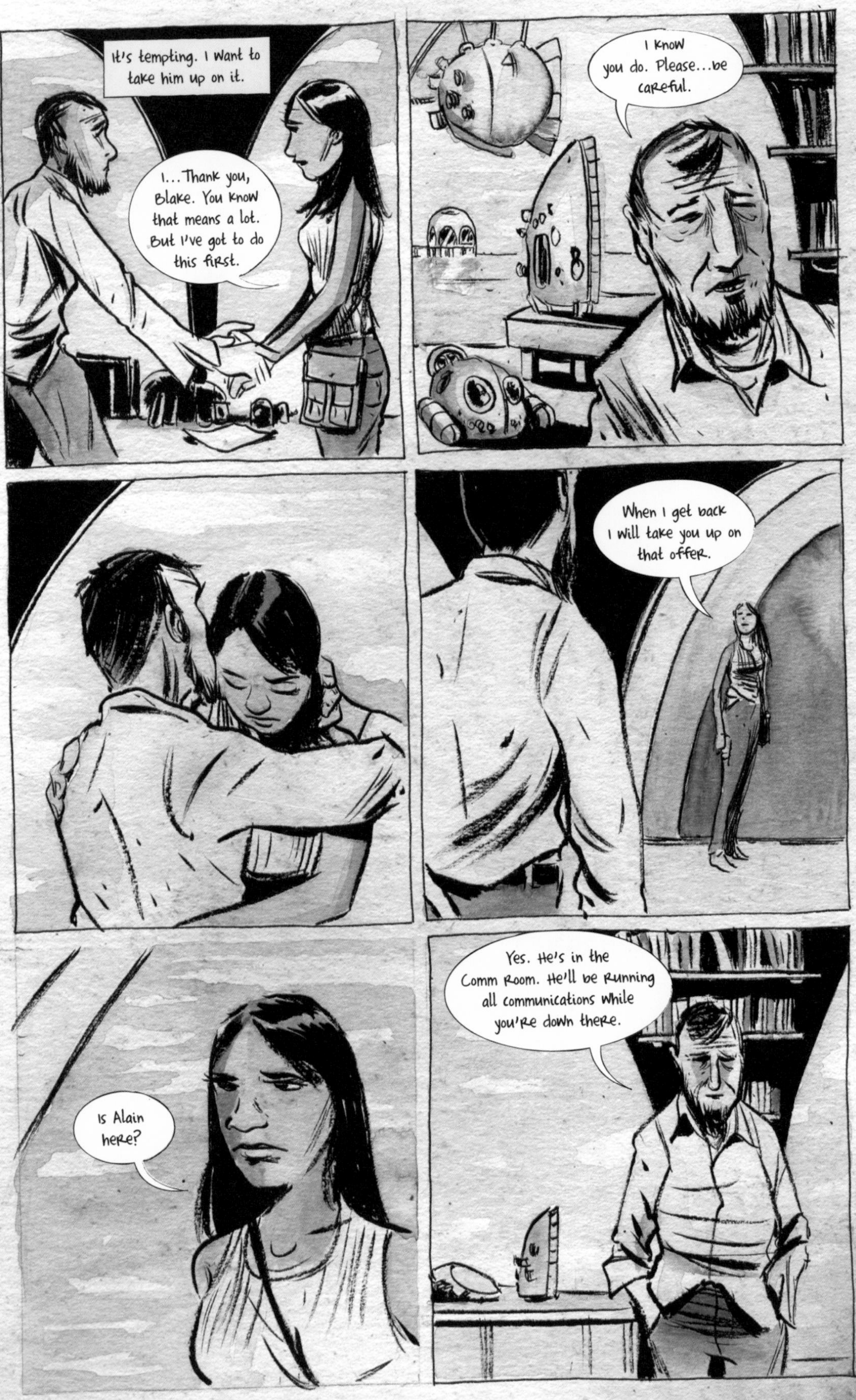
It's tempting. I want to take him up on it.
I... Thank you, Blake. You know that means a lot. But I've got to do this first.
I know you do. Please...be careful.
When I get back I will take you up on that offer.
Is Alain here?
Yes. He's in the Comm Room. He'll be running all communications while you're down there.

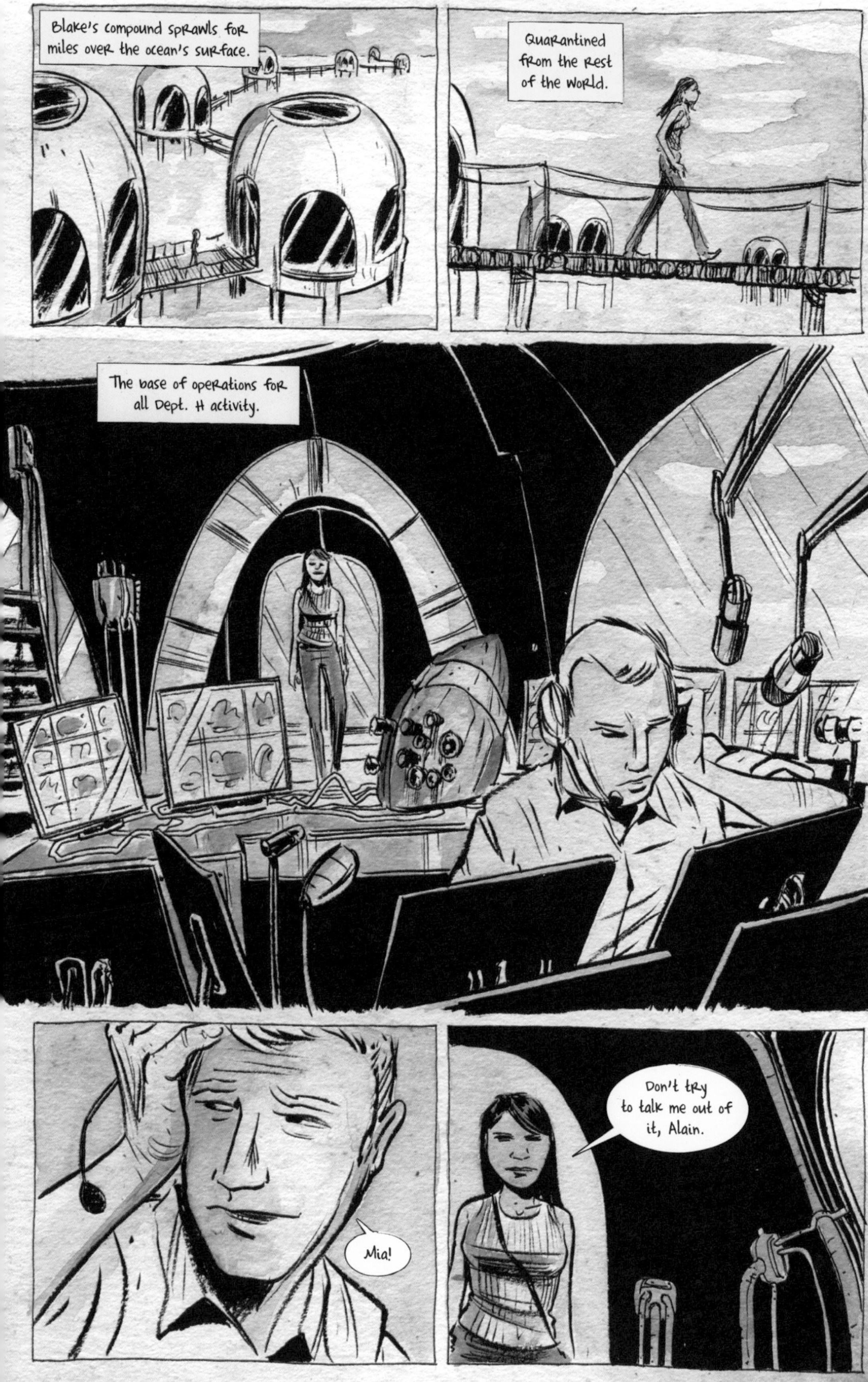
Blake's compound sprawls for miles over the ocean's surface.
Quarantined from the rest of the world.
The base of operations for all Dept. H activity.
Mia!
Don't try to talk me out of it, Alain.

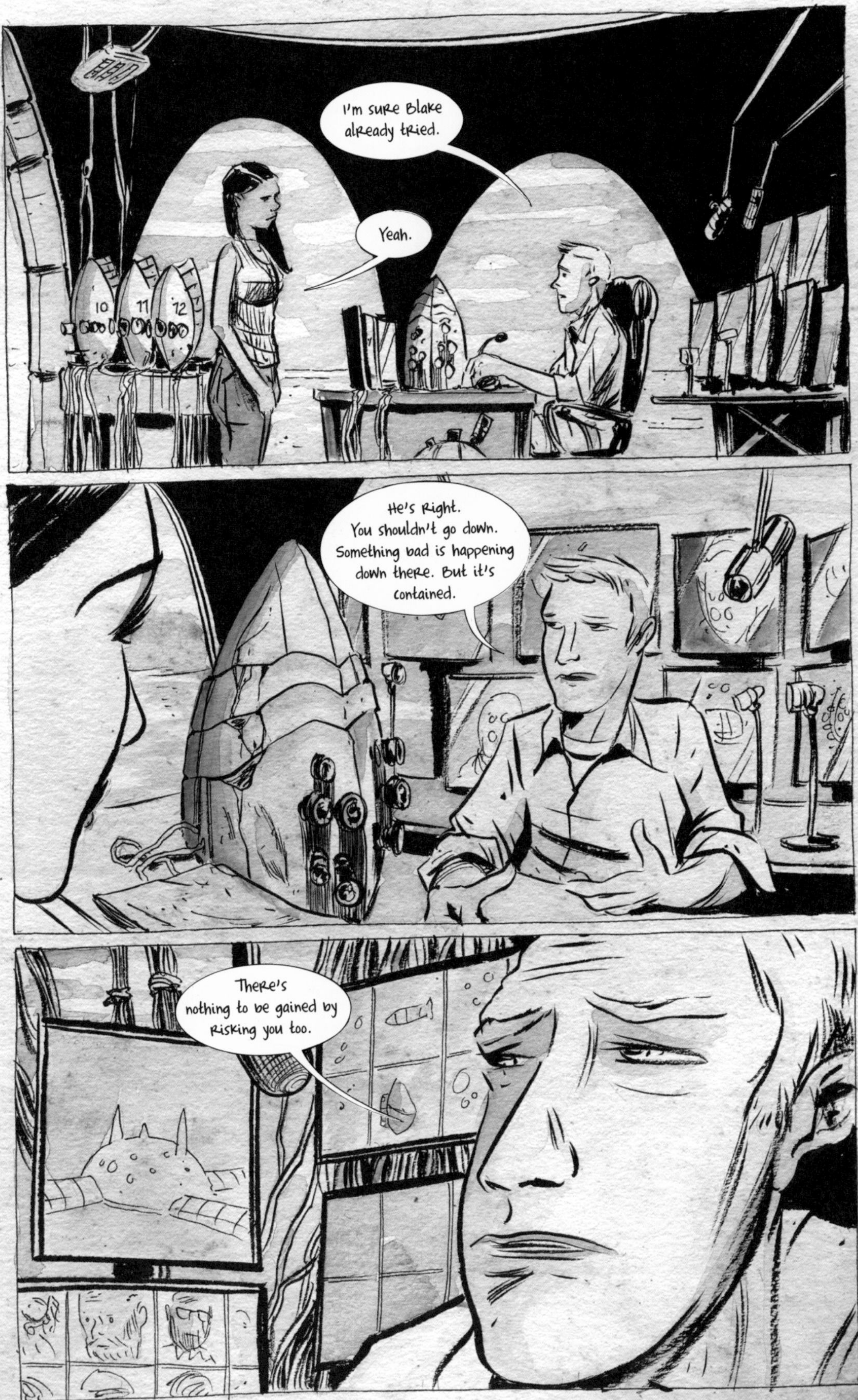
I'm sure Blake already tried.
Yeah.
10
11
12
He's right. You shouldn't go down. Something bad is happening down there. But it's contained.
There's nothing to be gained by risking you too.

There's the ~~truth~~, Alain. I'm going to have it.

Mia... please...

Don't go.

You know I have to.

Alain...

I can't think about him. Not now.

Not until this is all over.

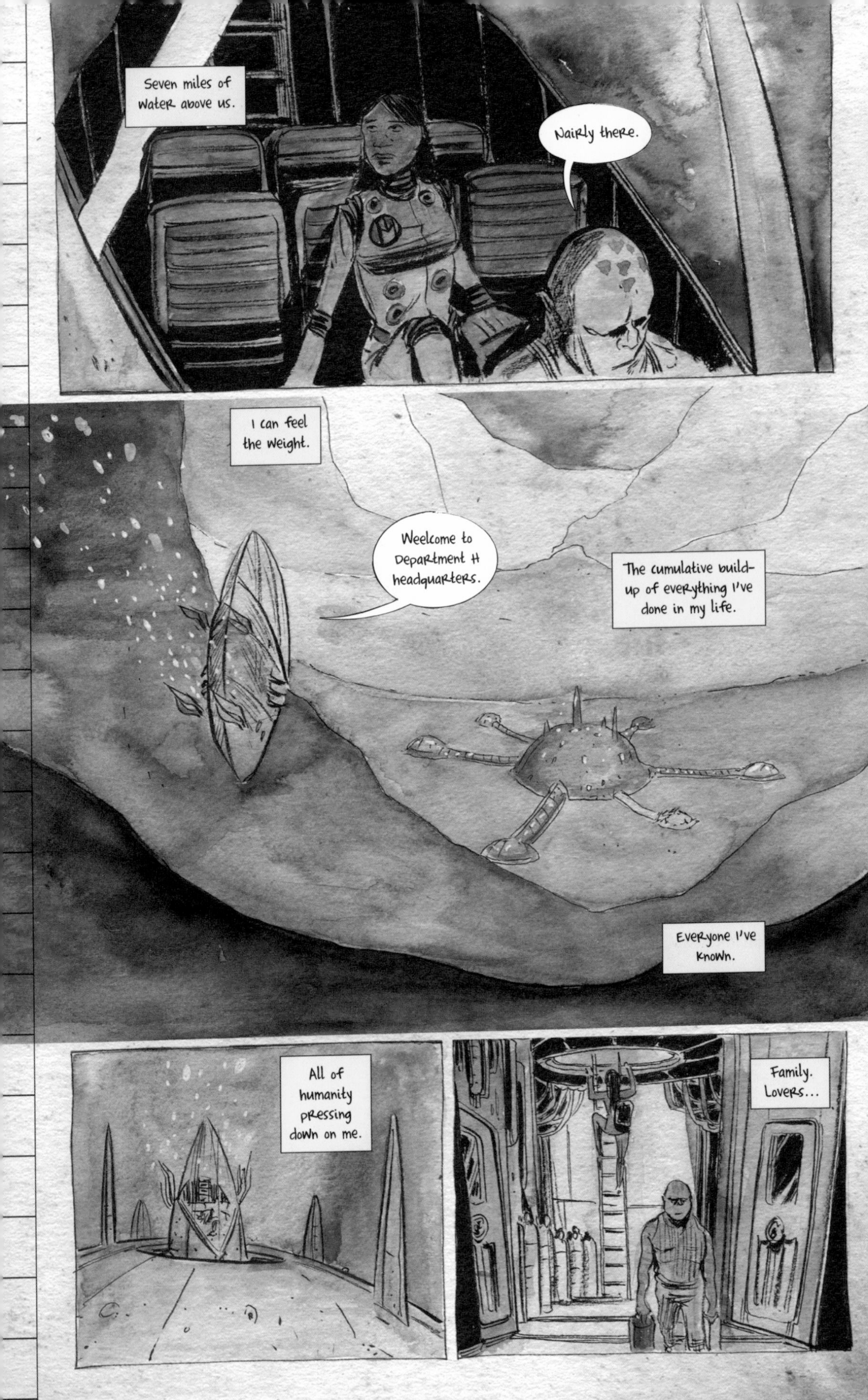
Seven miles of water above us.
Nairly there.
I can feel the weight.
Weelcome to Department H headquarters.
The cumulative build-up of everything I've done in my life.
Everyone I've known.
All of humanity pressing down on me.
Family. Lovers...

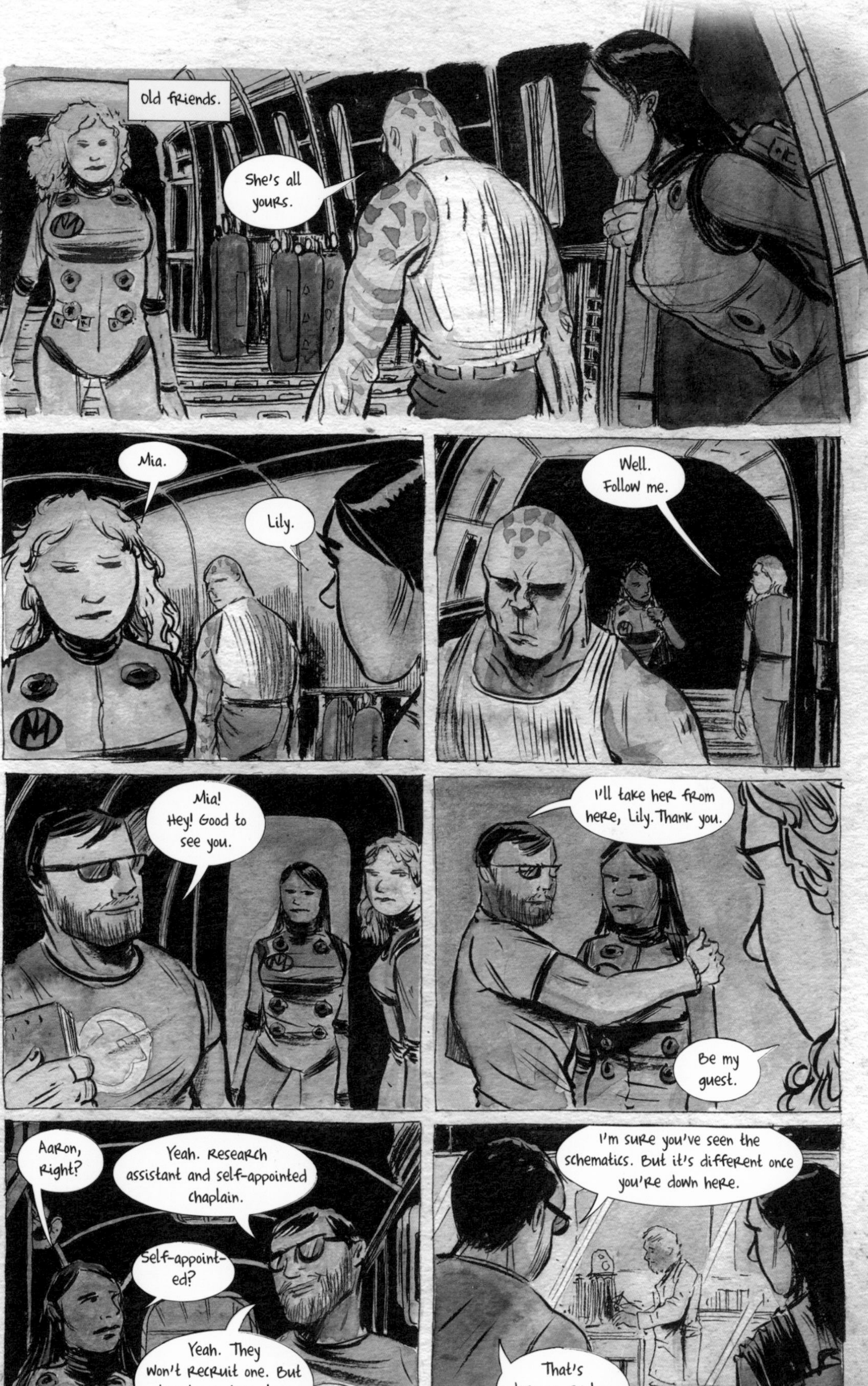
Old friends.
She's all yours.
Mia.
Lily.
Well. Follow me.
Mia! Hey! Good to see you.
I'll take her from here, Lily. Thank you.
Be my guest.
Aaron, right?
Yeah. Research assistant and self-appointed chaplain.
Self-appointed?
Yeah. They won't recruit one. But trust me, this place **needs** one.
I'm sure you've seen the schematics. But it's different once you're down here.
That's Jerome. Biology specialist.

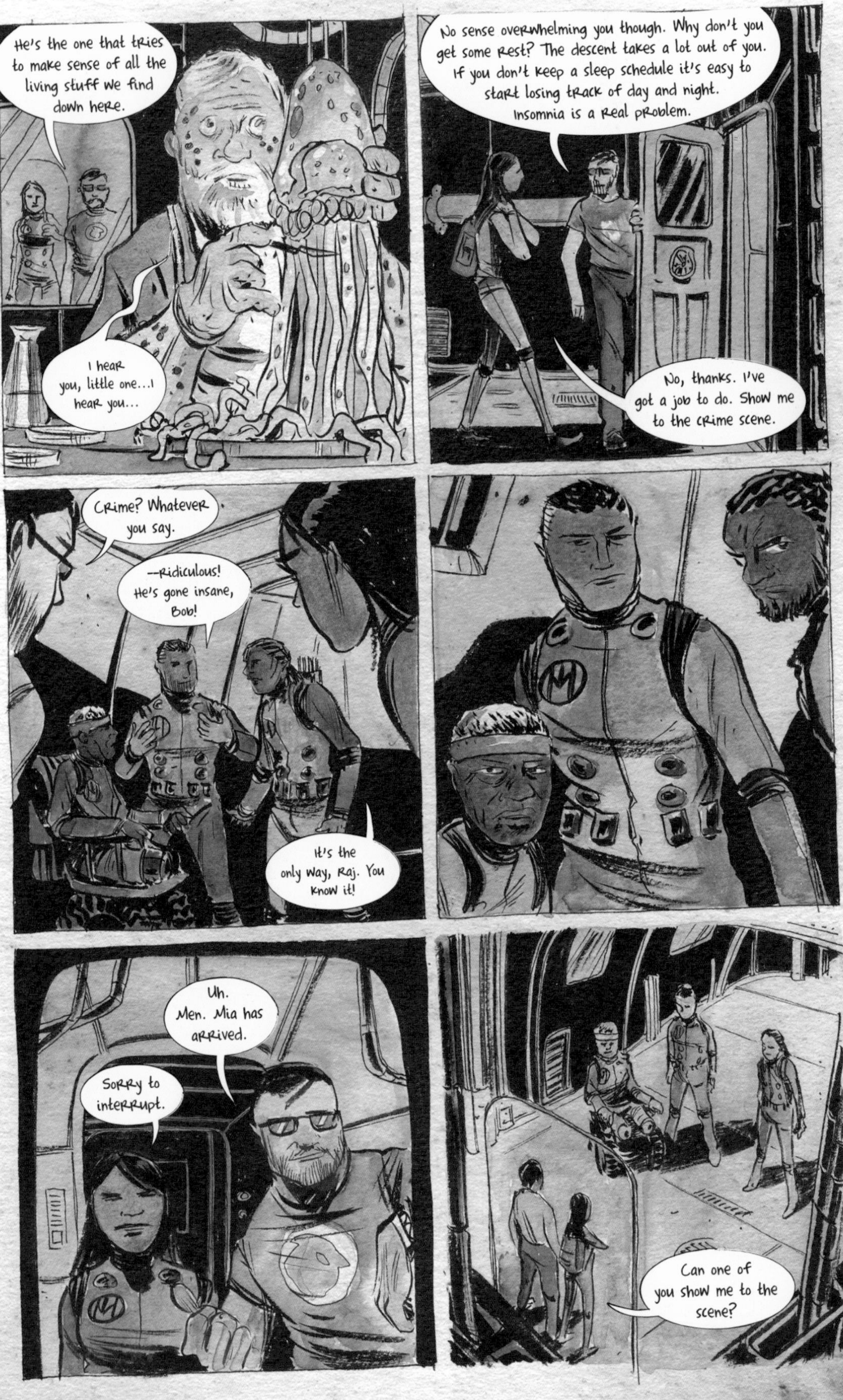
He's the one that tries to make sense of all the living stuff we find down here.
I hear you, little one...I hear you...
No sense overwhelming you though. Why don't you get some rest? The descent takes a lot out of you. If you don't keep a sleep schedule it's easy to start losing track of day and night. Insomnia is a real problem.
No, thanks. I've got a job to do. Show me to the crime scene.
Crime? Whatever you say.
--Ridiculous! He's gone insane, Bob!
It's the only way, Raj. You know it!
Uh. Men. Mia has arrived.
Sorry to interrupt.
Can one of you show me to the scene?

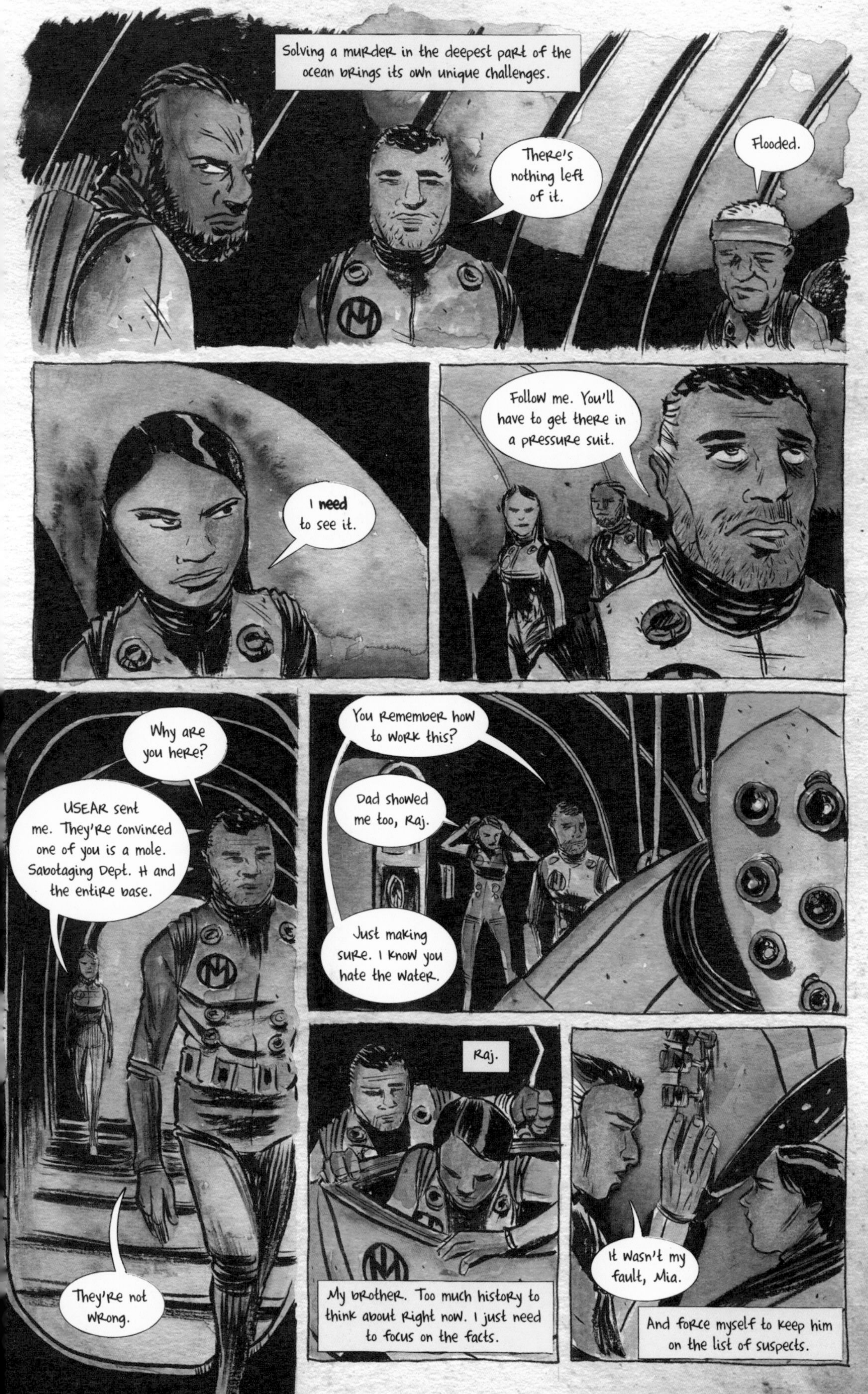
Solving a murder in the deepest part of the ocean brings its own unique challenges.
There's nothing left of it.
Flooded.
I **need** to see it.
Follow me. You'll have to get there in a pressure suit.
Why are you here?
USEAR sent me. They're convinced one of you is a mole. Sabotaging Dept. H and the entire base.
They're not wrong.
You remember how to work this?
Dad showed me too, Raj.
Just making sure. I know you hate the water.
Raj.
My brother. Too much history to think about right now. I just need to focus on the facts.
It wasn't my fault, Mia.
And force myself to keep him on the list of suspects.

That's what I'm here to find out.

FSSSH FSSSSH FSSSSH FSSSH

Deep diving is similar to space walking.

SQUEEK

Harsh elements. Millimeters separating you from near-instantaneous death.

THRUB BLUB

But there's something liberating about floating in a vacuum.

FSSSSH

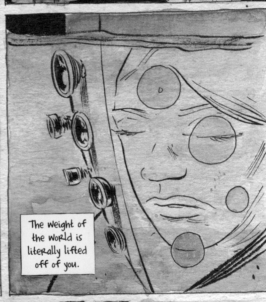

The weight of the world is literally lifted off of you.

It's the opposite down here.

Nothing light about it.

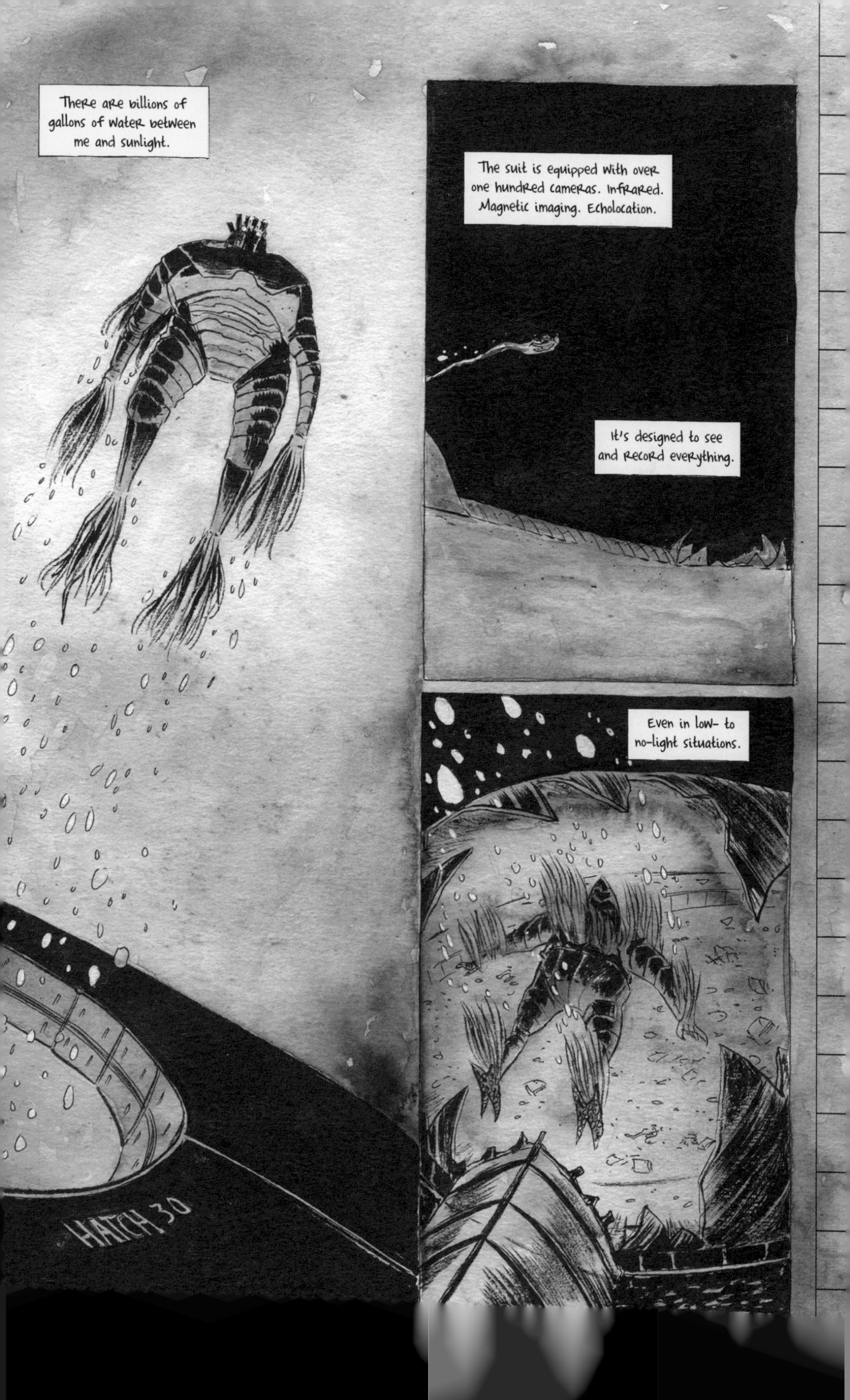
There are billions of gallons of water between me and sunlight.
The suit is equipped with over one hundred cameras. Infrared. Magnetic imaging. Echolocation.
It's designed to see and record everything.
Even in low- to no-light situations.
HATCH 30

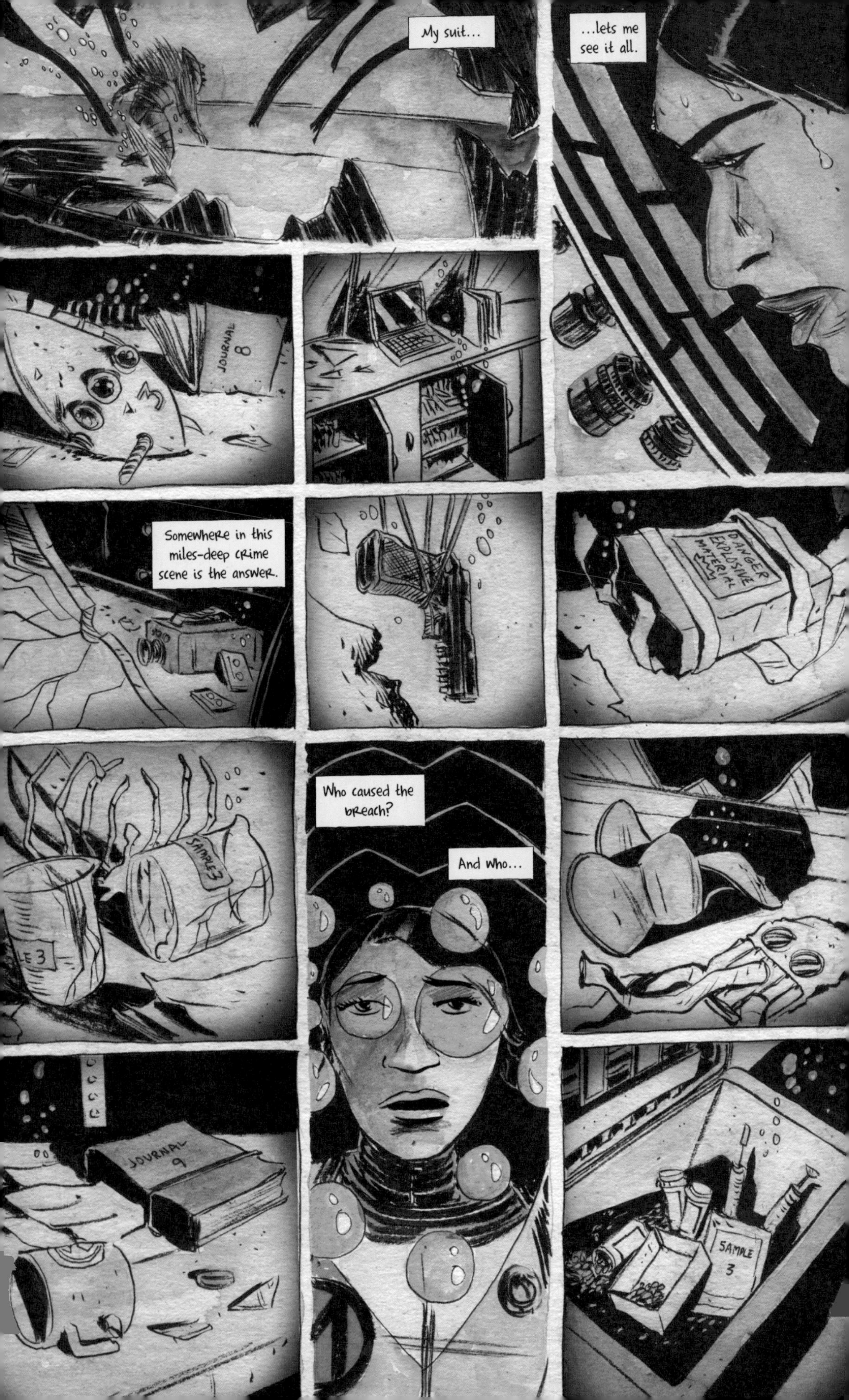
My suit...
...lets me see it all.
JOURNAL 8
Somewhere in this miles-deep crime scene is the answer.
DANGER EXPLOSIVE MATERIAL
SAMPLE 3
Who caused the breach?
And who...
JOURNAL 9
SAMPLE 3

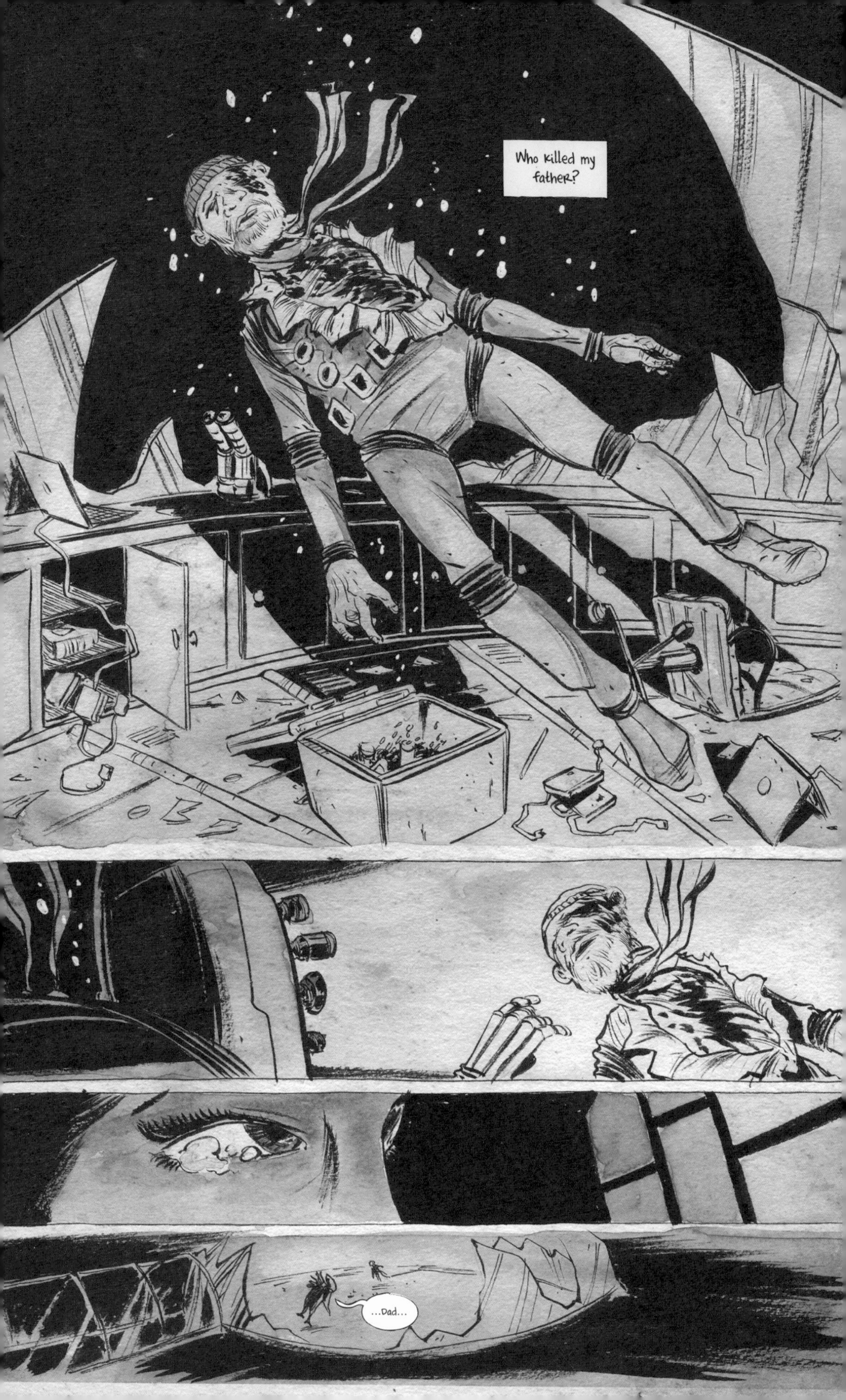
Who killed my father?
...Dad...

Open the lock. I'm coming back in.
I don't fear heights.
OR enclosed spaces.
SAMP
C
SAMP
B
SAMP
A
OR the dark.
JOURNAL
8
All of those things are quantifiable. Measurable.
Something you can prepare for.
I don't fear death.
Death is just a consequence of ineptitude or miscalculation.
And it only hurts for a second.
ngh...huf...
...huf...

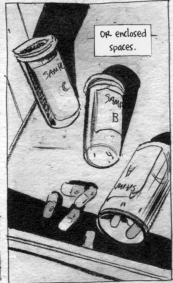

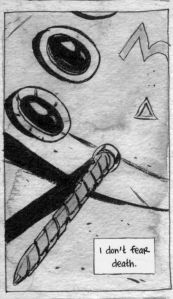

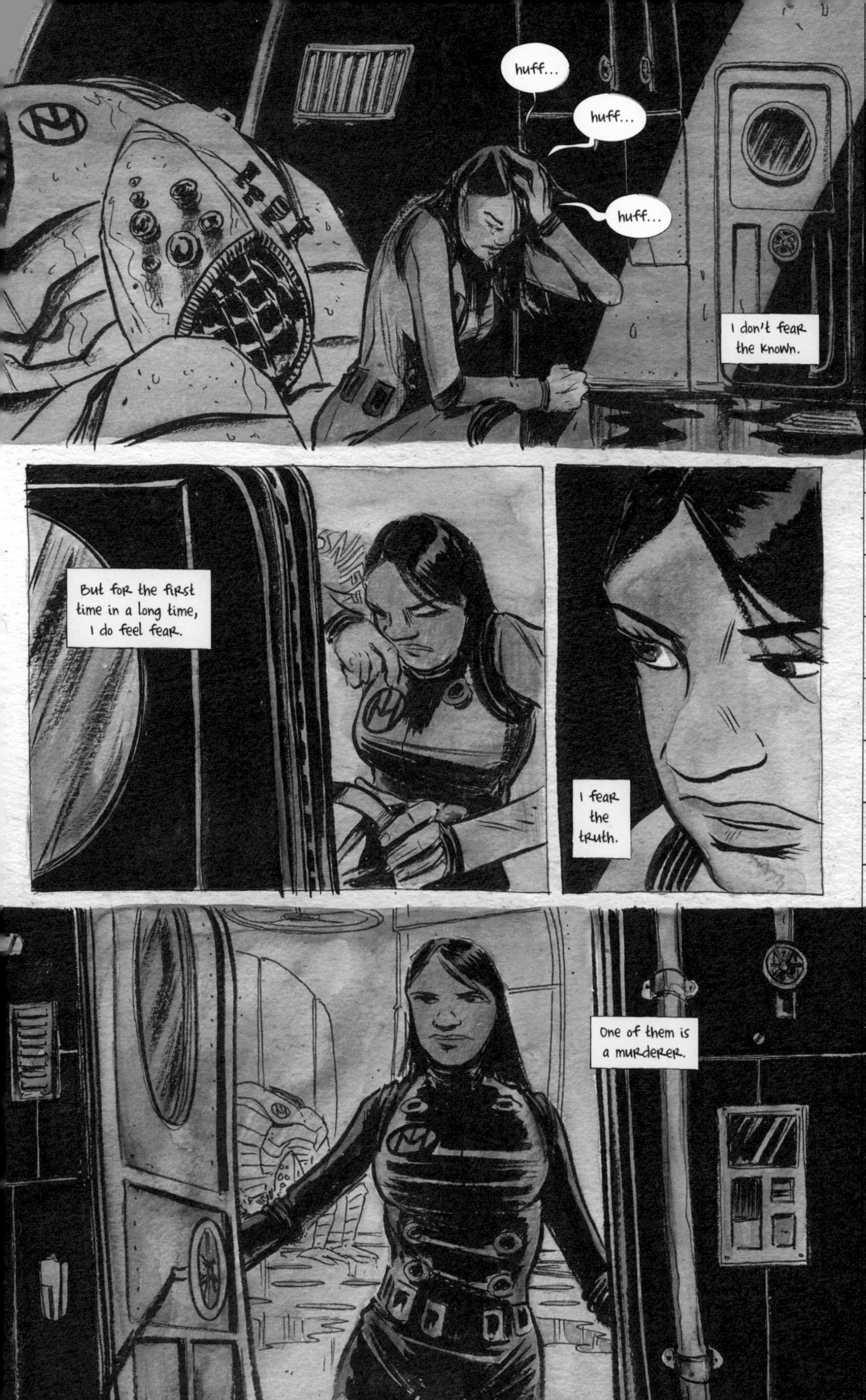

huff...
huff...
huff...
I don't fear the known.
But for the first time in a long time, I do feel fear.
I fear the truth.
One of them is a murderer.

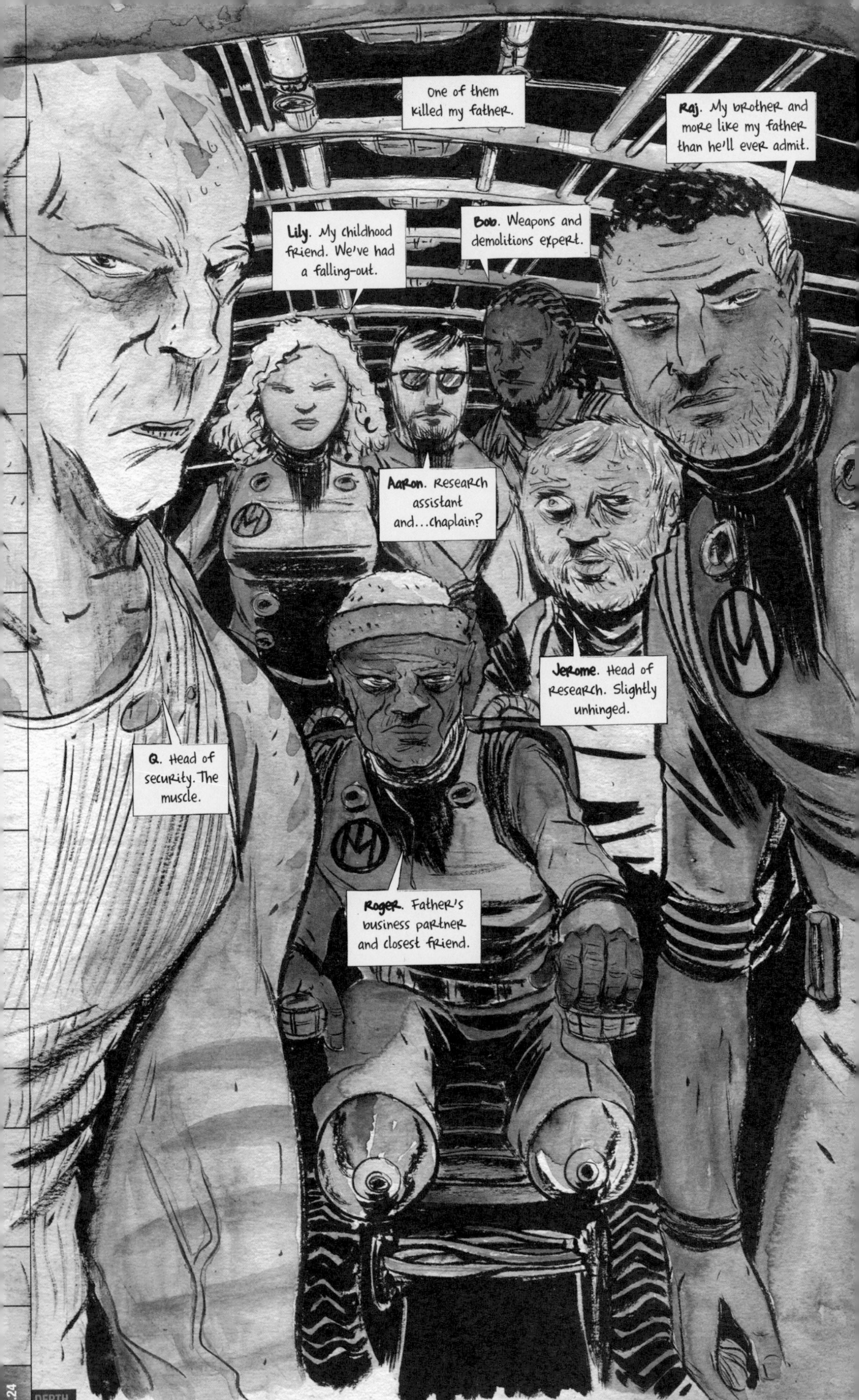
One of them killed my father.
Raj. My brother and more like my father than he'll ever admit.
Lily. My childhood friend. We've had a falling-out.
Bob. Weapons and demolitions expert.
Aaron. Research assistant and...chaplain?
Jerome. Head of research. Slightly unhinged.
Q. Head of security. The muscle.
Roger. Father's business partner and closest friend.

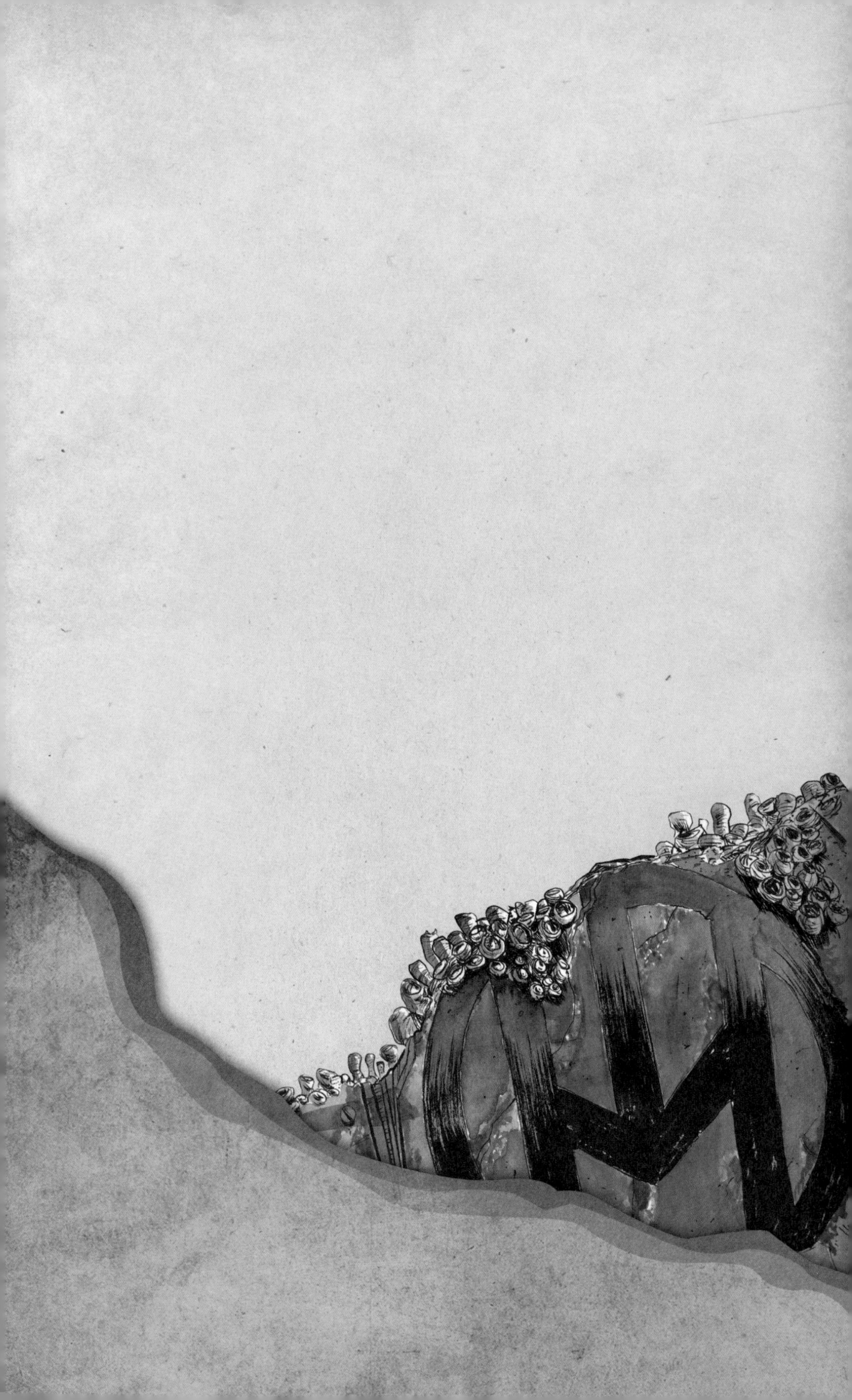

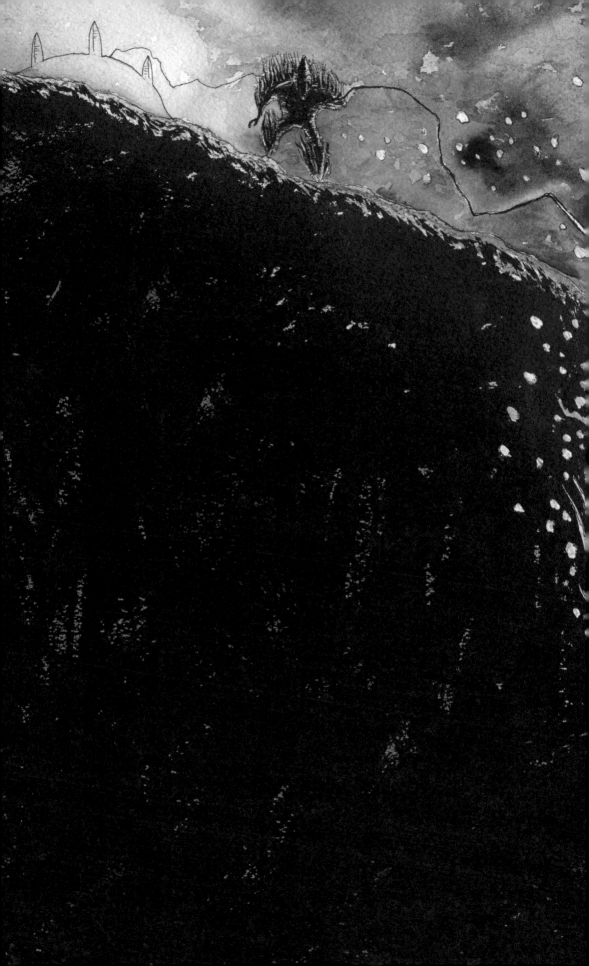

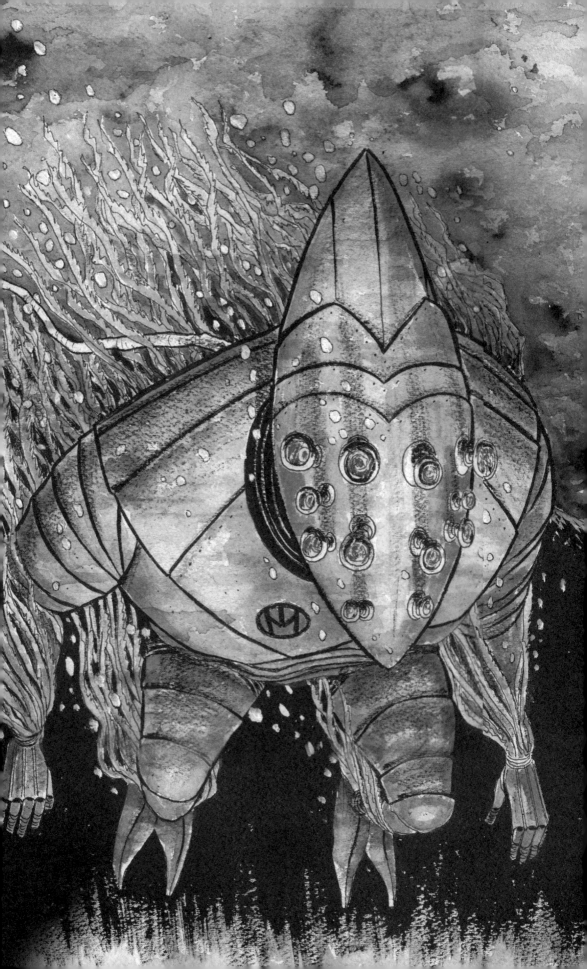

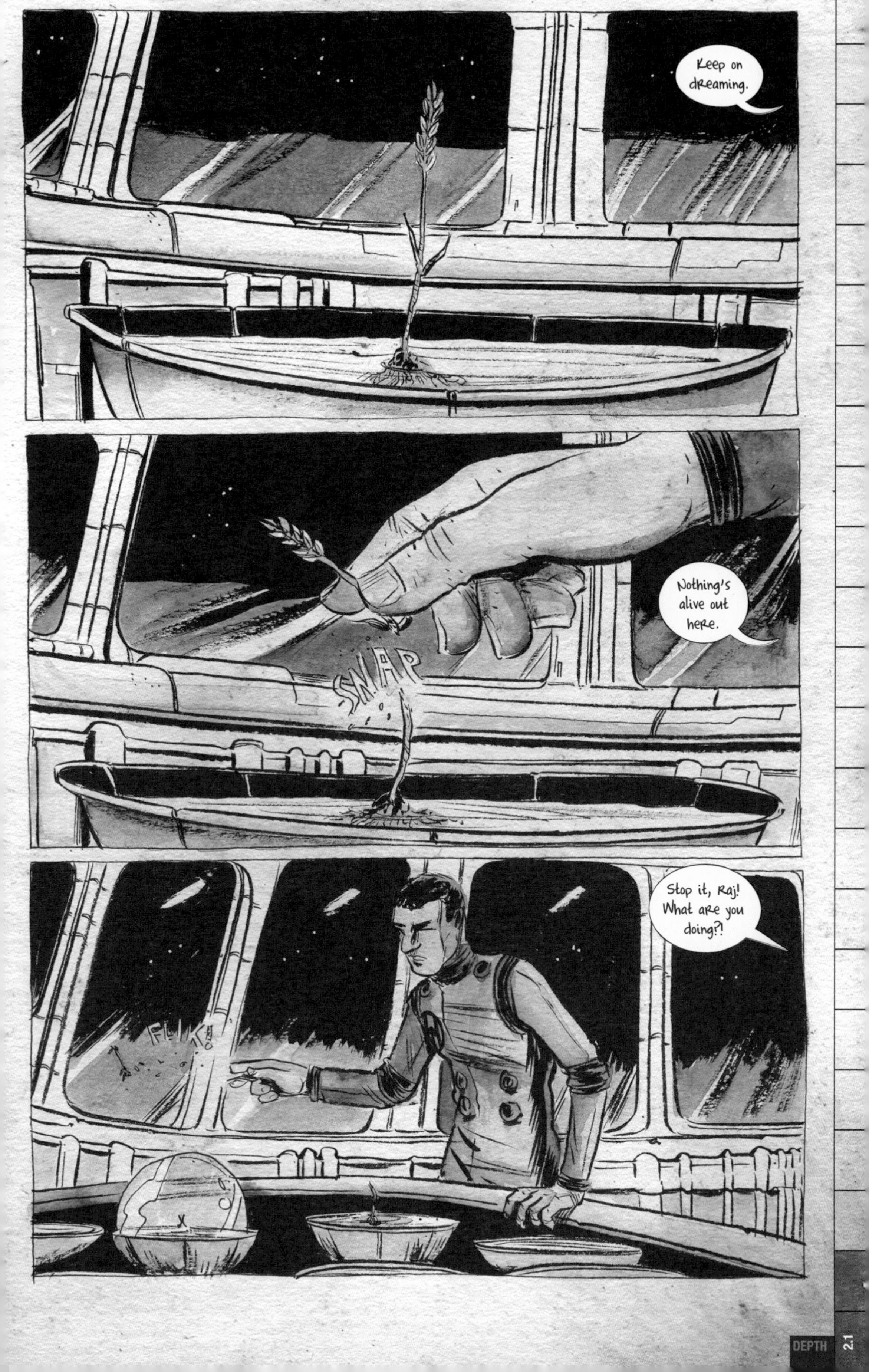
Keep on dreaming.
Nothing's alive out here.
SNAP
Stop it, Raj! What are you doing?!
FLIK

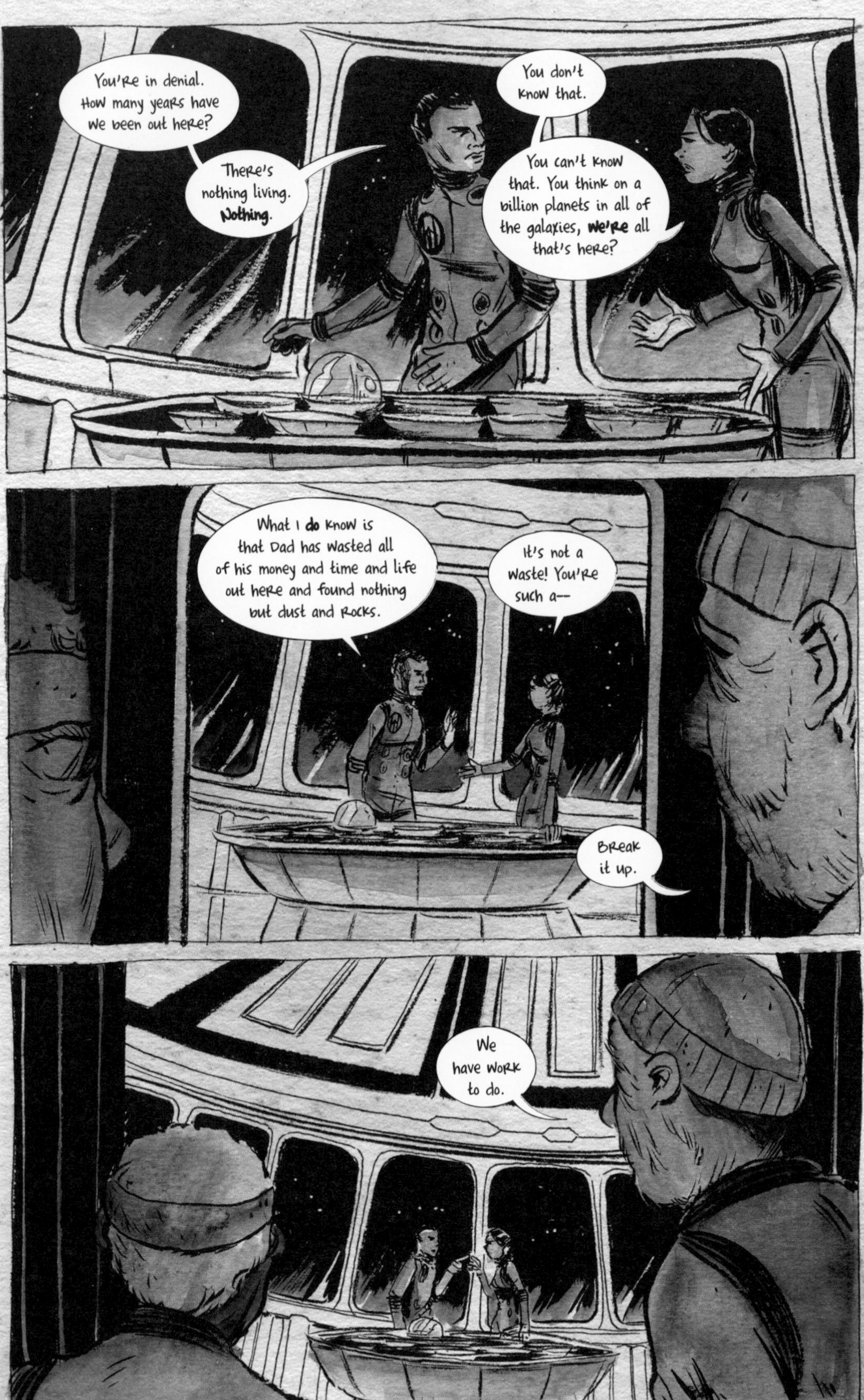
You're in denial. How many years have we been out here?
There's nothing living. **Nothing**.
You don't know that.
You can't know that. You think on a billion planets in all of the galaxies, **we're** all that's here?
What I **do** know is that Dad has wasted all of his money and time and life out here and found nothing but dust and rocks.
It's not a waste! You're such a--
Break it up.
We have work to do.

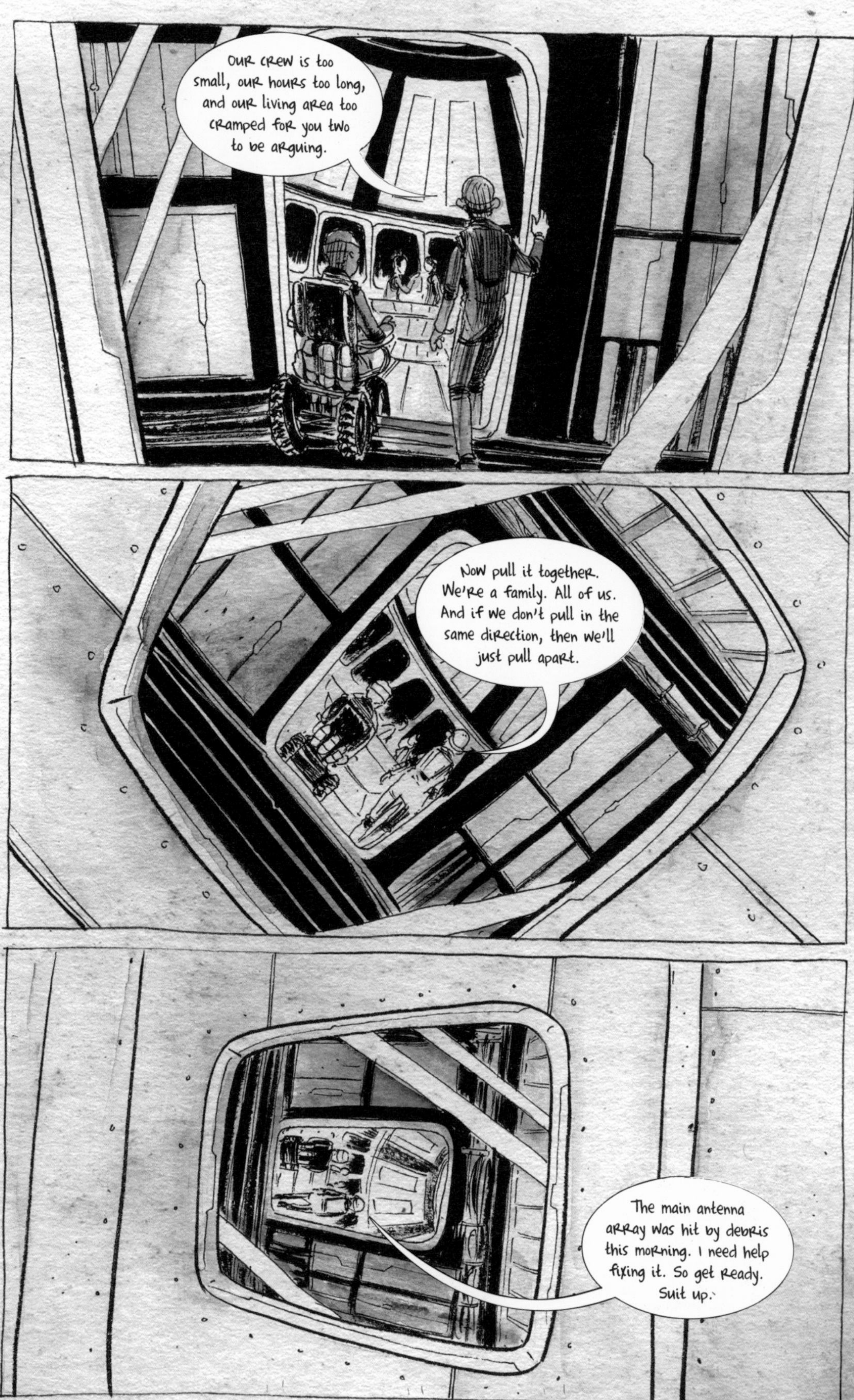
OUR CREW is too small, OUR hours too long, and OUR living area too cRamped for you two to be arguing.
Now pull it together. We're a family. All of us. And if we don't pull in the same direction, then we'll just pull apart.
The main antenna array was hit by debris this morning. I need help fixing it. So get Ready. Suit up.

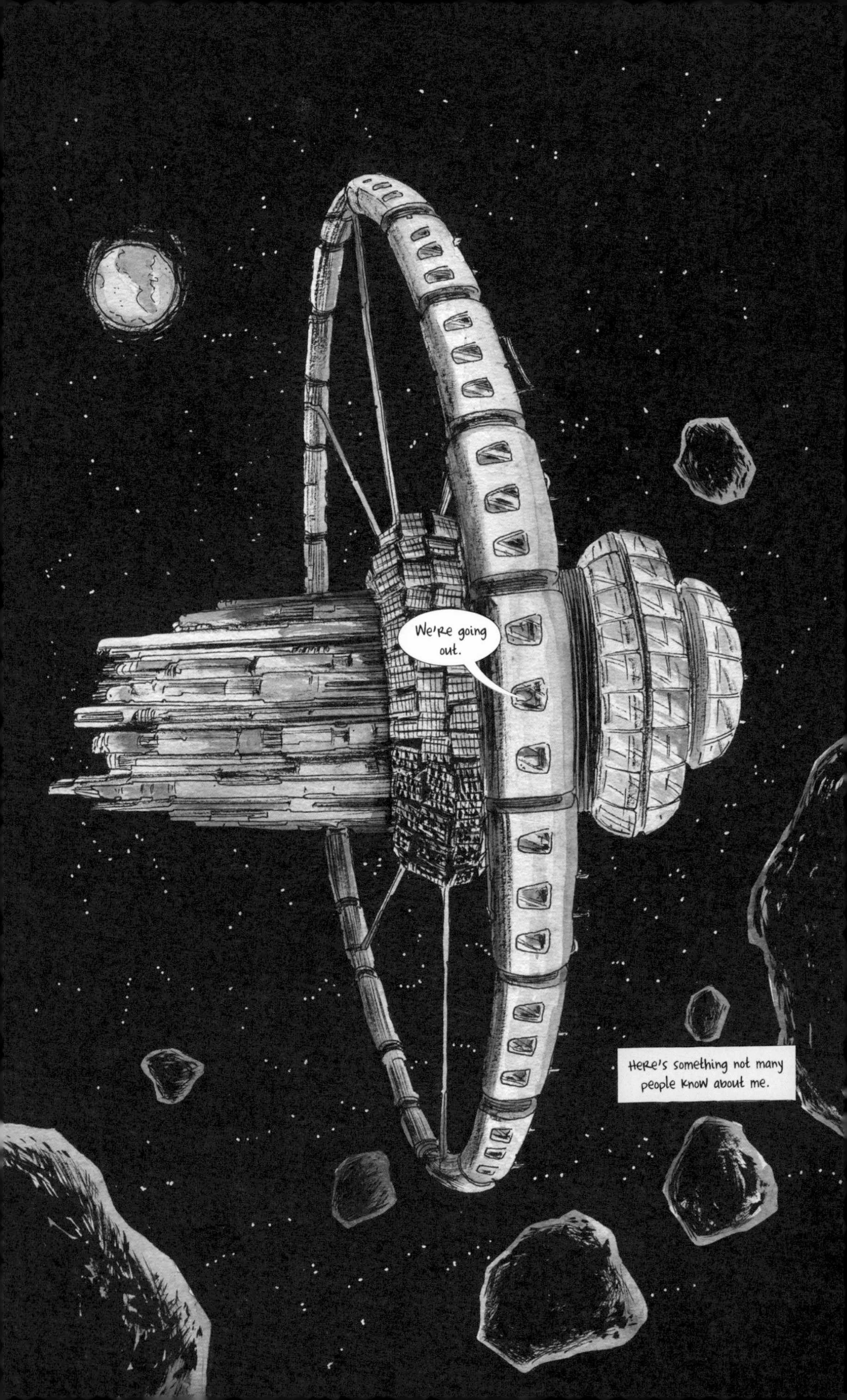
We're going out.
Here's something not many people know about me.

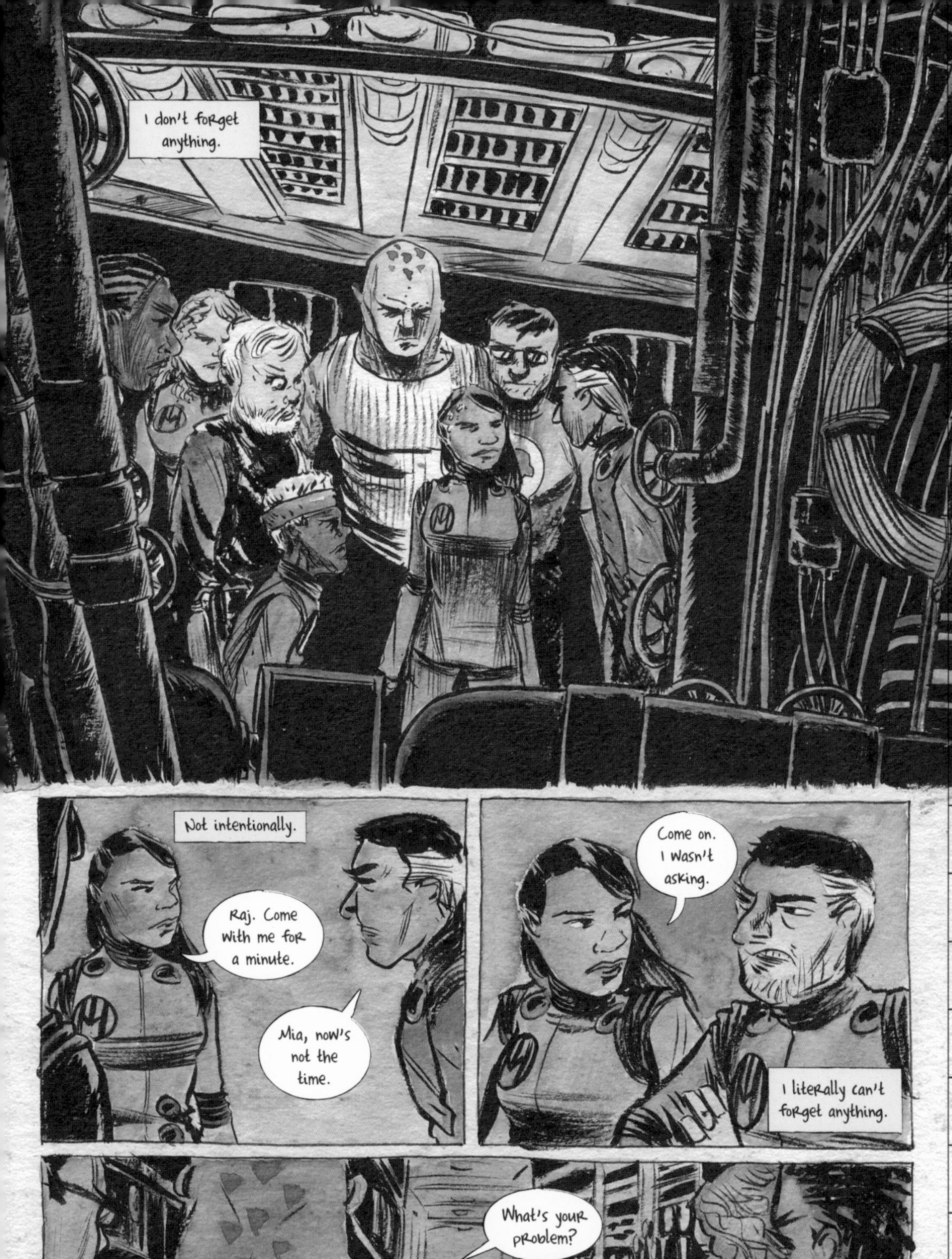
I don't forget anything.
Not intentionally.
Raj. Come with me for a minute.
Mia, now's not the time.
Come on. I wasn't asking.
I literally can't forget anything.
What's your problem?

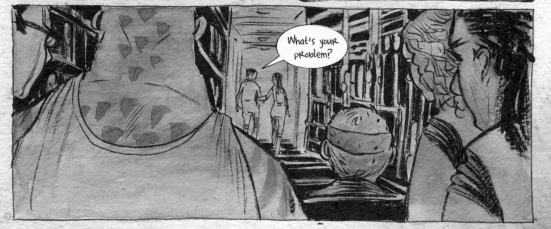

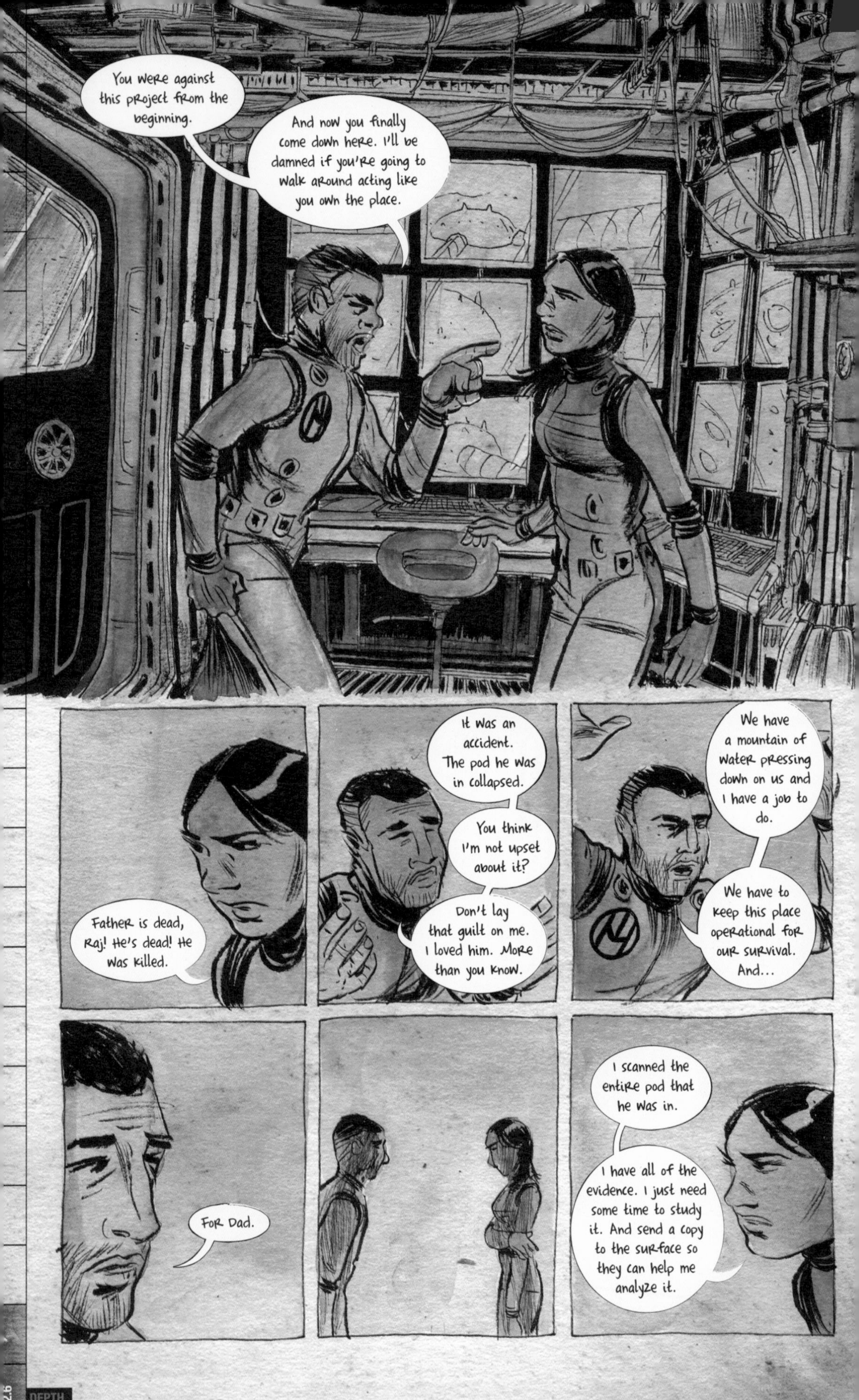
You were against this project from the beginning.
And now you finally come down here. I'll be damned if you're going to walk around acting like you own the place.
Father is dead, Raj! He's dead! He was killed.
It was an accident. The pod he was in collapsed.
You think I'm not upset about it?
Don't lay that guilt on me. I loved him. More than you know.
We have a mountain of water pressing down on us and I have a job to do.
We have to keep this place operational for our survival. And...
For Dad.
I scanned the entire pod that he was in.
I have all of the evidence. I just need some time to study it. And send a copy to the surface so they can help me analyze it.

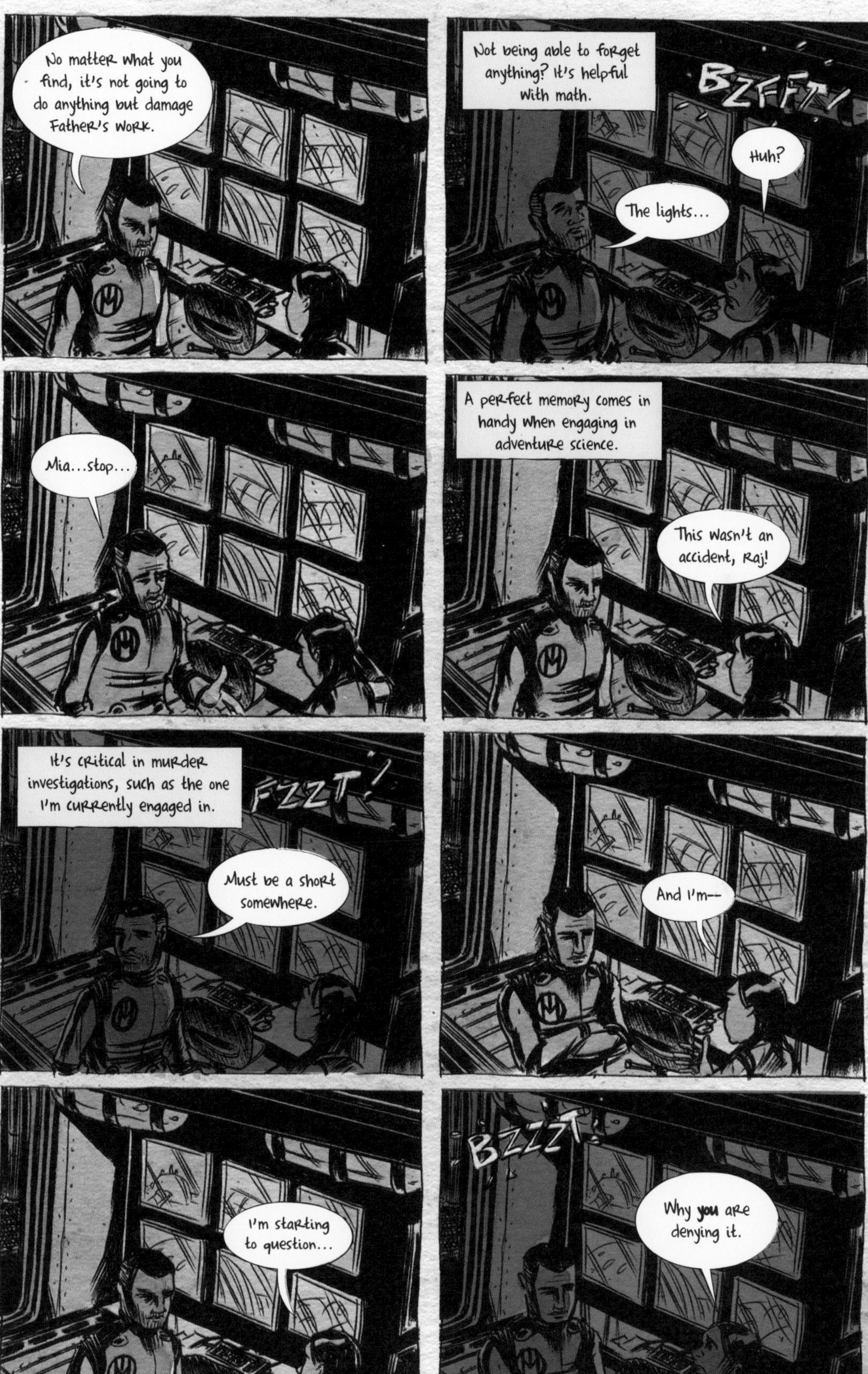
No matter what you find, it's not going to do anything but damage Father's work.
Not being able to forget anything? It's helpful with math.
BZFFT!
Huh?
The lights...
Mia...stop...
A perfect memory comes in handy when engaging in adventure science.
This wasn't an accident, Raj!
It's critical in murder investigations, such as the one I'm currently engaged in.
FZZT!
Must be a short somewhere.
And I'm--
I'm starting to question...
BZZZT!
Why you are denying it.

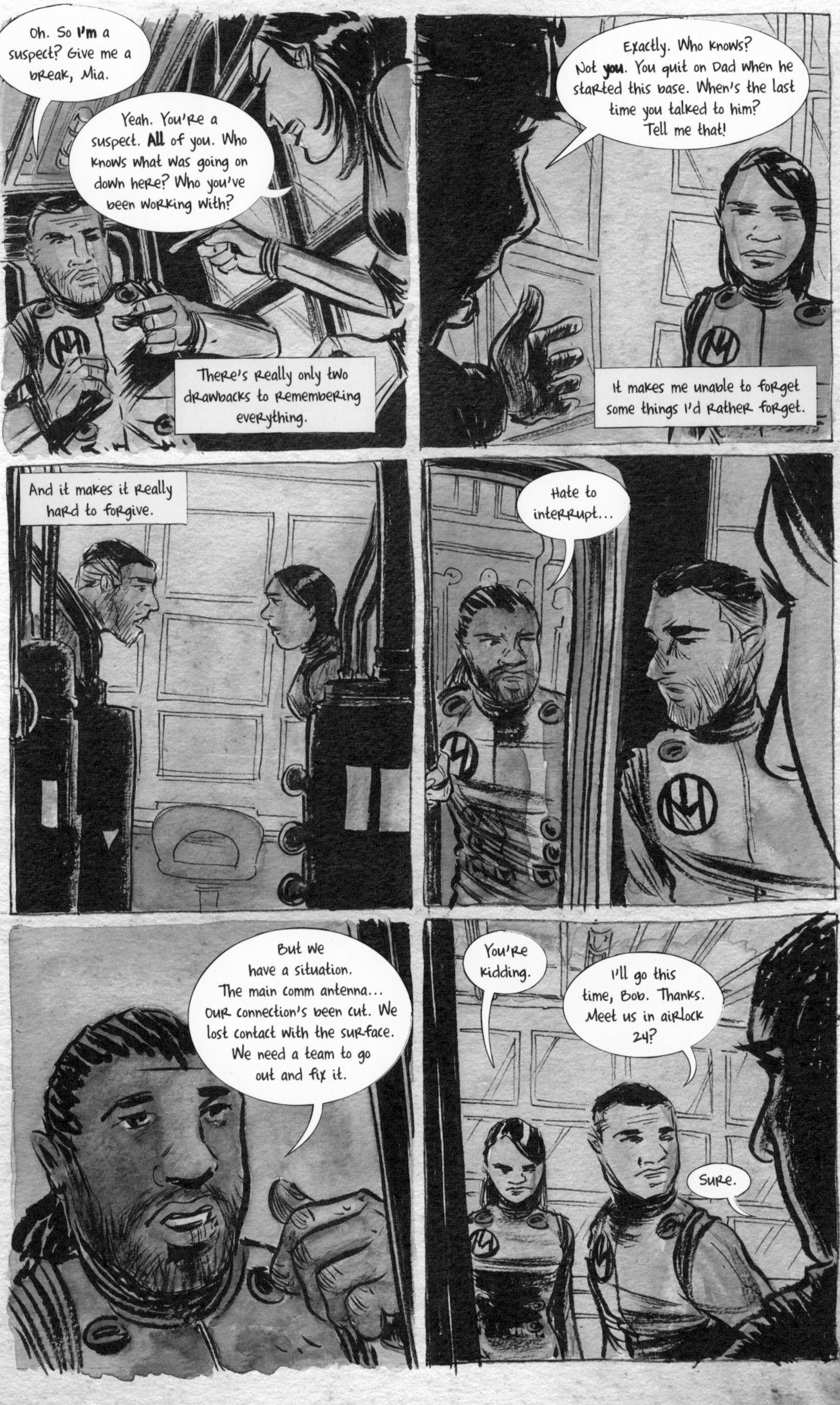
Oh. So I'm a suspect? Give me a break, Mia.
Yeah. You're a suspect. ALL of you. Who knows what was going on down here? Who you've been working with?
There's really only two drawbacks to remembering everything.
Exactly. Who knows? Not you. You quit on Dad when he started this base. When's the last time you talked to him? Tell me that!
It makes me unable to forget some things I'd rather forget.
And it makes it really hard to forgive.
Hate to interrupt...
But we have a situation. The main comm antenna... Our connection's been cut. We lost contact with the surface. We need a team to go out and fix it.
You're kidding.
I'll go this time, Bob. Thanks. Meet us in airlock 24?
Sure.

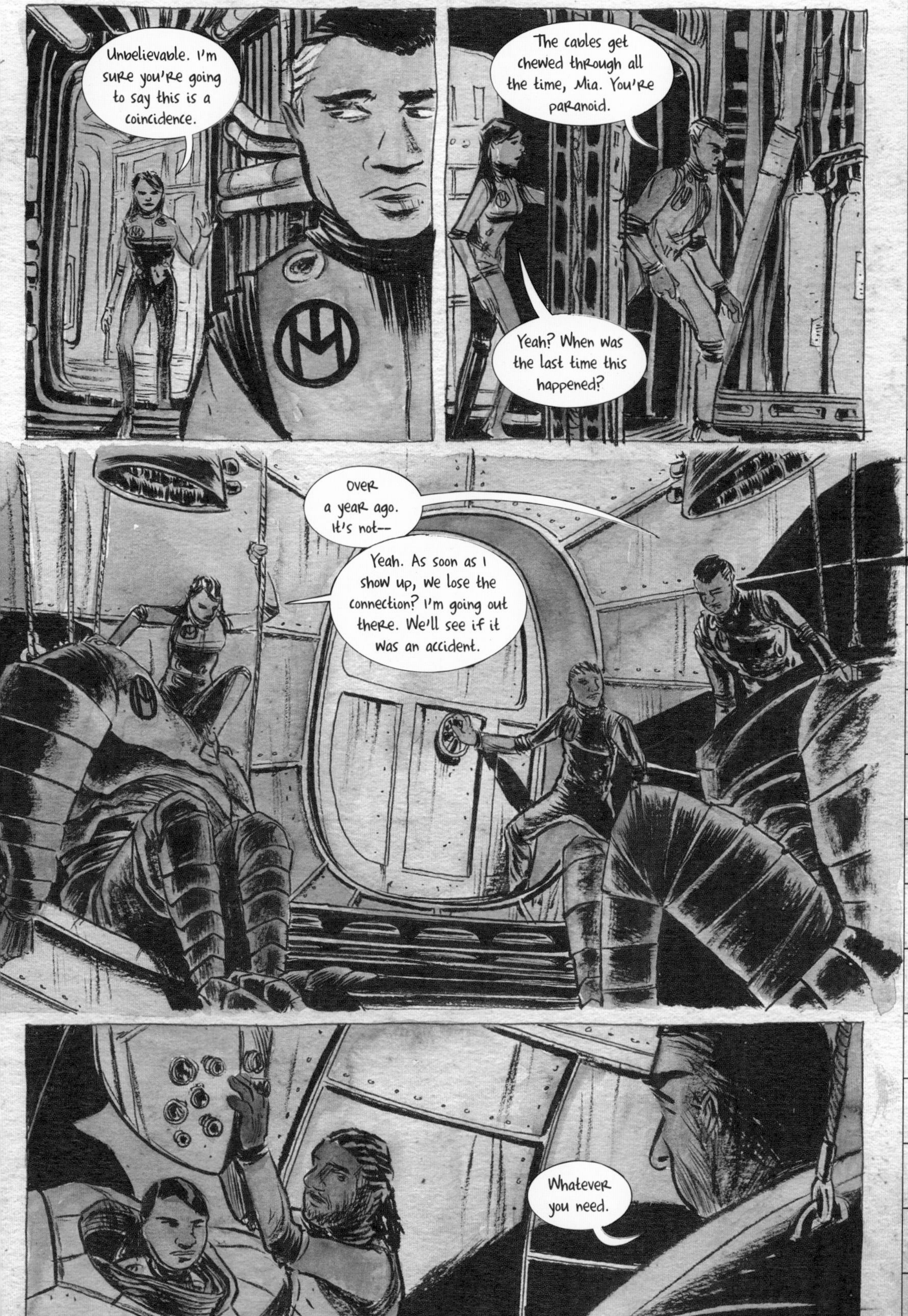
Unbelievable. I'm sure you're going to say this is a coincidence.
The cables get chewed through all the time, Mia. You're paranoid.
Yeah? When was the last time this happened?
Over a year ago. It's not--
Yeah. As soon as I show up, we lose the connection? I'm going out there. We'll see if it was an accident.
Whatever you need.

Probably a frayed cable. The damn bottom feeders will chew up anything.
Tools are in here. Radio back as soon as you have an assessment.
Will do.

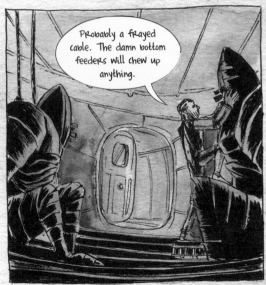

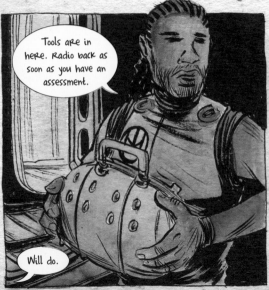

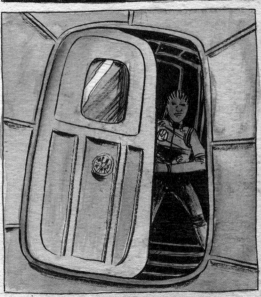

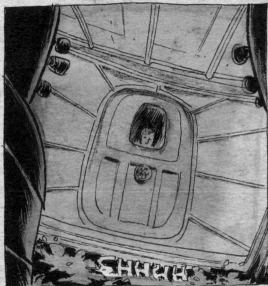

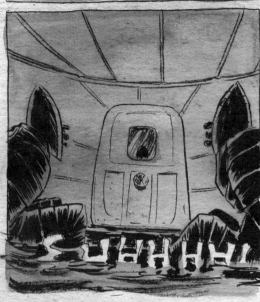

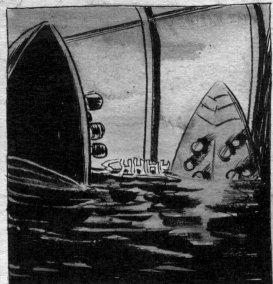

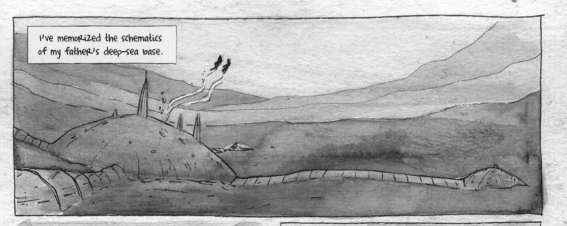

I've memorized the schematics of my father's deep-sea base.

He'd been developing it as long as he'd been working on the space station.

A lot of the technology overlapped.

He loved this station. He'd built in so many redundancies.

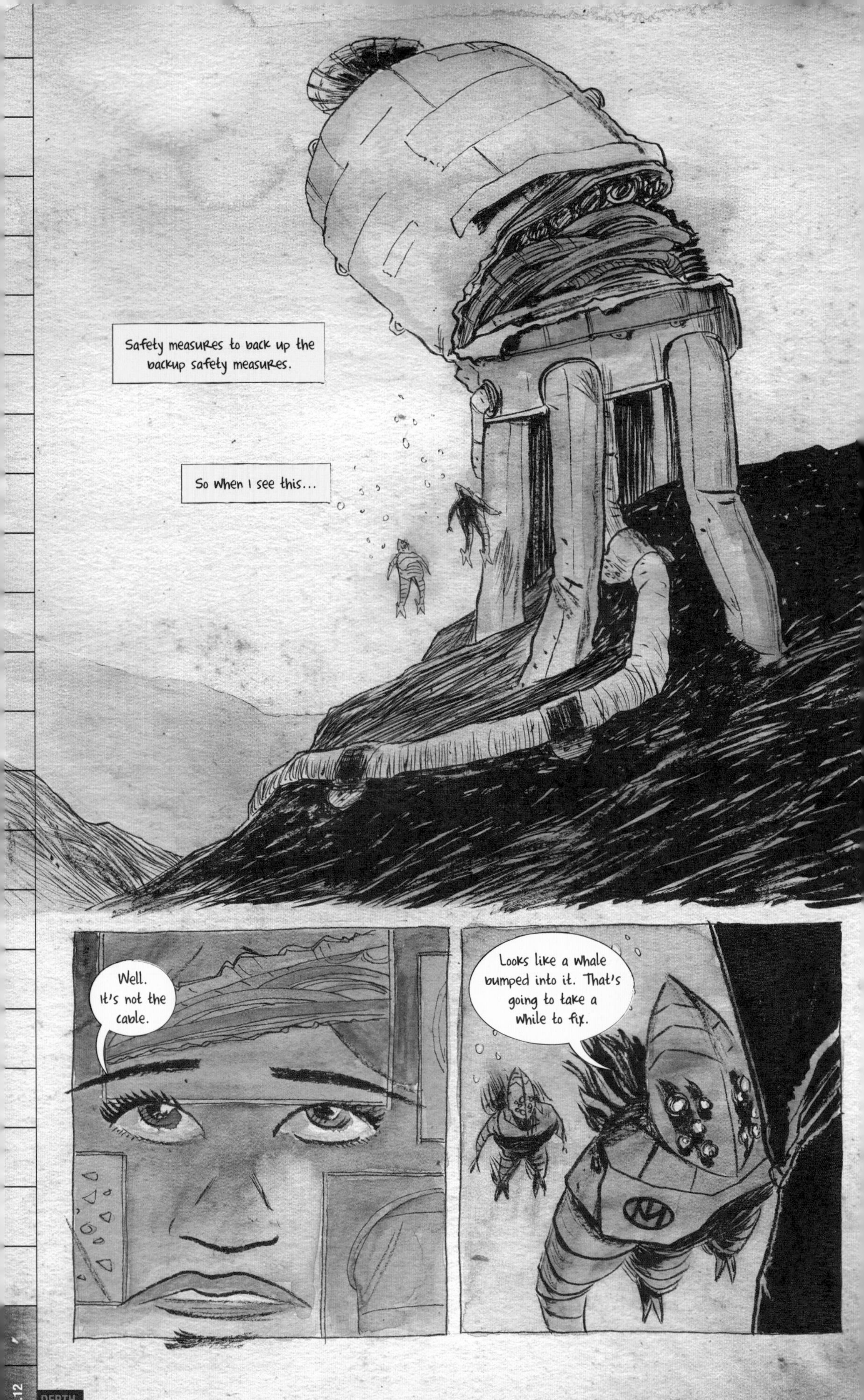
Safety measures to back up the backup safety measures.
So when I see this...
Well. It's not the cable.
Looks like a whale bumped into it. That's going to take a while to fix.

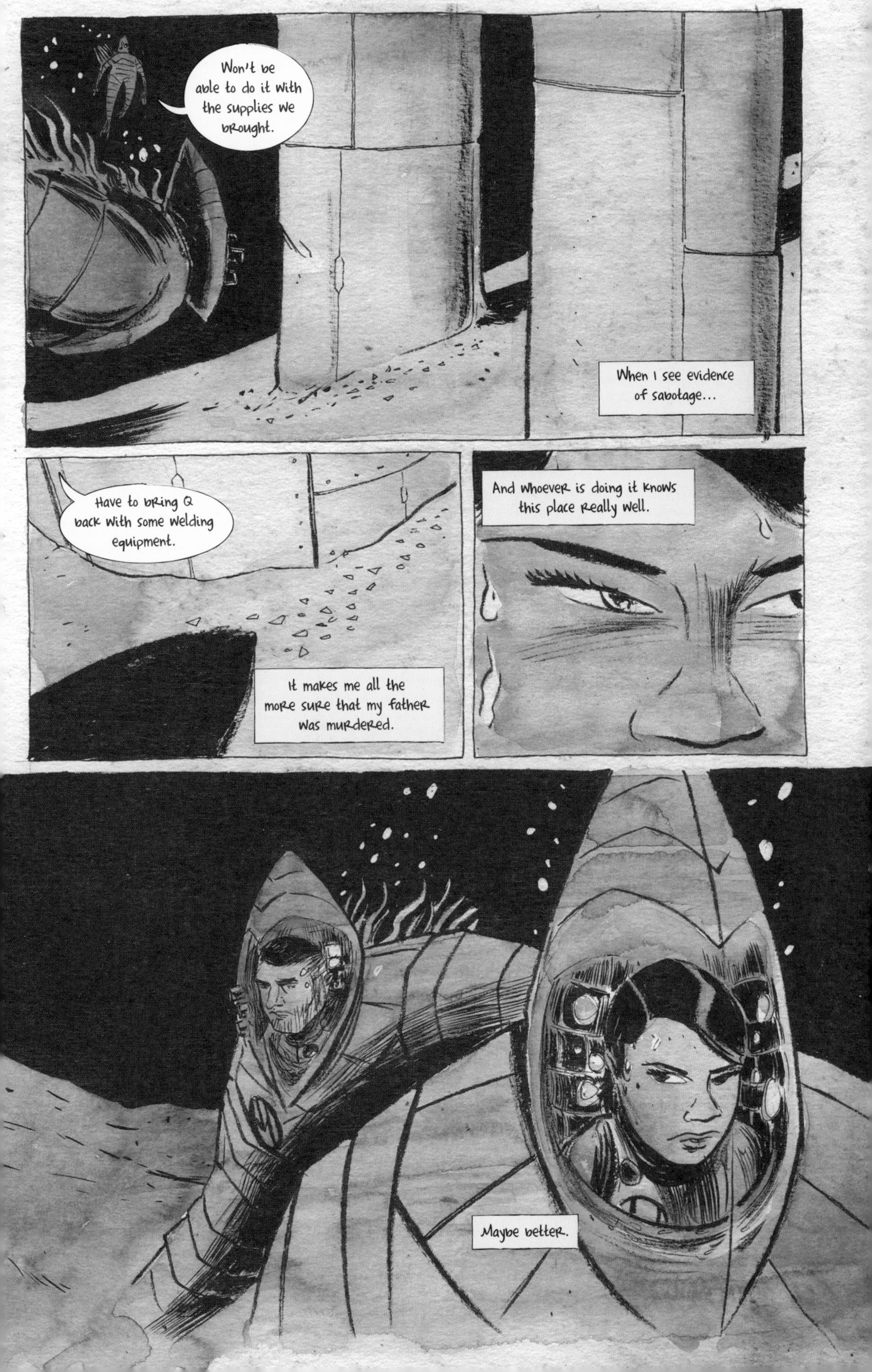
Won't be able to do it with the supplies we brought.
When I see evidence of sabotage...
Have to bring Q back with some welding equipment.
It makes me all the more sure that my father was murdered.
And whoever is doing it knows this place really well.
Maybe better.

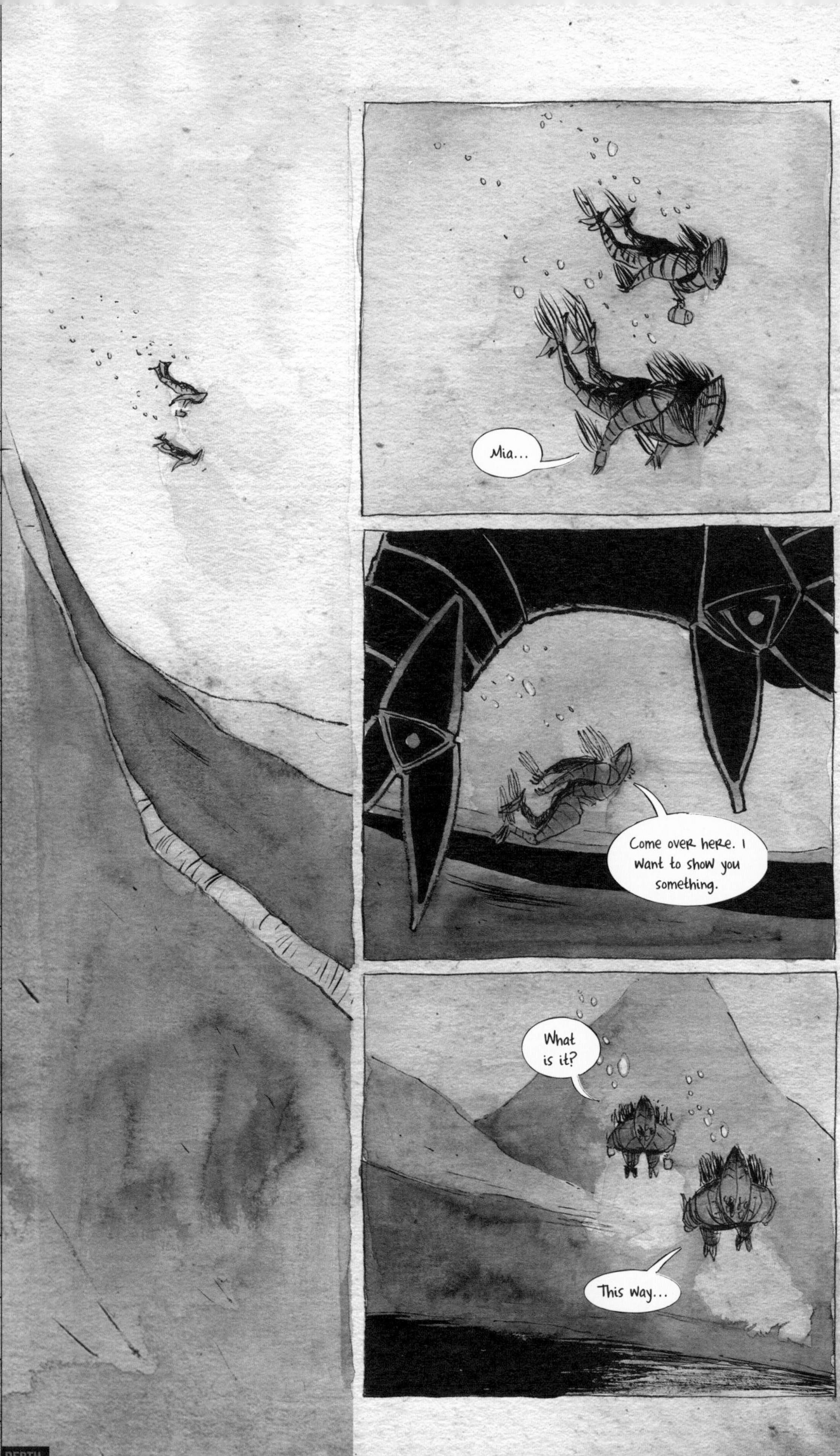
Mia...
Come over here. I want to show you something.
What is it?
This way...

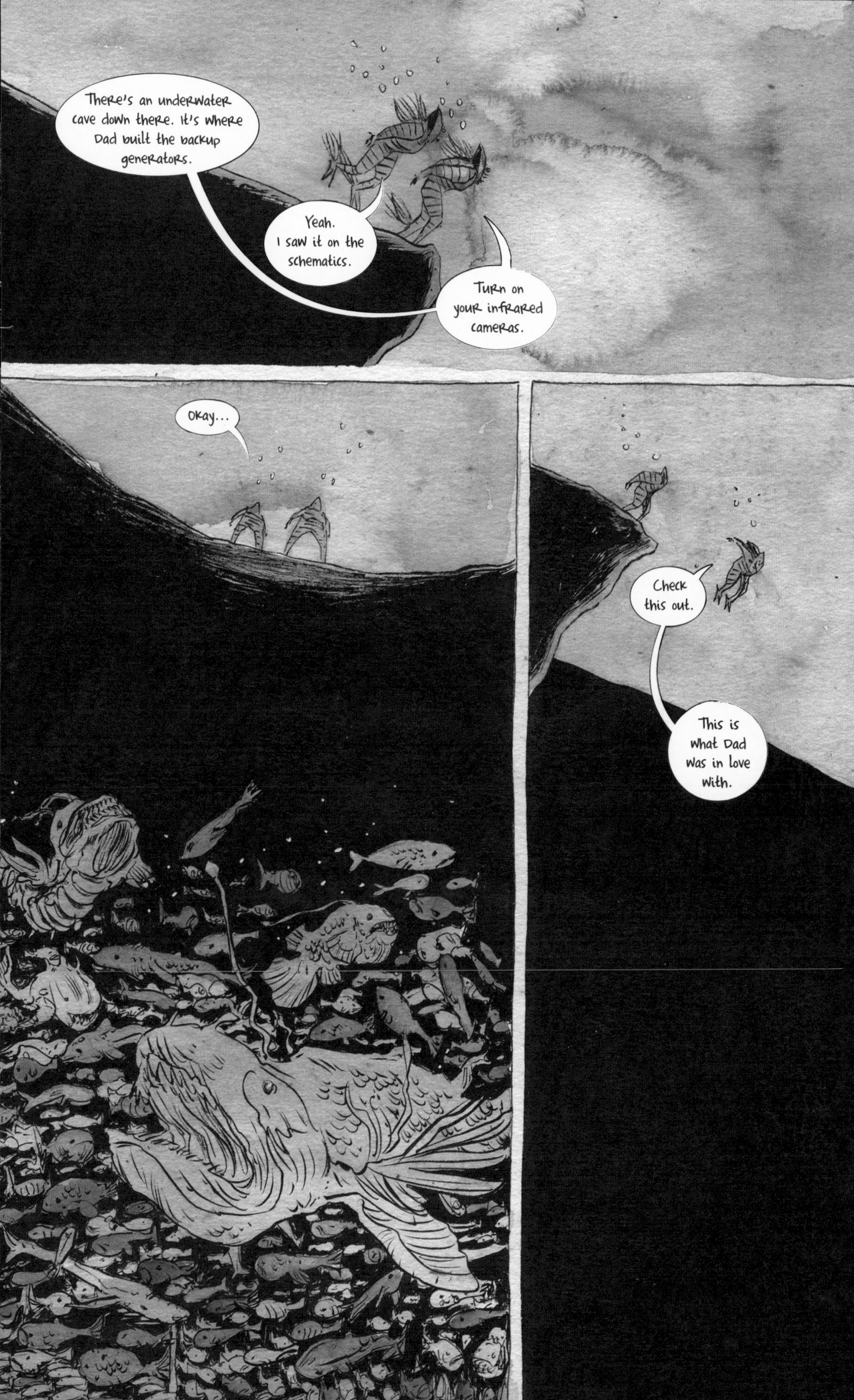
There's an underwater cave down there. It's where Dad built the backup generators.
Yeah. I saw it on the schematics.
Turn on your infrared cameras.
Okay...
Check this out.
This is what Dad was in love with.

There's a big difference between space exploration and ocean research.

This is why he came down here.

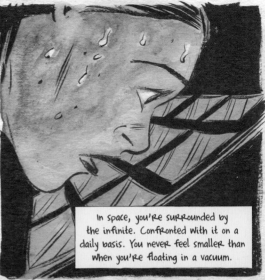

In space, you're surrounded by the infinite. Confronted with it on a daily basis. You never feel smaller than when you're floating in a vacuum.

The ocean is claustrophobic. Always pressing against you. Making you aware of its presence.

This was the first time in my experience that I really felt the expanse down here...

The infinite.

It was the first time I really felt...

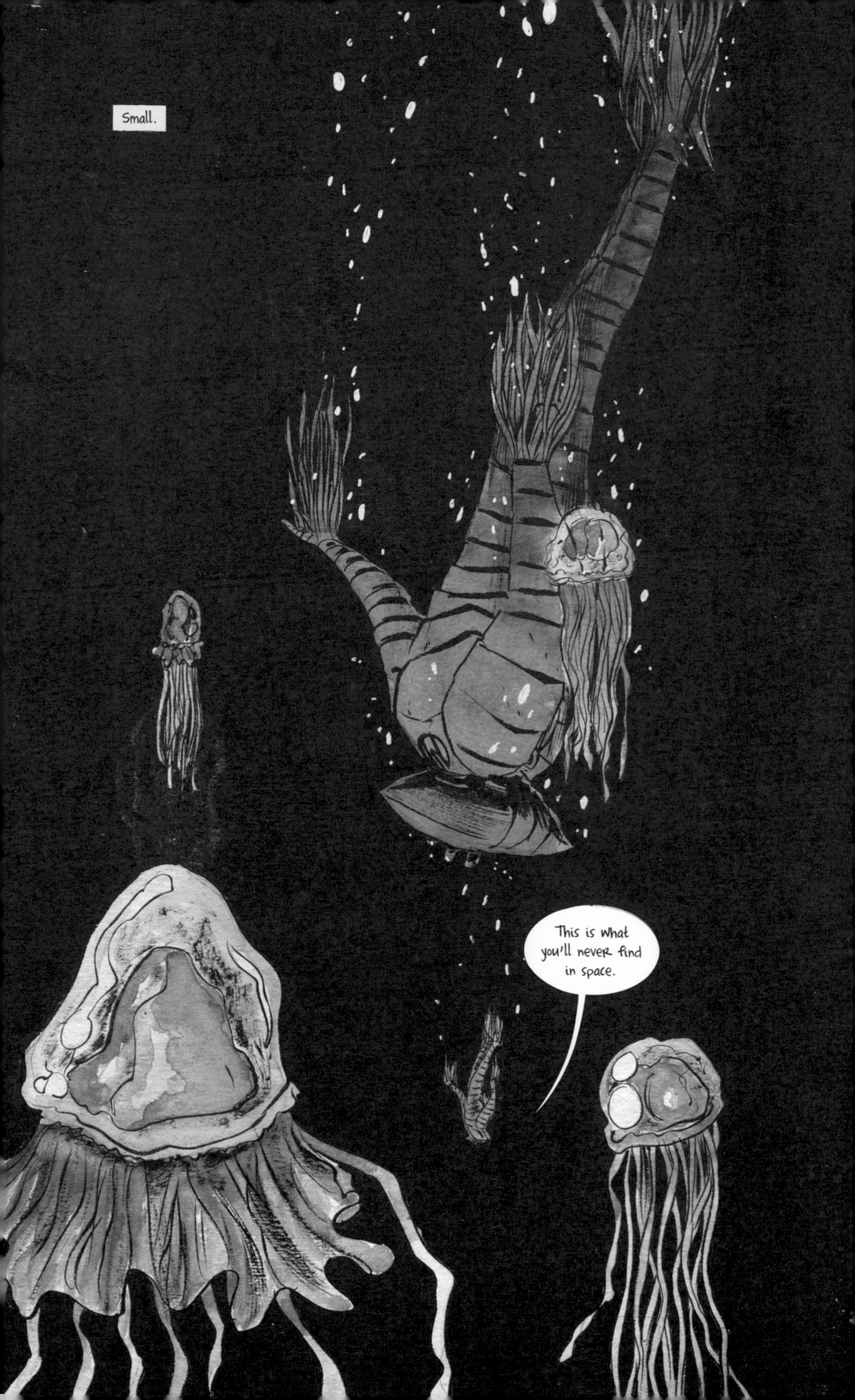
Small.
This is what you'll never find in space.

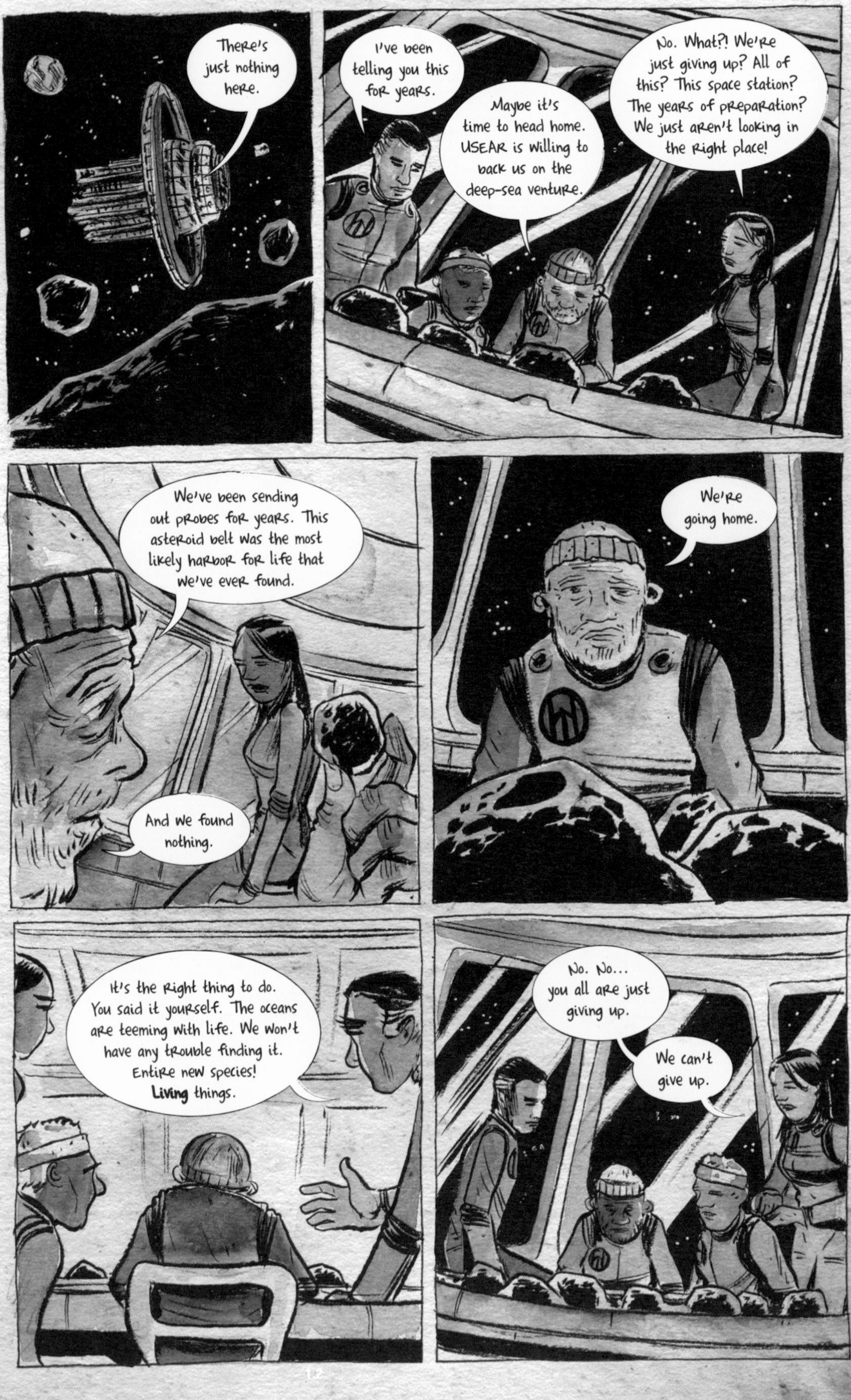
There's just nothing here.
I've been telling you this for years.
Maybe it's time to head home. USEAR is willing to back us on the deep-sea venture.
No. What?! We're just giving up? All of this? This space station? The years of preparation? We just aren't looking in the right place!
We've been sending out probes for years. This asteroid belt was the most likely harbor for life that we've ever found.
And we found nothing.
We're going home.
It's the right thing to do. You said it yourself. The oceans are teeming with life. We won't have any trouble finding it. Entire new species! **Living** things.
No. No... you all are just giving up.
We can't give up.

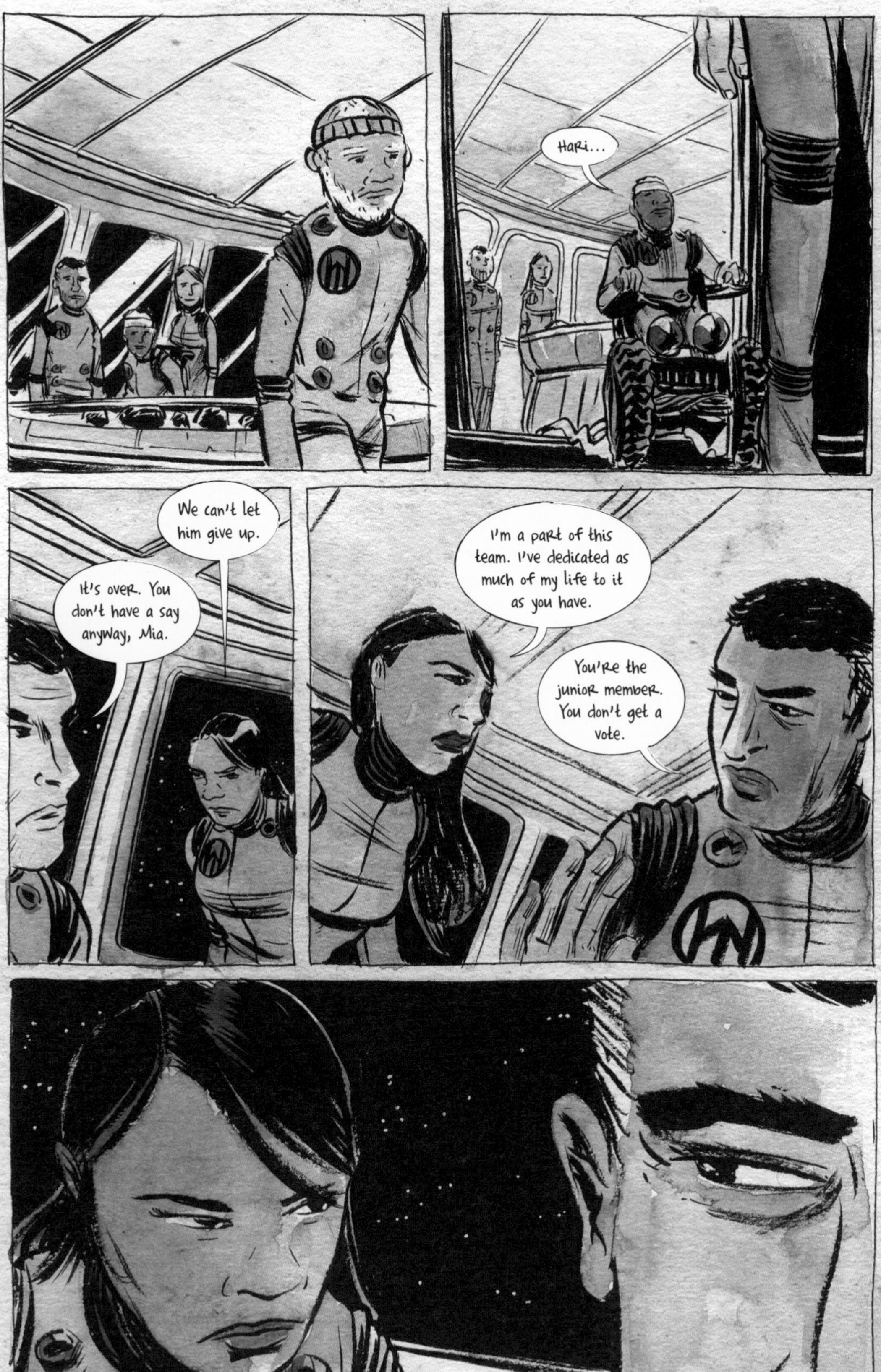
Hari...
We can't let him give up.
It's over. You don't have a say anyway, Mia.
I'm a part of this team. I've dedicated as much of my life to it as you have.
You're the junior member. You don't get a vote.

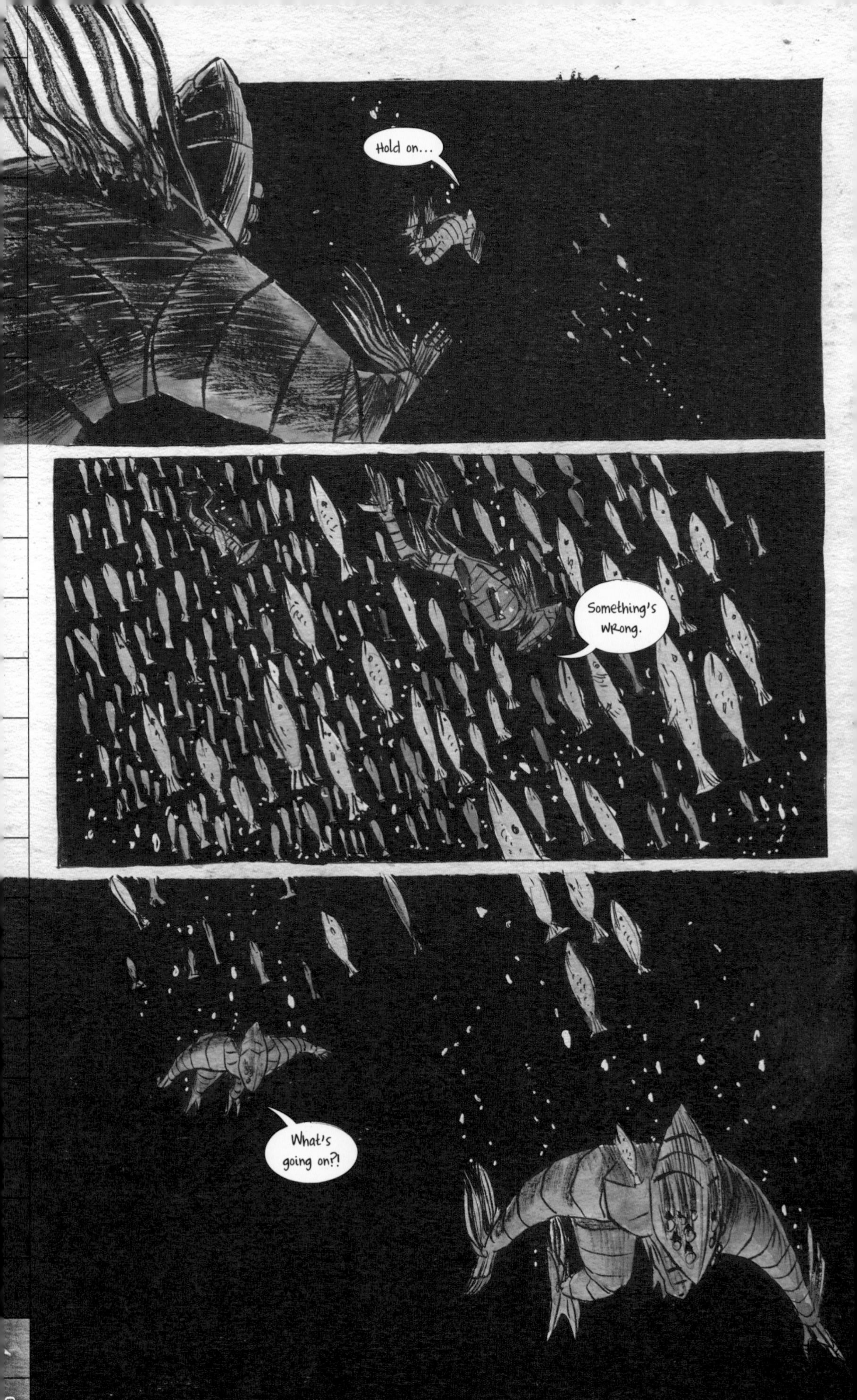
Hold on...
Something's wrong.
What's going on?!

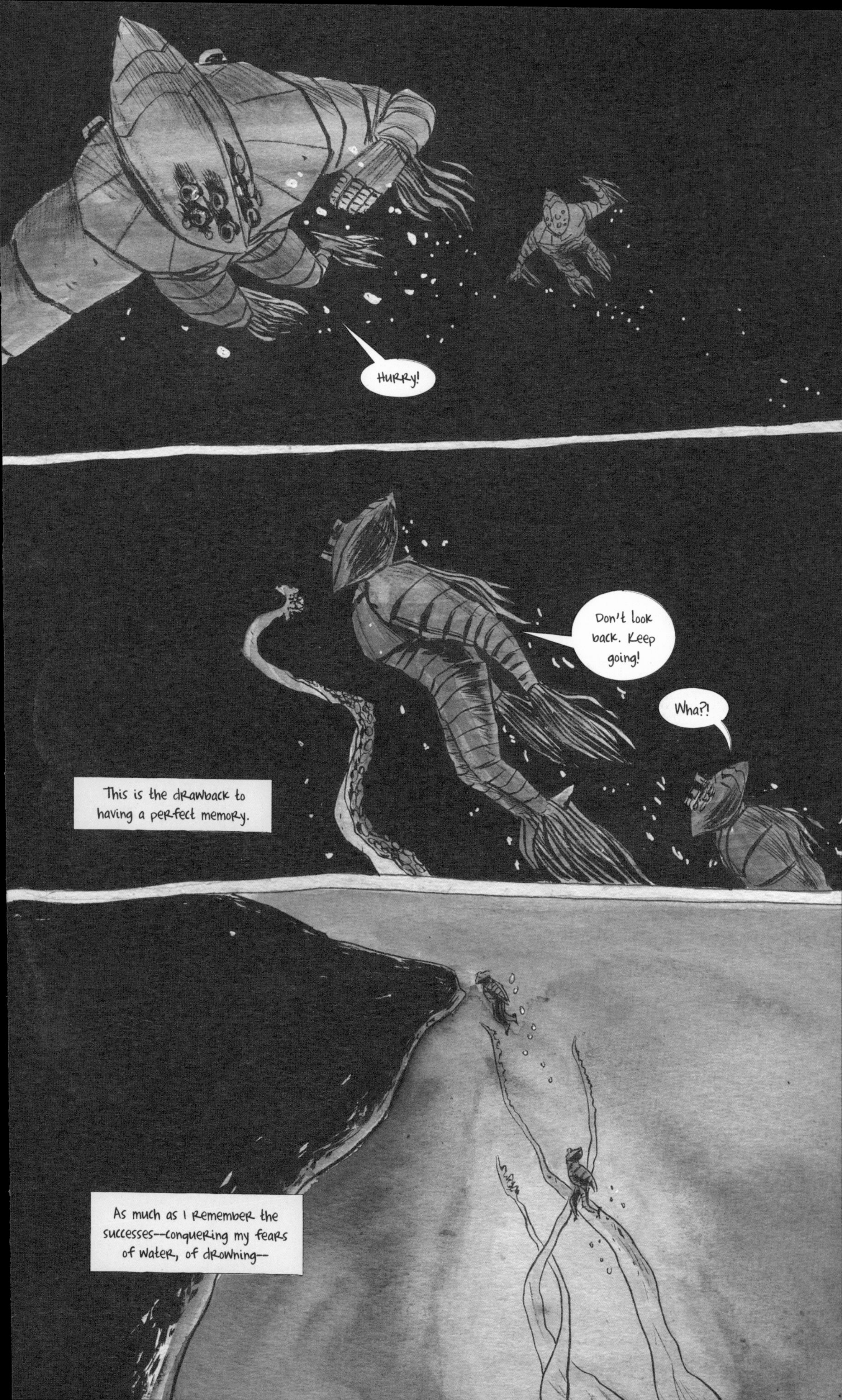
HURRY!
This is the drawback to having a perfect memory.
Don't look back. Keep going!
Wha?!
As much as I remember the successes--conquering my fears of water, of drowning--

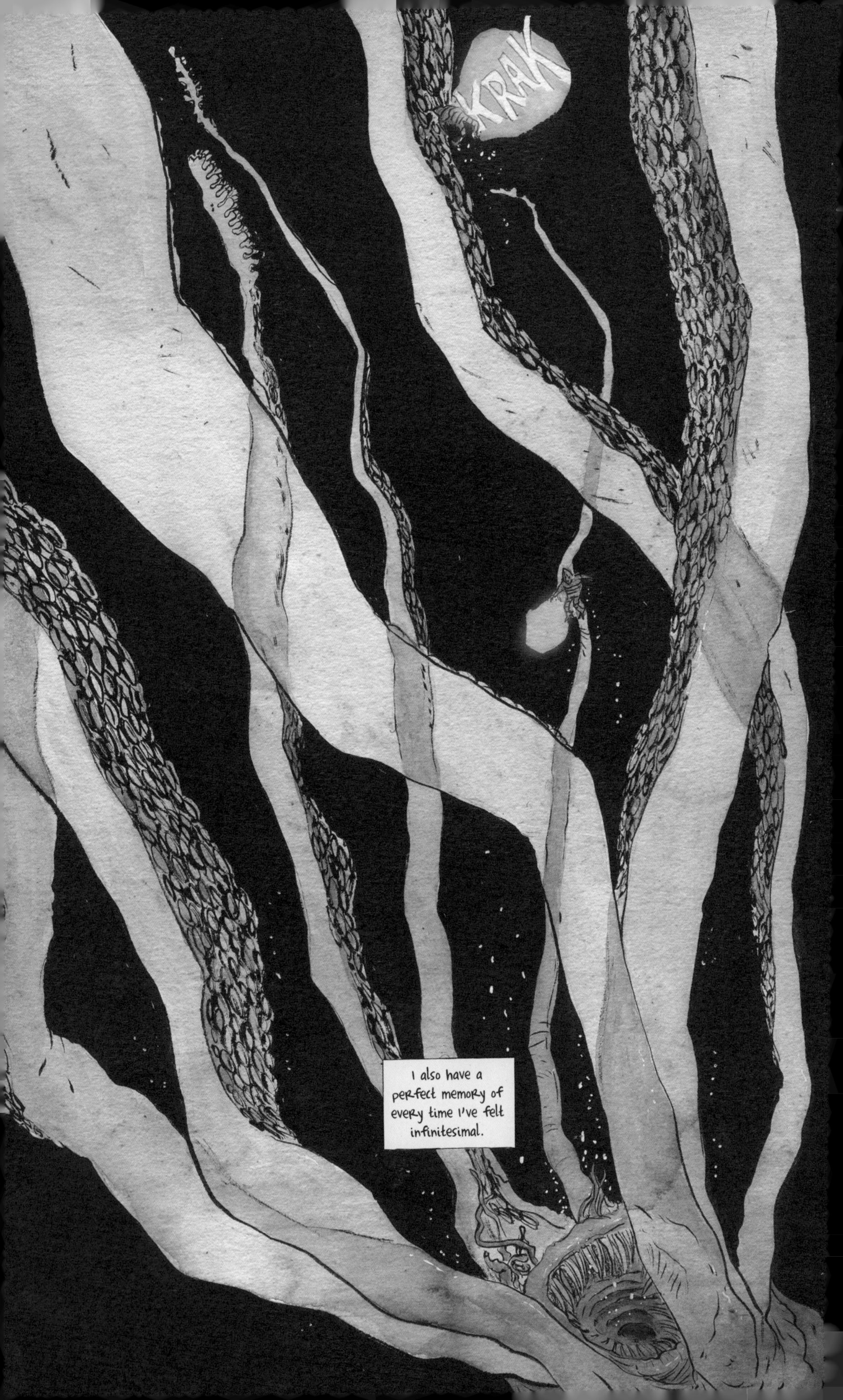
KRAK
I also have a perfect memory of every time I've felt infinitesimal.

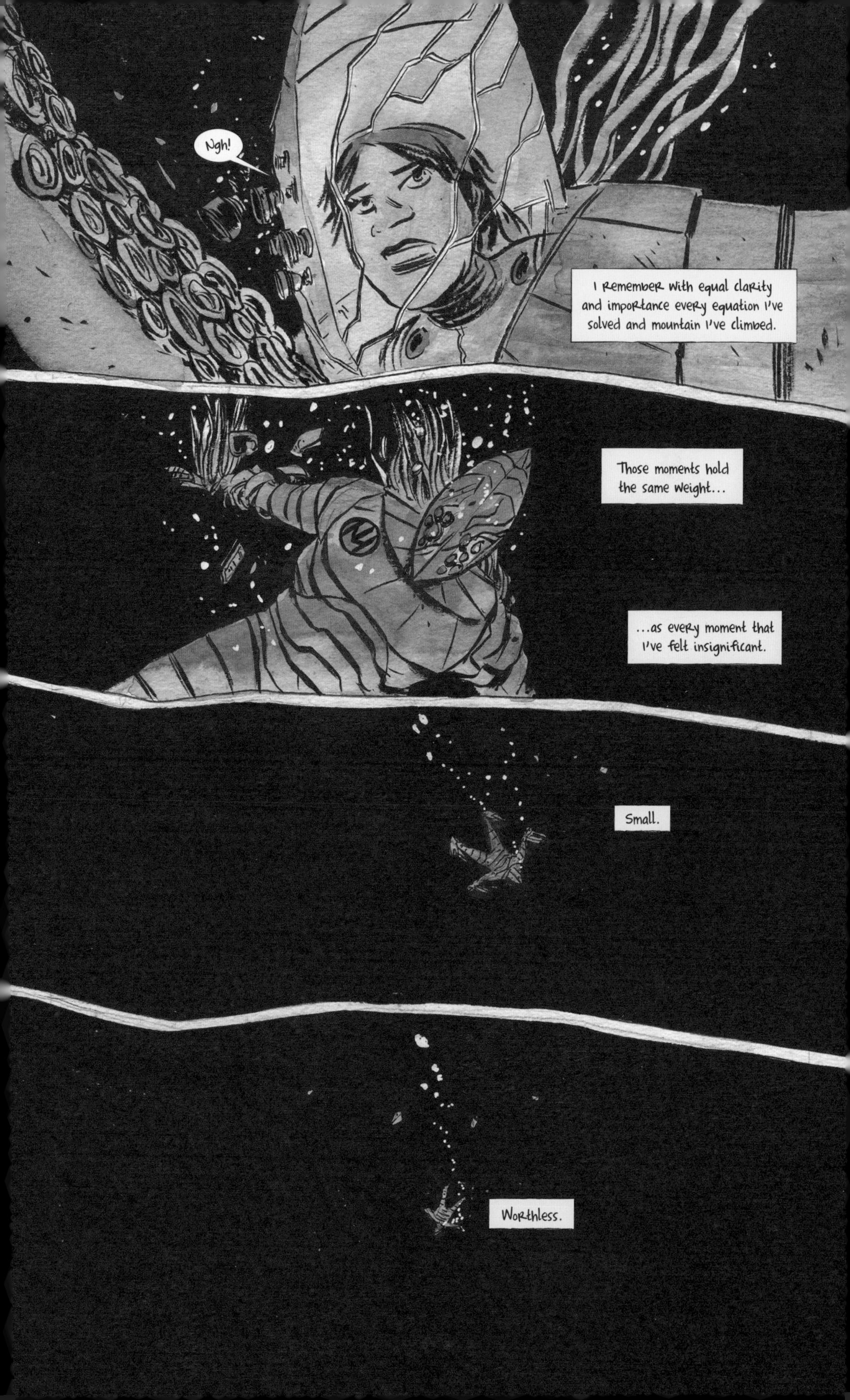
Ngh!
I remember with equal clarity and importance every equation I've solved and mountain I've climbed.
Those moments hold the same weight...
...as every moment that I've felt insignificant.
Small.
Worthless.

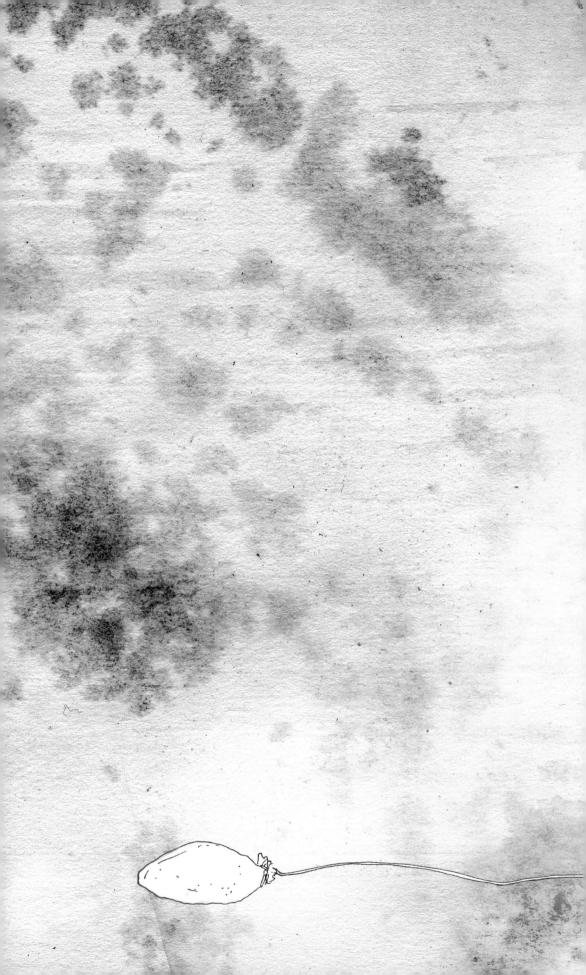

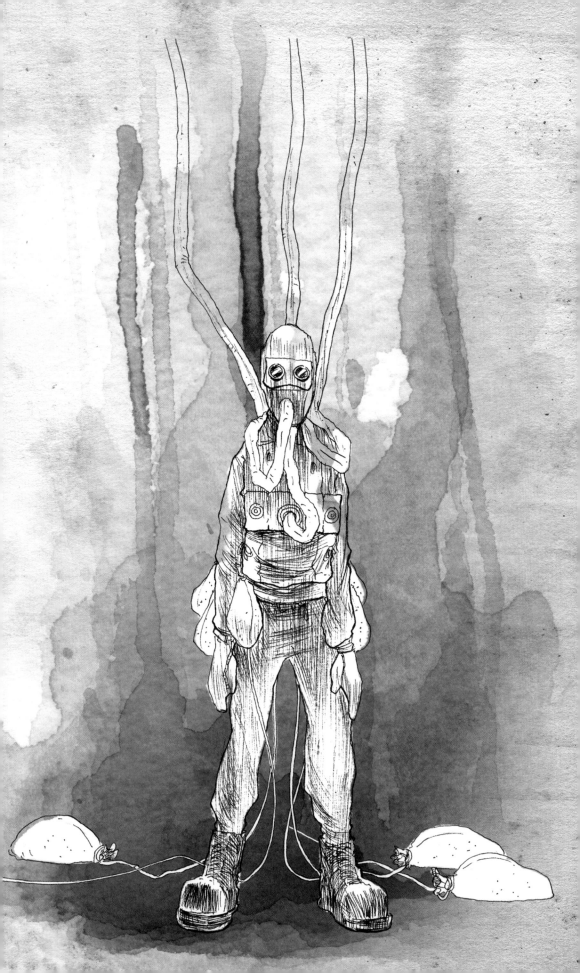

...fifty-nine...
...sixty!
...sixty-one...
...sixty-two...
...sixty-three...
...sixty-four...
Ghahh!
Huff! Huff!
Two minutes! That's a new record!
EXHALE

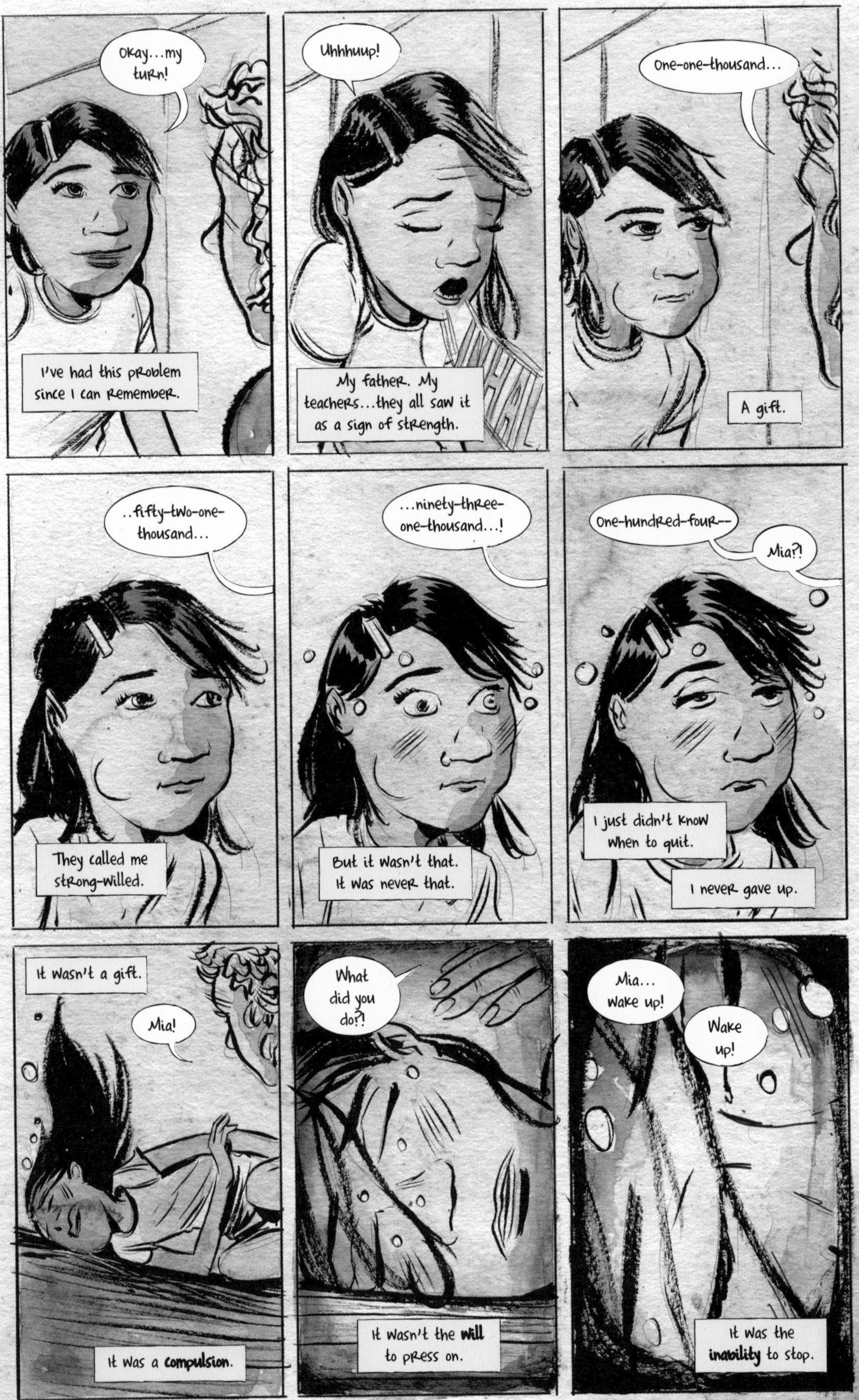
Okay...my turn!
I've had this problem since I can remember.
Uhhhuup!
My father. My teachers...they all saw it as a sign of strength.
One-one-thousand...
A gift.
...fifty-two-one-thousand...
They called me strong-willed.
...ninety-three-one-thousand...!
But it wasn't that. It was never that.
One-hundred-four--
Mia?!
I just didn't know when to quit.
I never gave up.
It wasn't a gift.
Mia!
It was a **compulsion**.
What did you do?!
It wasn't the **will** to press on.
Mia... Wake up!
Wake up!
It was the **inability** to stop.

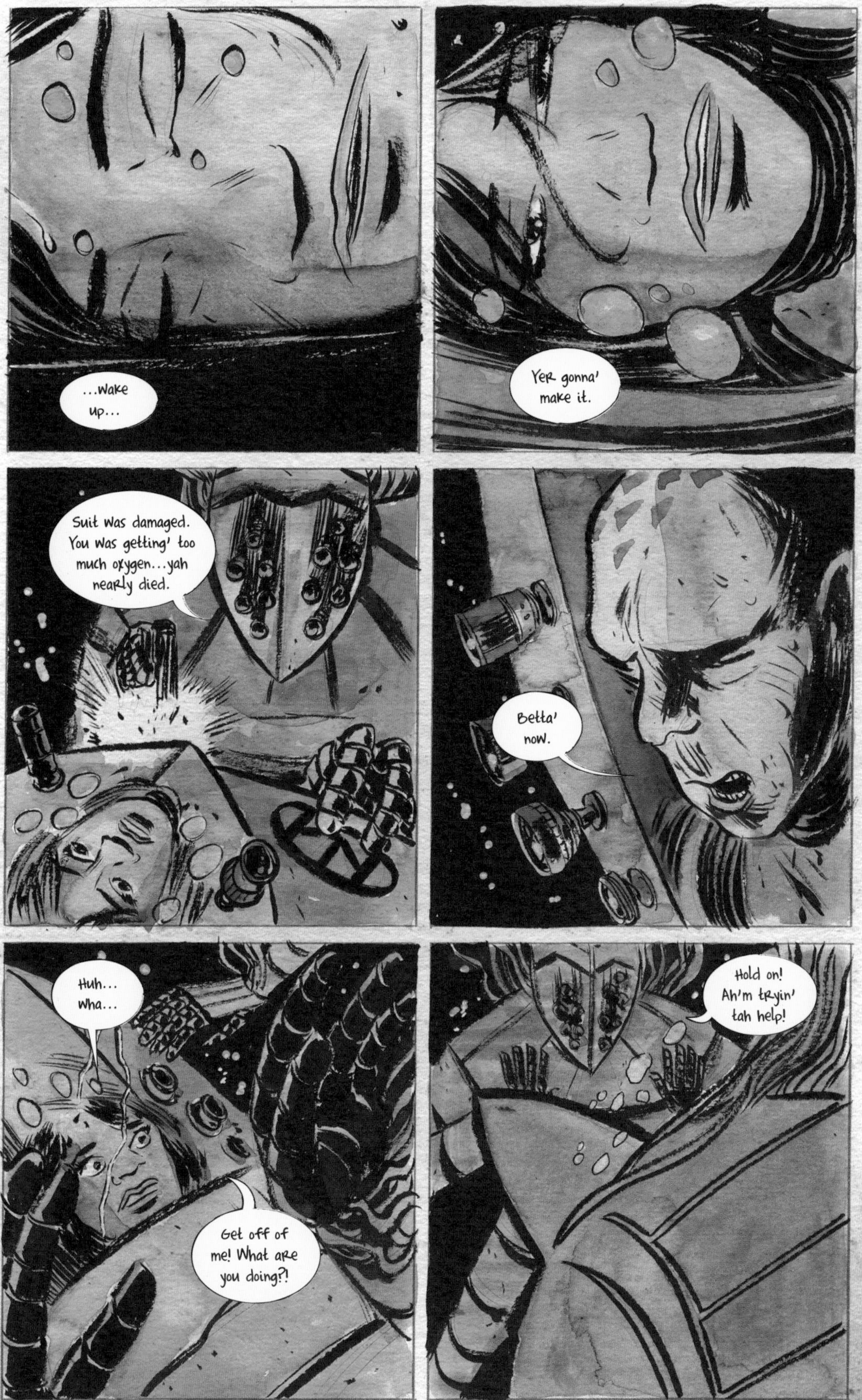
...Wake up...
Yer gonna' make it.
Suit was damaged. You was getting' too much oxygen...yah nearly died.
Betta' now.
Huh... Wha...
Get off of me! What are you doing?!
Hold on! Ah'm tryin' tah help!

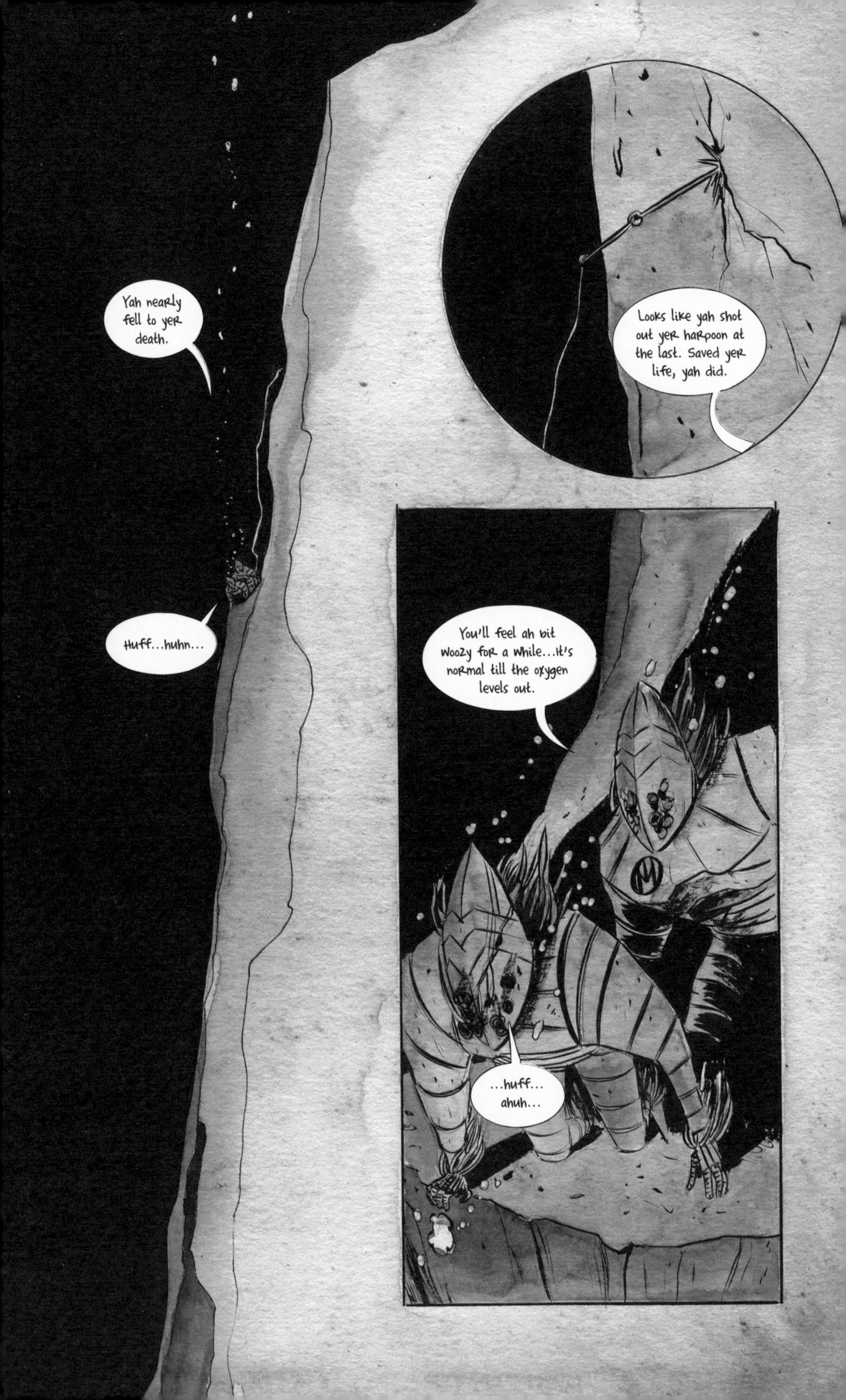

Yah nearly fell to yer death.
Looks like yah shot out yer harpoon at the last. Saved yer life, yah did.
Huff...huhn...
You'll feel ah bit woozy for a while...It's normal till the oxygen levels out.
...huff... ahuh...

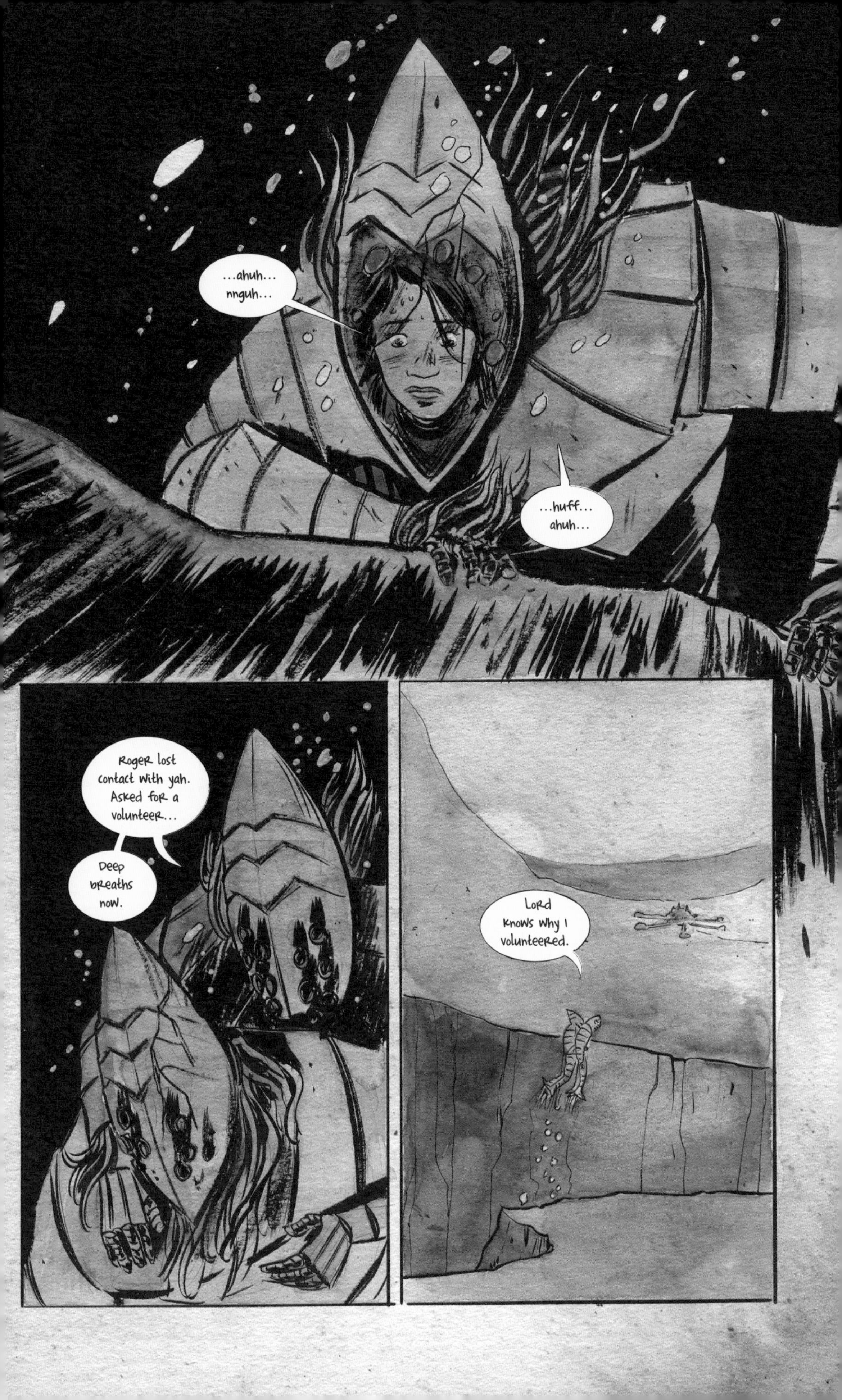
...ahuh...
nnguh...
...huff...
ahuh...
Roger lost contact with yah. Asked for a volunteer...
Deep breaths now.
Lord knows why I volunteered.

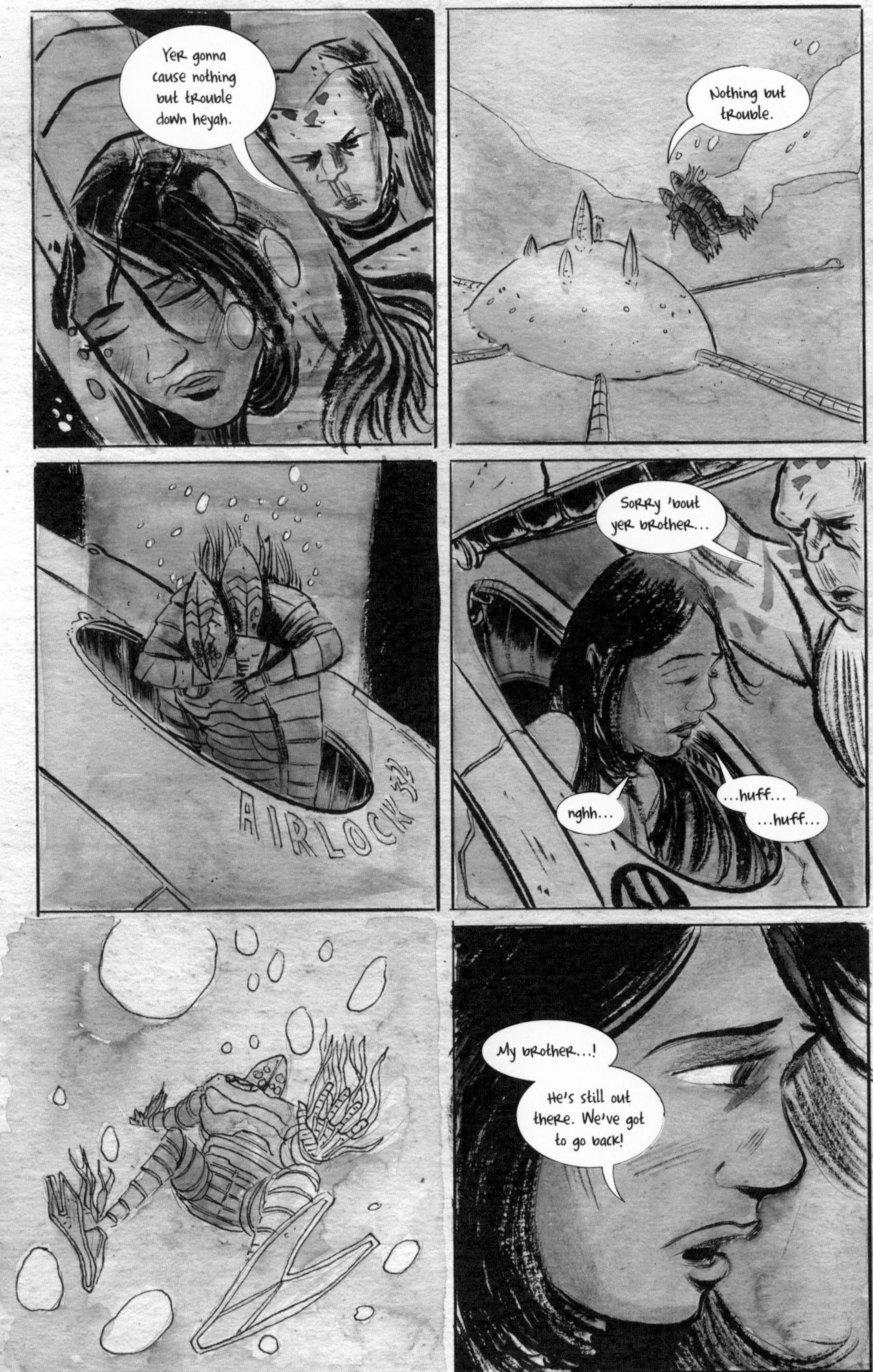
Yer gonna cause nothing but trouble down heyah.
Nothing but trouble.
Sorry 'bout yer brother...
nghh...
...huff...
...huff...
AIRLOCK 32
My brother...!
He's still out there. We've got to go back!

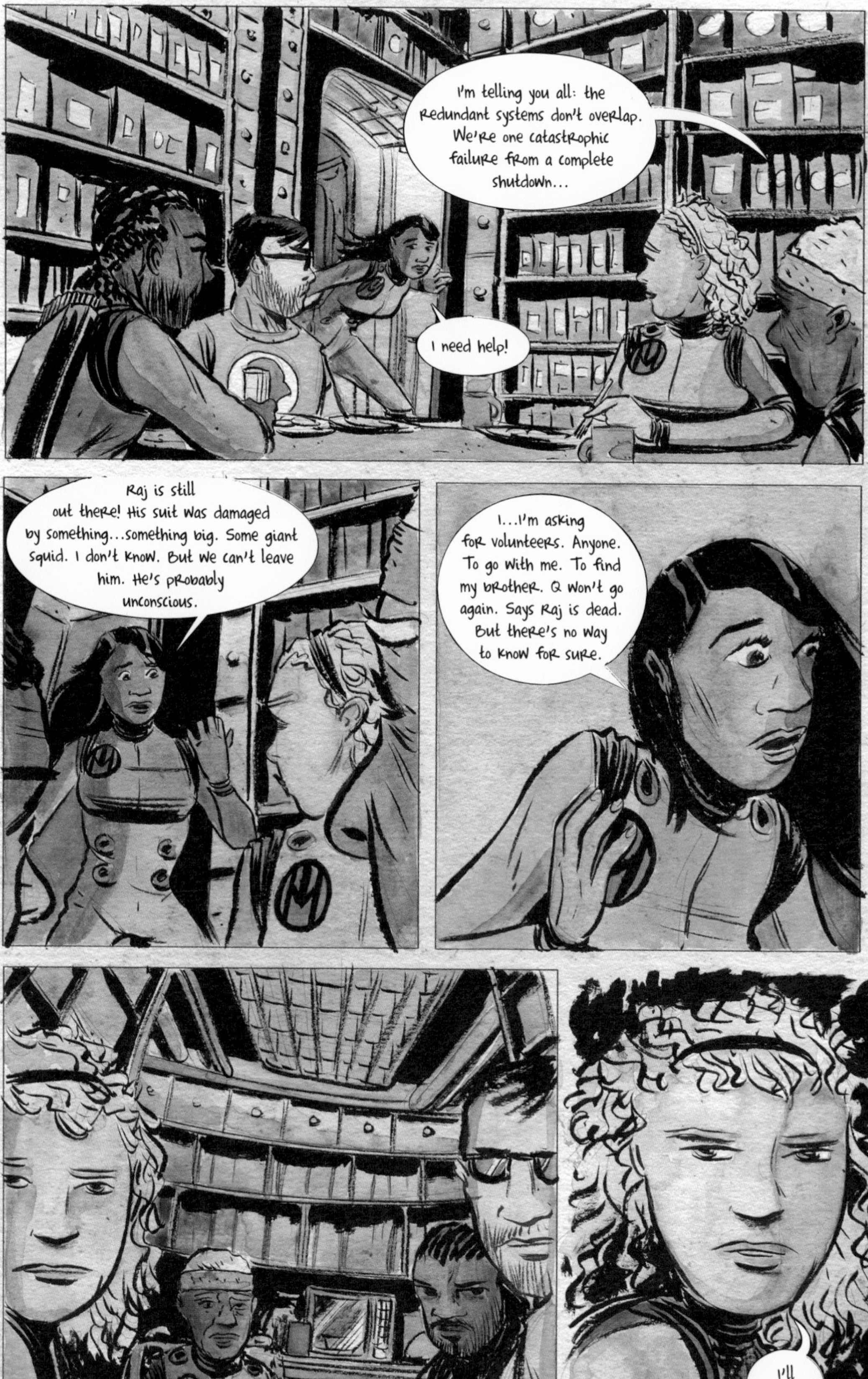
I'm telling you all: the redundant systems don't overlap. We're one catastrophic failure from a complete shutdown...
I need help!
Raj is still out there! His suit was damaged by something...something big. Some giant squid. I don't know. But we can't leave him. He's probably unconscious.
I...I'm asking for volunteers. Anyone. To go with me. To find my brother. Q won't go again. Says Raj is dead. But there's no way to know for sure.
I'll help.

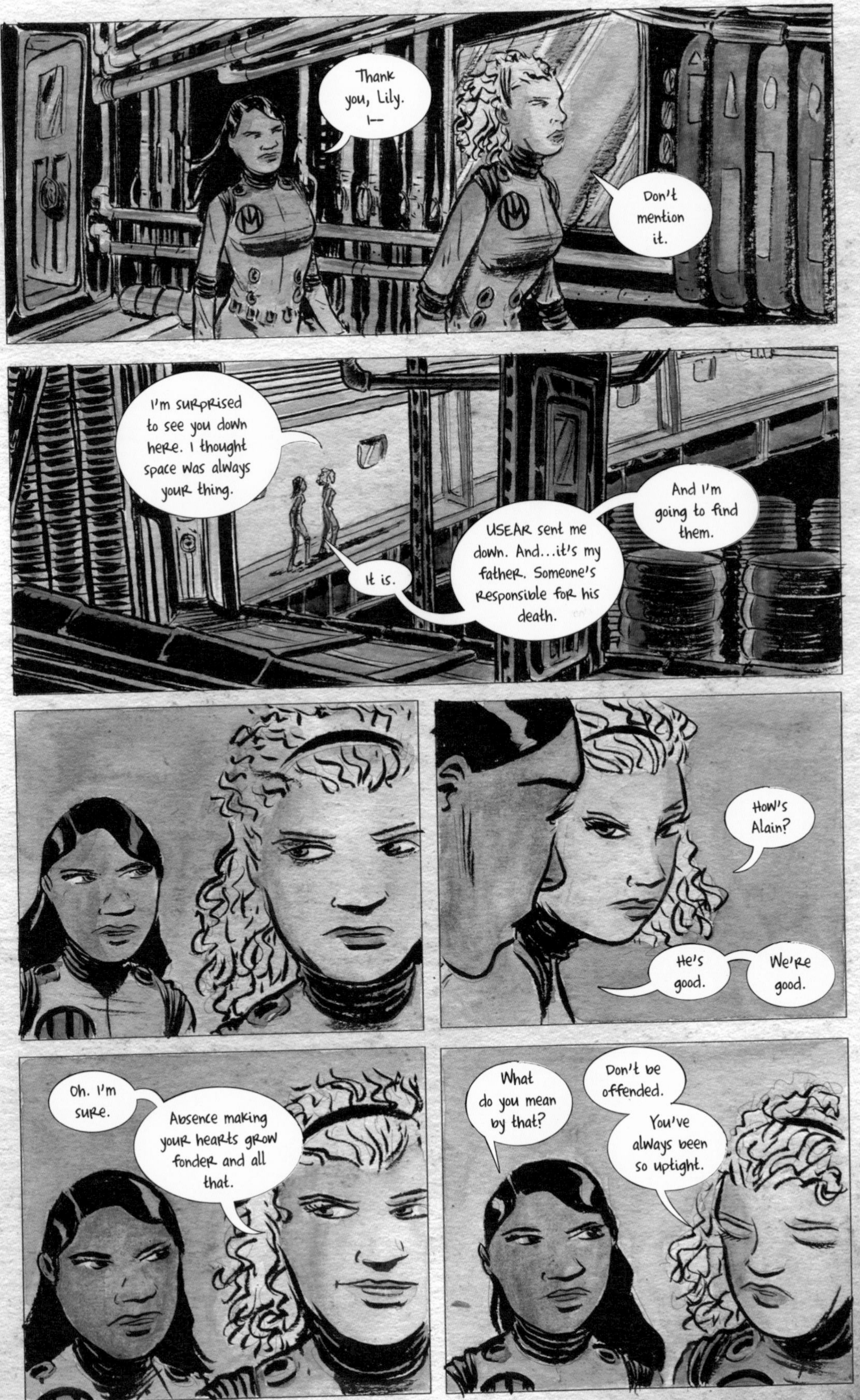
Thank you, Lily. I--
Don't mention it.
I'm surprised to see you down here. I thought space was always your thing.
It is.
USEAR sent me down. And...it's my father. Someone's responsible for his death.
And I'm going to find them.
How's Alain?
He's good.
We're good.
Oh. I'm sure.
Absence making your hearts grow fonder and all that.
What do you mean by that?
Don't be offended.
You've always been so uptight.

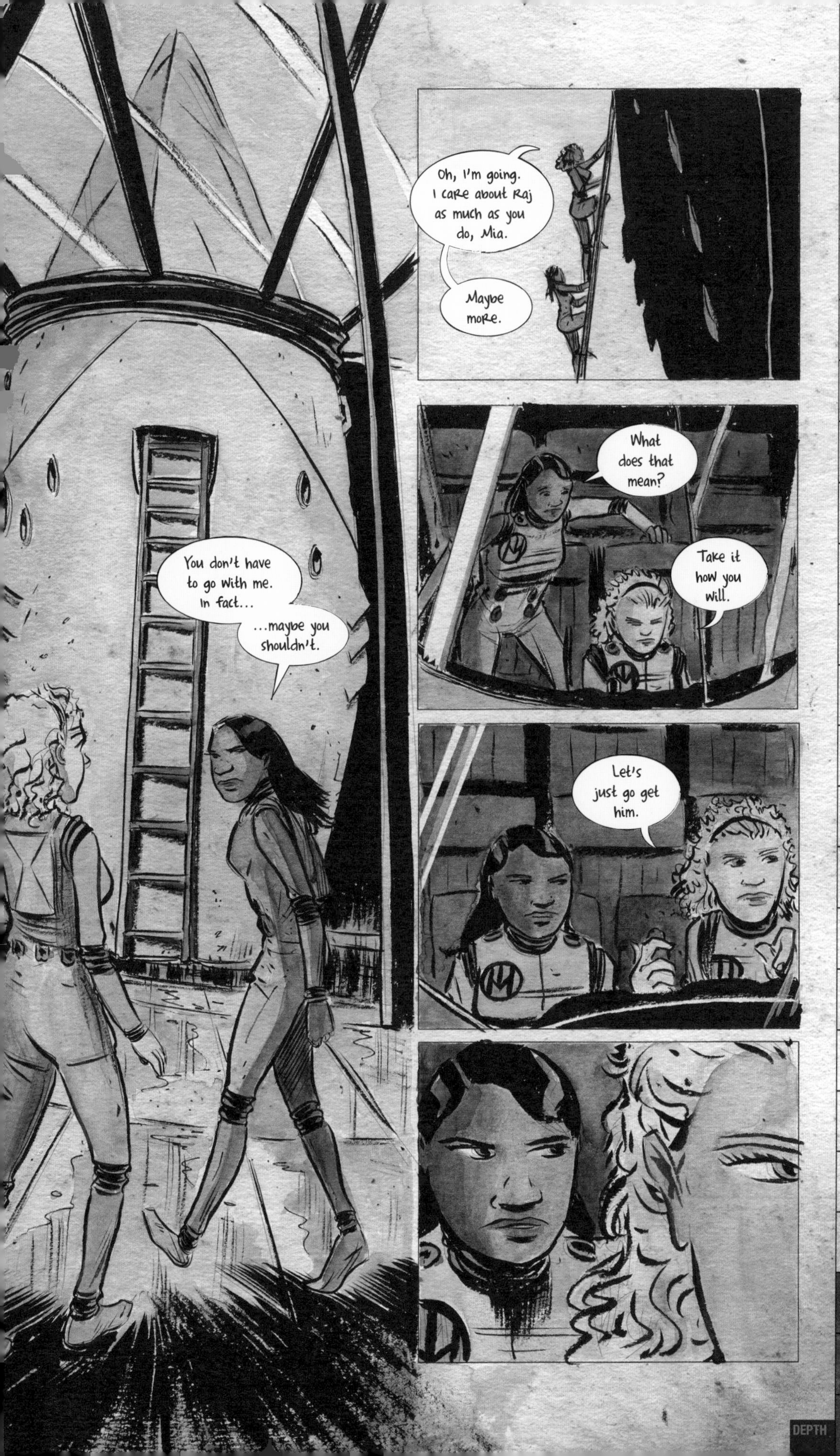
You don't have to go with me. In fact...
...maybe you shouldn't.
Oh, I'm going. I care about Raj as much as you do, Mia.
Maybe more.
What does that mean?
Take it how you will.
Let's just go get him.

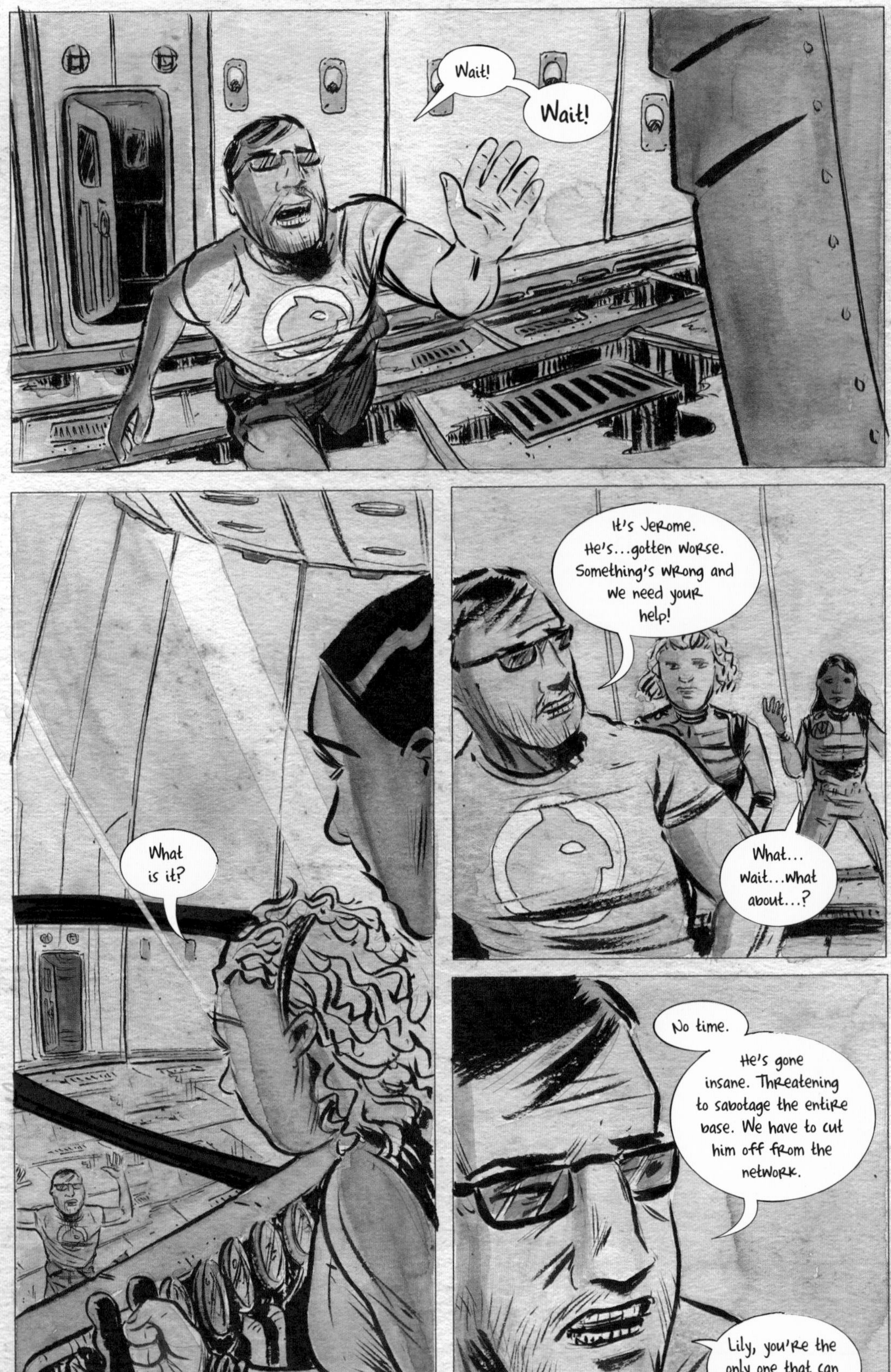
Wait!
Wait!
What is it?
It's Jerome. He's...gotten worse. Something's wrong and we need your help!
What... wait...what about...?
No time.
He's gone insane. Threatening to sabotage the entire base. We have to cut him off from the network.
Lily, you're the only one that can limit his access!

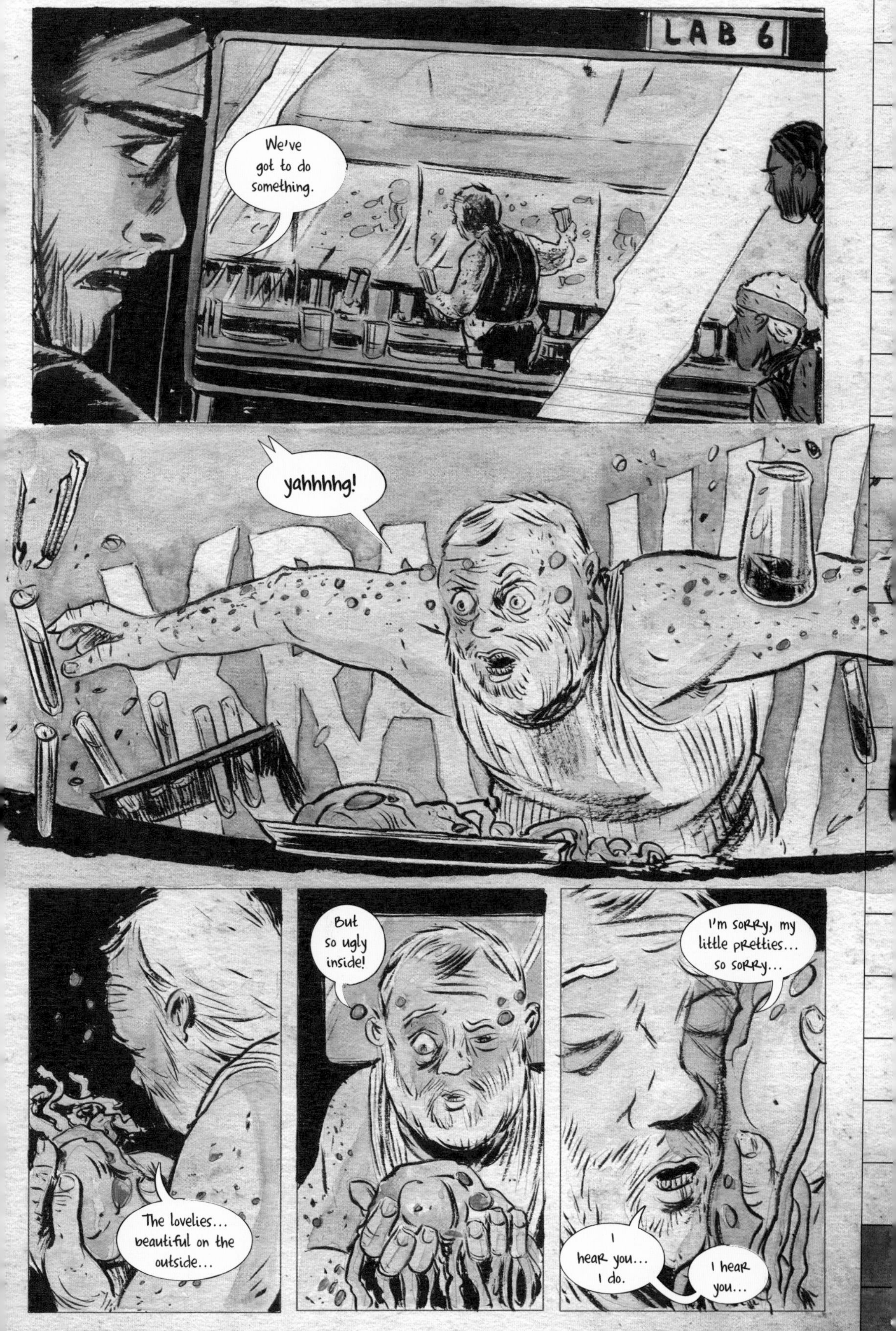

LAB 6
We've got to do something.
yahhhhg!
The lovelies... beautiful on the outside...
But so ugly inside!
I'm sorry, my little pretties... so sorry...
I hear you... I do.
I hear you...

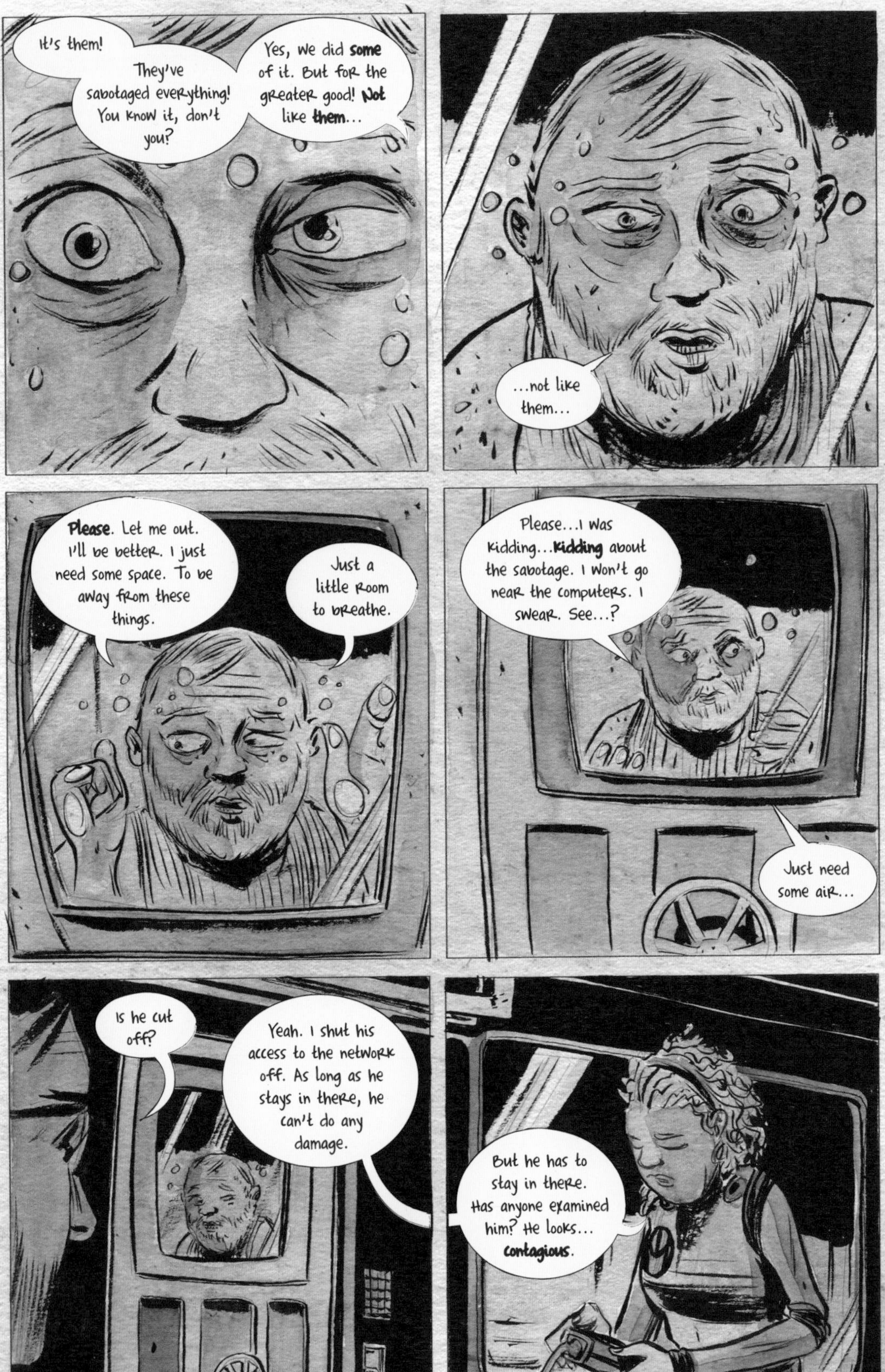
It's them!
They've sabotaged everything! You know it, don't you?
Yes, we did **some** of it. But for the greater good! **Not** like **them**...
...not like them...
Please. Let me out. I'll be better. I just need some space. To be away from these things.
Just a little room to breathe.
Please...I was kidding...**Kidding** about the sabotage. I won't go near the computers. I swear. See...?
Just need some air...
Is he cut off?
Yeah. I shut his access to the network off. As long as he stays in there, he can't do any damage.
But he has to stay in there. Has anyone examined him? He looks... **contagious**.

Have you seen my dad?
Research lab, I think.
Thanks.
...See? The beauty is in these small details. It's all around us...
...we just have to take notice.
It's amazing, Hari. You're amazing.

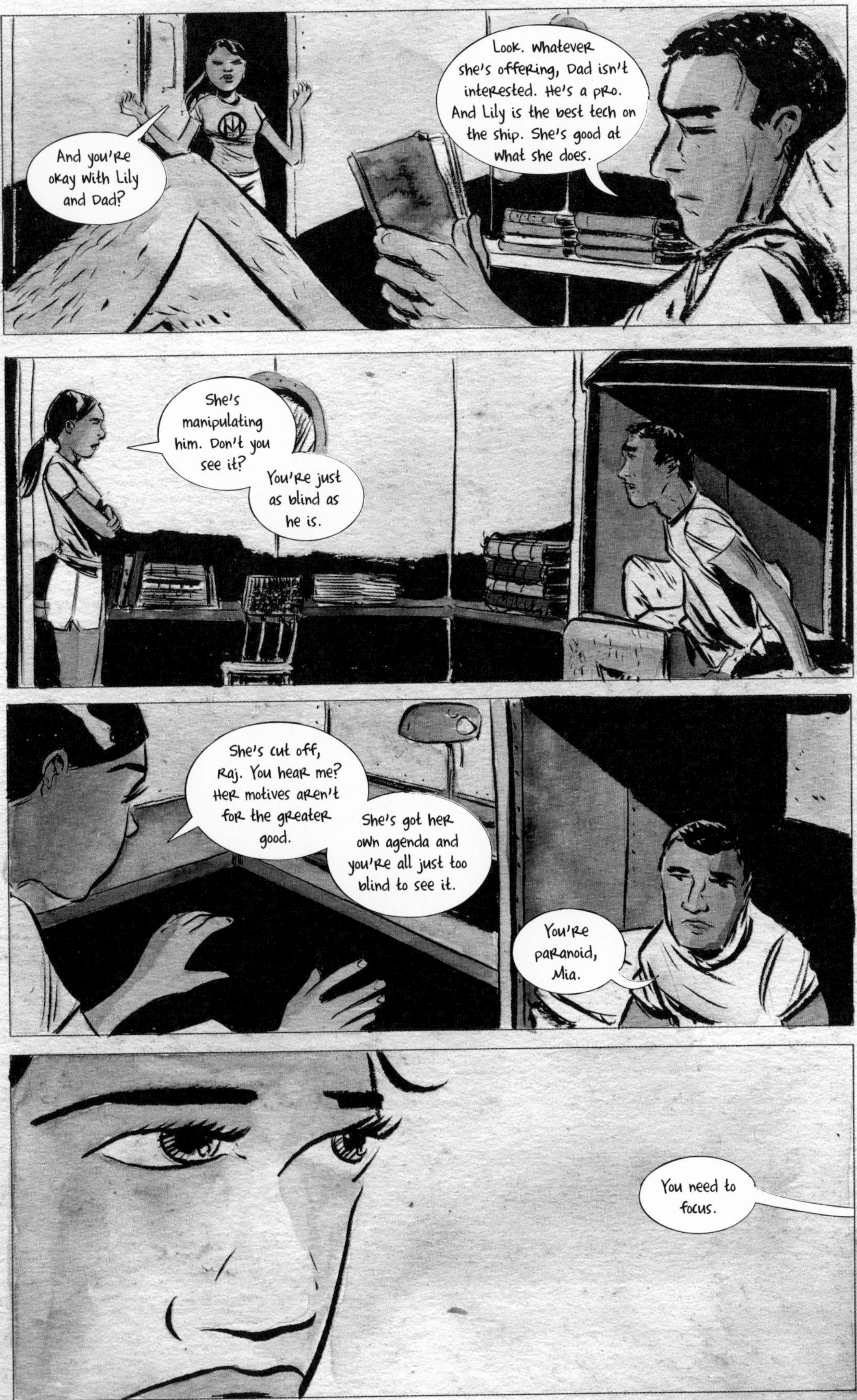

And you're okay with Lily and Dad?
Look. Whatever she's offering, Dad isn't interested. He's a pro. And Lily is the best tech on the ship. She's good at what she does.
She's manipulating him. Don't you see it?
You're just as blind as he is.
She's cut off, Raj. You hear me? Her motives aren't for the greater good.
She's got her own agenda and you're all just too blind to see it.
You're paranoid, Mia.
You need to focus.

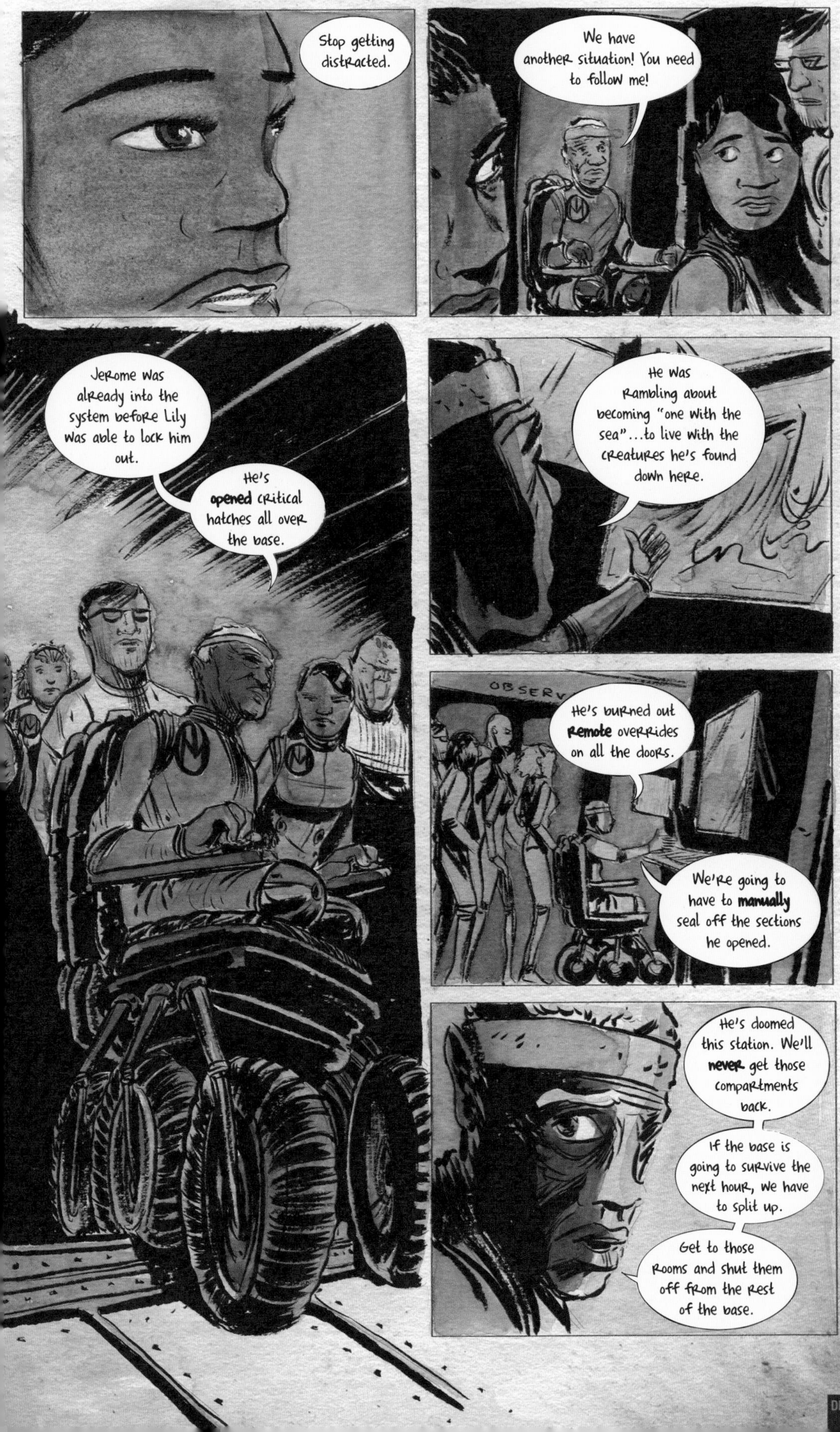

Stop getting distracted.
We have another situation! You need to follow me!
Jerome was already into the system before Lily was able to lock him out.
He's **opened** critical hatches all over the base.
He was rambling about becoming "one with the sea"...to live with the creatures he's found down here.
OBSERV
He's burned out **remote** overrides on all the doors.
We're going to have to **manually** seal off the sections he opened.
He's doomed this station. We'll **never** get those compartments back.
If the base is going to survive the next hour, we have to split up.
Get to those rooms and shut them off from the rest of the base.

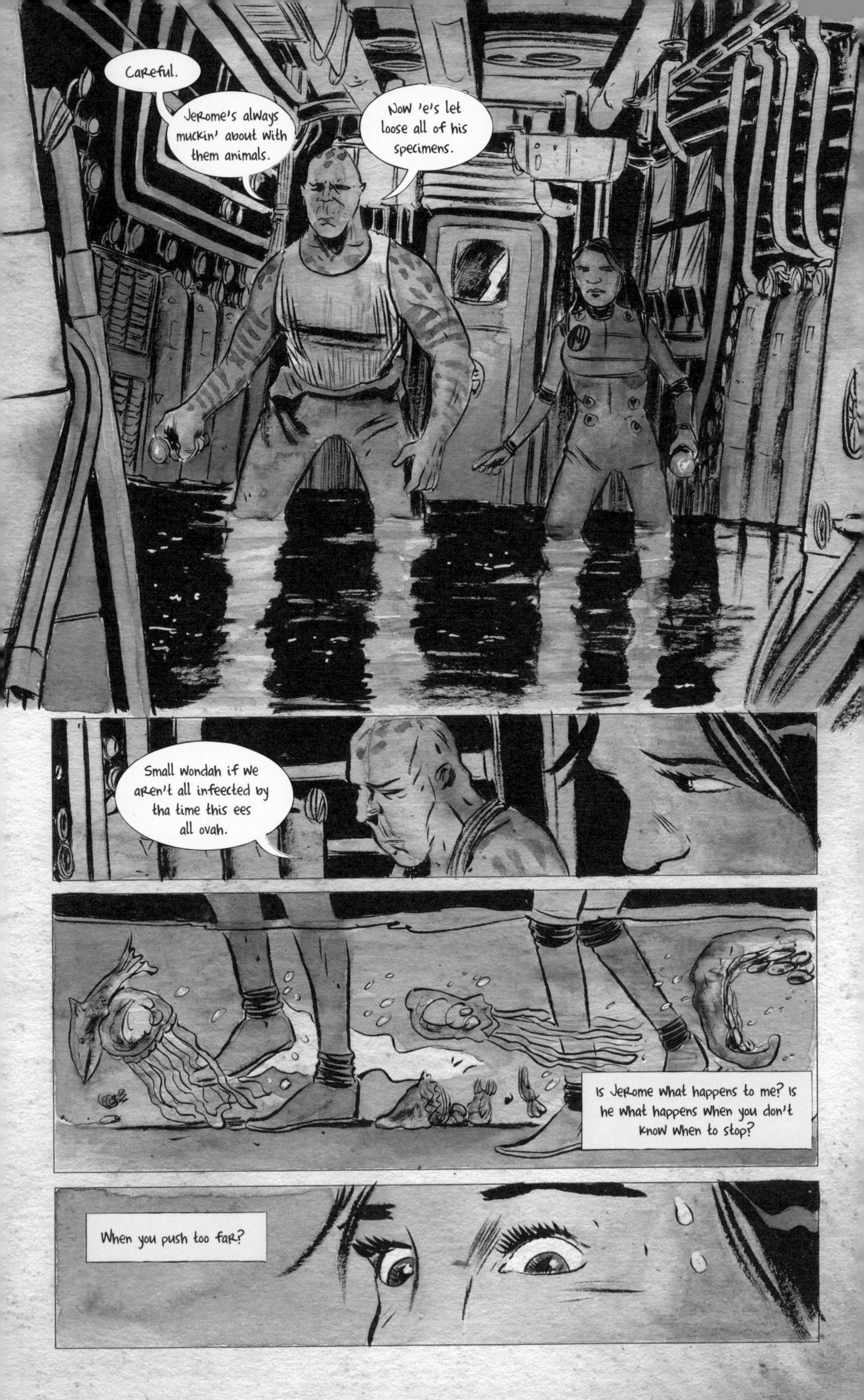
Careful.
Jerome's always muckin' about with them animals.
Now 'e's let loose all of his specimens.
Small wondah if we aren't all infeected by tha time this ees all ovah.
Is Jerome what happens to me? Is he what happens when you don't know when to stop?
When you push too far?

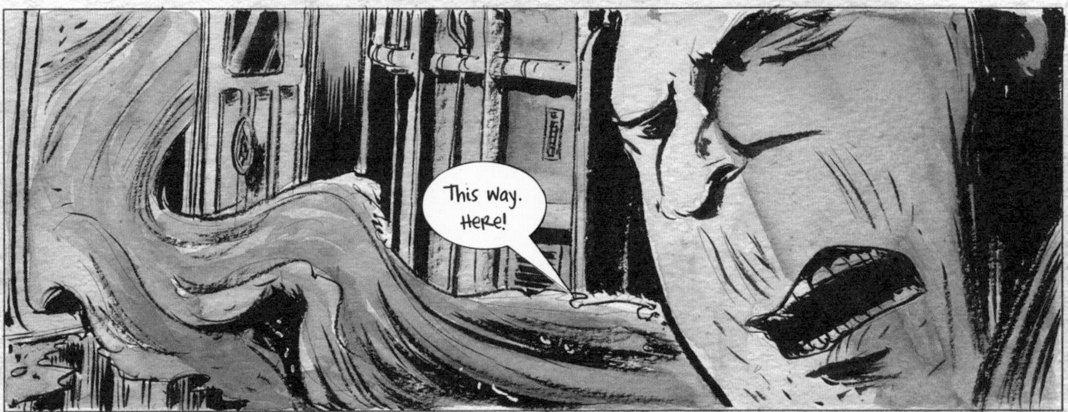
This way. Here!

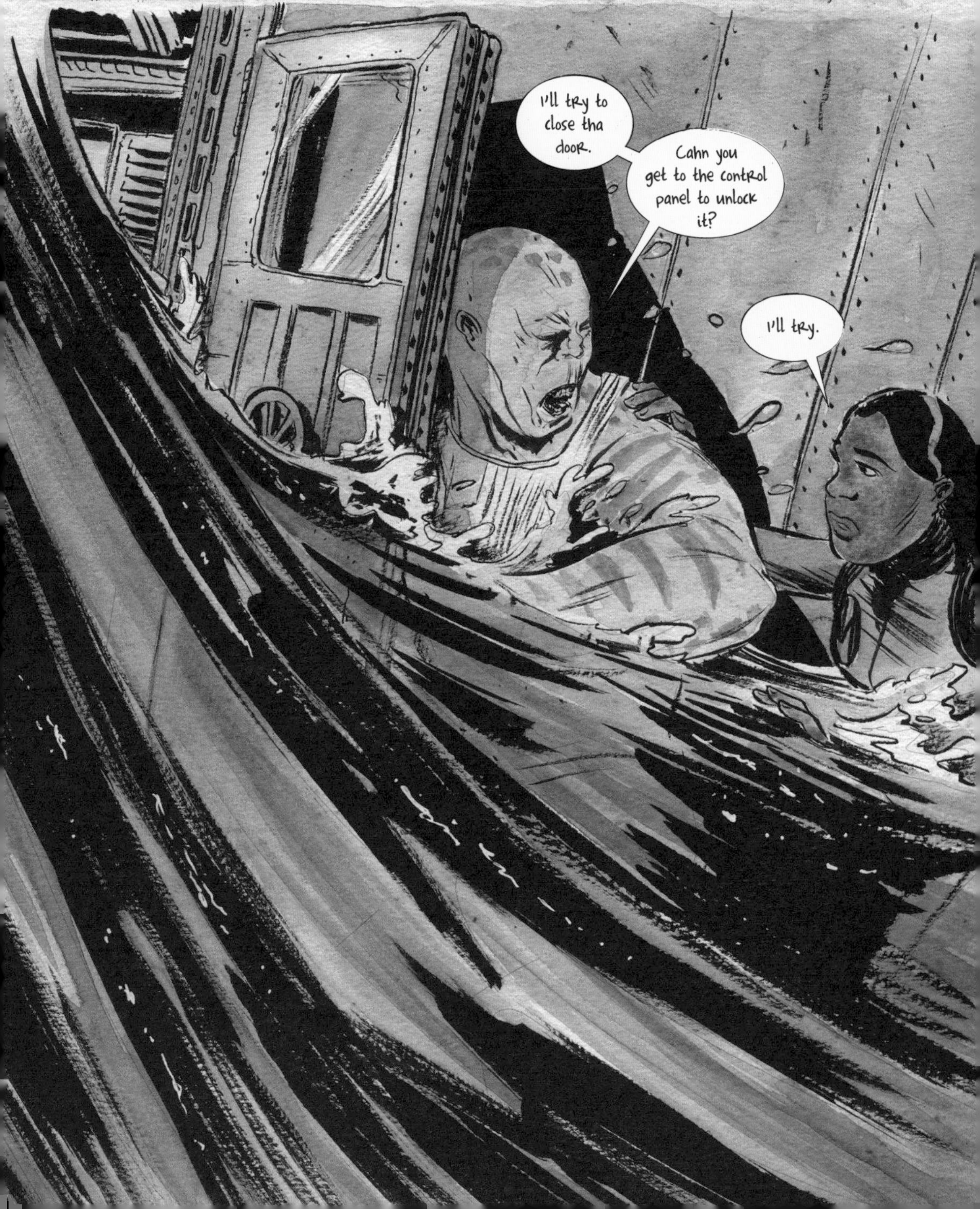
I'll try to close tha door.
Cahn you get to the control panel to unlock it?
I'll try.

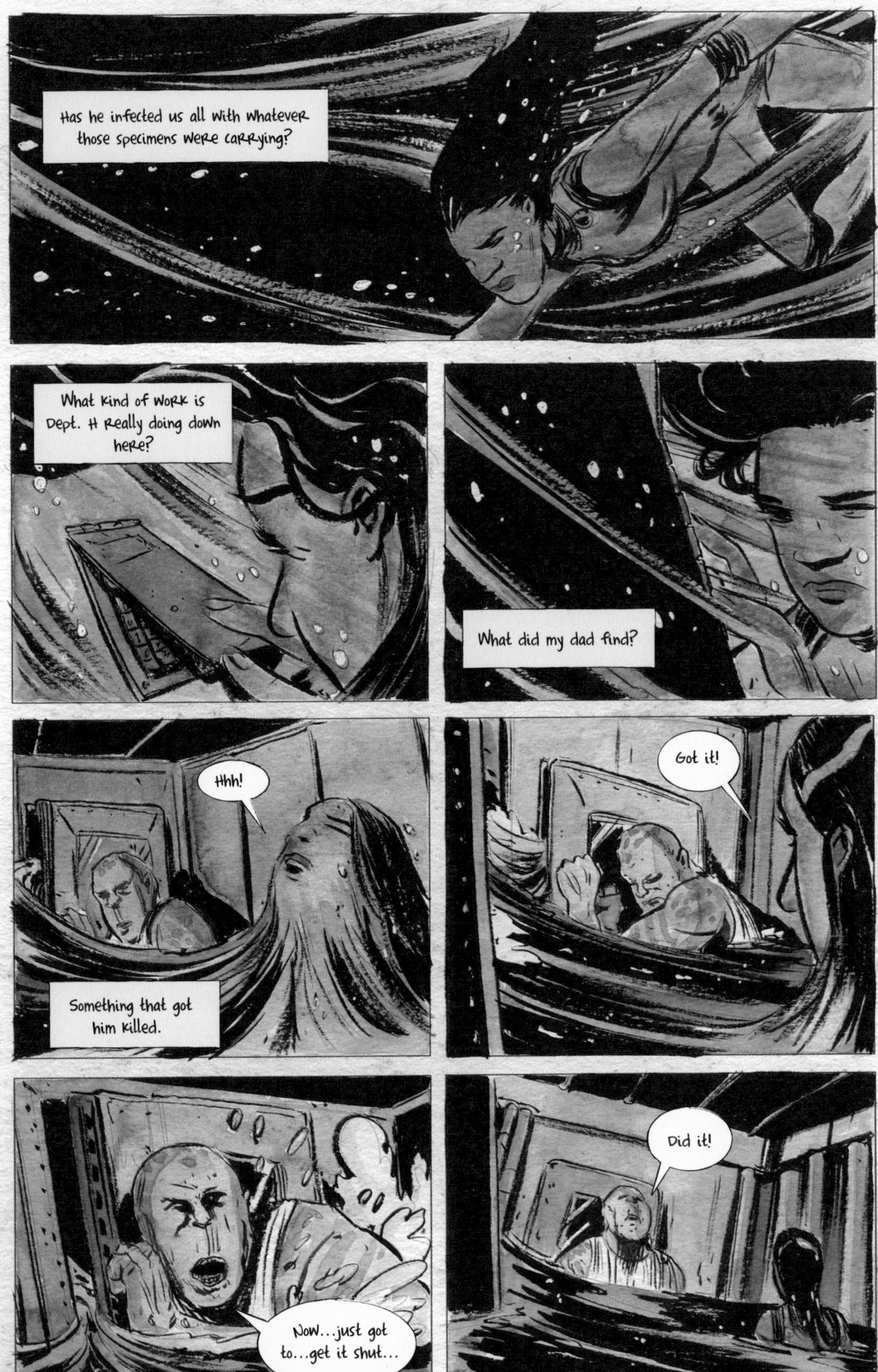

Has he infected us all with whatever those specimens were carrying?
What kind of work is Dept. H really doing down here?
What did my dad find?
Hhh!
Something that got him killed.
Got it!
Now...just got to...get it shut...
Did it!

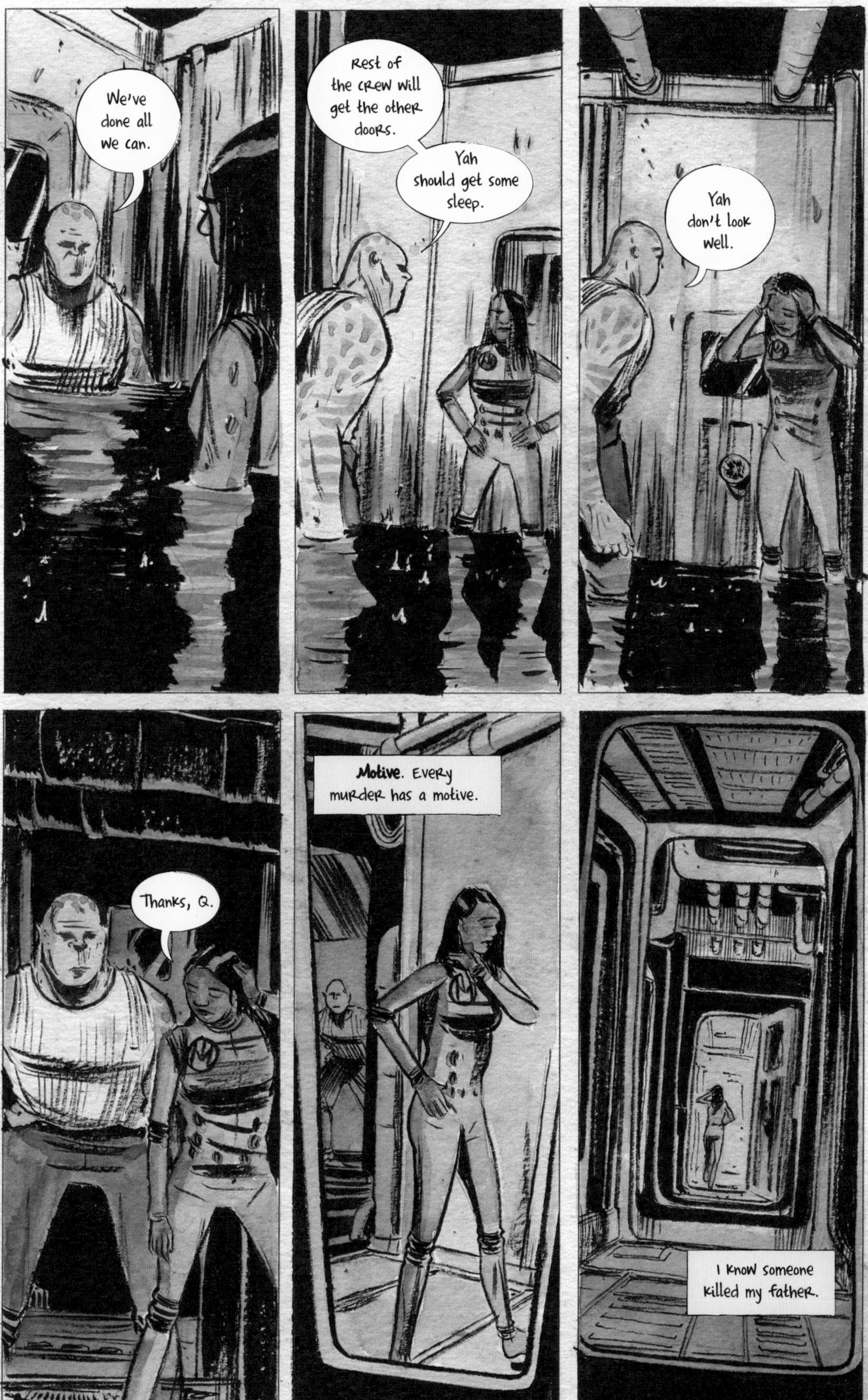
We've done all we can.
Rest of the crew will get the other doors.
Yah should get some sleep.
Yah don't look well.
Thanks, Q.
Motive. Every murder has a motive.
I know someone killed my father.

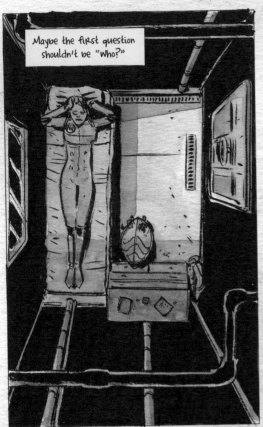

Maybe the first question shouldn't be "Who?"

Maybe it should be "Why?"

I have to know. I won't stop until I find out. But so tired...haven't slept for three days.

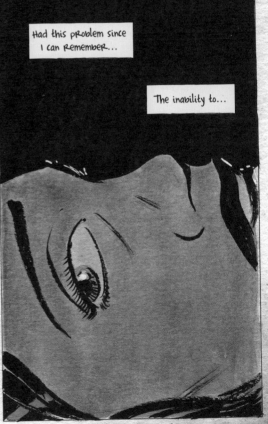

Had this problem since I can remember...

The inability to...

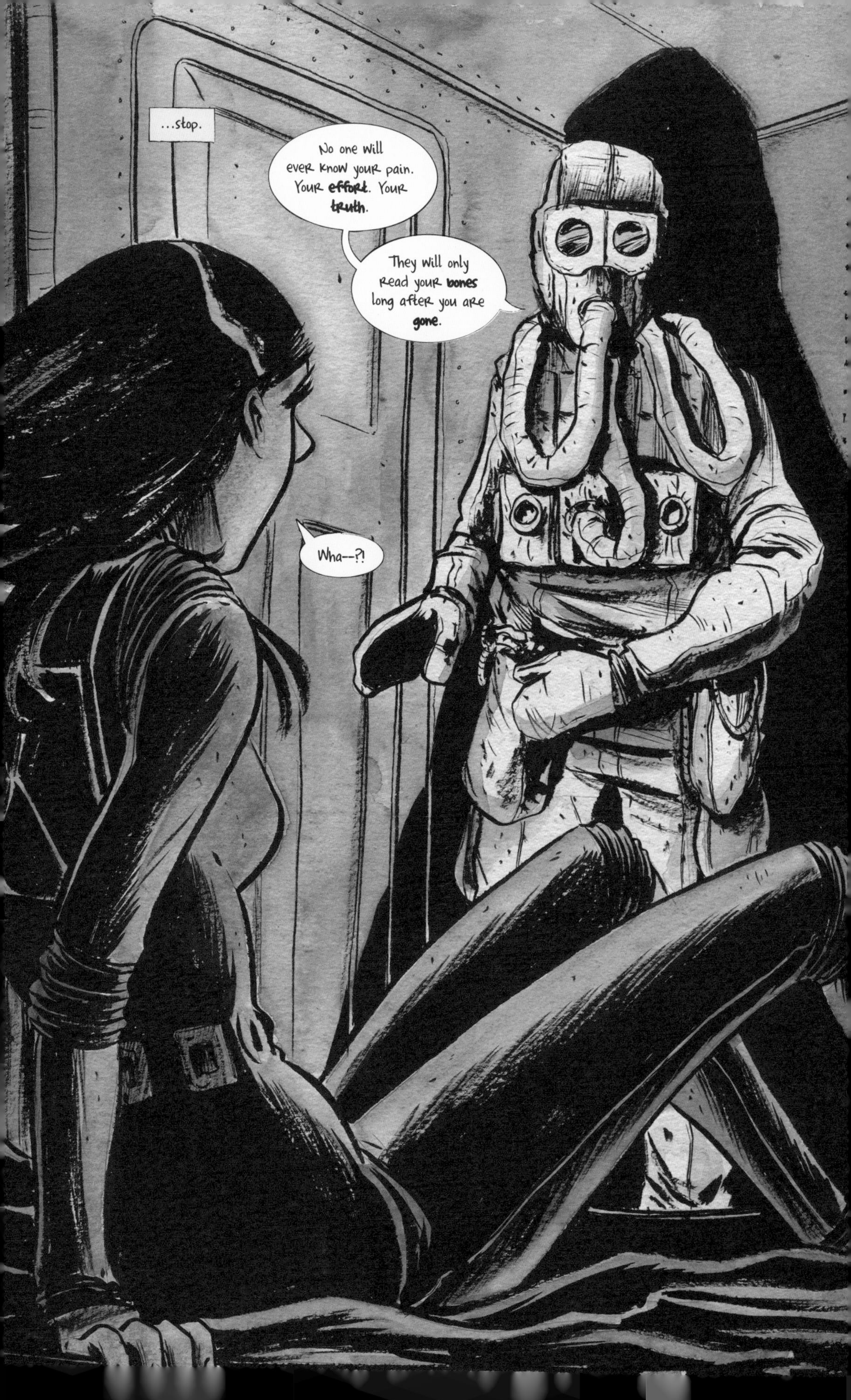
...stop.
No one will ever know your pain. Your effort. Your truth.
They will only read your bones long after you are gone.
Wha--?!

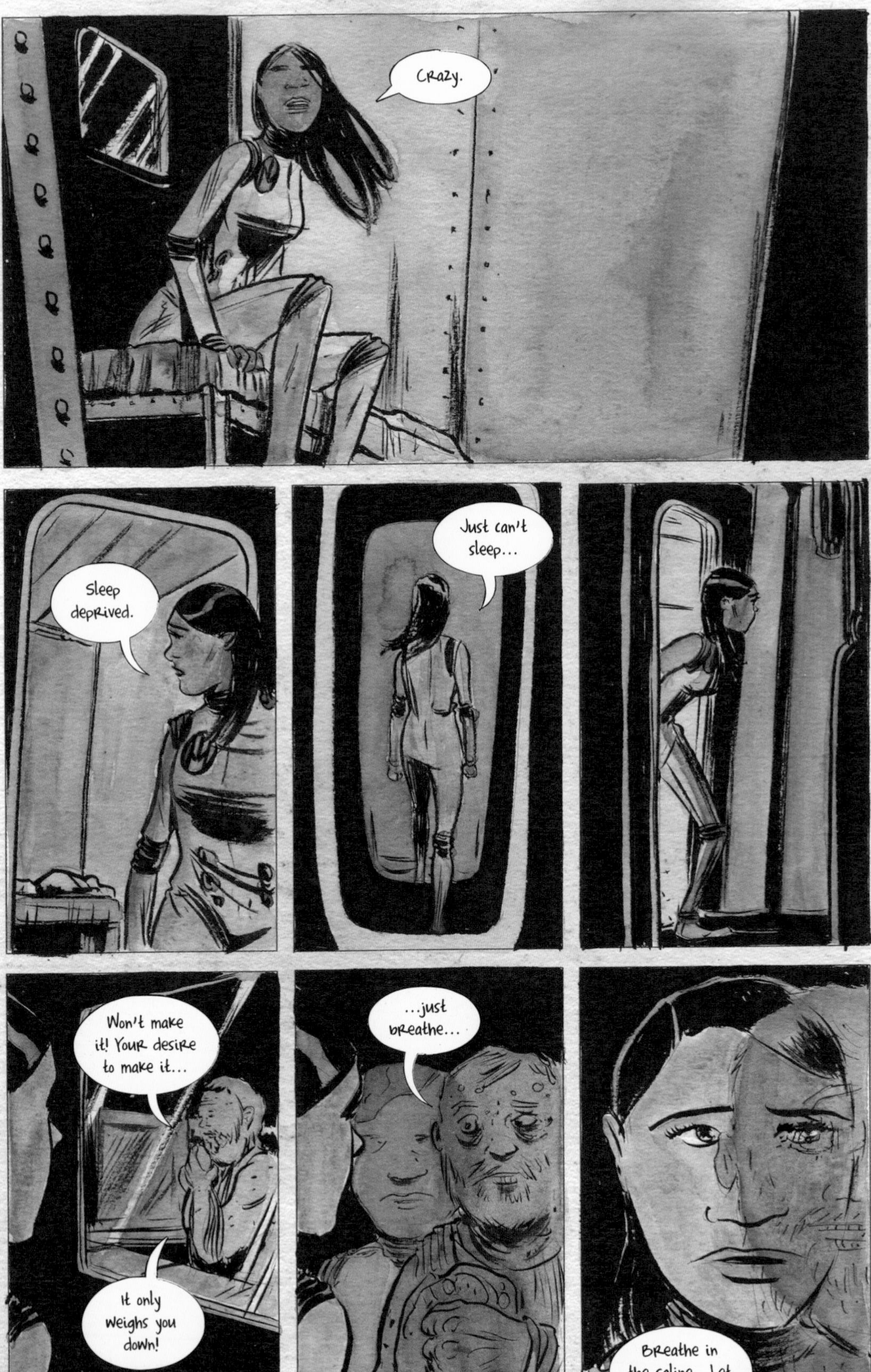
Crazy.
Sleep deprived.
Just can't sleep...
Won't make it! Your desire to make it...
It only weighs you down!
...just breathe...
Breathe in the saline...Let it fill you...

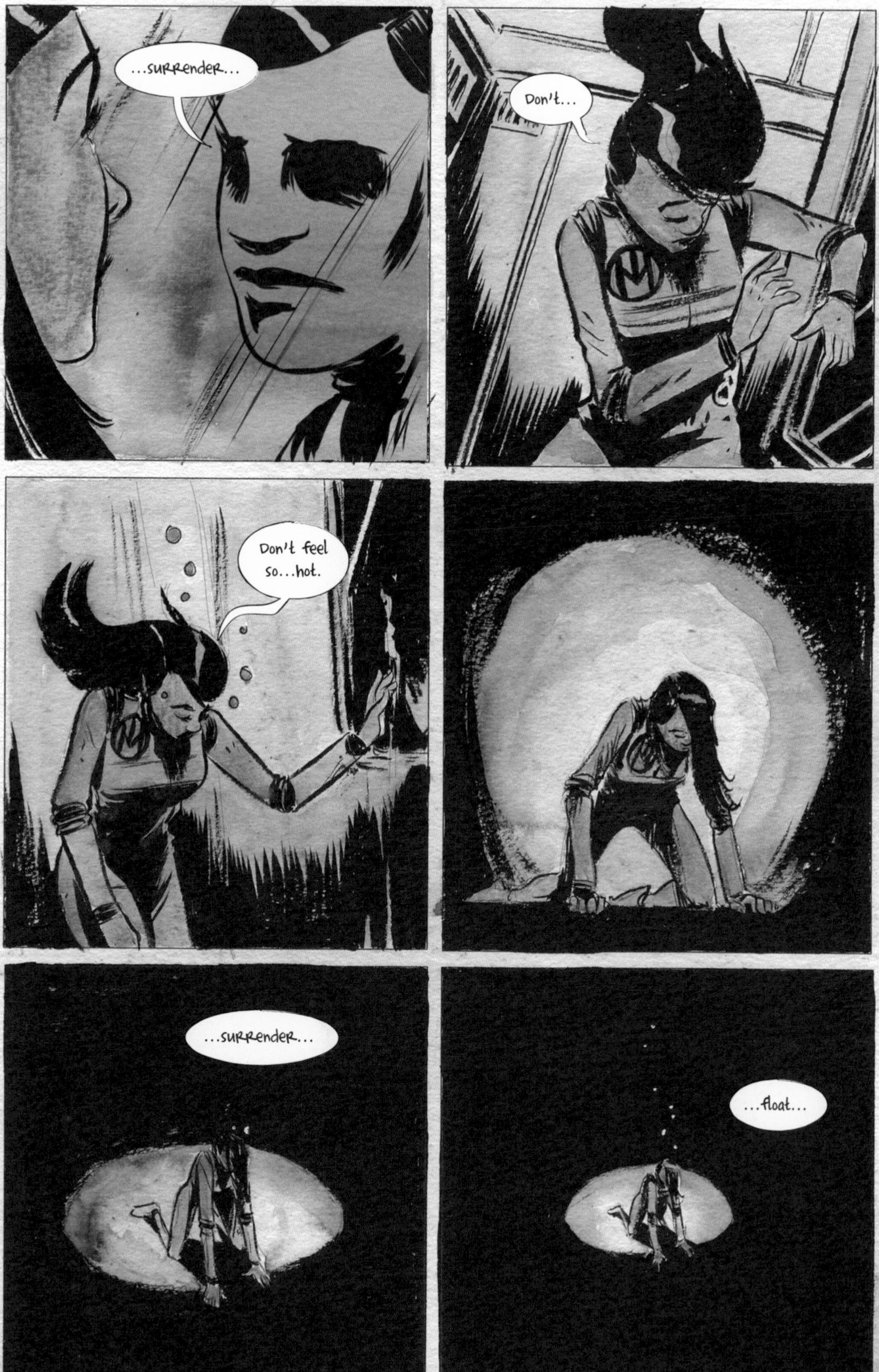
...surrender...
Don't...
Don't feel so...hot.
...surrender...
...float...

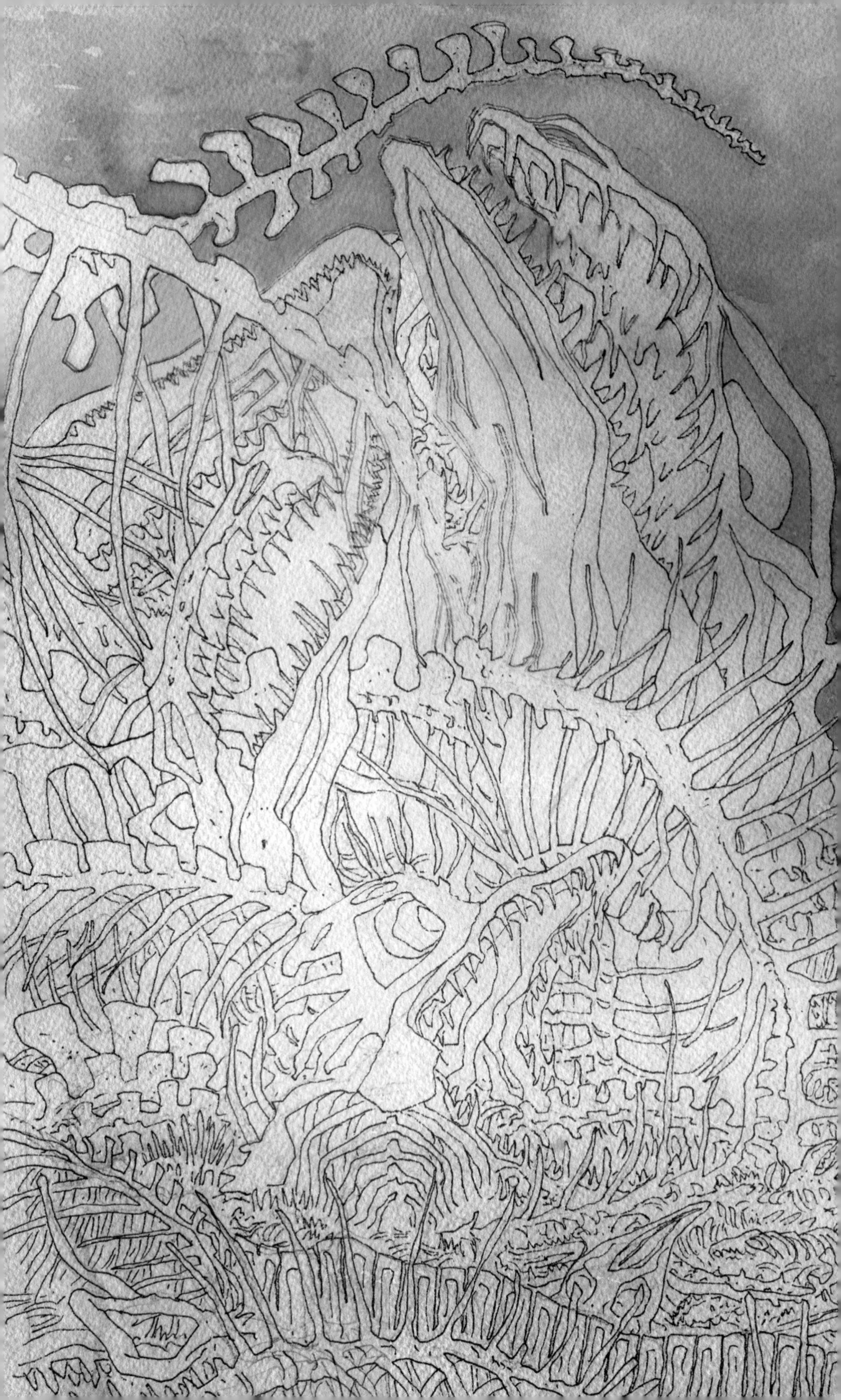

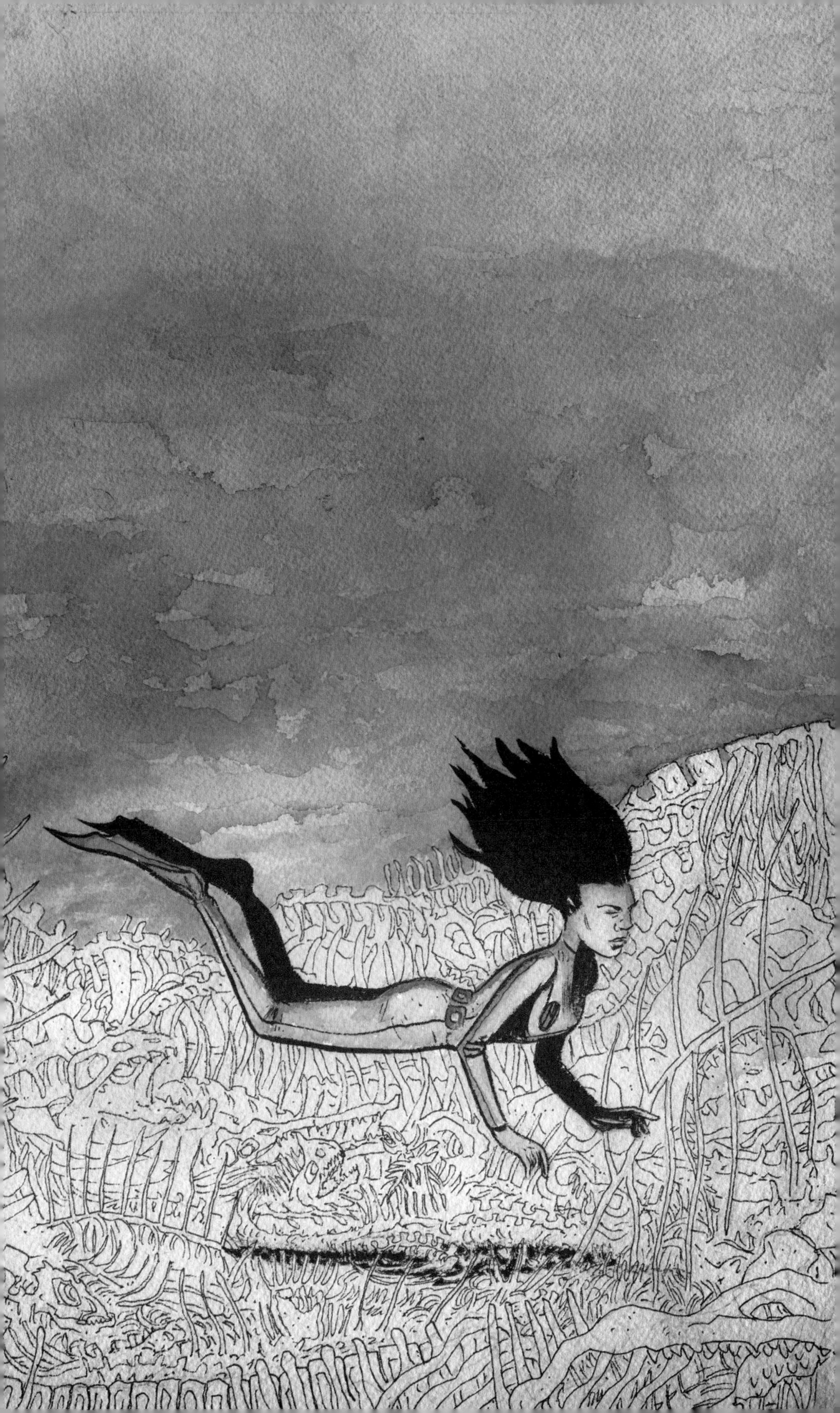

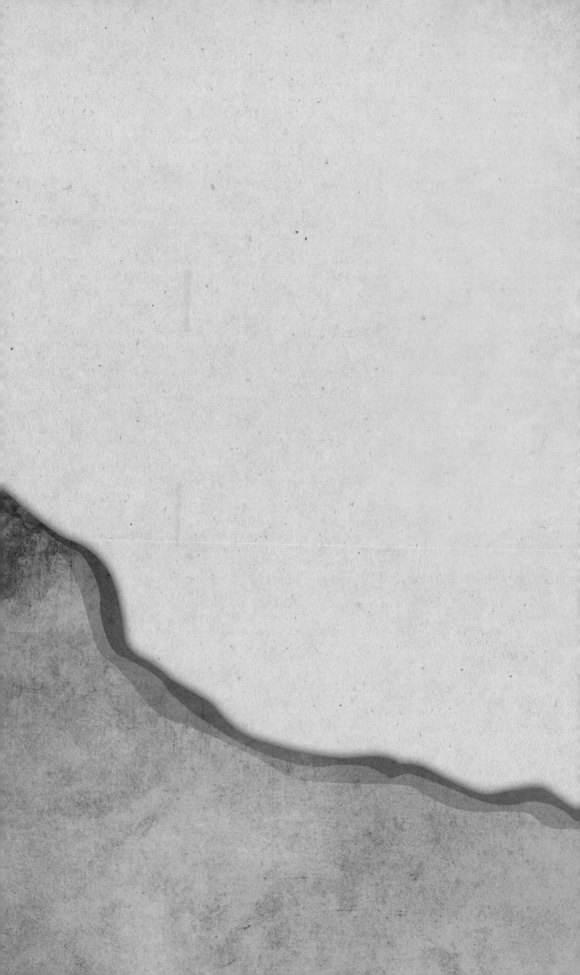

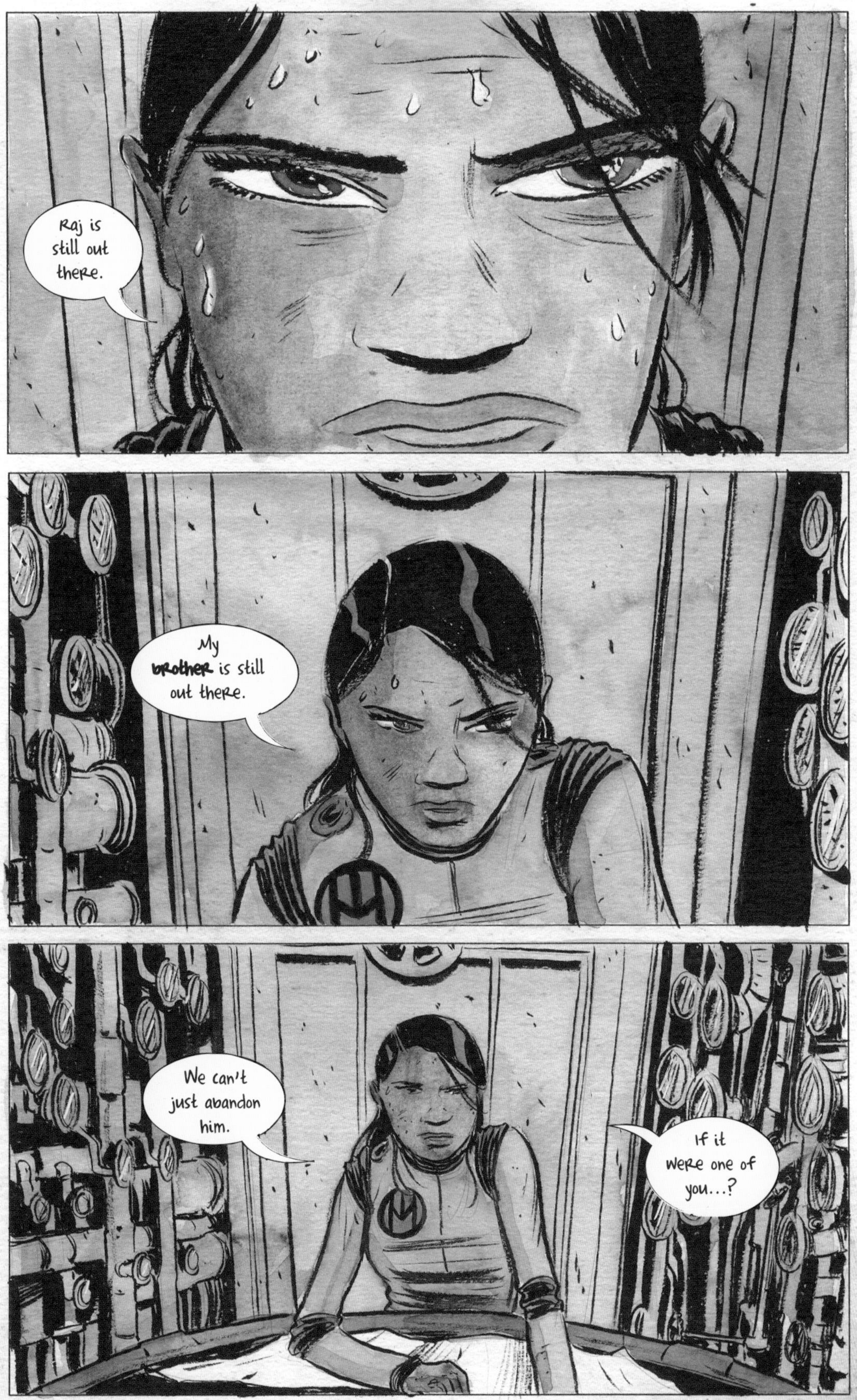
Raj is still out there.
My brother is still out there.
We can't just abandon him.
If it were one of you...?

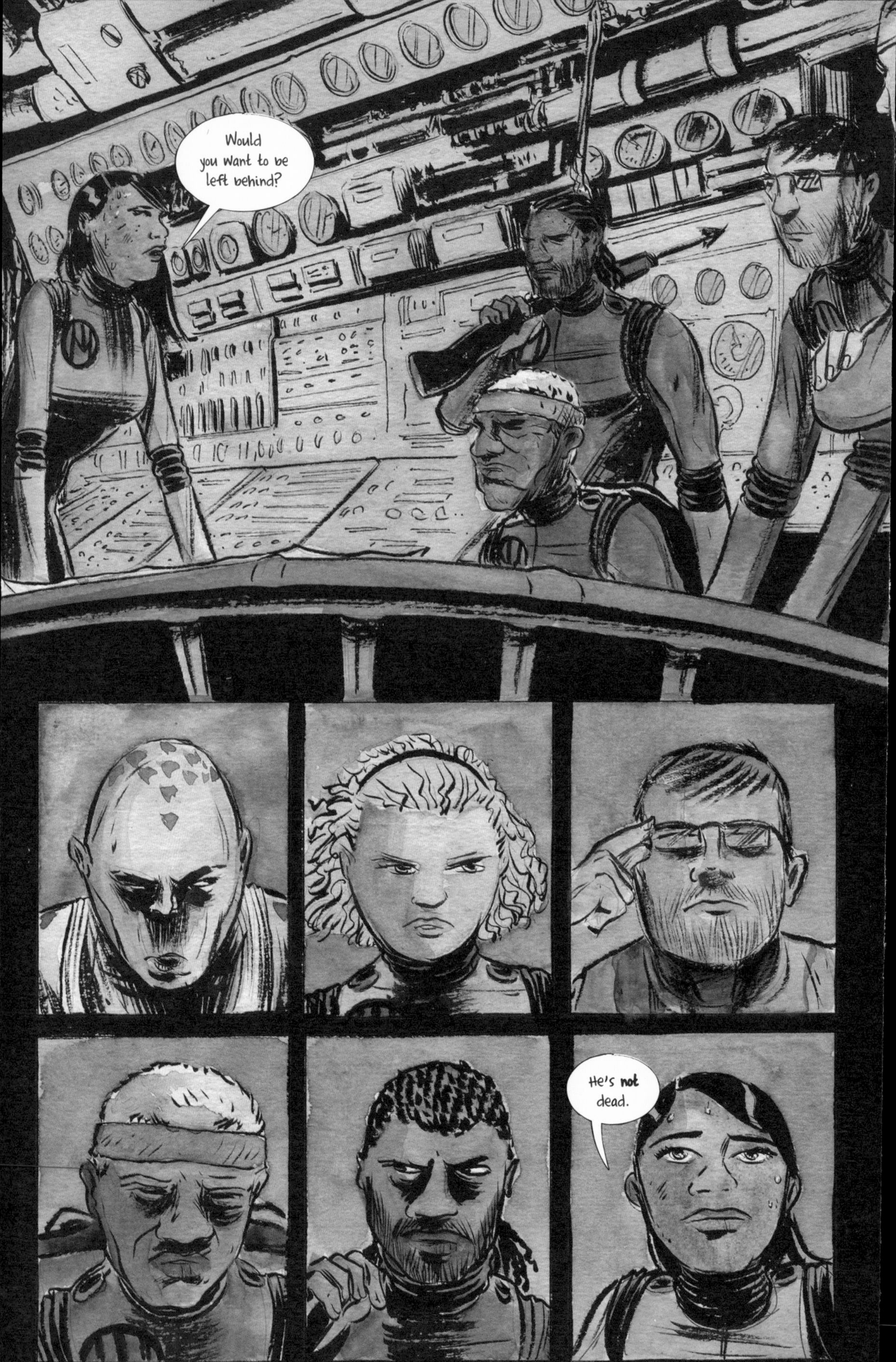
Would you want to be left behind?
He's **not** dead.

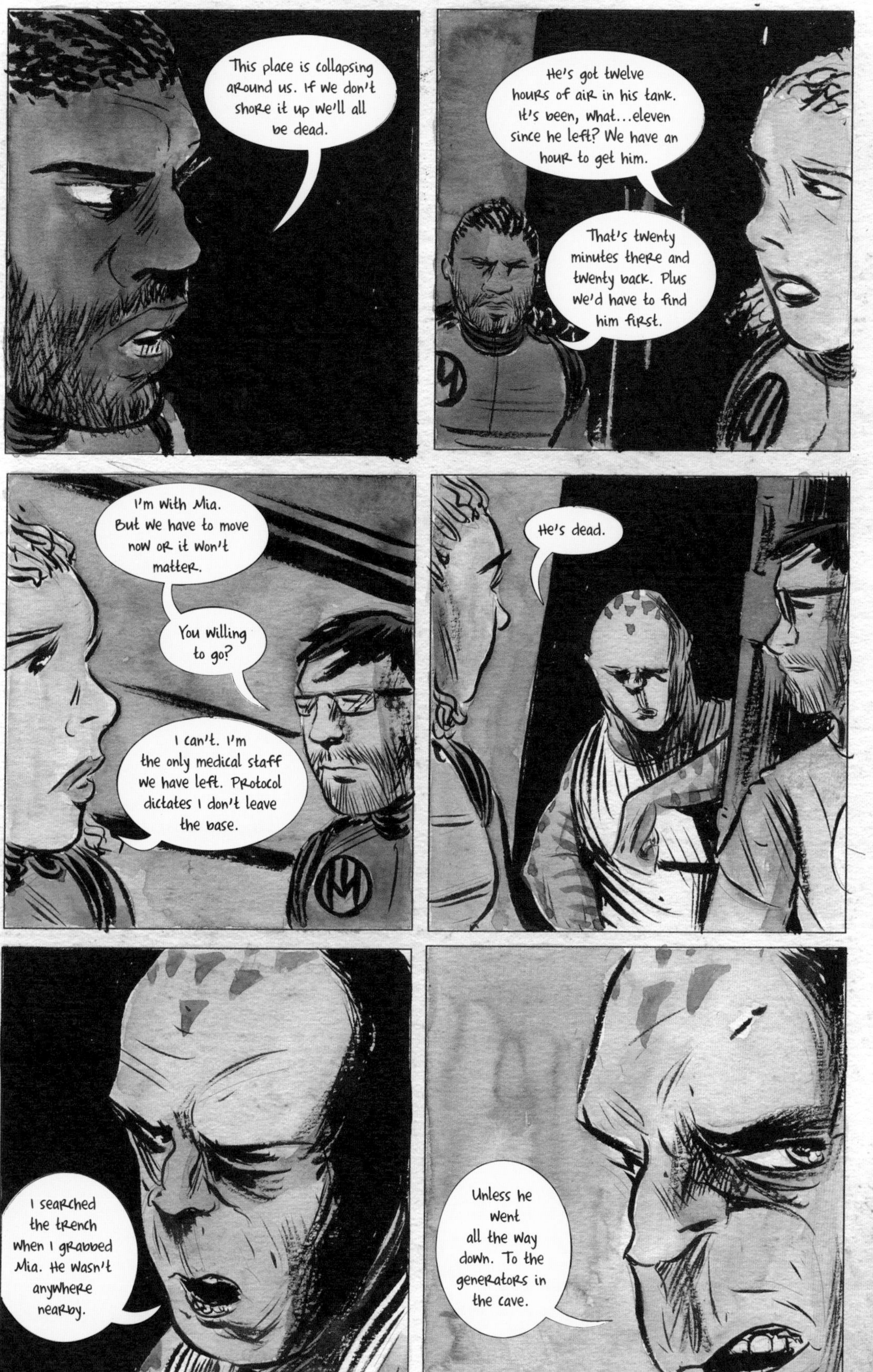
This place is collapsing around us. If we don't shore it up we'll all be dead.
He's got twelve hours of air in his tank. It's been, what...eleven since he left? We have an hour to get him.
That's twenty minutes there and twenty back. Plus we'd have to find him first.
I'm with Mia. But we have to move now or it won't matter.
You willing to go?
I can't. I'm the only medical staff we have left. Protocol dictates I don't leave the base.
He's dead.
I searched the trench when I grabbed Mia. He wasn't anywhere nearby.
Unless he went all the way down. To the generators in the cave.

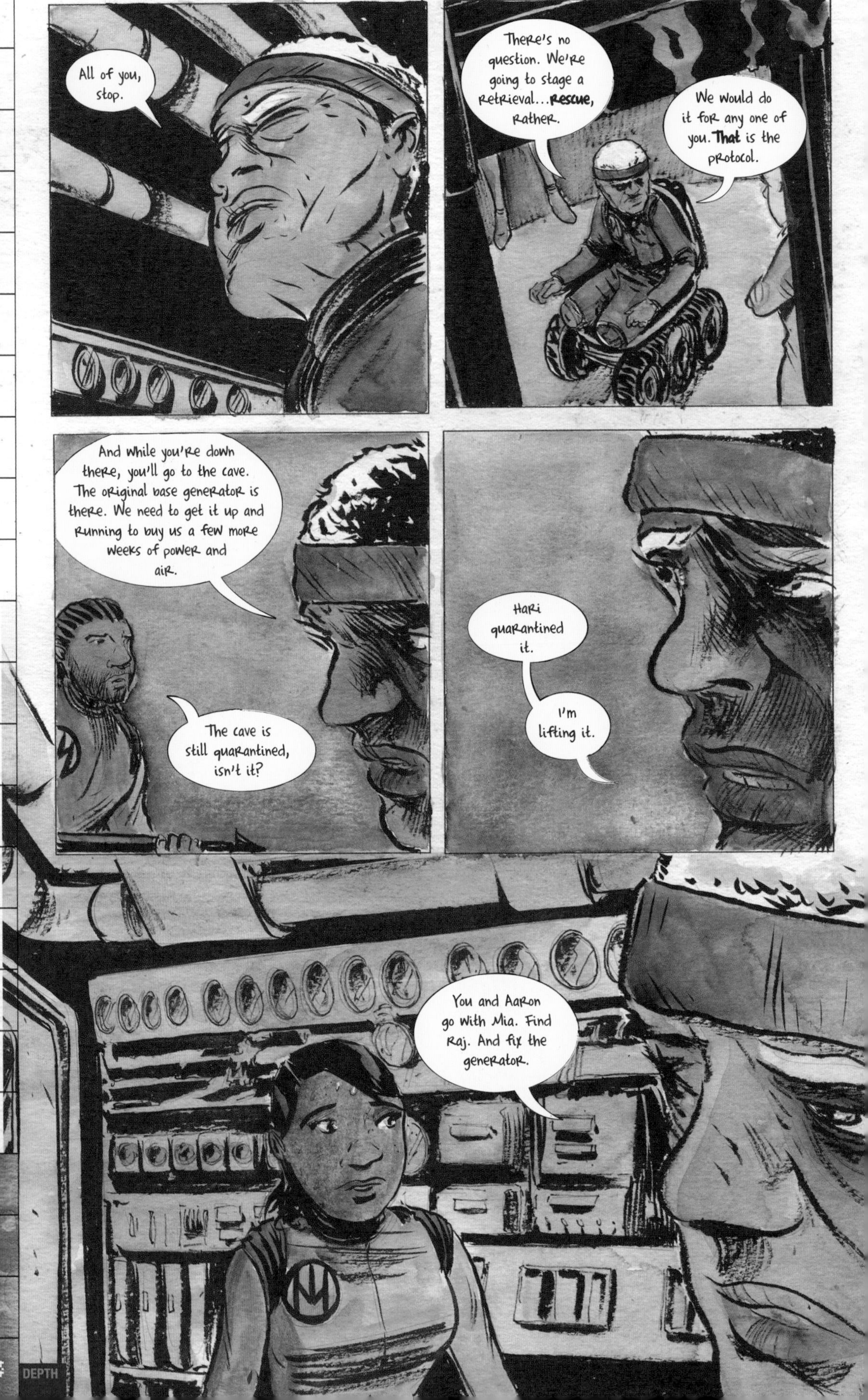
All of you, stop.
There's no question. We're going to stage a retrieval... **rescue,** rather.
We would do it for any one of you. **That** is the protocol.
And while you're down there, you'll go to the cave. The original base generator is there. We need to get it up and running to buy us a few more weeks of power and air.
The cave is still quarantined, isn't it?
Hari quarantined it.
I'm lifting it.
You and Aaron go with Mia. Find Raj. And fix the generator.

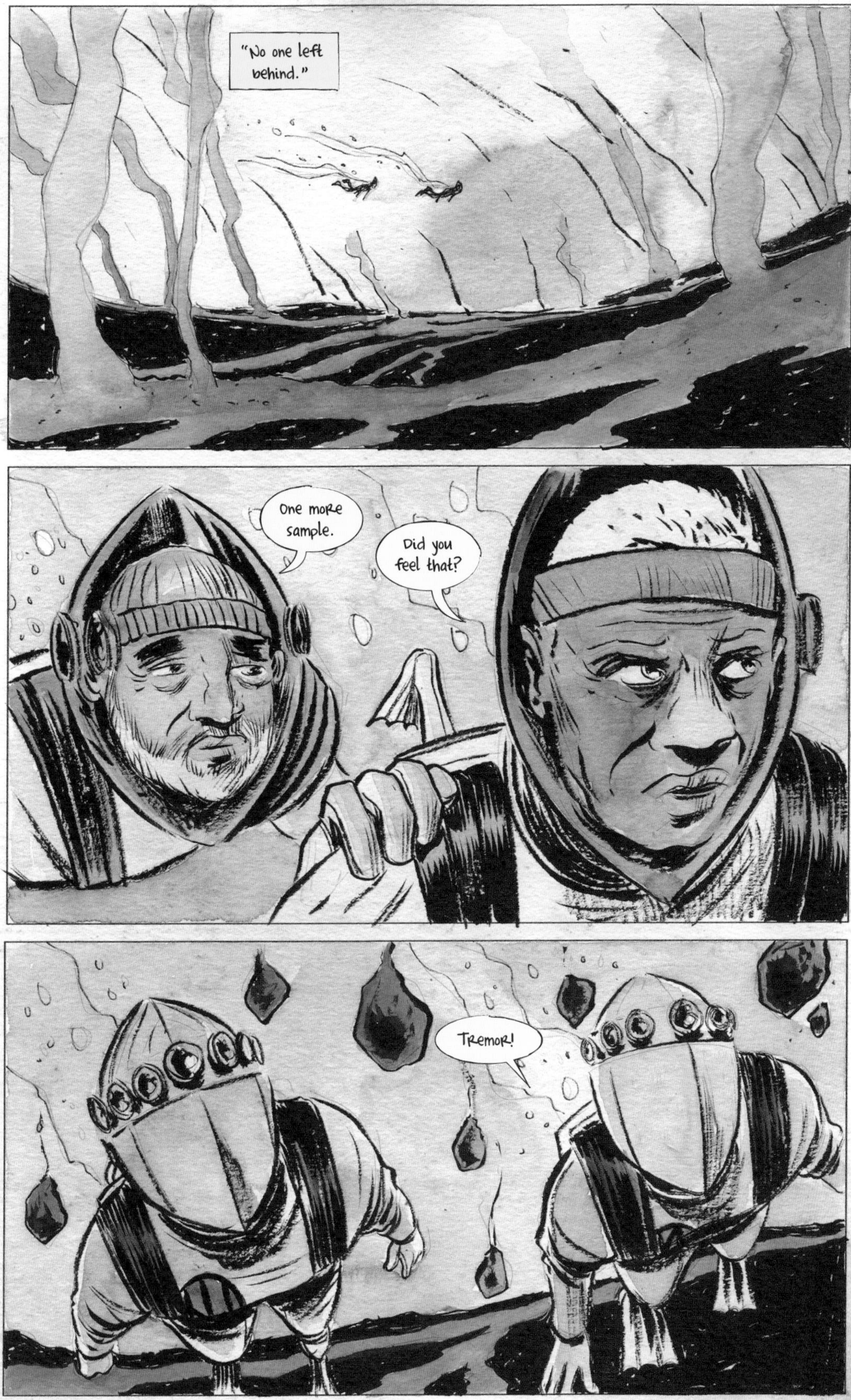
"No one left behind."
One more sample.
Did you feel that?
Tremor!

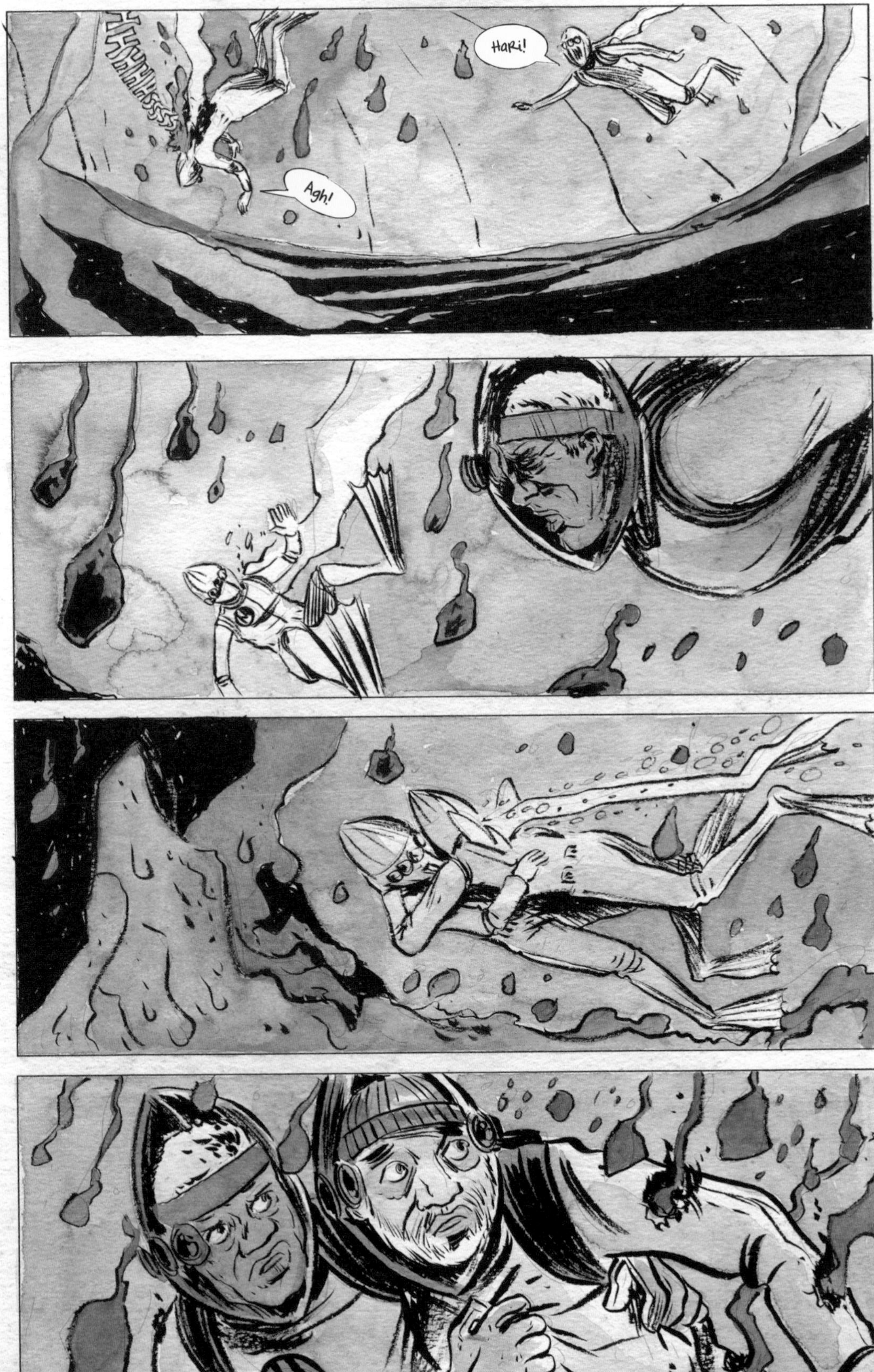
Hari!
Agh!

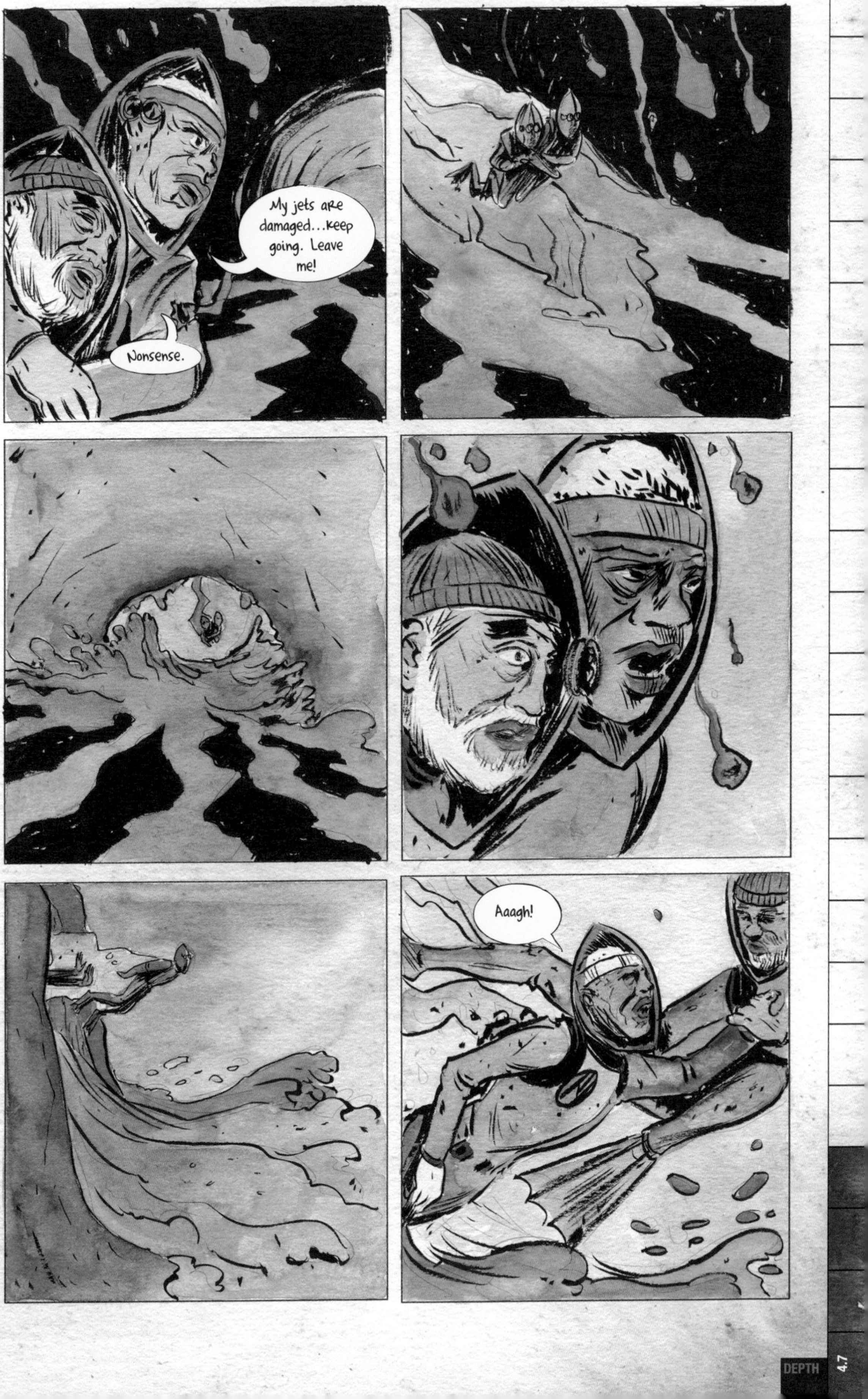
My jets are damaged...keep going. Leave me!
Nonsense.
Aaagh!

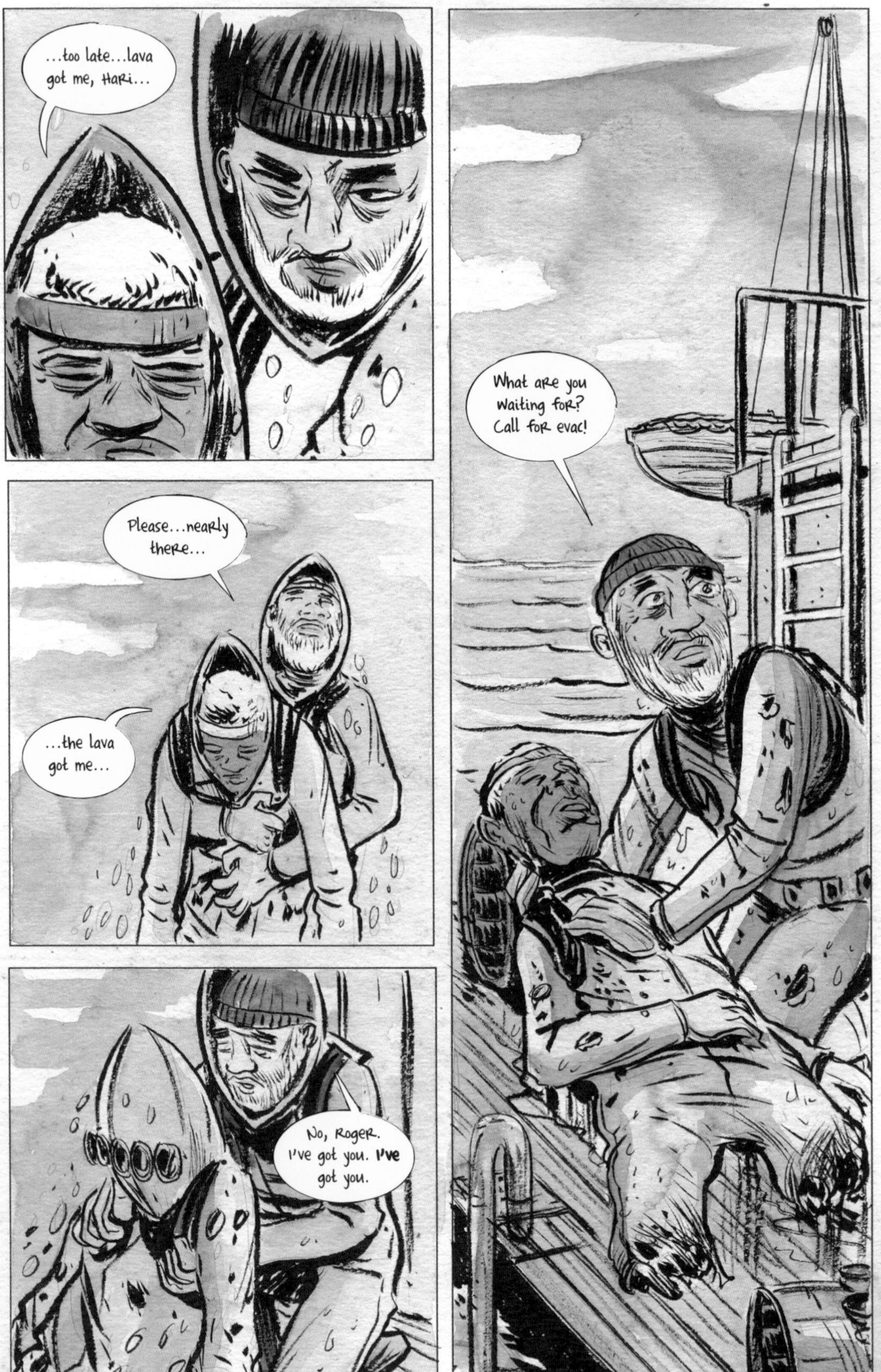
...too late...lava got me, Hari...
Please...nearly there...
...the lava got me...
No, Roger. I've got you. I've got you.
What are you waiting for? Call for evac!

I appreciate it, you two. I really do.

We need the generatah fixed. Rogah was jus' humoring you, little miss.

Raj is long dead.

Q...do you have to...?

Truth, Aaron. Best yah all stop lyin' to yerselves.

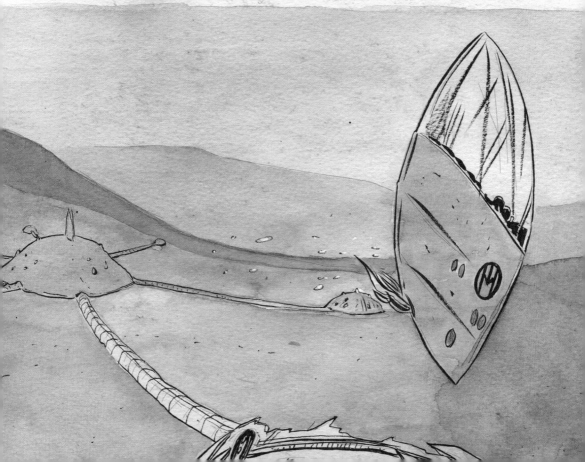

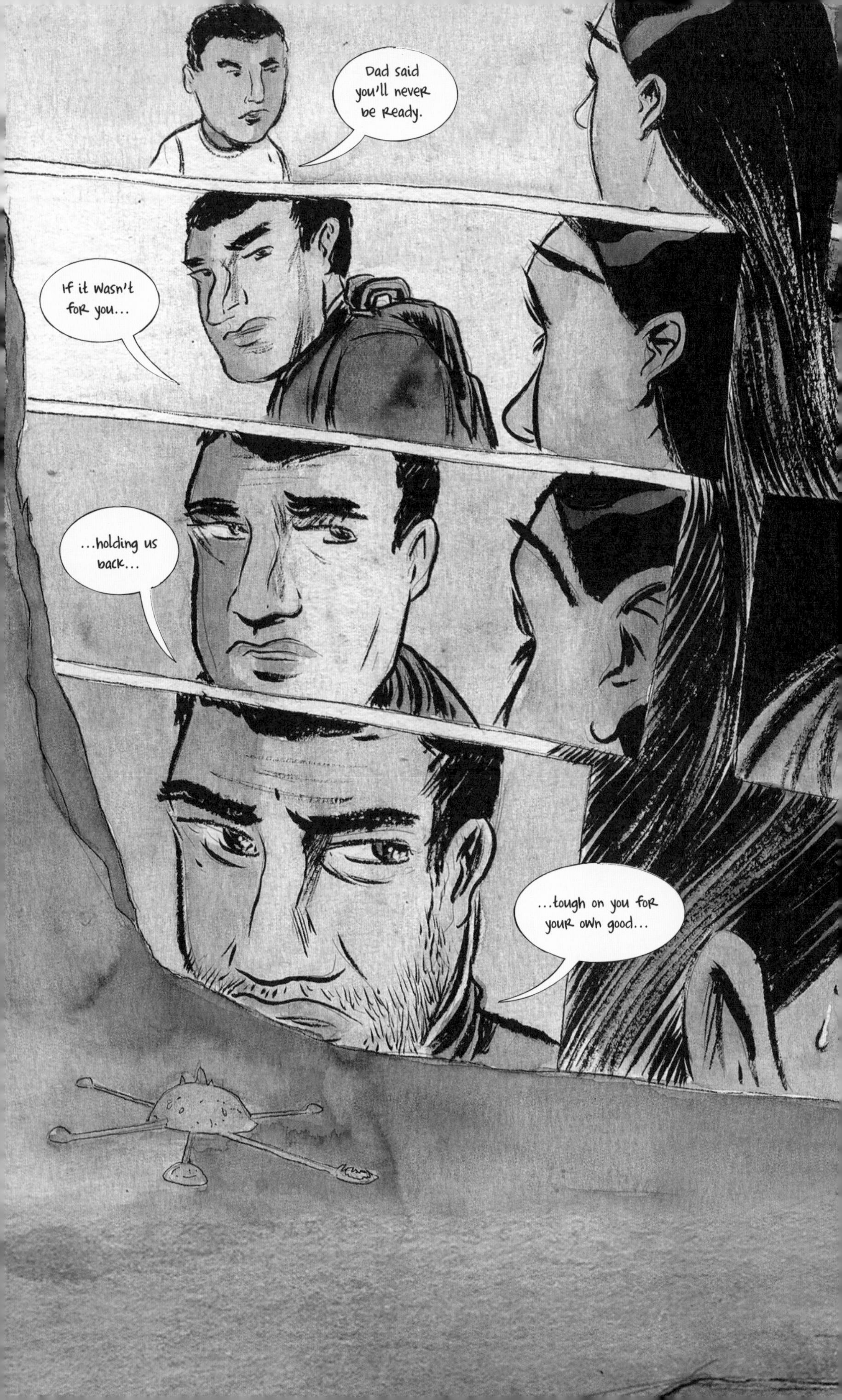
Dad said you'll never be ready.
If it wasn't for you...
...holding us back...
...tough on you for your own good...

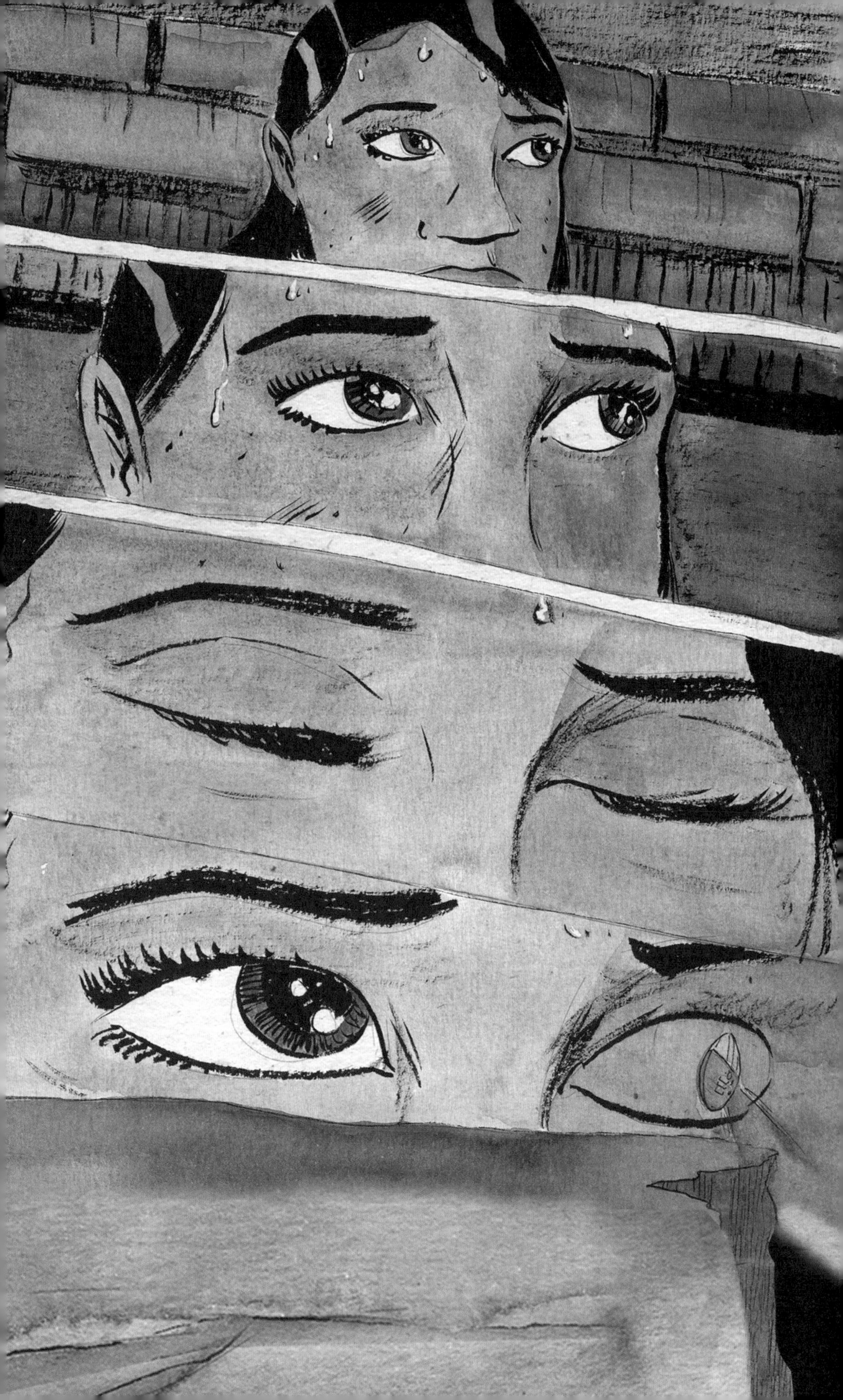

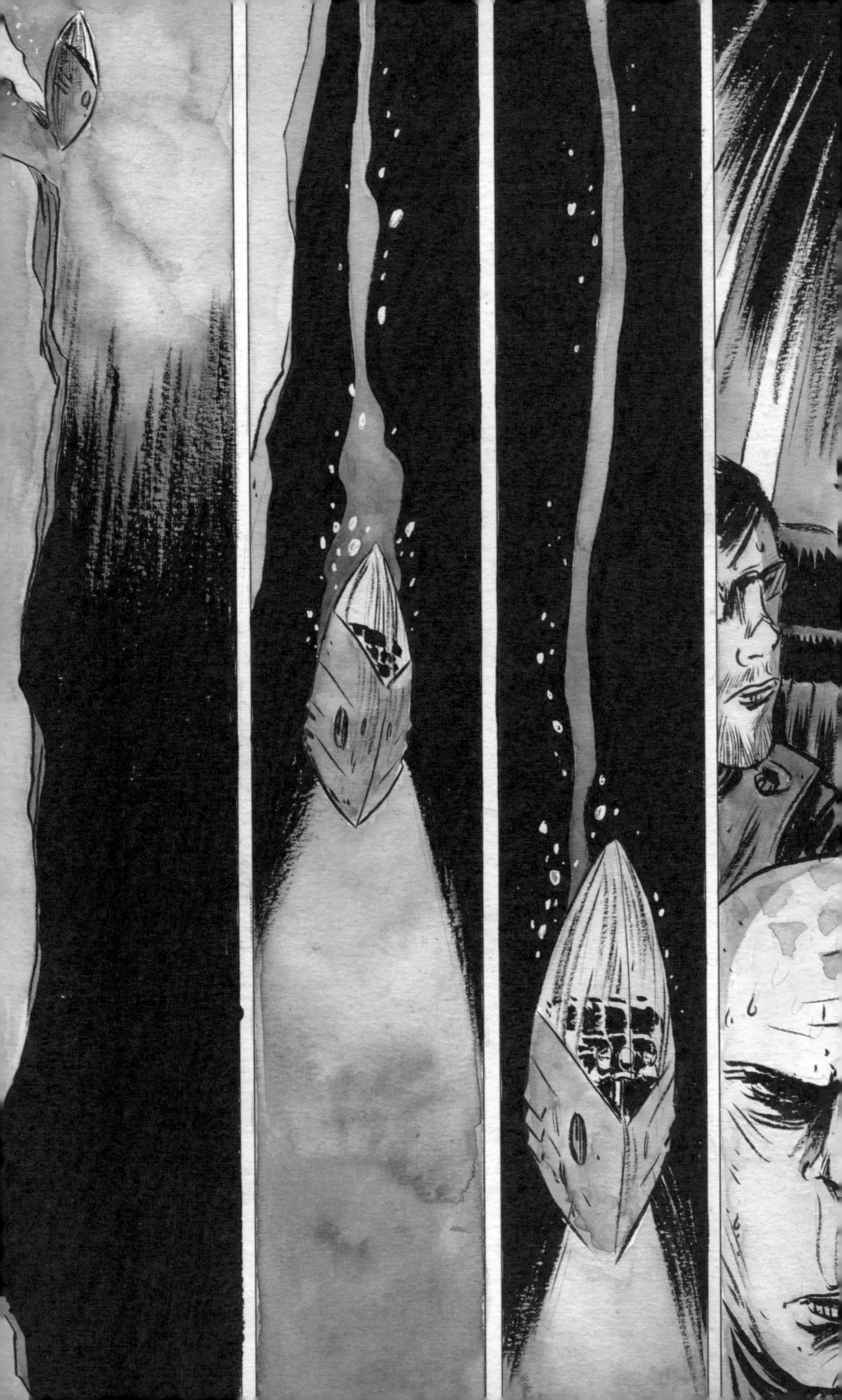

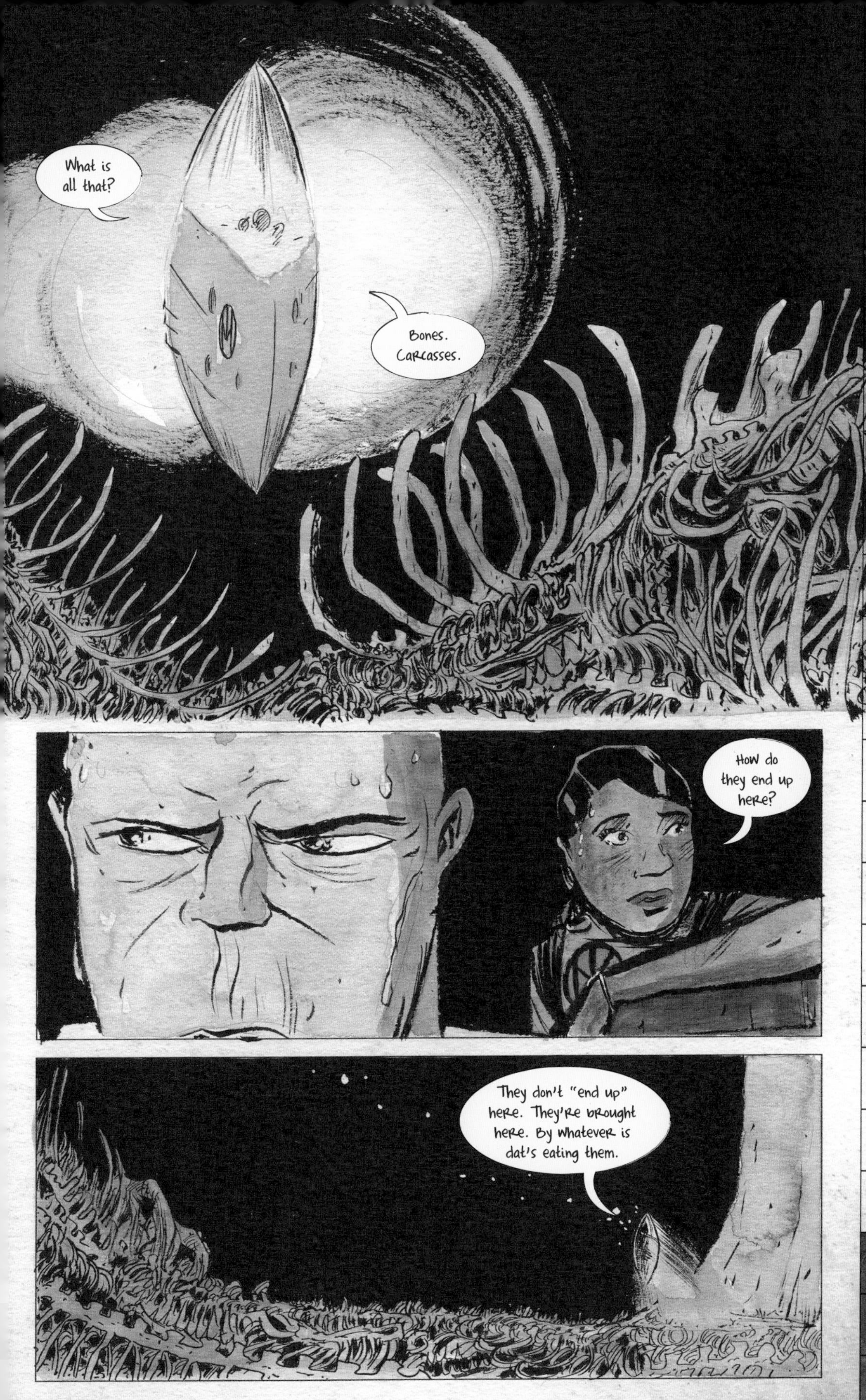

What is all that?
Bones. Carcasses.
How do they end up here?
They don't "end up" here. They're brought here. By whatever is dat's eating them.

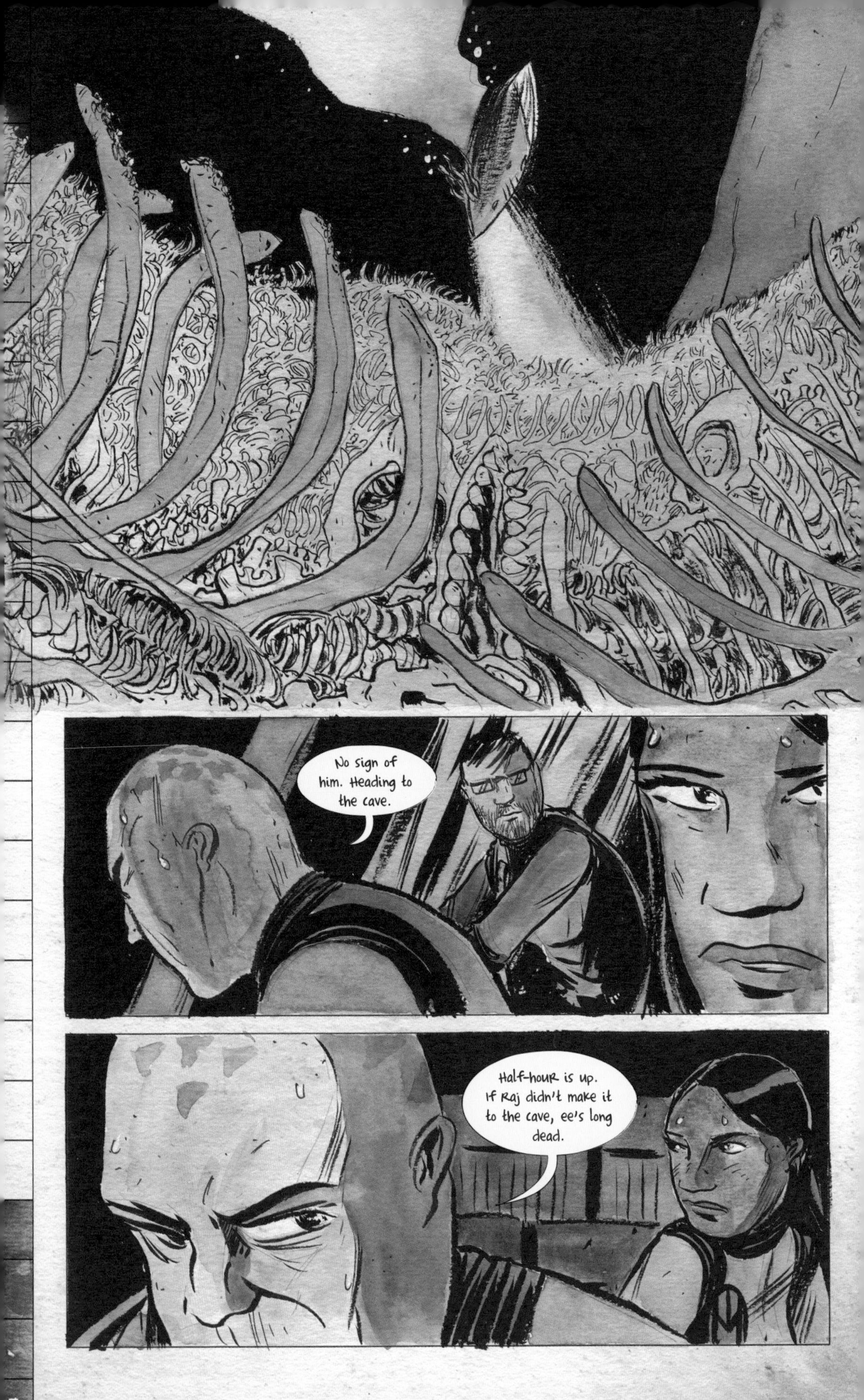
No sign of him. Heading to the cave.
Half-hour is up. If Raj didn't make it to the cave, ee's long dead.

Your father found this cave on the first dive.

It was the site of the first power generator. It powered the base in the early days.

As the base developed, current and saline drives were brought down. More efficient. More reliable. This generator wasn't needed anymore.

But it should still be intact.

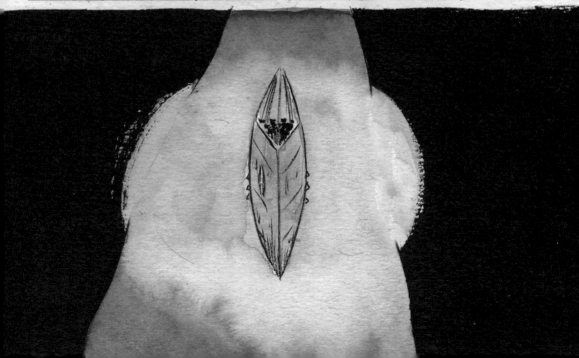

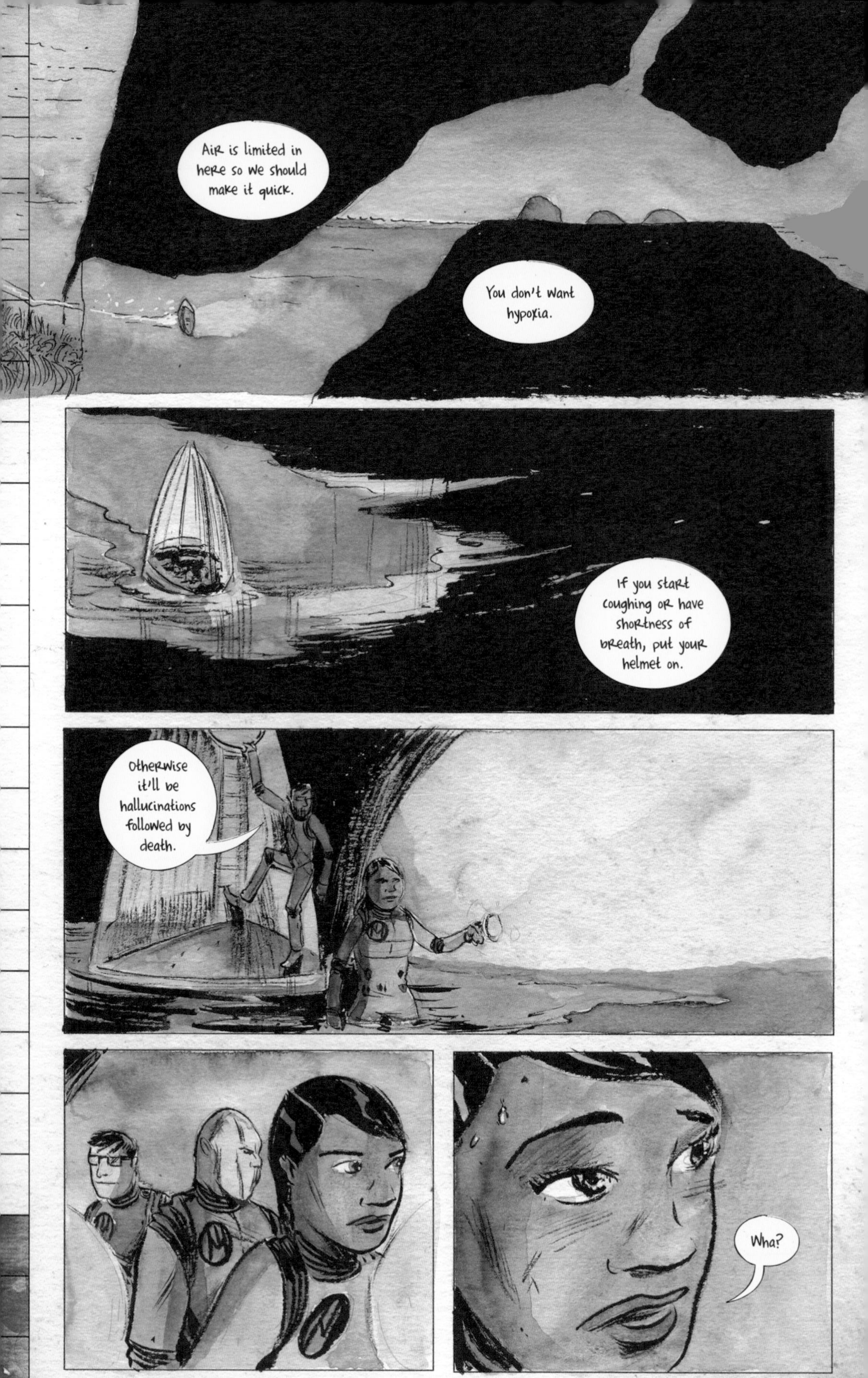
Air is limited in here so we should make it quick.
You don't want hypoxia.
If you start coughing or have shortness of breath, put your helmet on.
Otherwise it'll be hallucinations followed by death.
Wha?

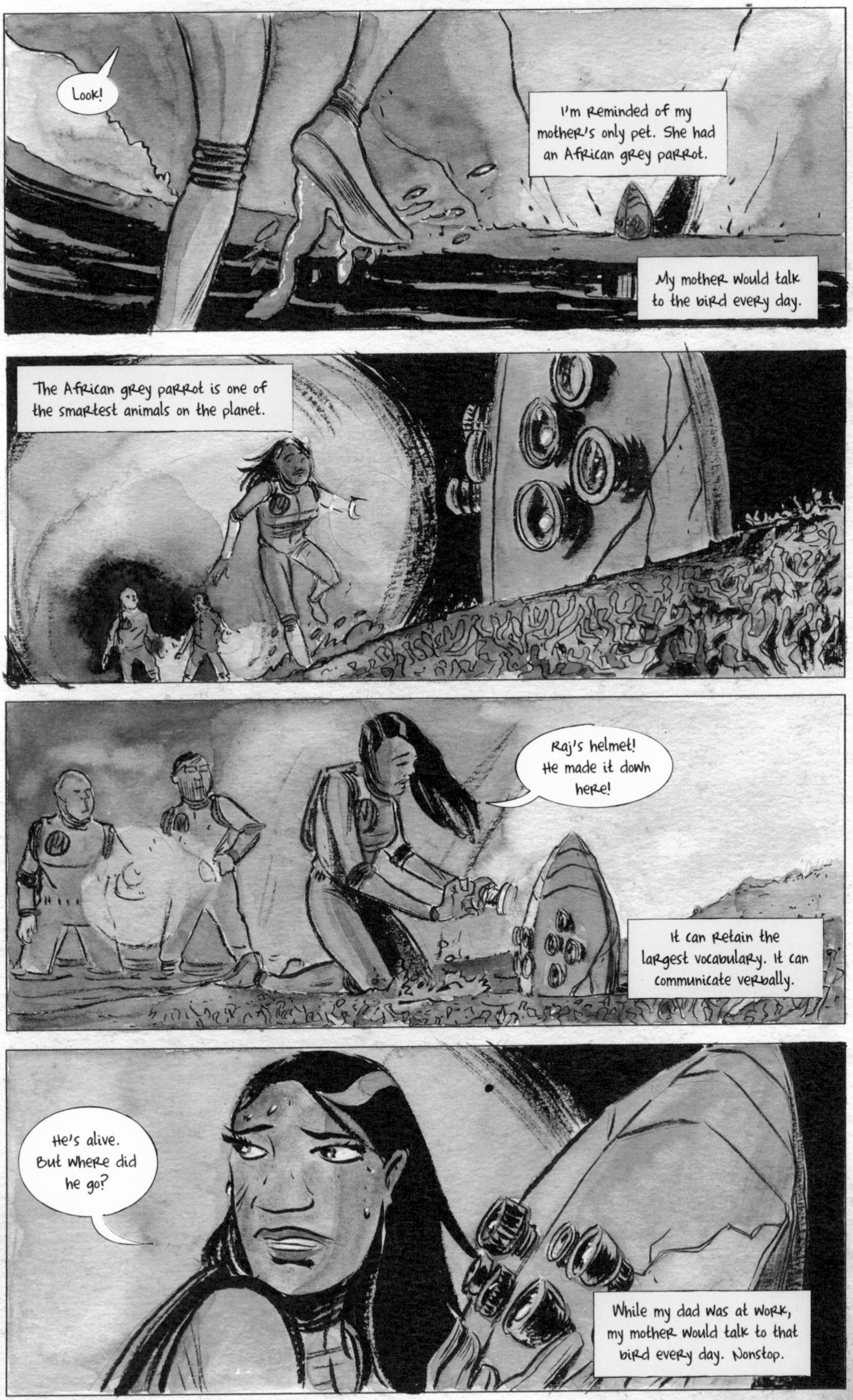
Look!
I'm reminded of my mother's only pet. She had an African grey parrot.
My mother would talk to the bird every day.
The African grey parrot is one of the smartest animals on the planet.
Raj's helmet! He made it down here!
It can retain the largest vocabulary. It can communicate verbally.
He's alive. But where did he go?
While my dad was at work, my mother would talk to that bird every day. Nonstop.

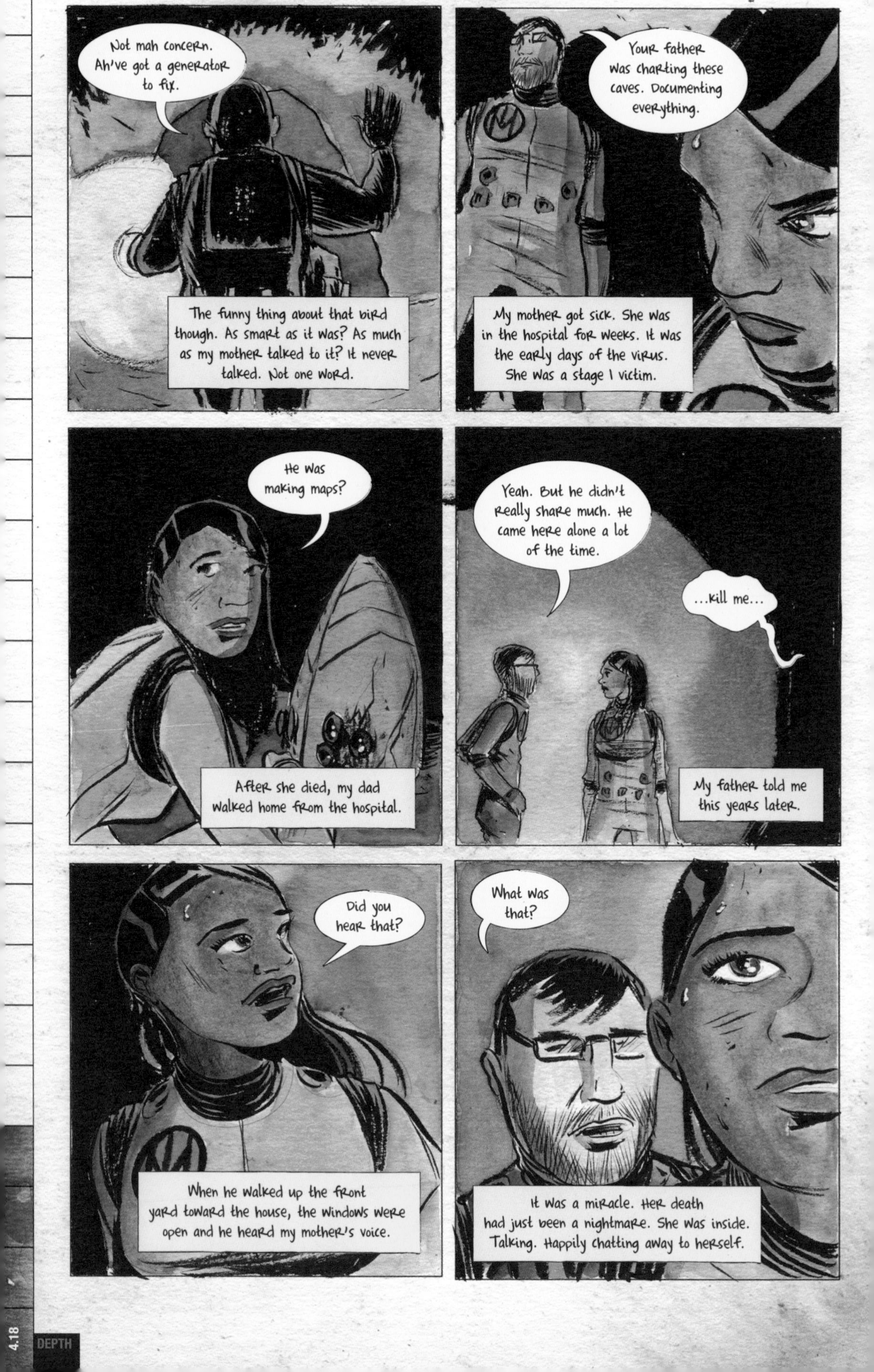
Not mah concern. Ah've got a generator to fix.
The funny thing about that bird though. As smart as it was? As much as my mother talked to it? It never talked. Not one word.
Your father was charting these caves. Documenting everything.
My mother got sick. She was in the hospital for weeks. It was the early days of the virus. She was a stage I victim.
He was making maps?
After she died, my dad walked home from the hospital.
Yeah. But he didn't really share much. He came here alone a lot of the time.
...kill me...
My father told me this years later.
Did you hear that?
When he walked up the front yard toward the house, the windows were open and he heard my mother's voice.
What was that?
It was a miracle. Her death had just been a nightmare. She was inside. Talking. Happily chatting away to herself.

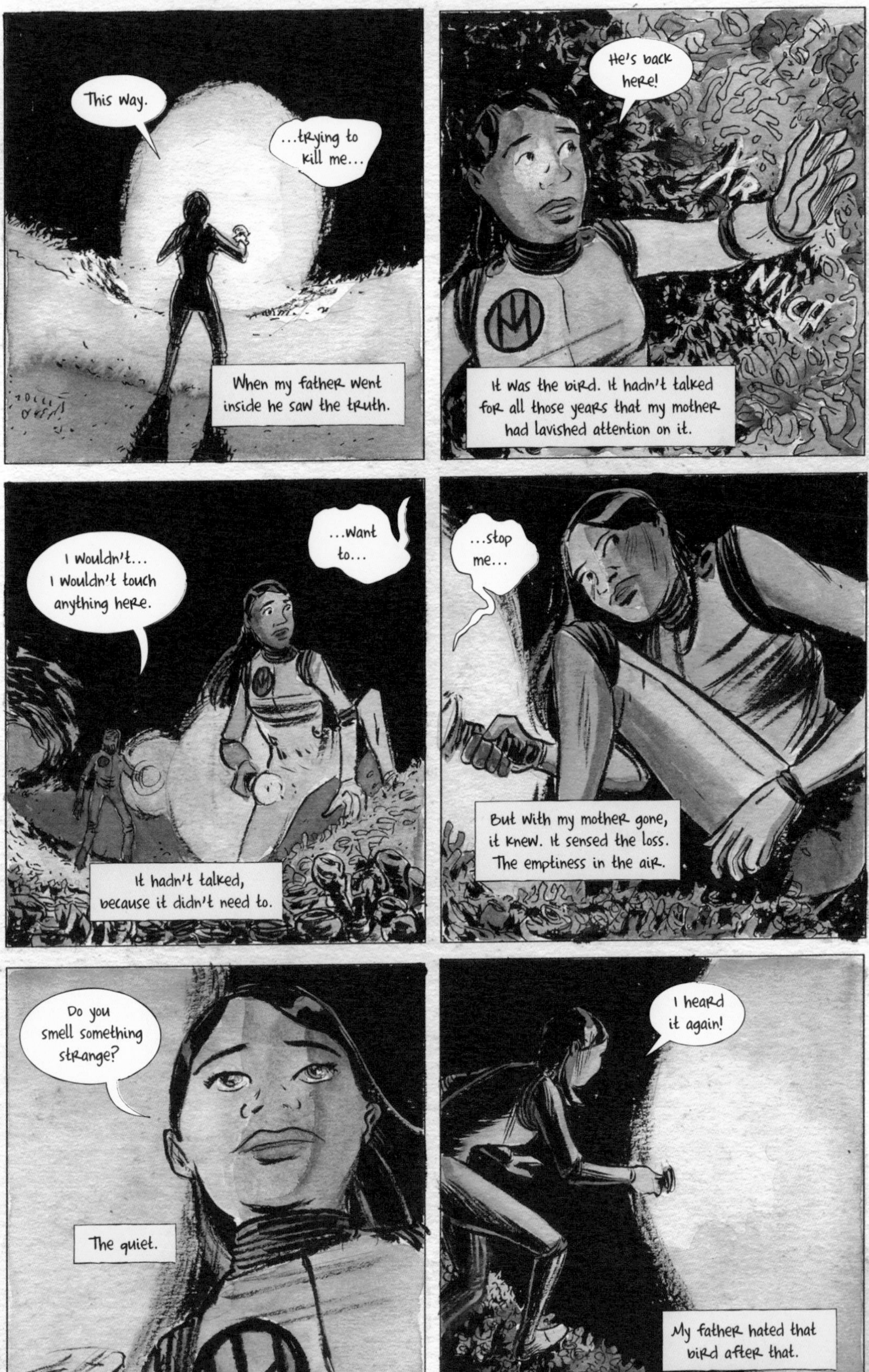
This way.
...trying to kill me...
When my father went inside he saw the truth.
He's back here!
KRNNCH
It was the bird. It hadn't talked for all those years that my mother had lavished attention on it.
I wouldn't... I wouldn't touch anything here.
...want to...
It hadn't talked, because it didn't need to.
...stop me...
But with my mother gone, it knew. It sensed the loss. The emptiness in the air.
Do you smell something strange?
The quiet.
I heard it again!
My father hated that bird after that.

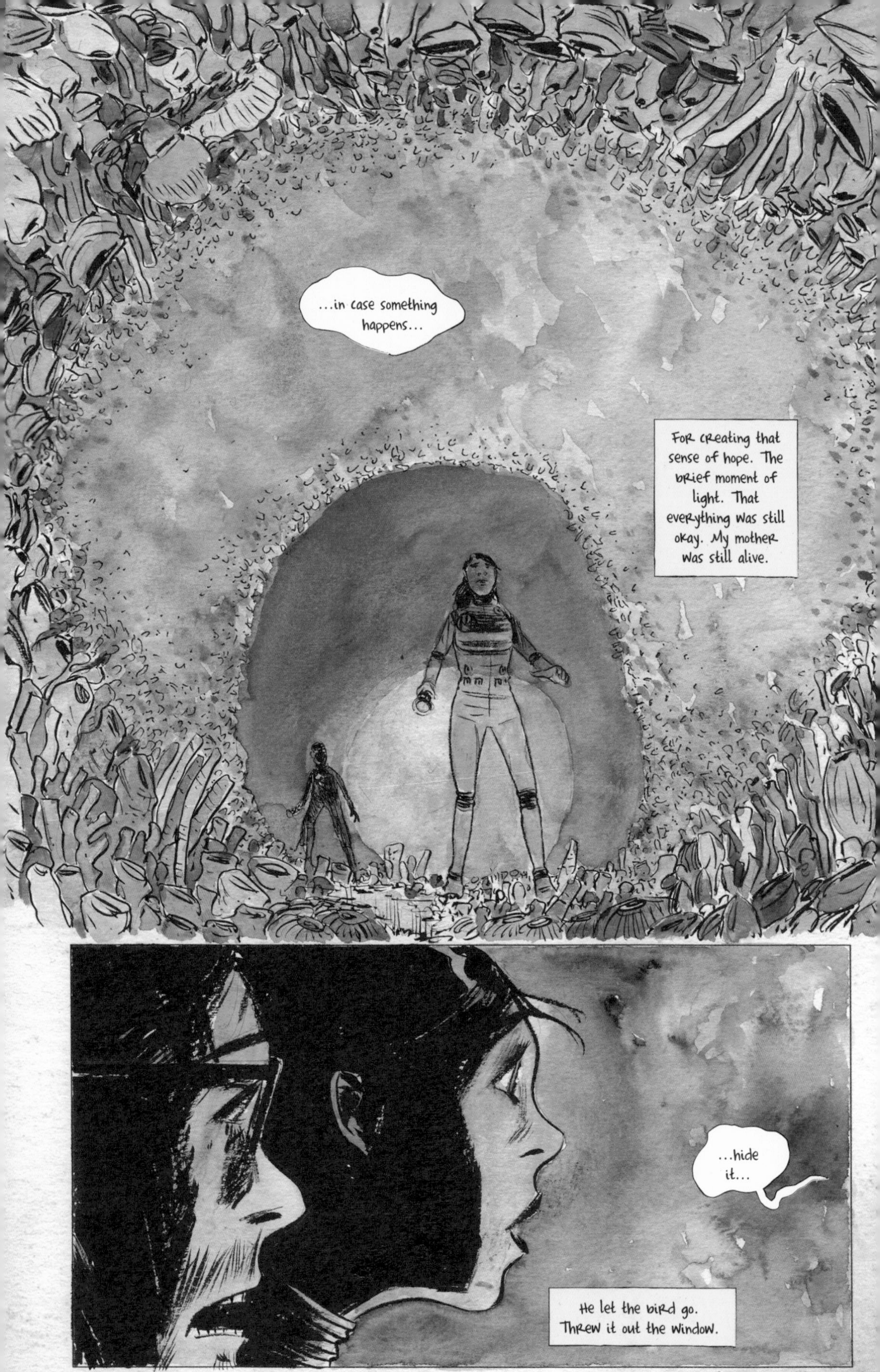
...in case something happens...
For creating that sense of hope. The brief moment of light. That everything was still okay. My mother was still alive.
...hide it...
He let the bird go. Threw it out the window.

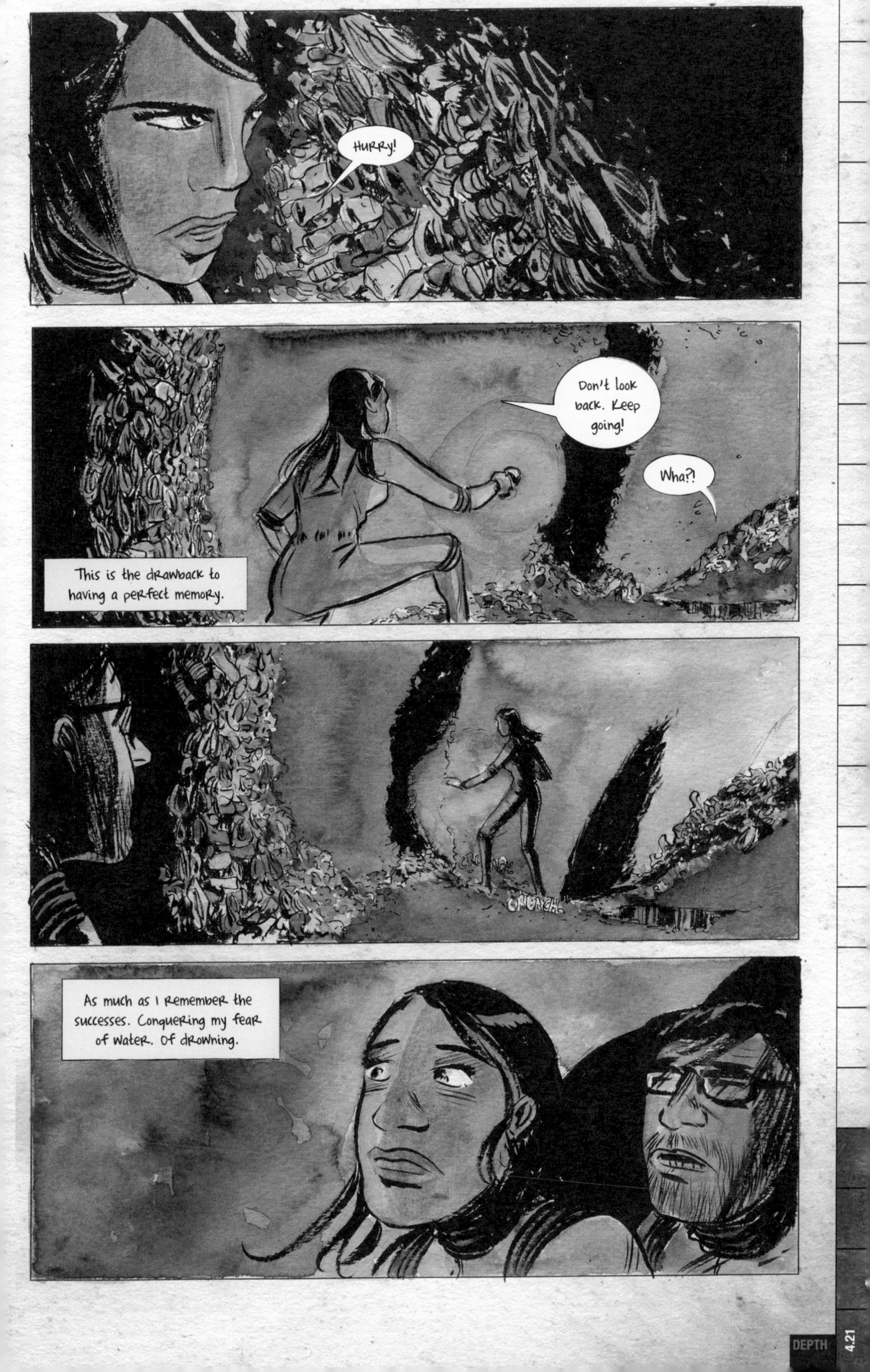
HURRY!
Don't look back. Keep going!
Wha?!
This is the drawback to having a perfect memory.
CRUNCH!
As much as I remember the successes. Conquering my fear of water. Of drowning.

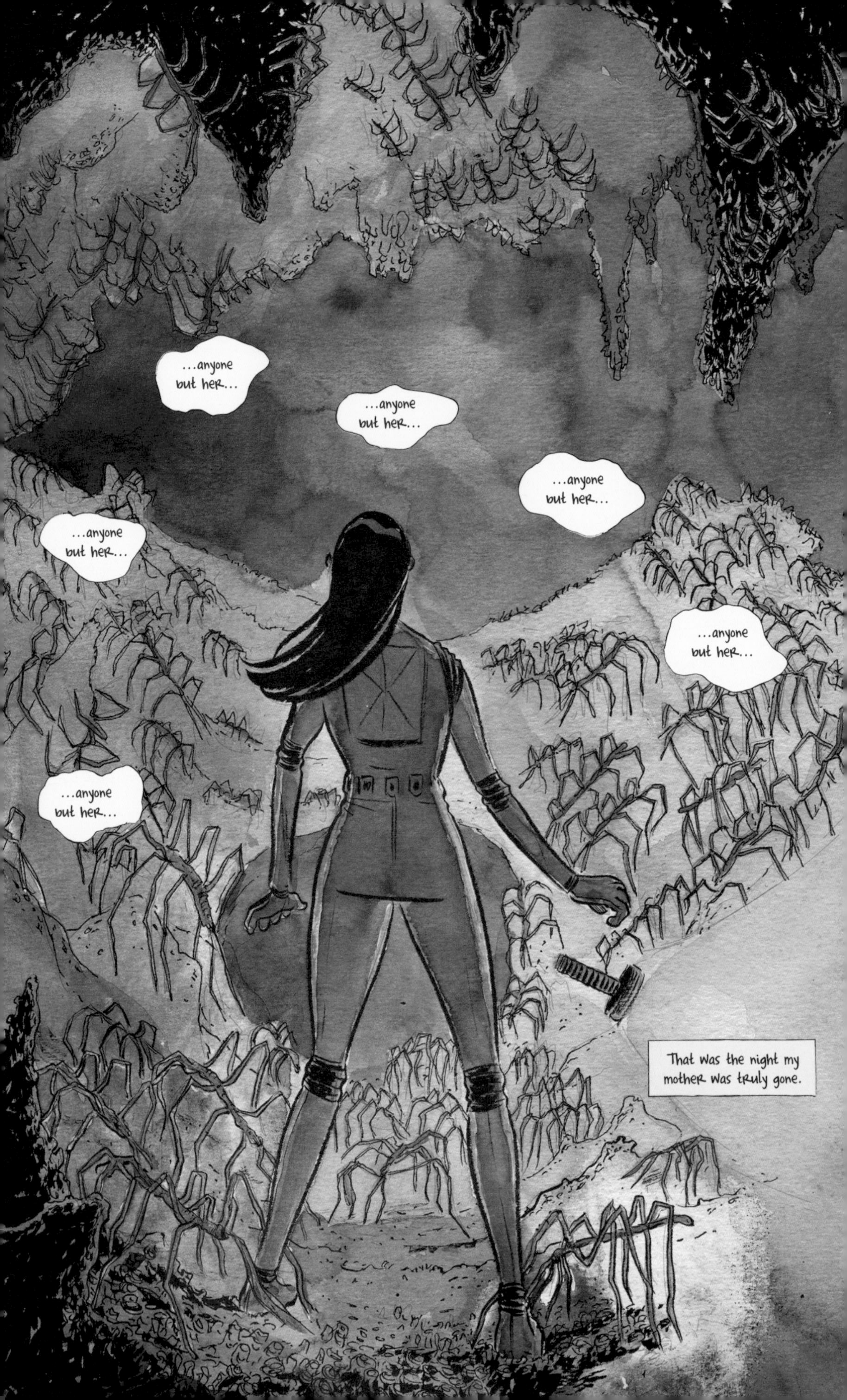
...anyone but her...
...anyone but her...
...anyone but her...
...anyone but her...
...anyone but her...
...anyone but her...
That was the night my mother was truly gone.

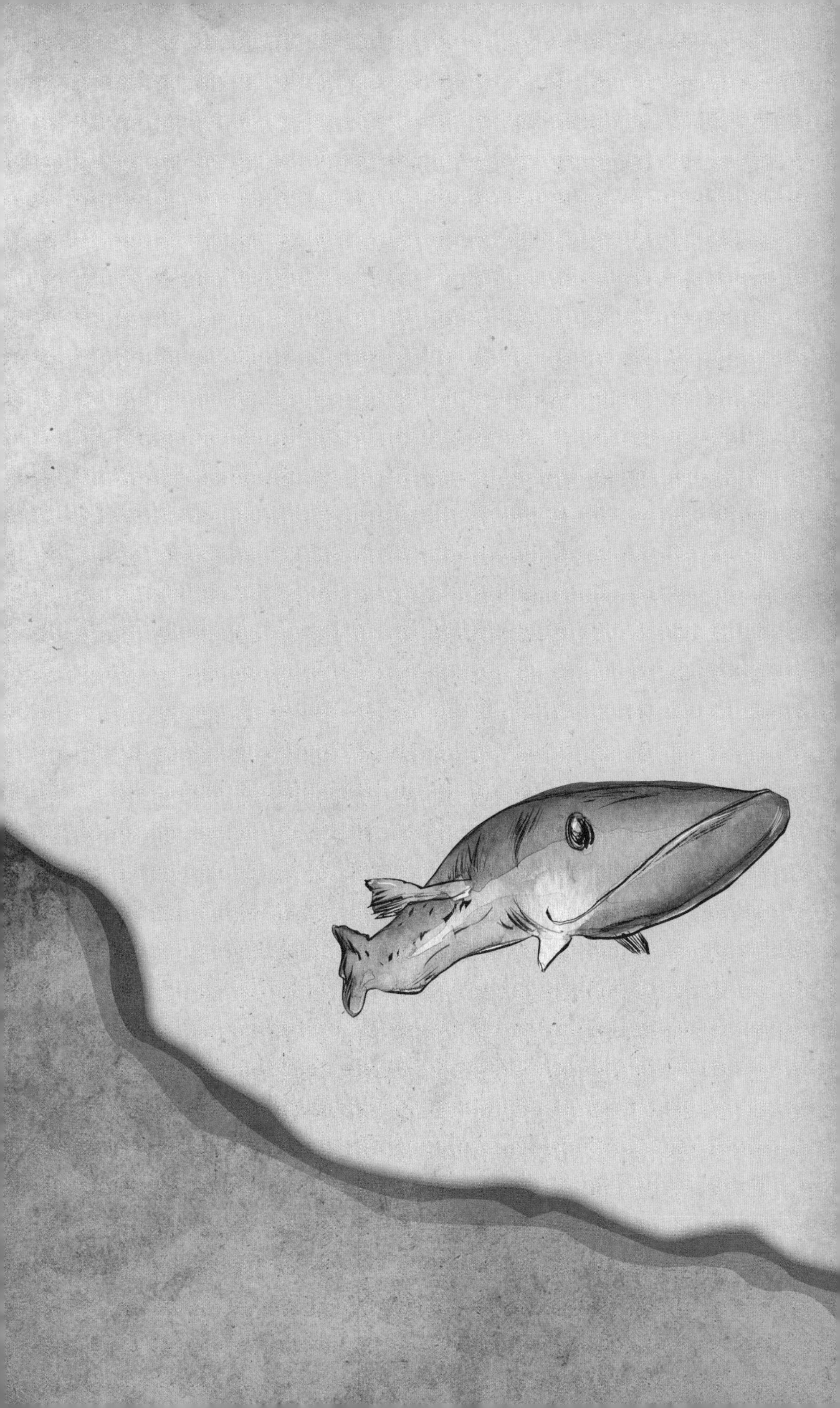

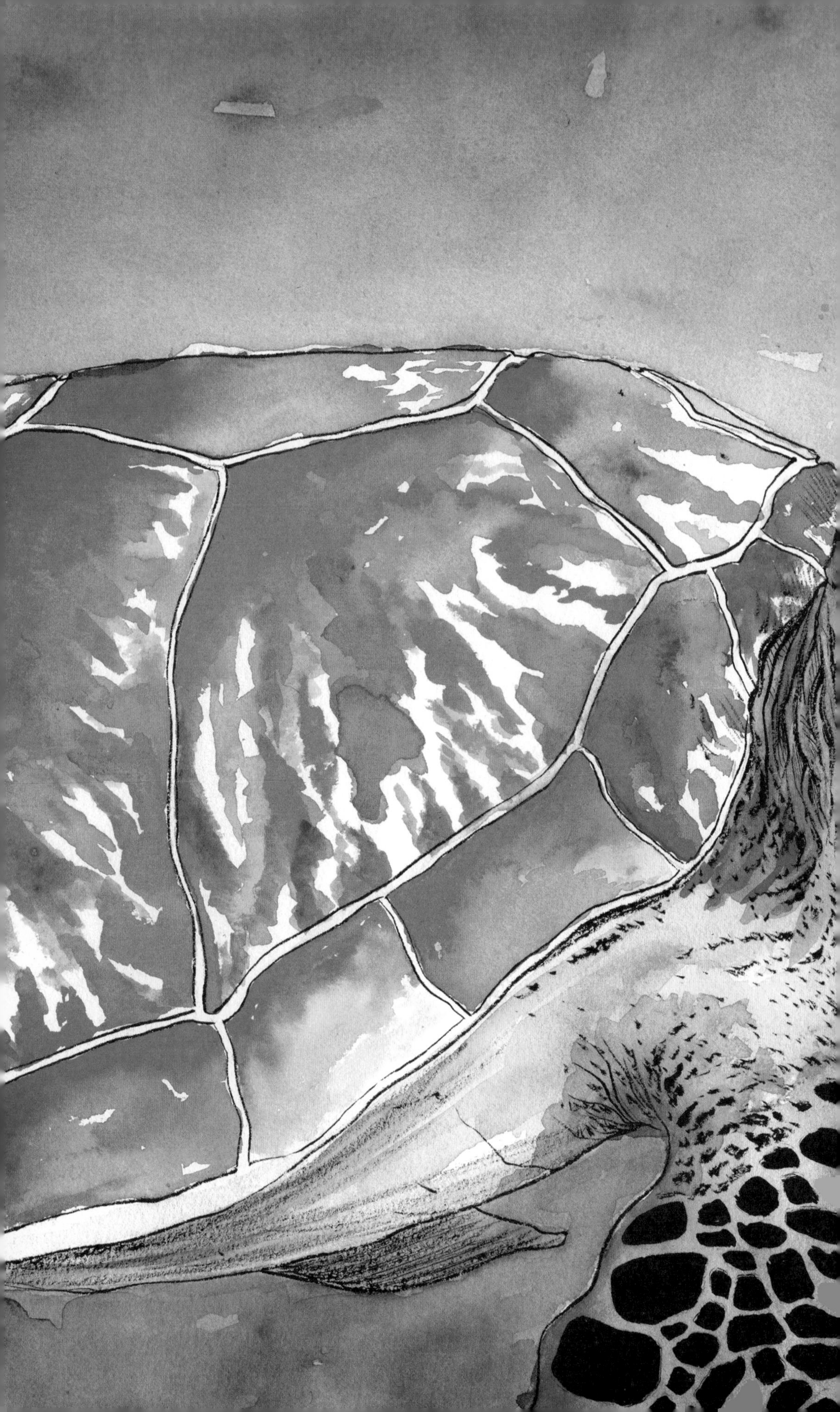

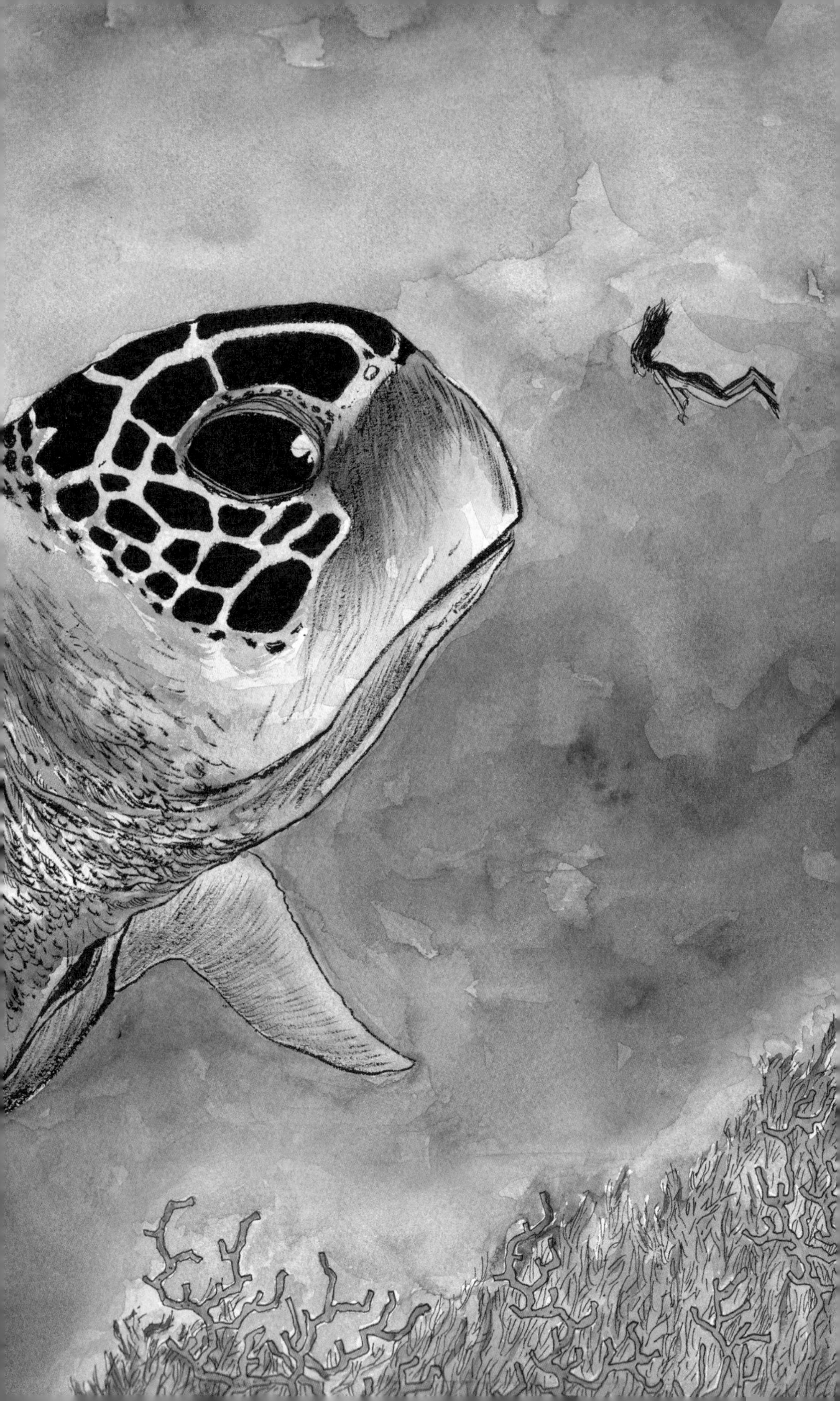

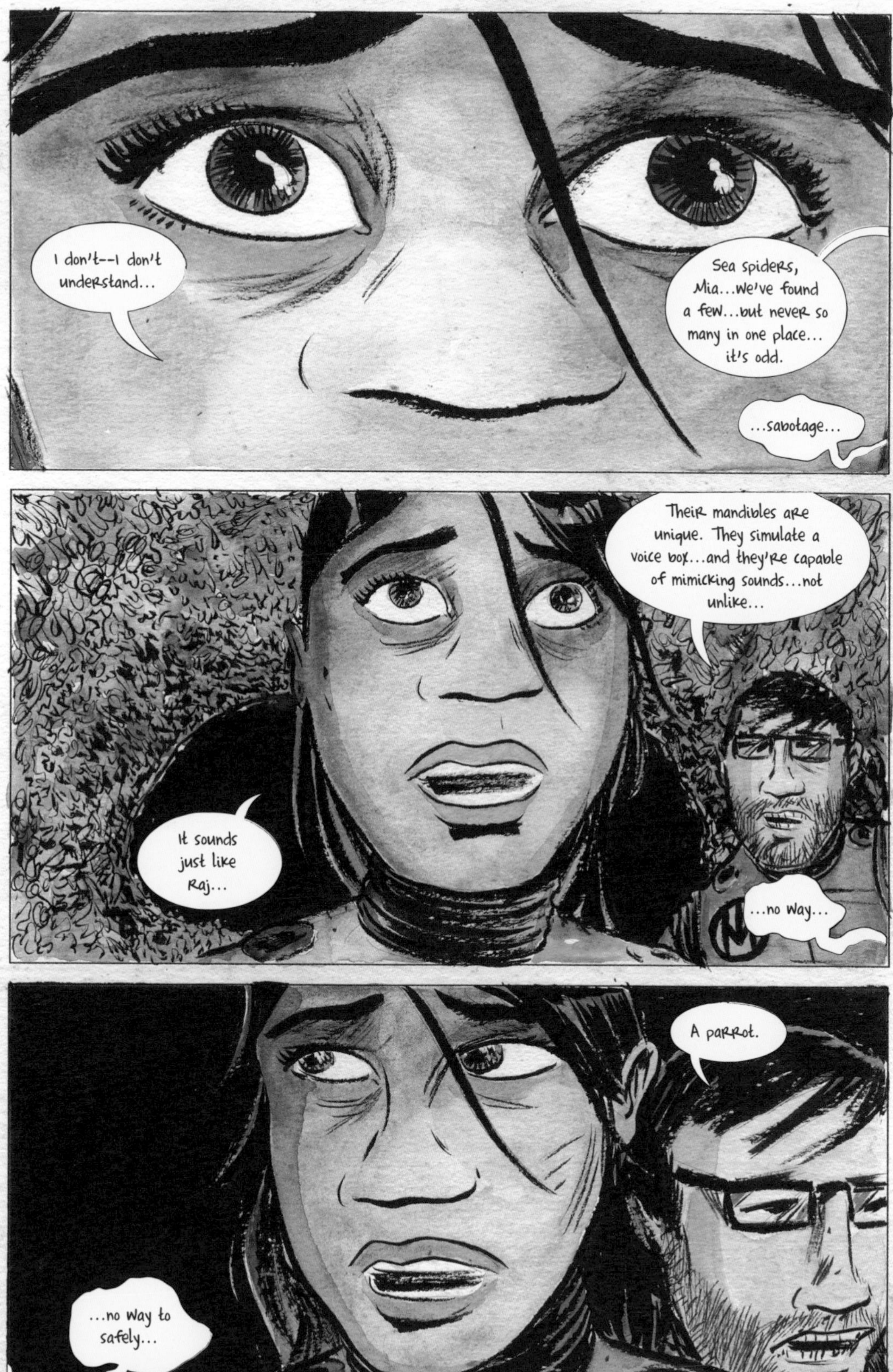
I don't--I don't understand...
Sea spiders, Mia...we've found a few...but never so many in one place... it's odd.
...sabotage...
Their mandibles are unique. They simulate a voice box...and they're capable of mimicking sounds...not unlike...
It sounds just like Raj...
...no way...
A parrot.
...no way to safely...

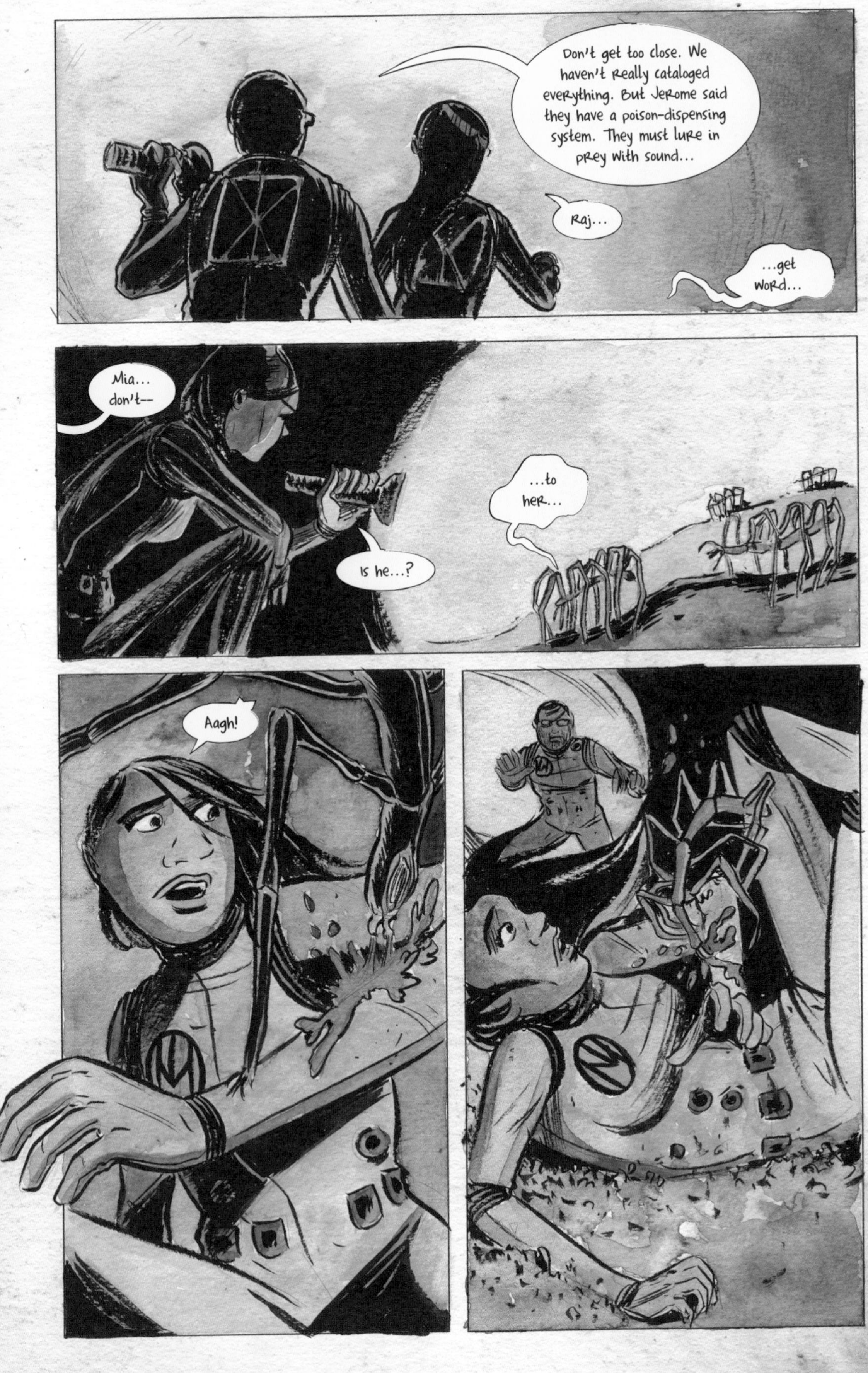
Don't get too close. We haven't really cataloged everything. But Jerome said they have a poison-dispensing system. They must lure in prey with sound...
Raj...
...get word...
Mia... don't--
...to her...
Is he...?
Aagh!

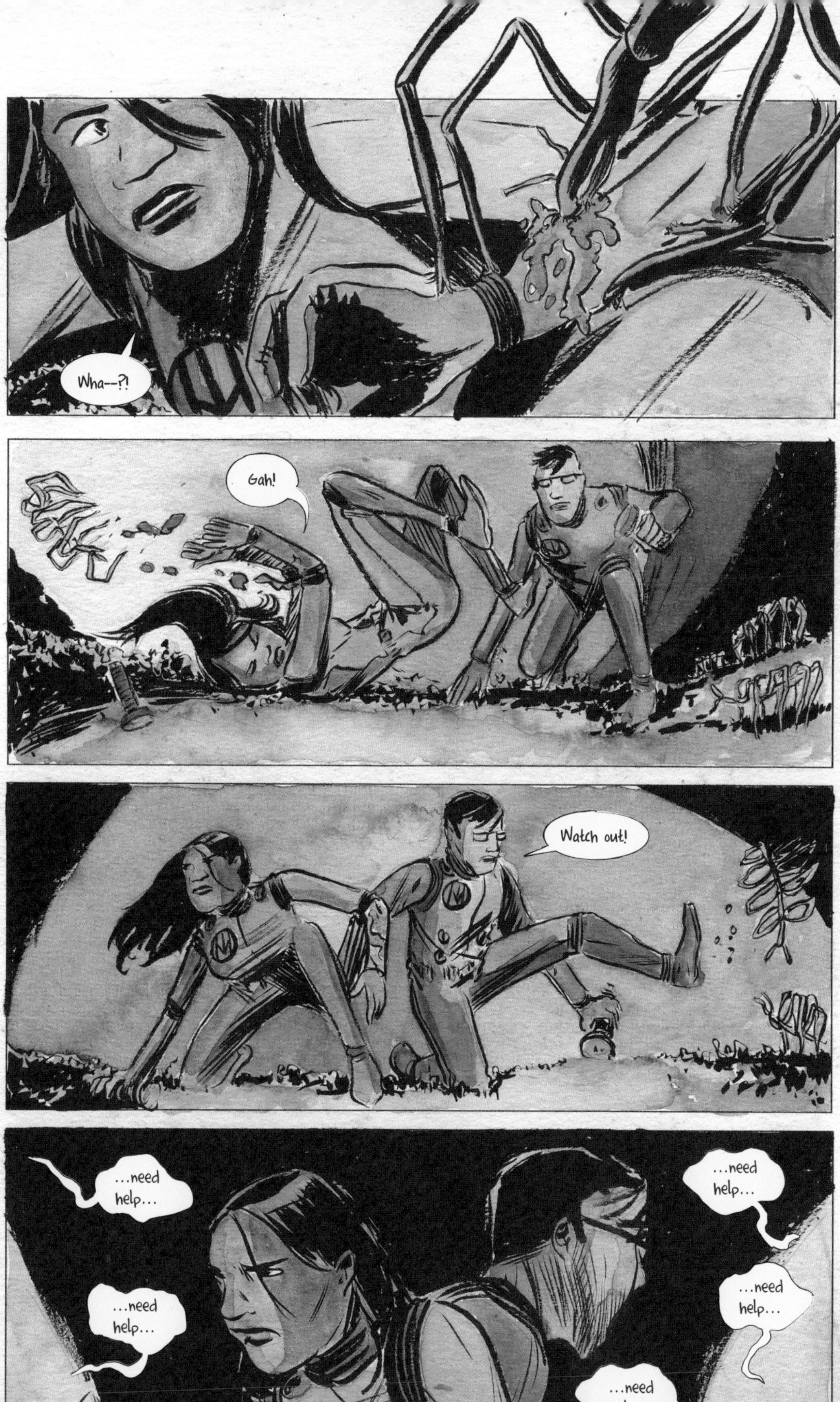
Wha--?!
Gah!
Watch out!
...need help...
...need help...
...need help...
...need help...
...need help...

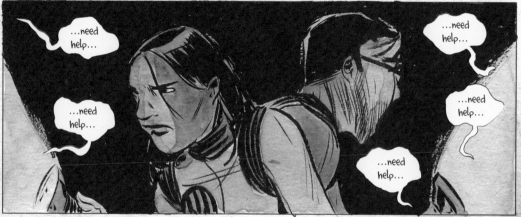

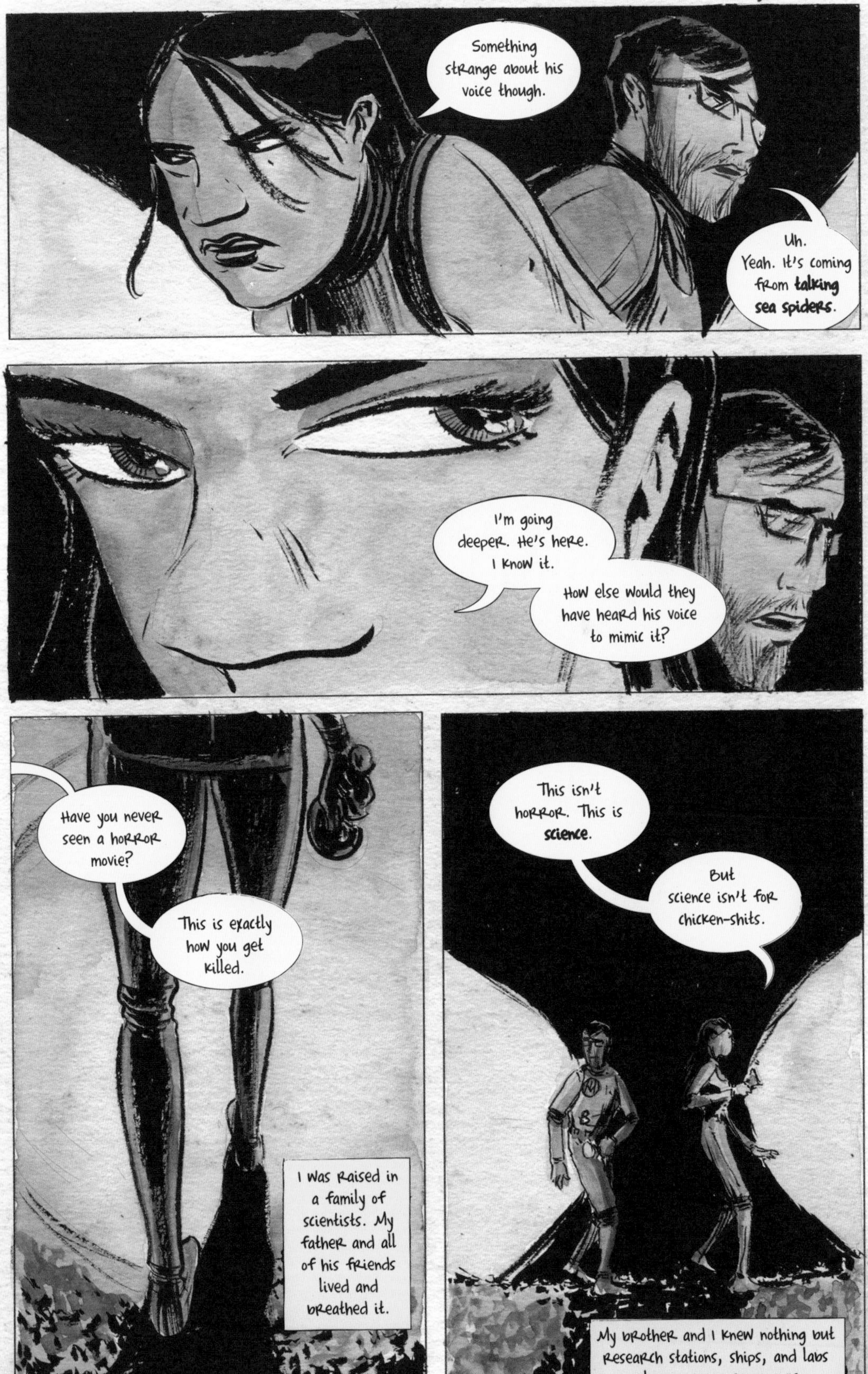
Something strange about his voice though.
Uh. Yeah. It's coming from **talking sea spiders**.
I'm going deeper. He's here. I know it.
How else would they have heard his voice to mimic it?
Have you never seen a horror movie?
This is exactly how you get killed.
I was raised in a family of scientists. My father and all of his friends lived and breathed it.
This isn't horror. This is **science**.
But science isn't for chicken-shits.
My brother and I knew nothing but research stations, ships, and labs as long as I can remember.

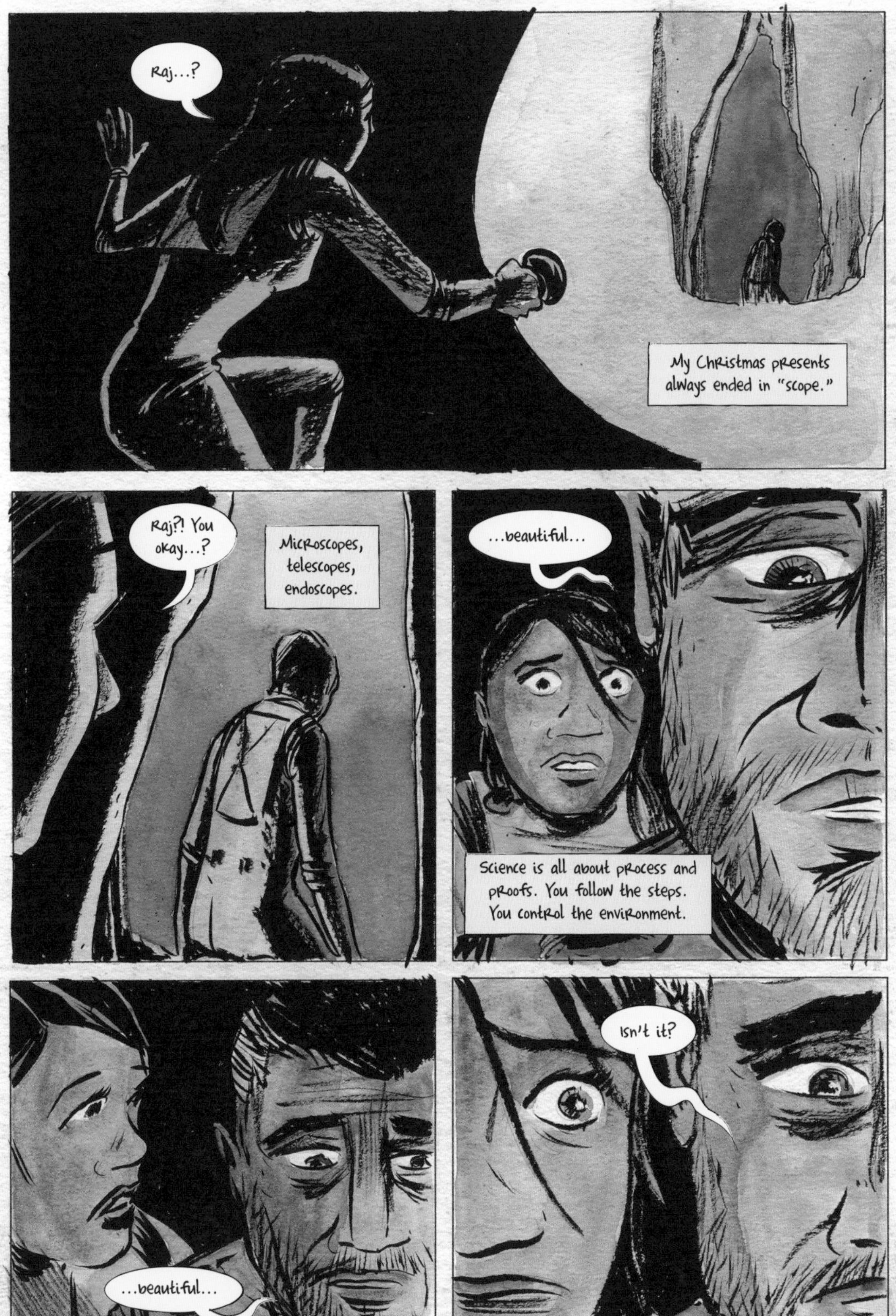
Raj...?
My Christmas presents always ended in "scope."
Raj?! You okay...?
Microscopes, telescopes, endoscopes.
...beautiful...
Science is all about process and proofs. You follow the steps. You control the environment.
...beautiful...
You gather facts. And you prove something.
Isn't it?
You would think...with that kind of background, I wouldn't believe in coincidence. In fate. In destiny.

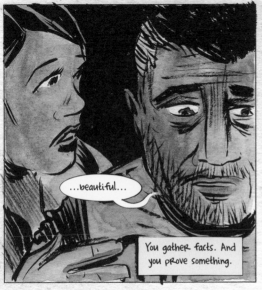

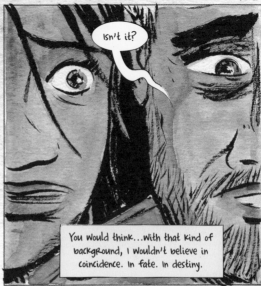

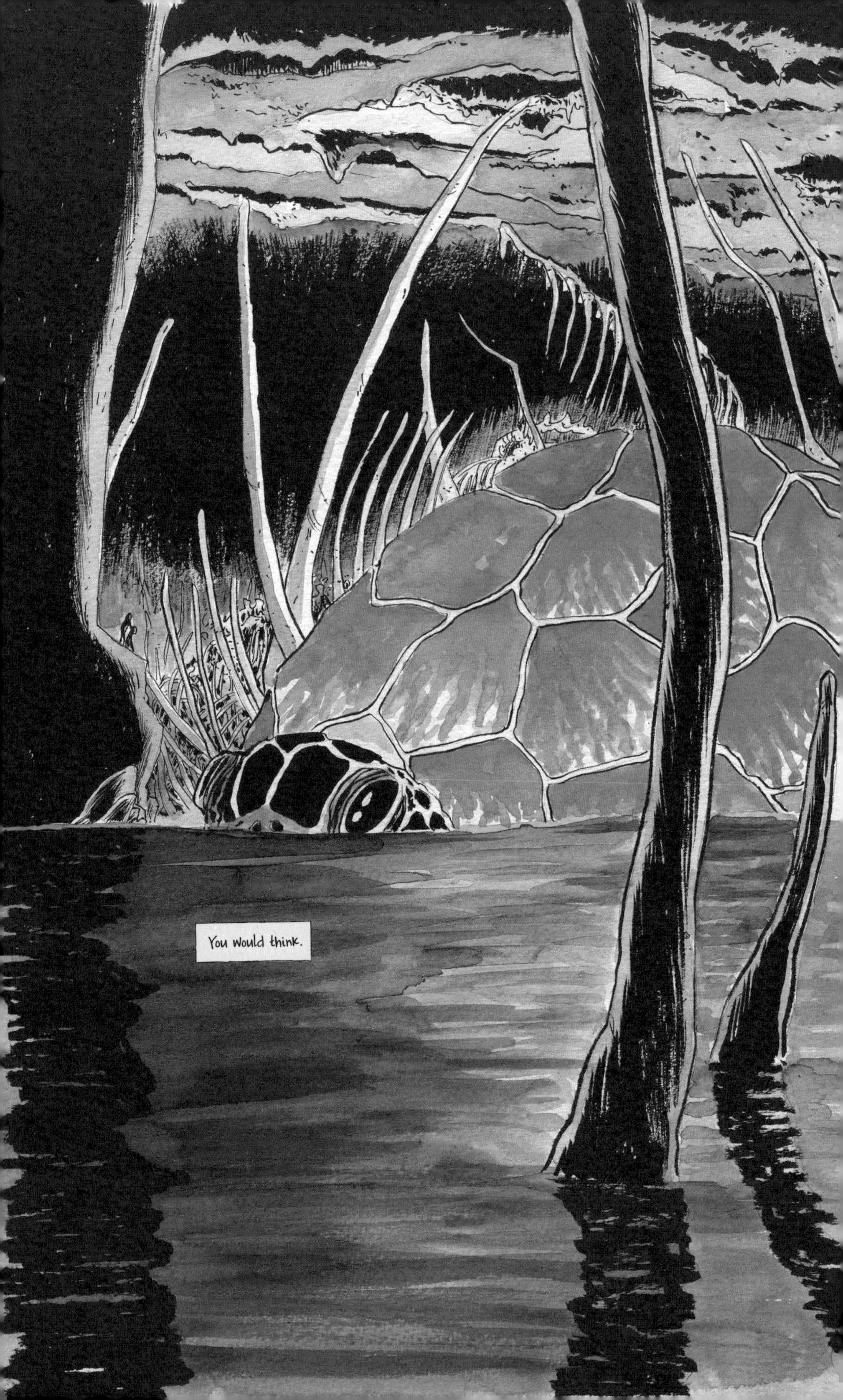
You would think.

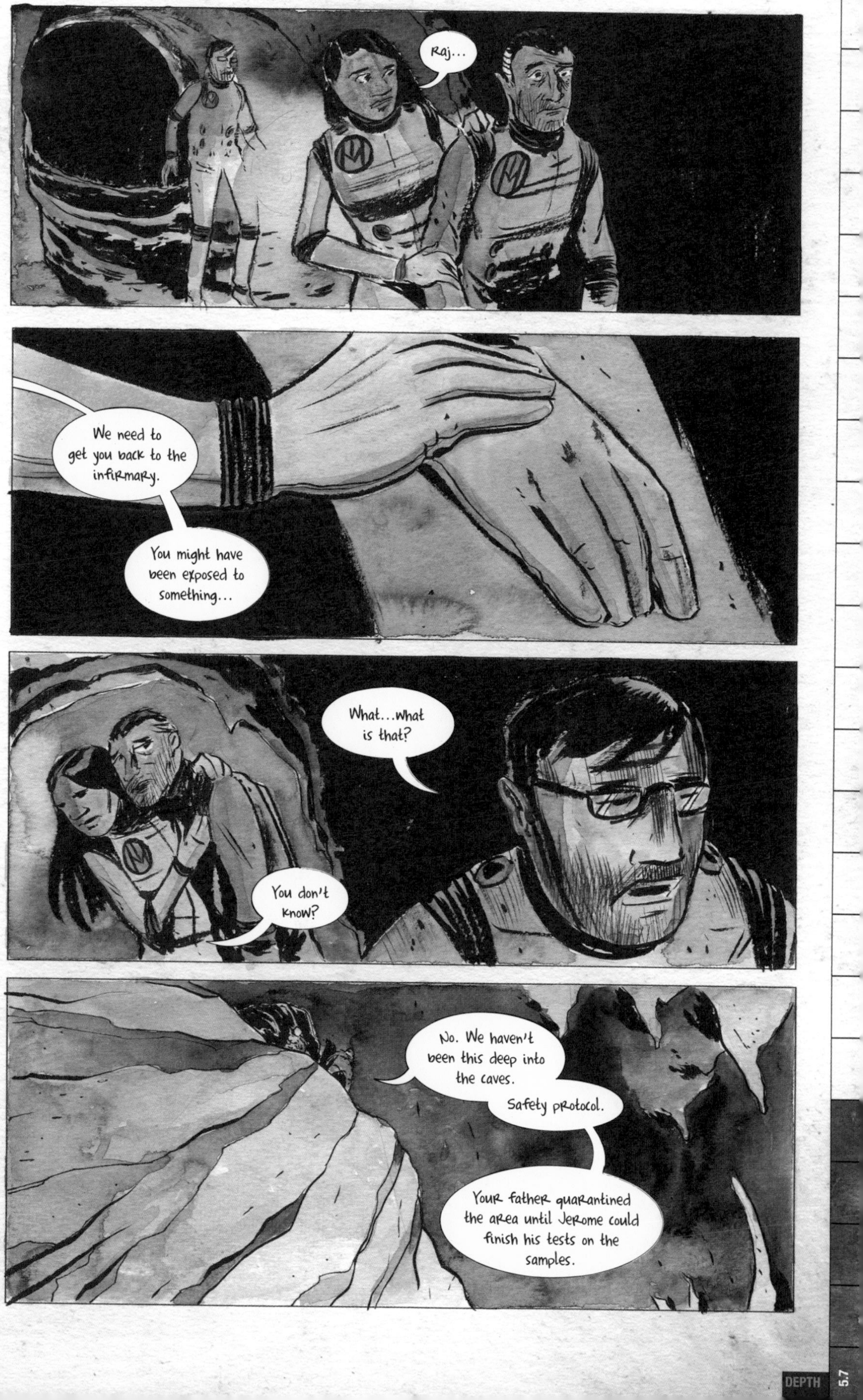
Raj...
We need to get you back to the infirmary.
You might have been exposed to something...
What...what is that?
You don't know?
No. We haven't been this deep into the caves.
Safety protocol.
Your father quarantined the area until Jerome could finish his tests on the samples.

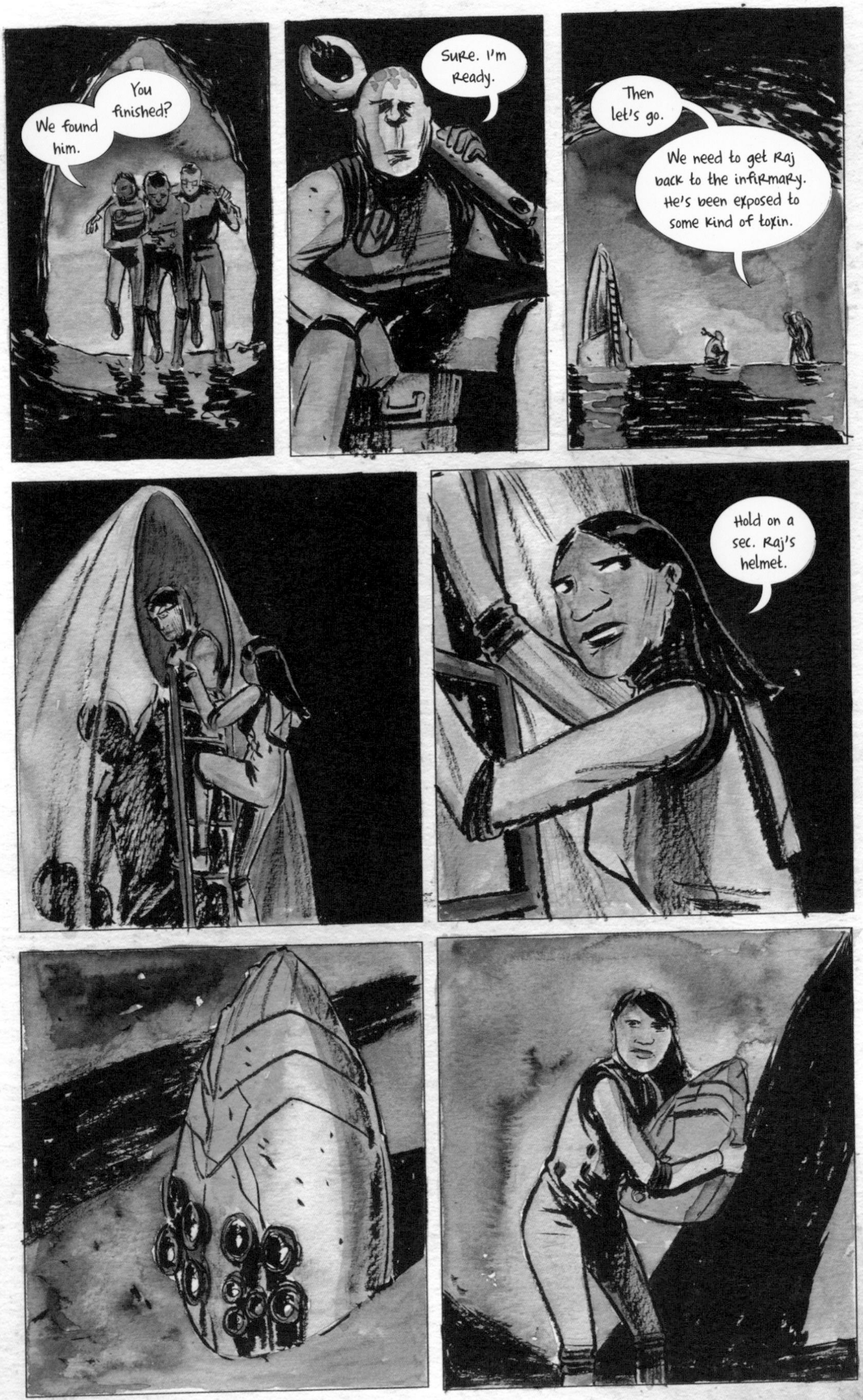
You finished?
We found him.
Sure. I'm ready.
Then let's go.
We need to get Raj back to the infirmary. He's been exposed to some kind of toxin.
Hold on a sec. Raj's helmet.

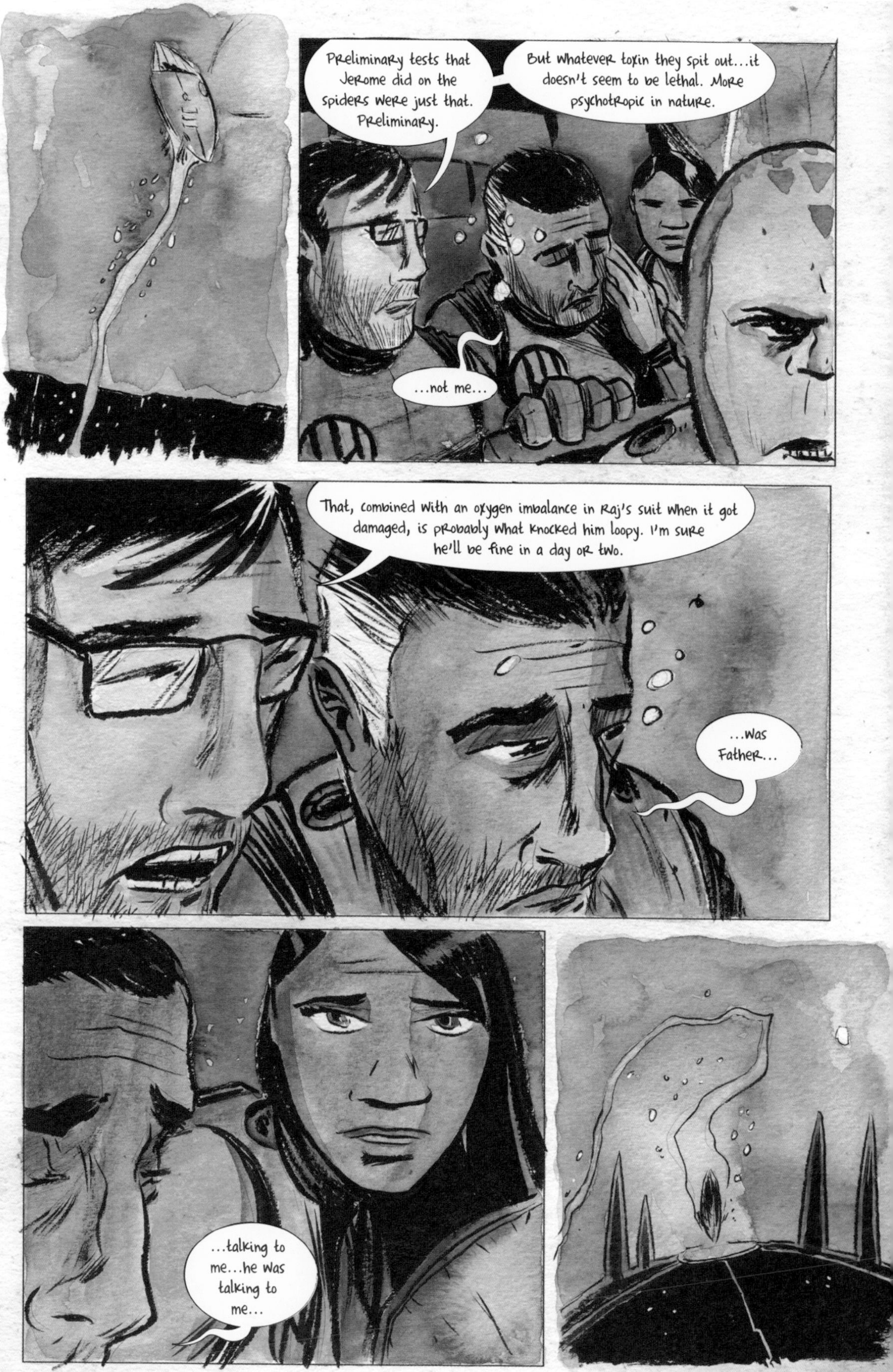

Preliminary tests that Jerome did on the spiders were just that. Preliminary.
But whatever toxin they spit out...it doesn't seem to be lethal. More psychotropic in nature.
...not me...
That, combined with an oxygen imbalance in Raj's suit when it got damaged, is probably what knocked him loopy. I'm sure he'll be fine in a day or two.
...was Father...
...talking to me...he was talking to me...

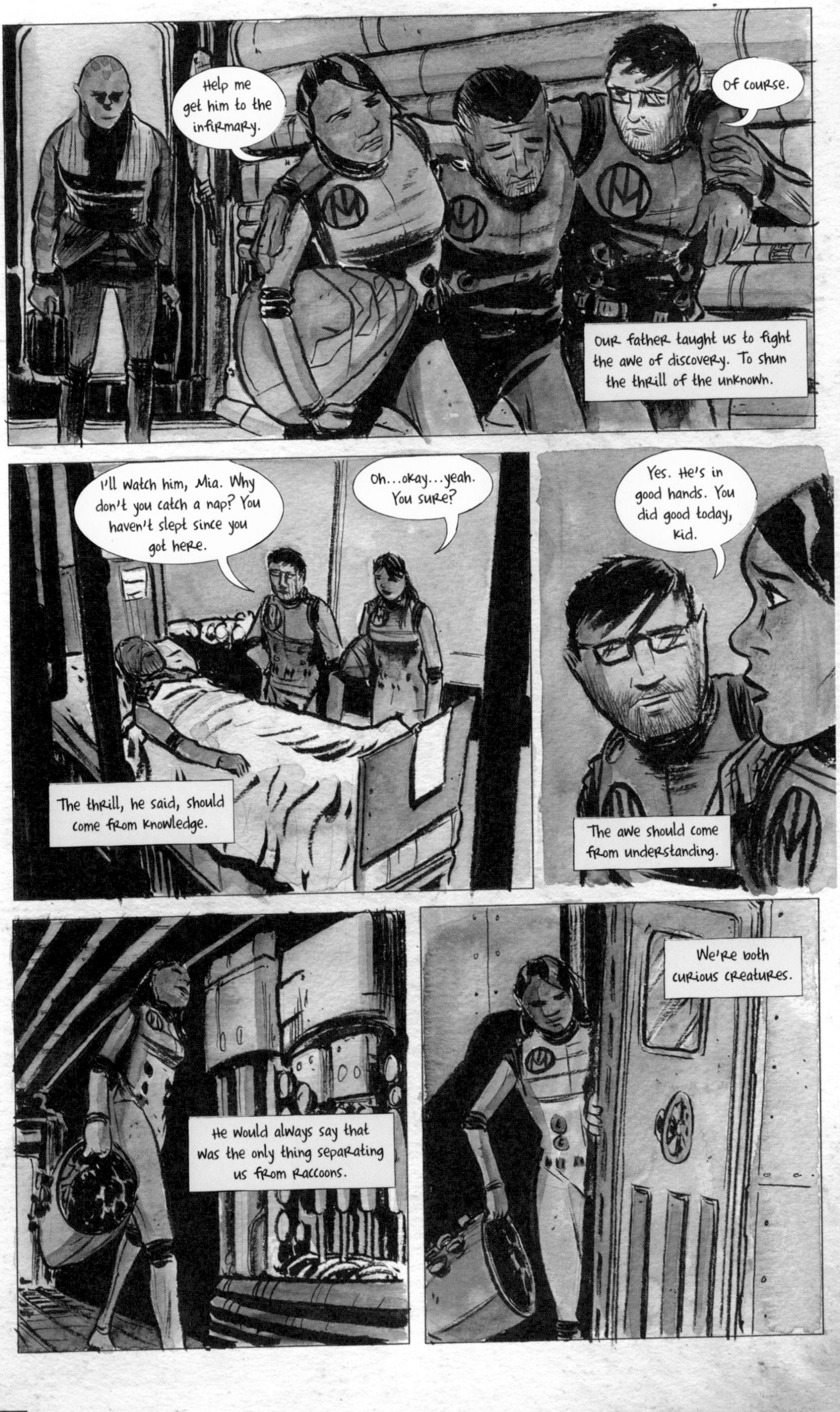
Help me get him to the infirmary.
Of course.
Our father taught us to fight the awe of discovery. To shun the thrill of the unknown.
I'll watch him, Mia. Why don't you catch a nap? You haven't slept since you got here.
Oh...okay...yeah. You sure?
The thrill, he said, should come from knowledge.
Yes. He's in good hands. You did good today, kid.
The awe should come from understanding.
He would always say that was the only thing separating us from raccoons.
We're both curious creatures.

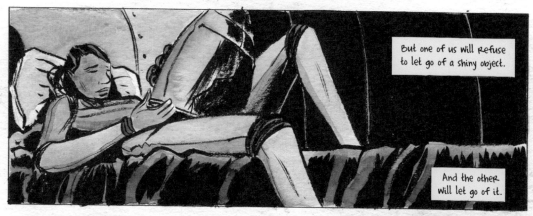

But one of us will refuse to let go of a shiny object.

And the other will let go of it.

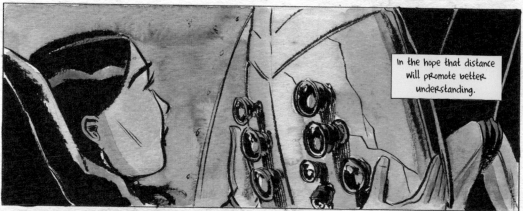

In the hope that distance will promote better understanding.

Need sleep. Badly.

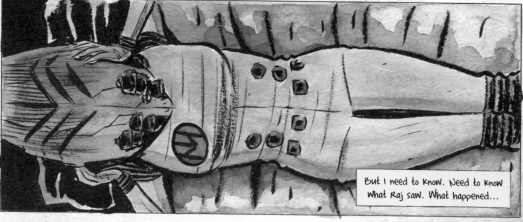

But I need to know. Need to know what Raj saw. What happened...

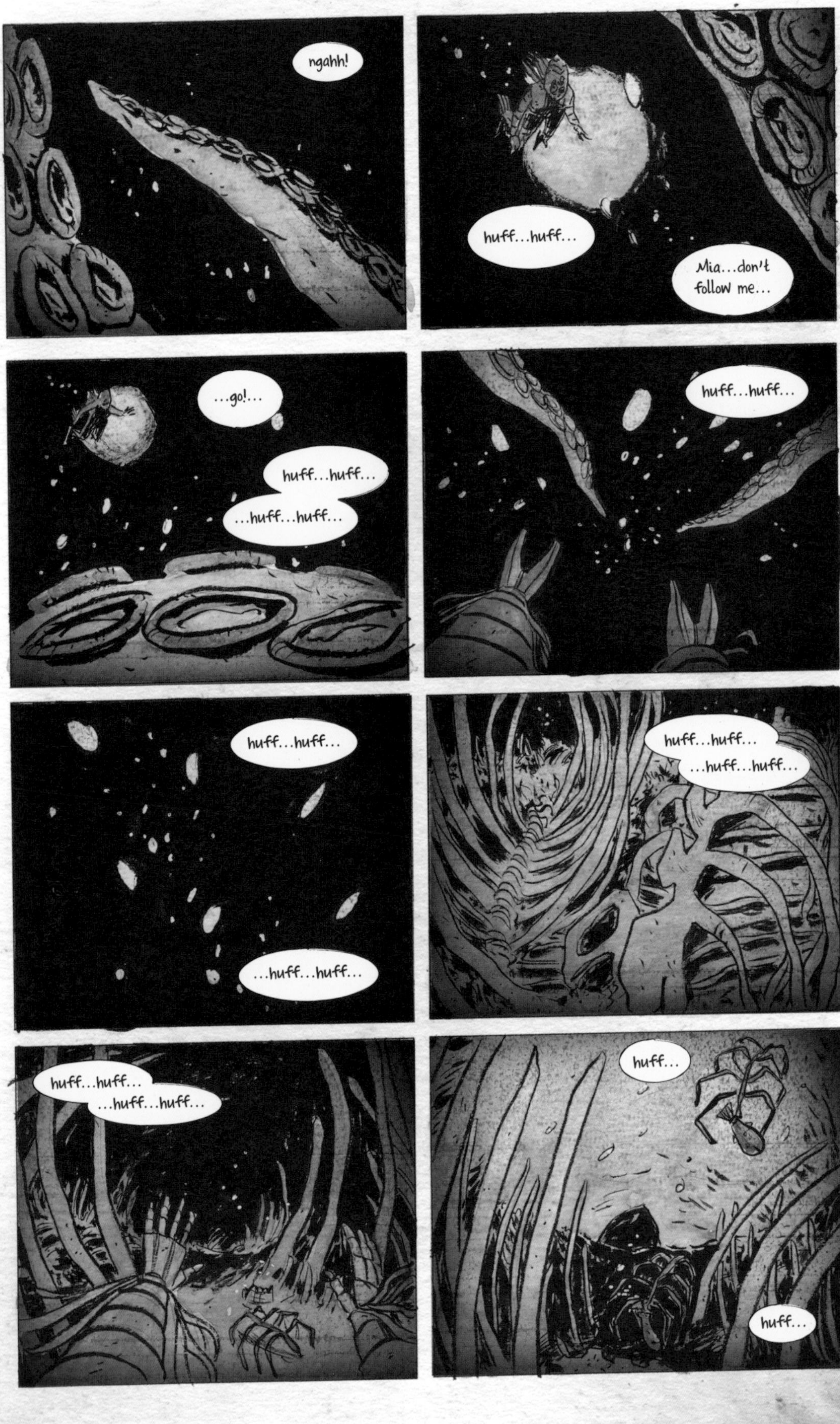
ngahh!
huff...huff...
Mia...don't follow me...
...go!...
huff...huff...
...huff...huff...
huff...huff...
huff...huff...
...huff...huff...
huff...huff...
...huff...huff...
huff...huff...
...huff...huff...
huff...huff...
...huff...huff...
huff...
huff...

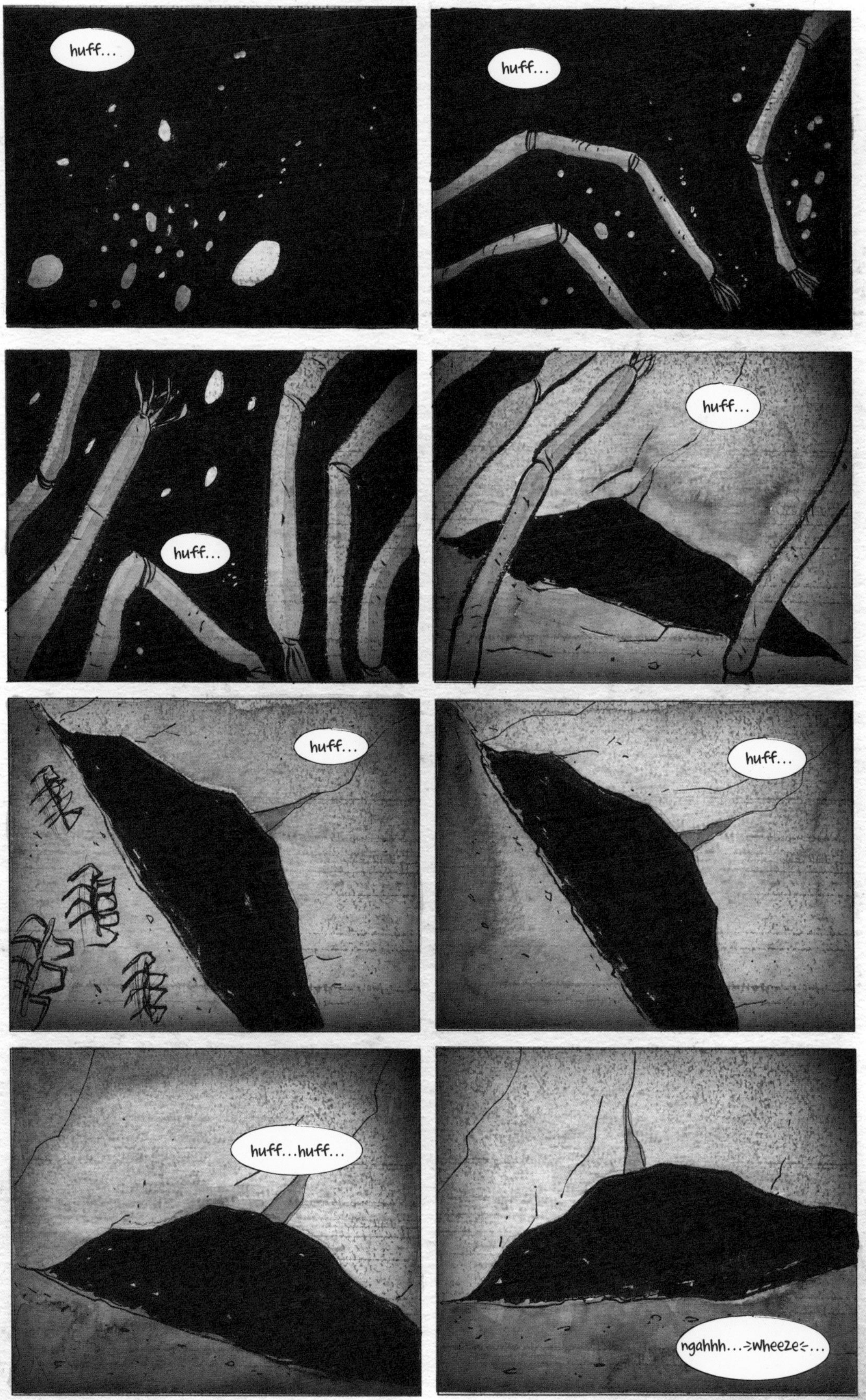
huff...
huff...
huff...
huff...
huff...
huff...
huff...huff...
ngahhh...≈wheeze≈...

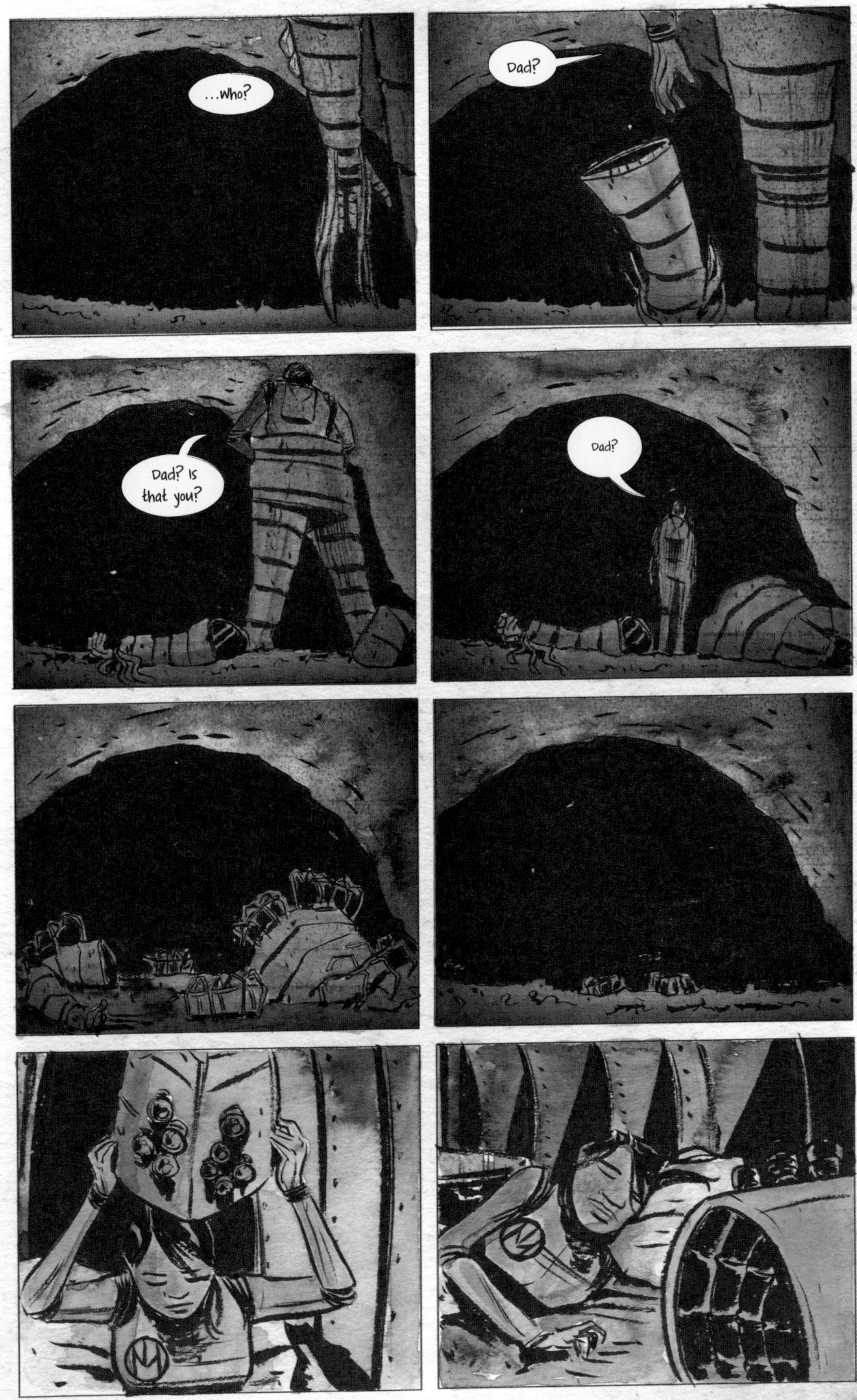
...Who?
Dad?
Dad? Is that you?
Dad?

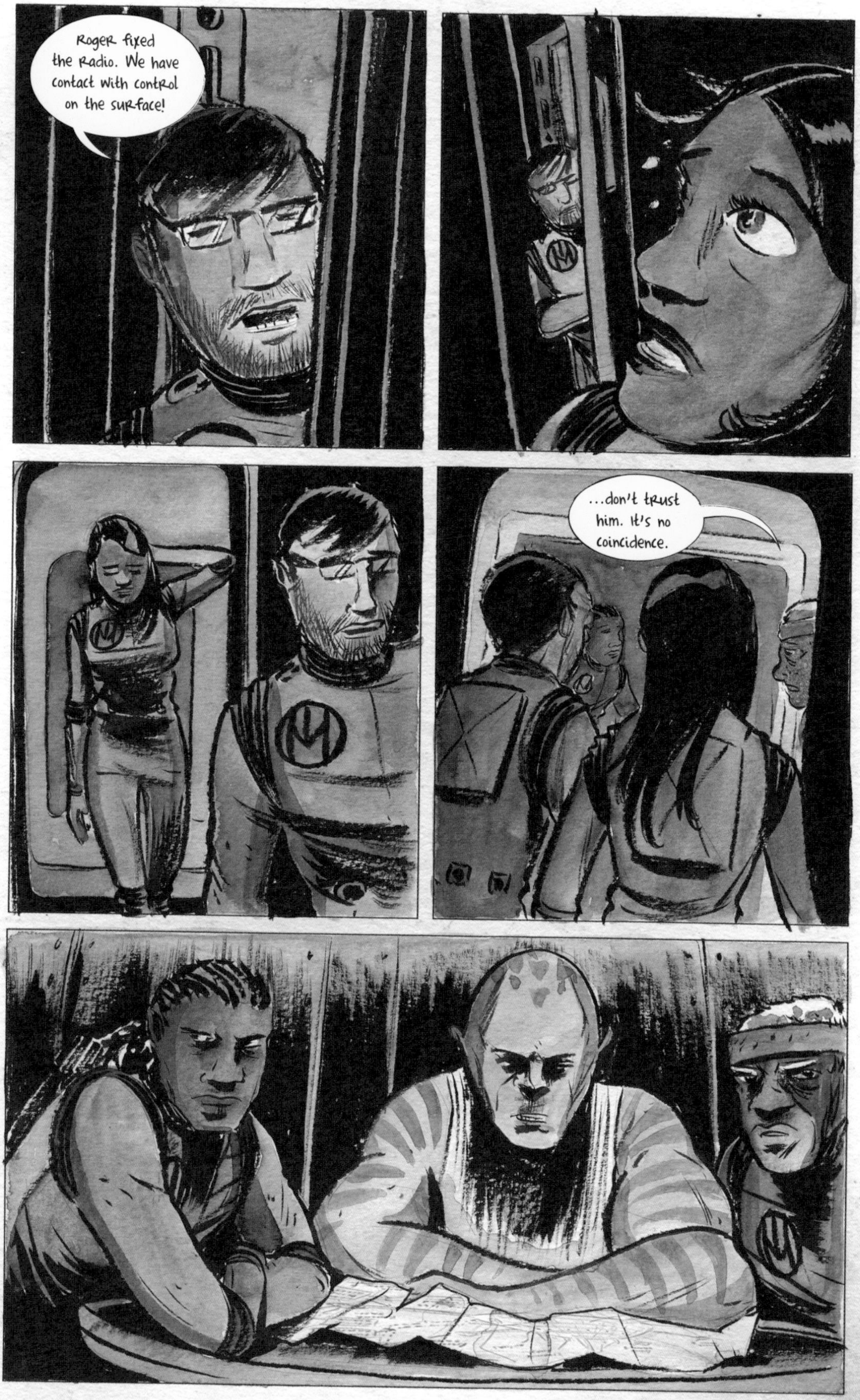
Roger fixed the Radio. We have contact with control on the surface!
...don't trust him. It's no coincidence.

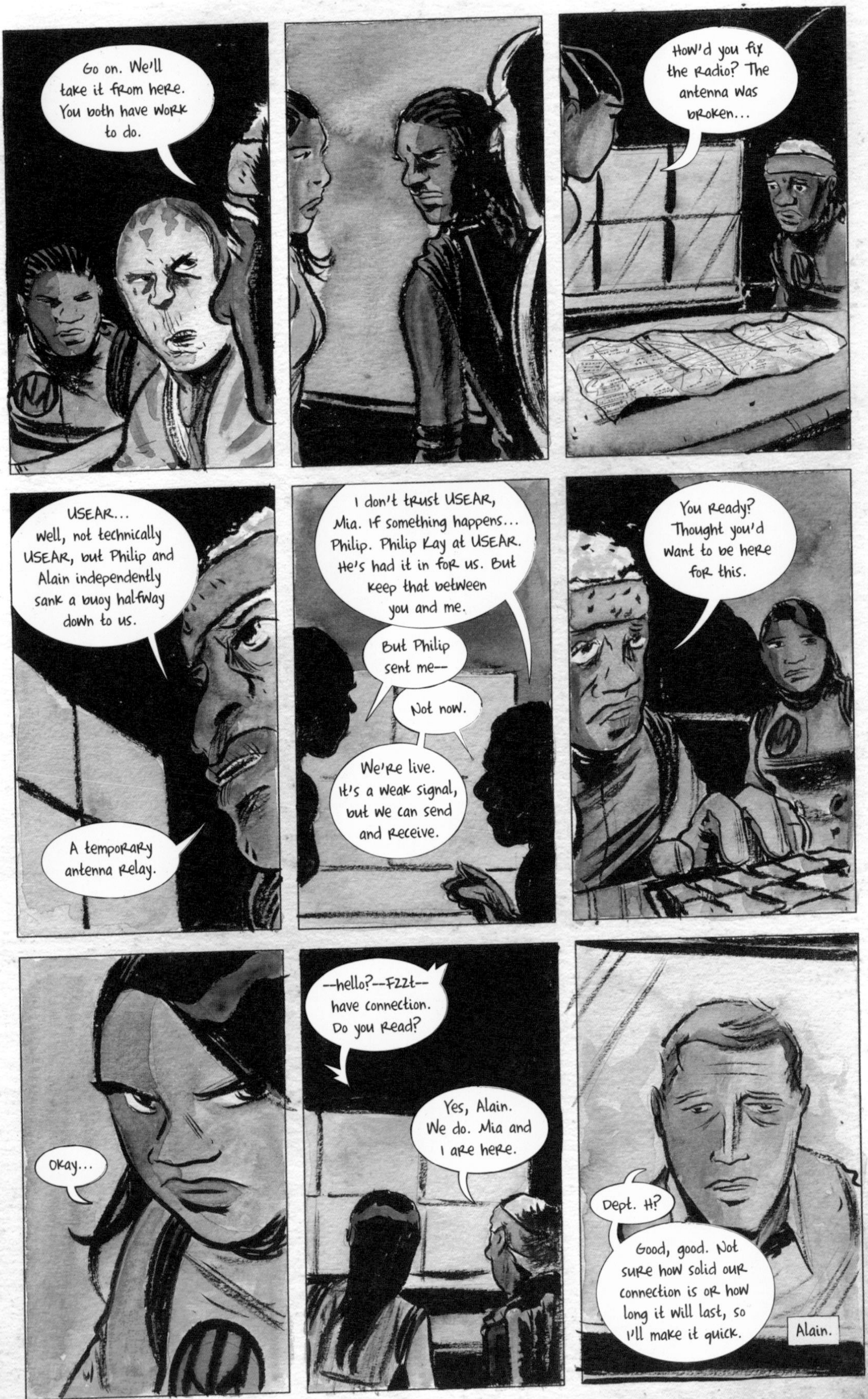
Go on. We'll take it from here. You both have work to do.
How'd you fix the radio? The antenna was broken...
USEAR... well, not technically USEAR, but Philip and Alain independently sank a buoy halfway down to us.
A temporary antenna relay.
I don't trust USEAR, Mia. If something happens... Philip. Philip Kay at USEAR. He's had it in for us. But keep that between you and me.
But Philip sent me--
Not now.
We're live. It's a weak signal, but we can send and receive.
You ready? Thought you'd want to be here for this.
Okay...
--hello?--fzzt-- have connection. Do you read?
Yes, Alain. We do. Mia and I are here.
Dept. H?
Good, good. Not sure how solid our connection is or how long it will last, so I'll make it quick.
Alain.

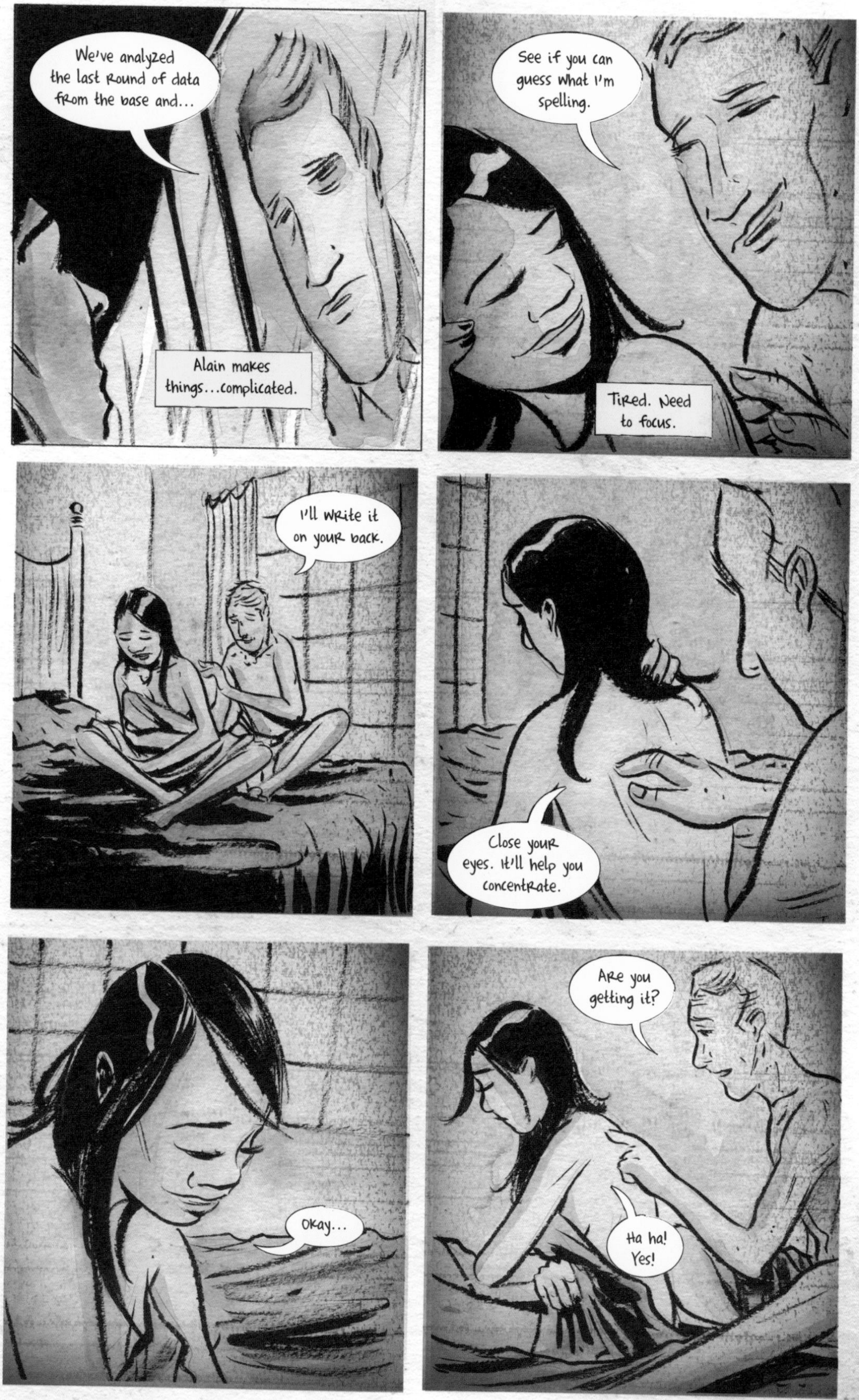
We've analyzed the last Round of data from the base and...
Alain makes things...complicated.
See if you can guess what I'm spelling.
Tired. Need to focus.
I'll write it on your back.
Close your eyes. It'll help you concentrate.
Okay...
Are you getting it?
Ha ha! Yes!

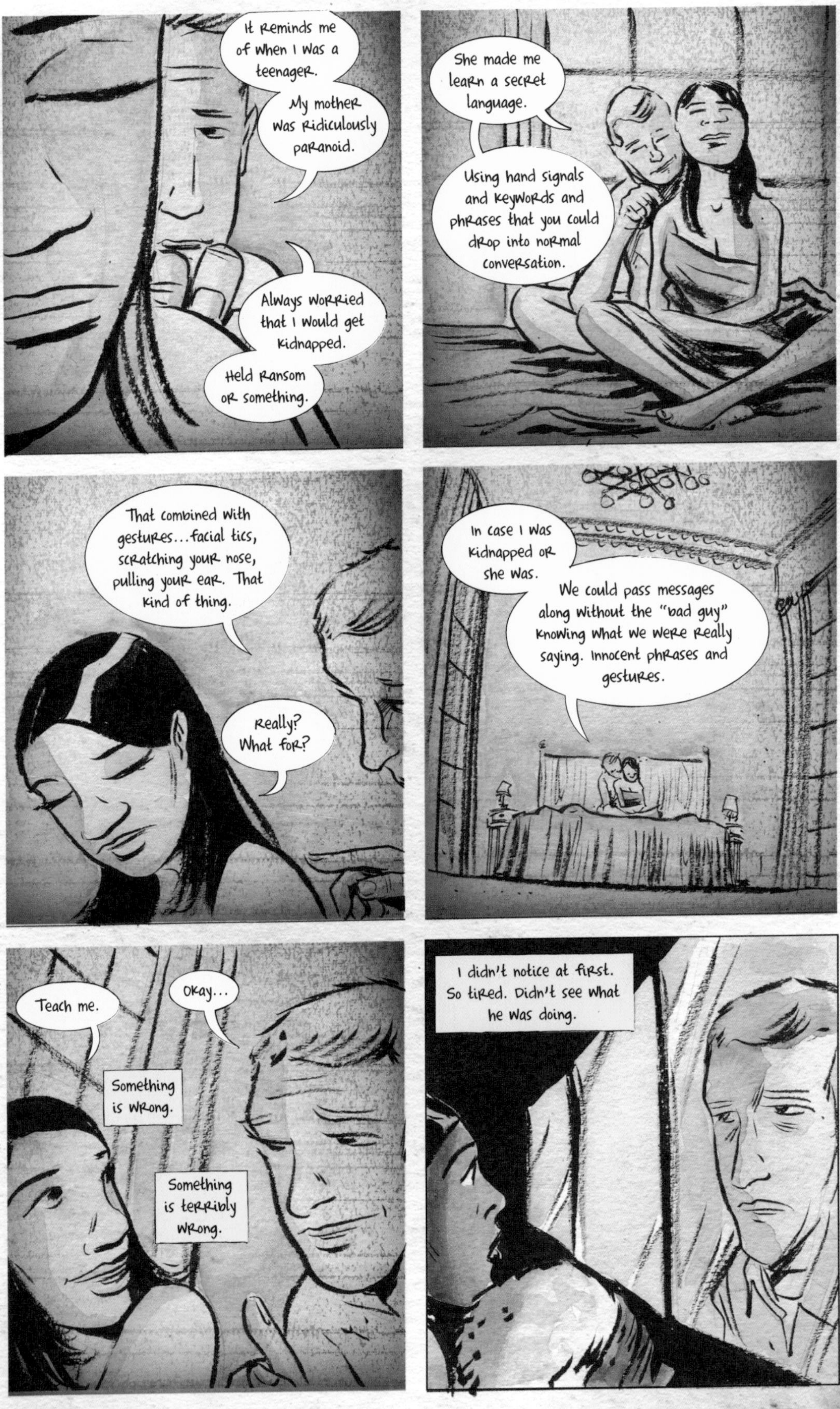

It reminds me of when I was a teenager.
My mother was ridiculously paranoid.
Always worried that I would get kidnapped.
Held ransom or something.
She made me learn a secret language.
Using hand signals and keywords and phrases that you could drop into normal conversation.
That combined with gestures... facial tics, scratching your nose, pulling your ear. That kind of thing.
Really? What for?
In case I was kidnapped or she was.
We could pass messages along without the "bad guy" knowing what we were really saying. Innocent phrases and gestures.
Teach me.
Okay...
Something is wrong.
Something is terribly wrong.
I didn't notice at first. So tired. Didn't see what he was doing.

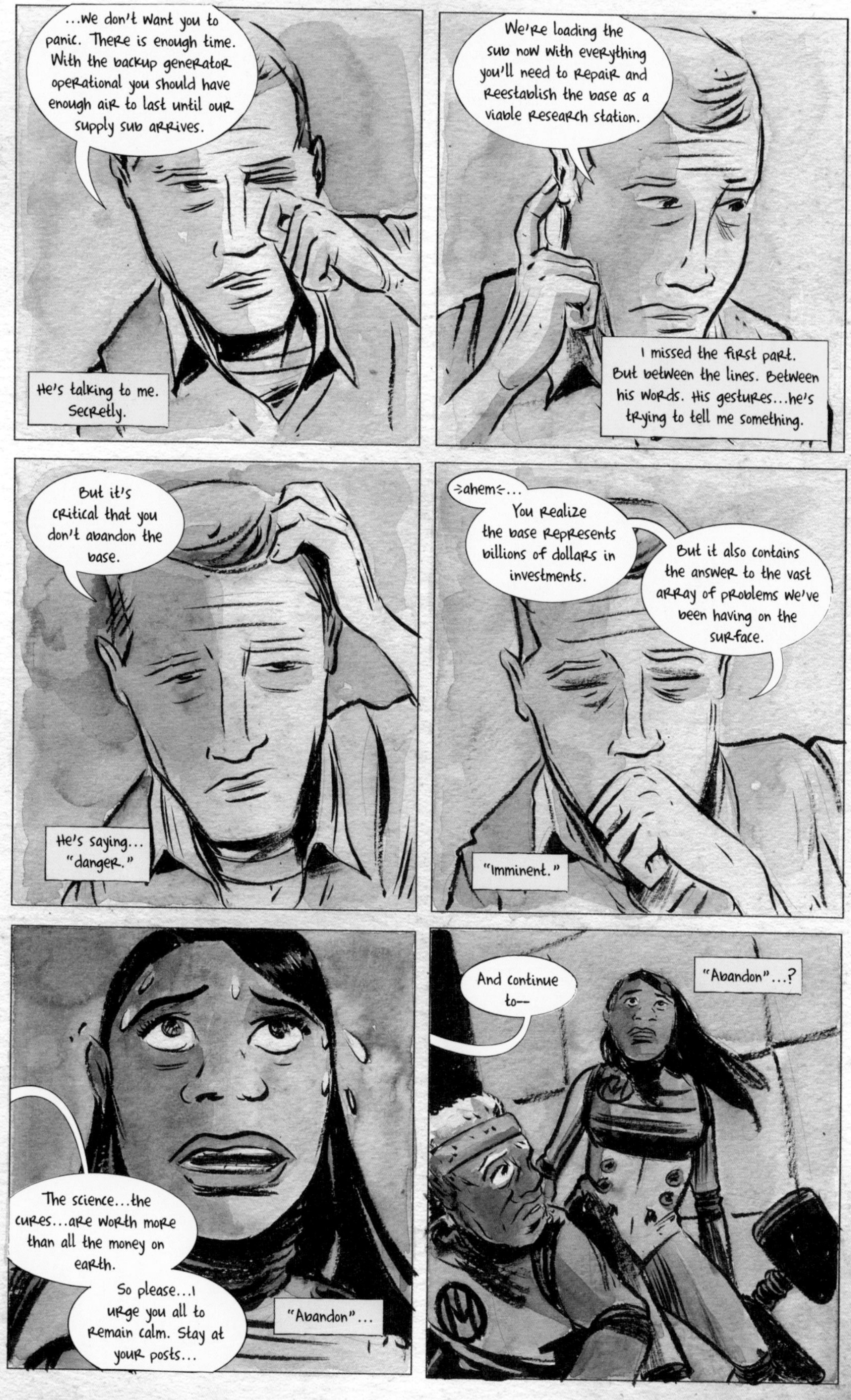
...We don't want you to panic. There is enough time. With the backup generator operational you should have enough air to last until our supply sub arrives.
He's talking to me. Secretly.
We're loading the sub now with everything you'll need to repair and reestablish the base as a viable research station.
I missed the first part. But between the lines. Between his words. His gestures...he's trying to tell me something.
But it's critical that you don't abandon the base.
He's saying... "danger."
>ahem<...
You realize the base represents billions of dollars in investments.
But it also contains the answer to the vast array of problems we've been having on the surface.
"Imminent."
The science...the cures...are worth more than all the money on earth.
So please...I urge you all to remain calm. Stay at your posts...
"Abandon"...
And continue to--
"Abandon"...?

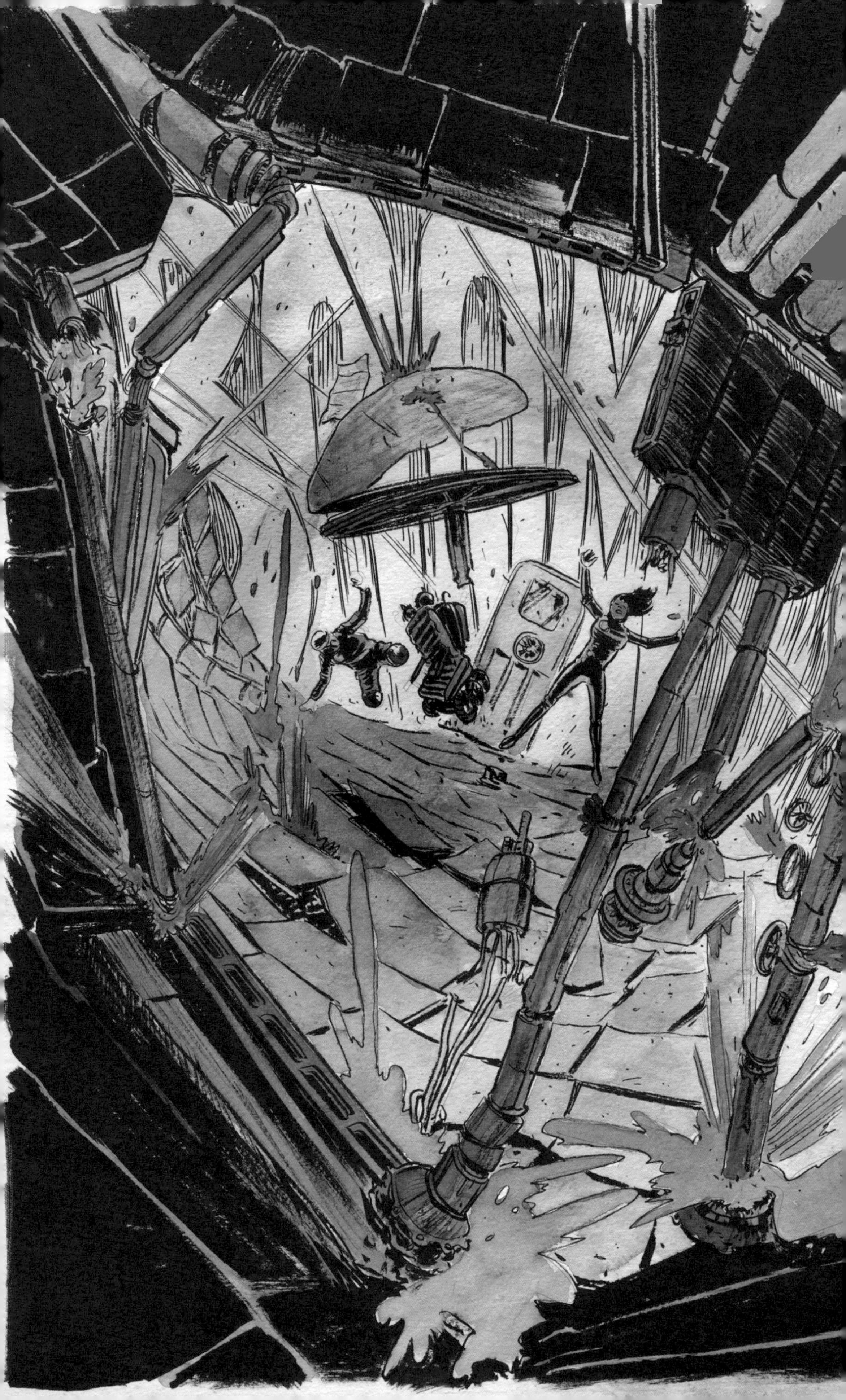

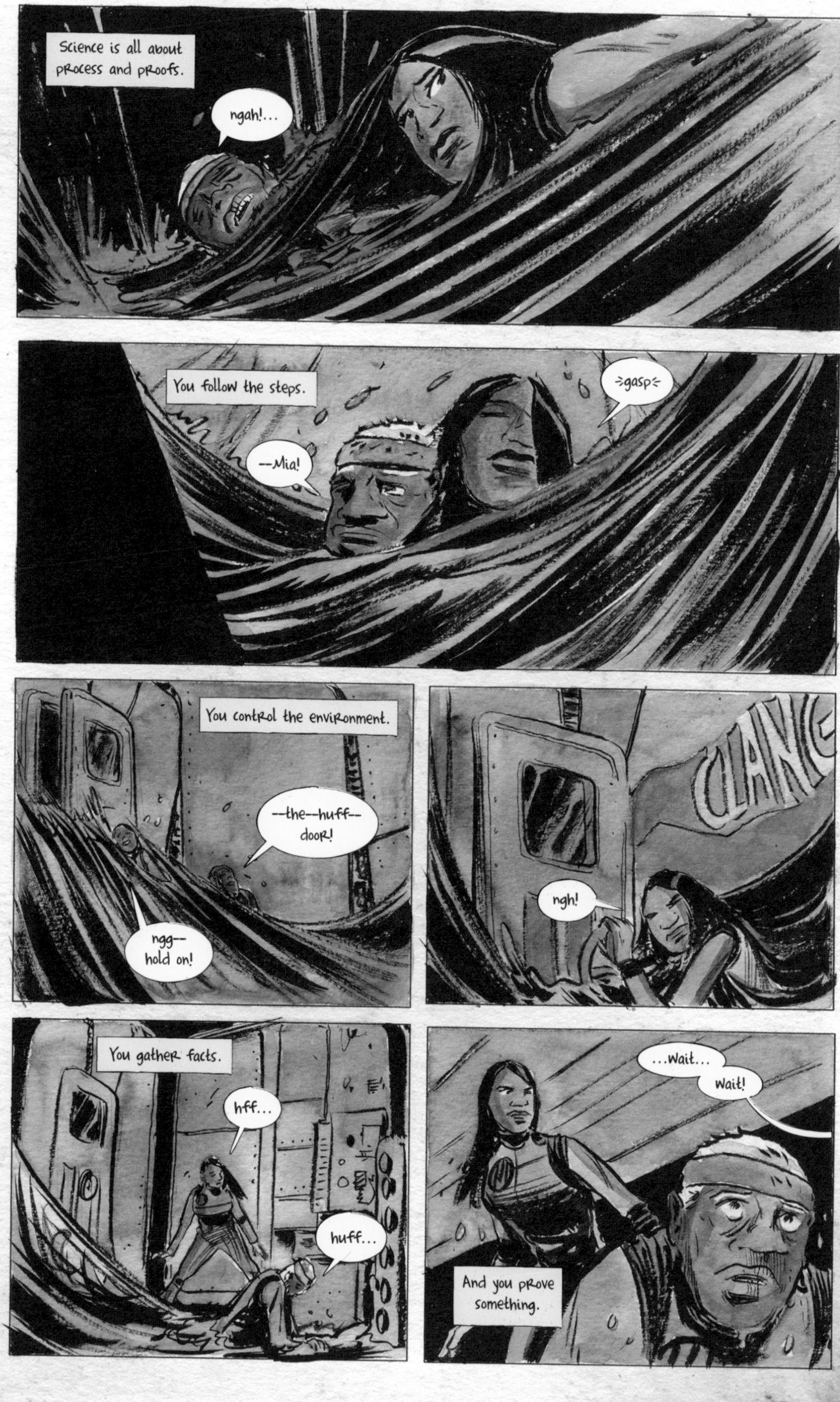
Science is all about process and proofs.
ngah!...
You follow the steps.
=gasp=
--Mia!
You control the environment.
--the--huff--door!
ngg--hold on!
CLANG
ngh!
You gather facts.
hff...
huff...
...Wait...
Wait!
And you prove something.

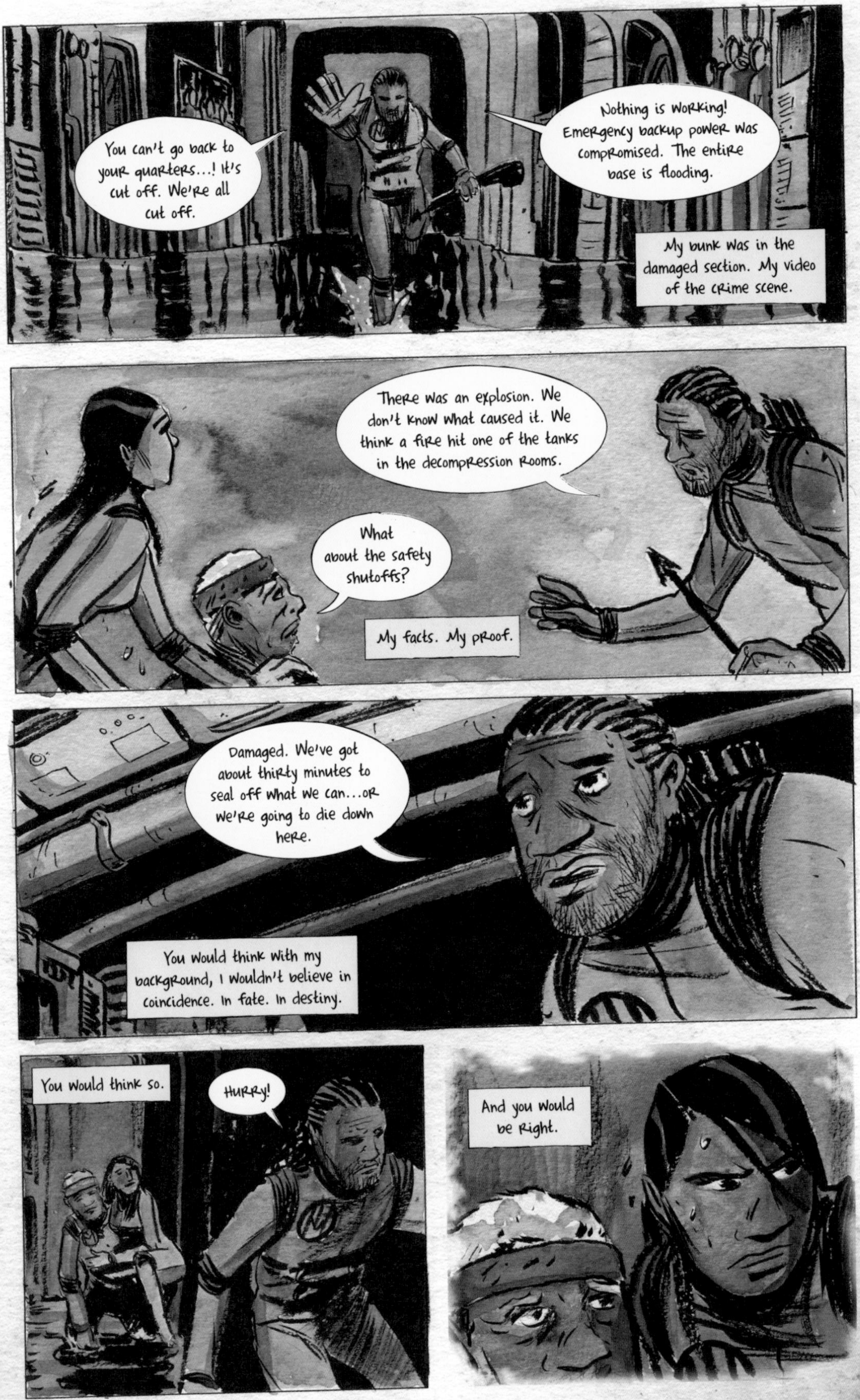
You can't go back to your quarters...! It's cut off. We're all cut off.
Nothing is working! Emergency backup power was compromised. The entire base is flooding.
My bunk was in the damaged section. My video of the crime scene.
There was an explosion. We don't know what caused it. We think a fire hit one of the tanks in the decompression rooms.
What about the safety shutoffs?
My facts. My proof.
Damaged. We've got about thirty minutes to seal off what we can...or we're going to die down here.
You would think with my background, I wouldn't believe in coincidence. In fate. In destiny.
You would think so.
Hurry!
And you would be right.

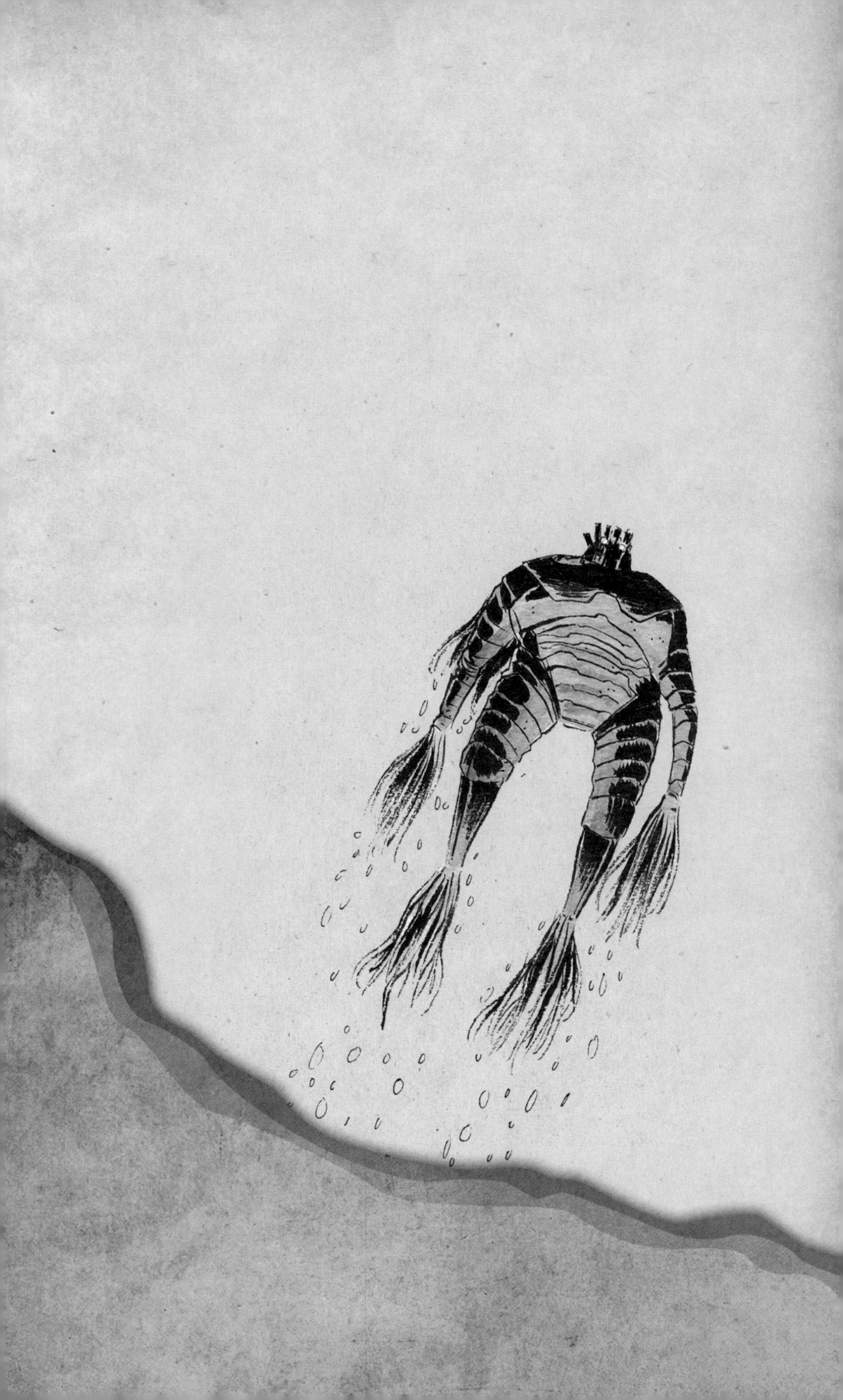

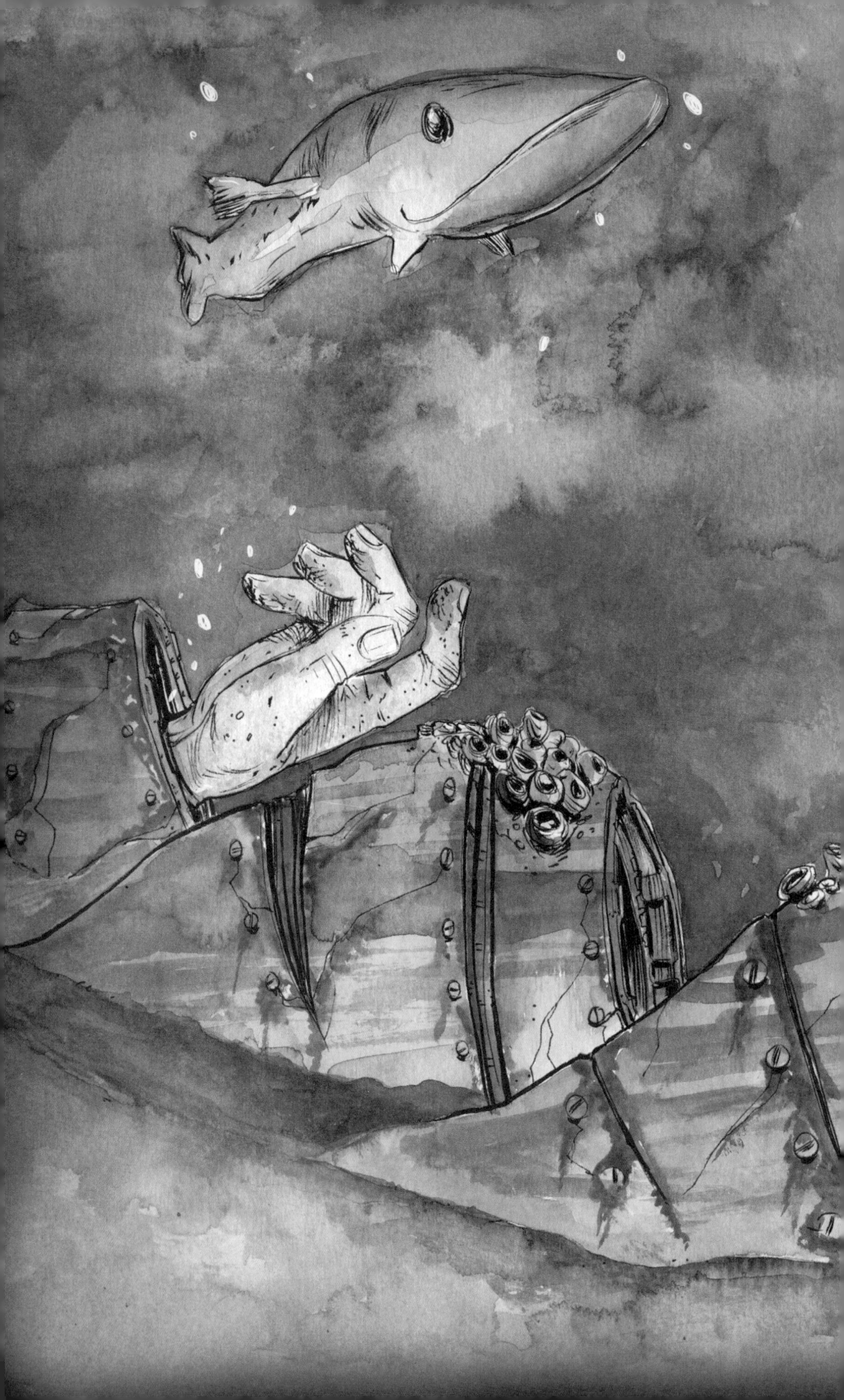

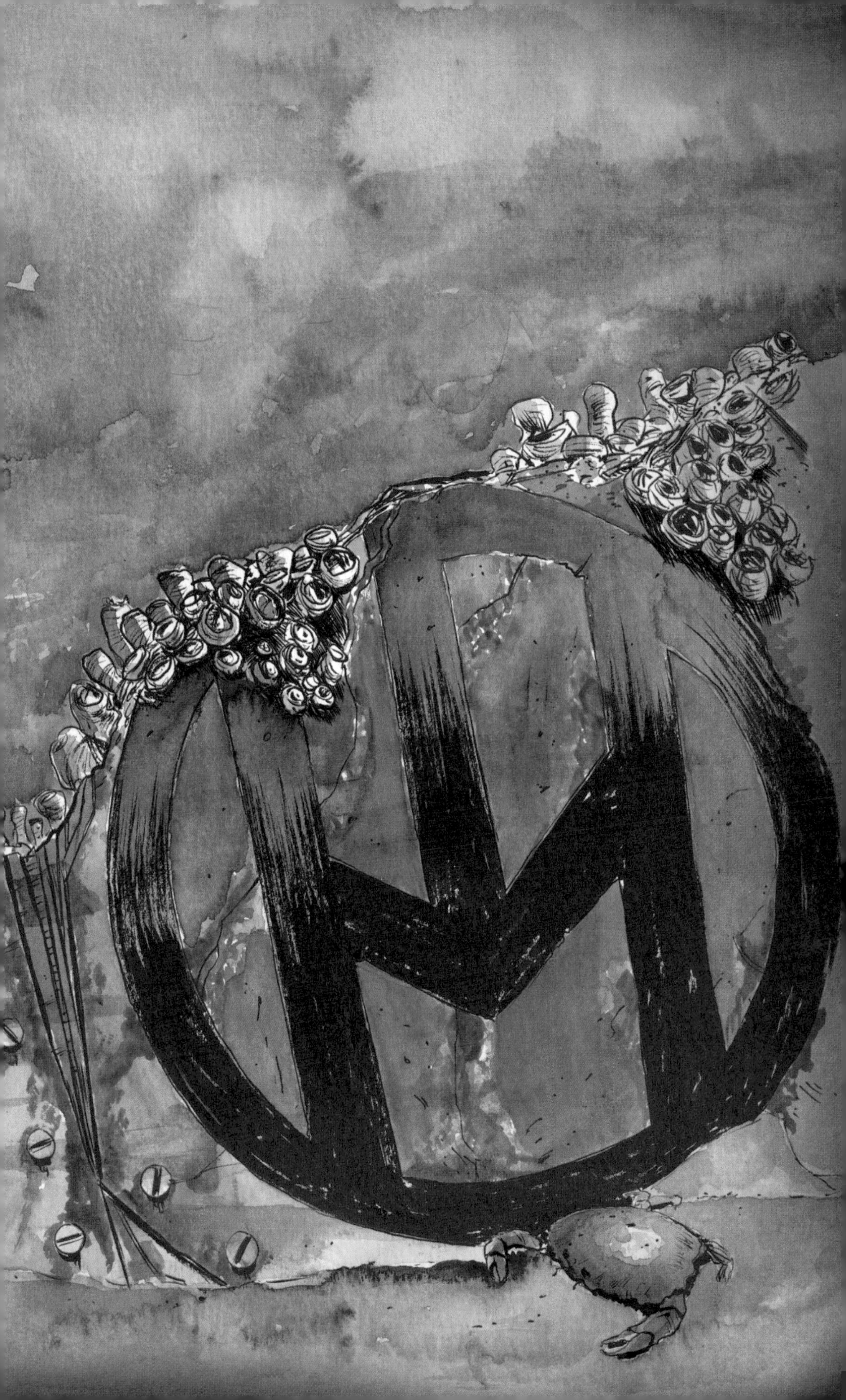

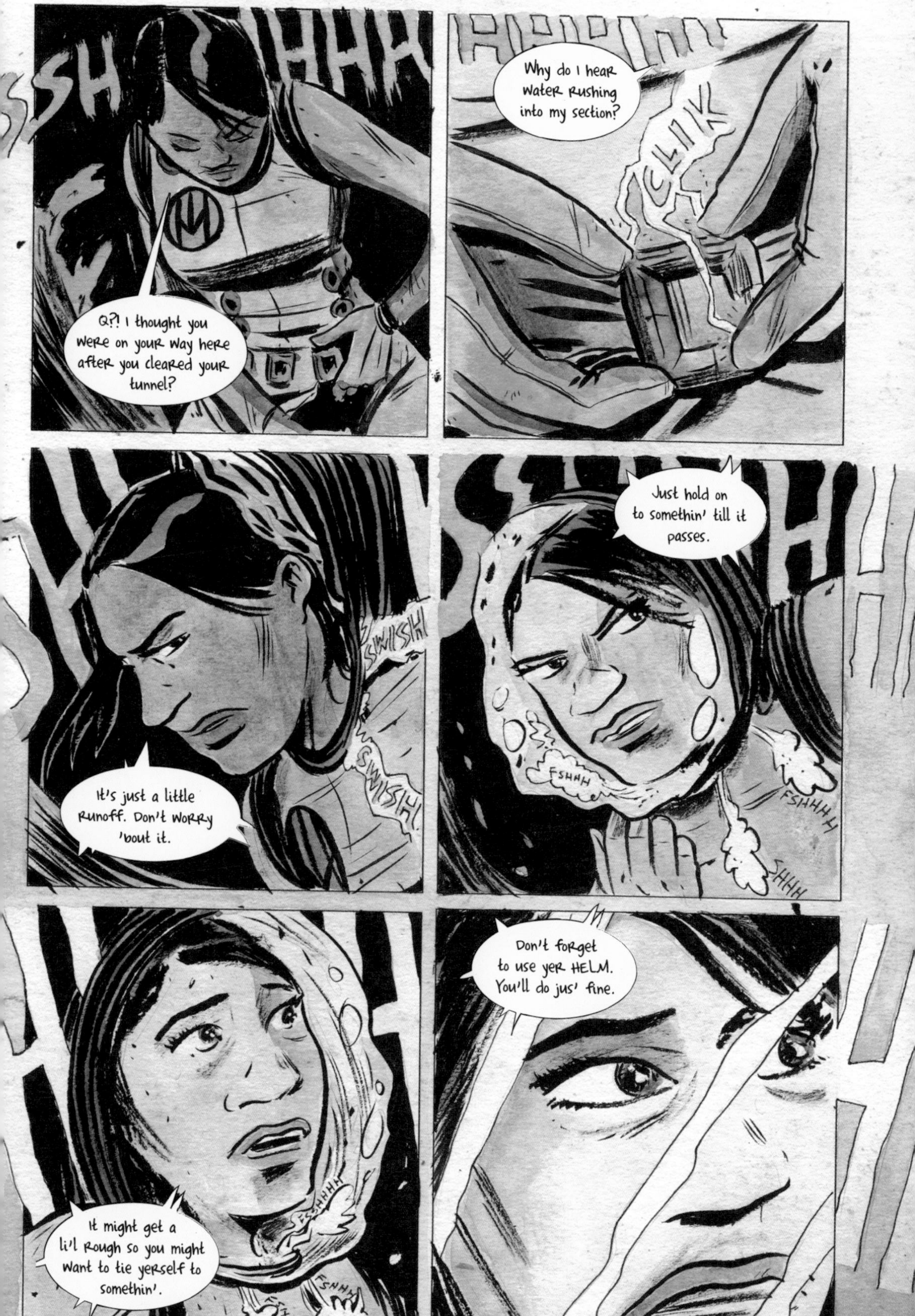
SSHHHHH
Q?! I thought you were on your way here after you cleared your tunnel?
Why do I hear water rushing into my section?
CLIK
It's just a little runoff. Don't worry 'bout it.
SWISH
SWISH
Just hold on to somethin' till it passes.
FSHHH
FSHHHH
SHHH
It might get a li'l rough so you might want to tie yerself to somethin'.
Don't forget to use yer HELM. You'll do jus' fine.

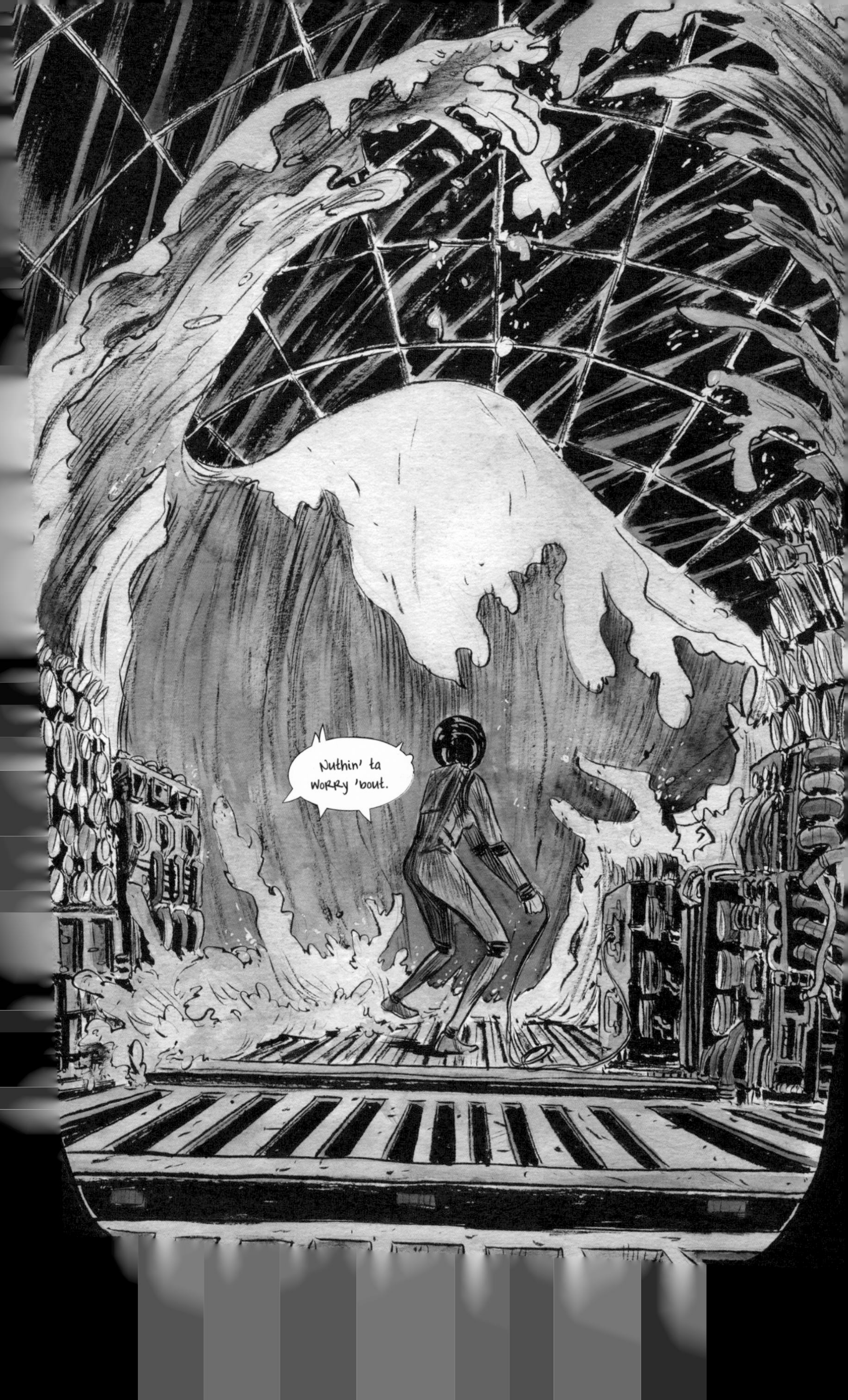
Nuthin' ta worry 'bout.

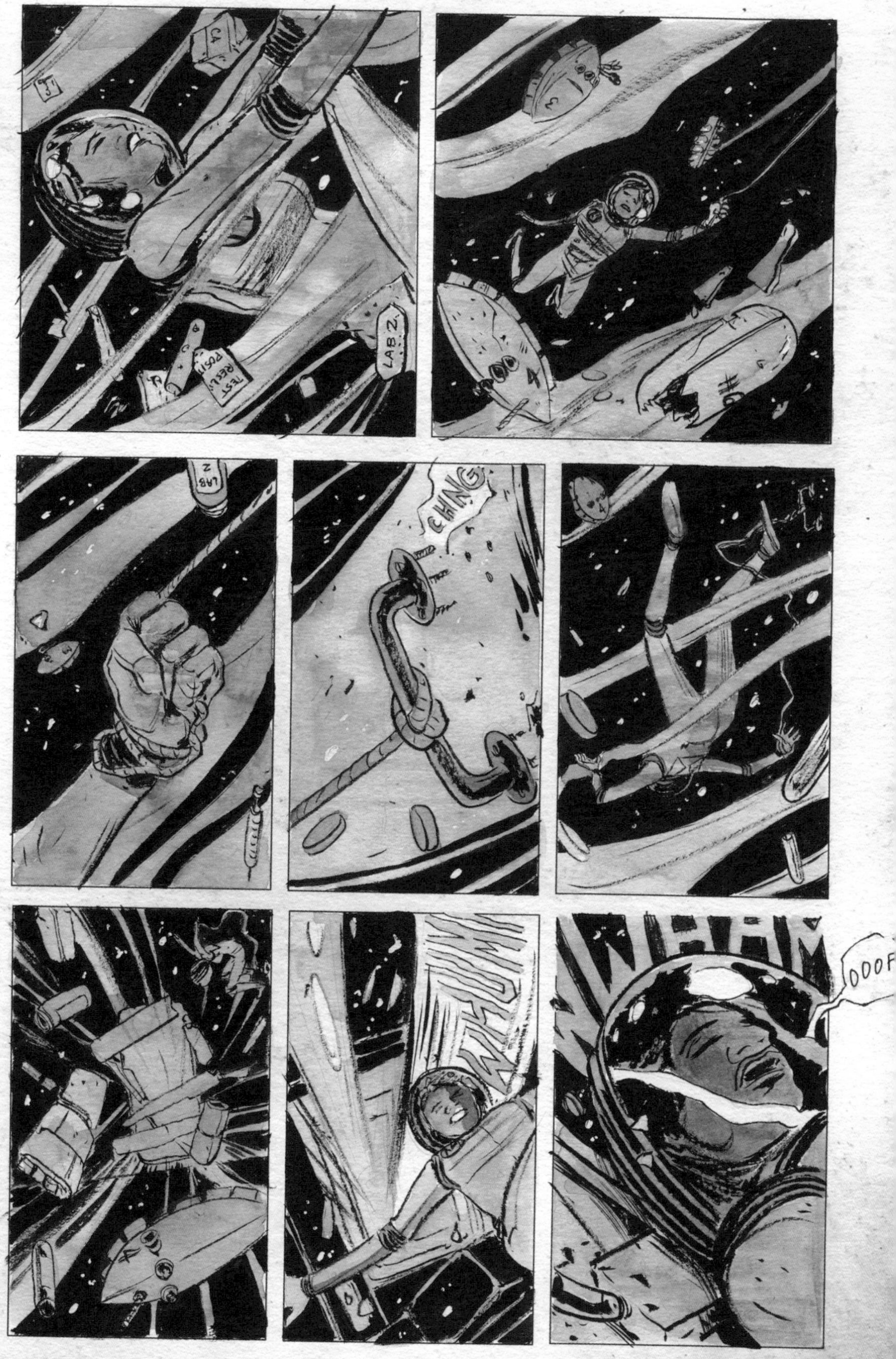
LAB 2.
LAB 2
CHNG
WHAM
OOOF

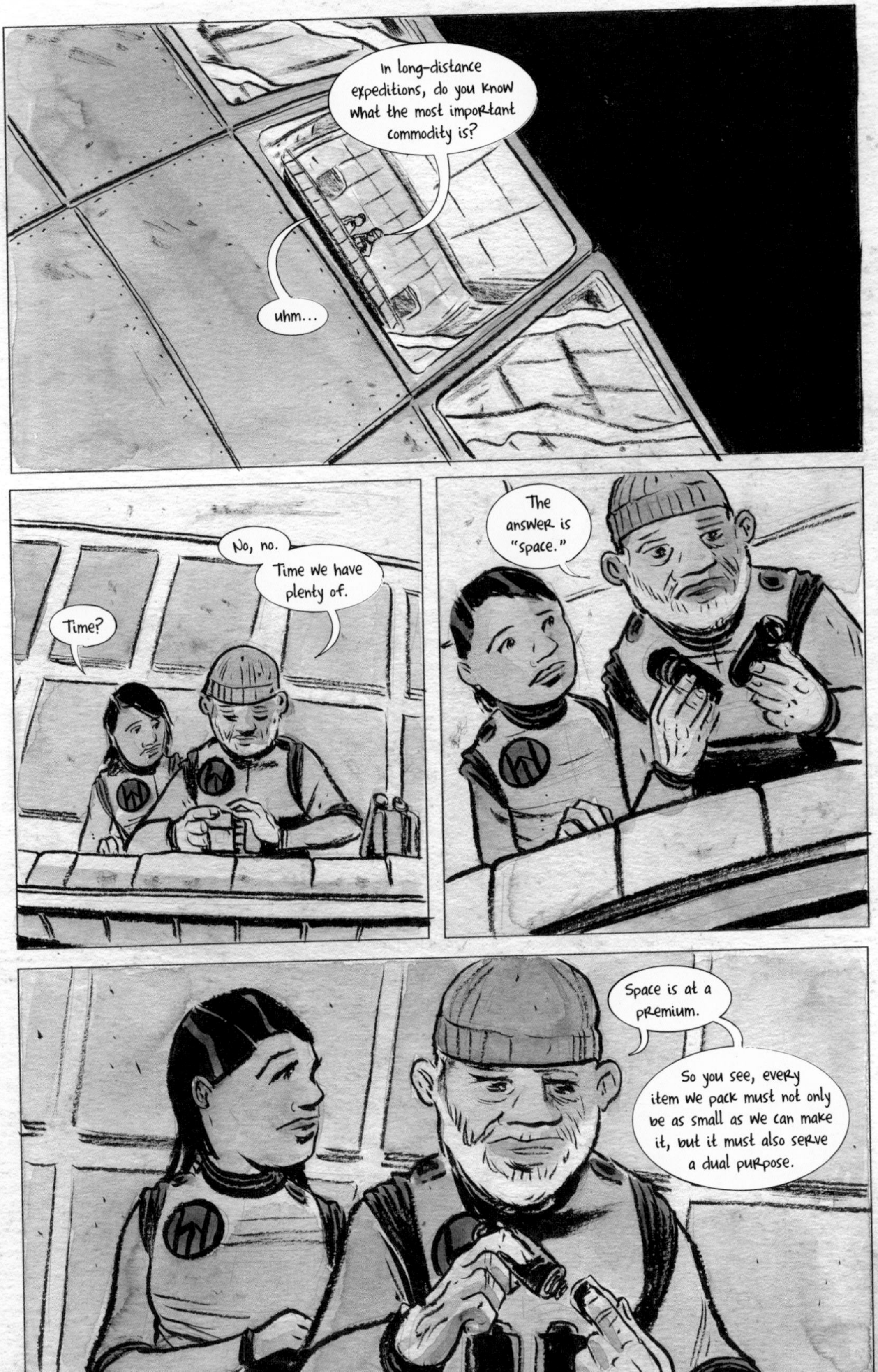

In long-distance expeditions, do you know what the most important commodity is?
uhm...
No, no.
Time we have plenty of.
Time?
The answer is "space."
Space is at a premium.
So you see, every item we pack must not only be as small as we can make it, but it must also serve a dual purpose.

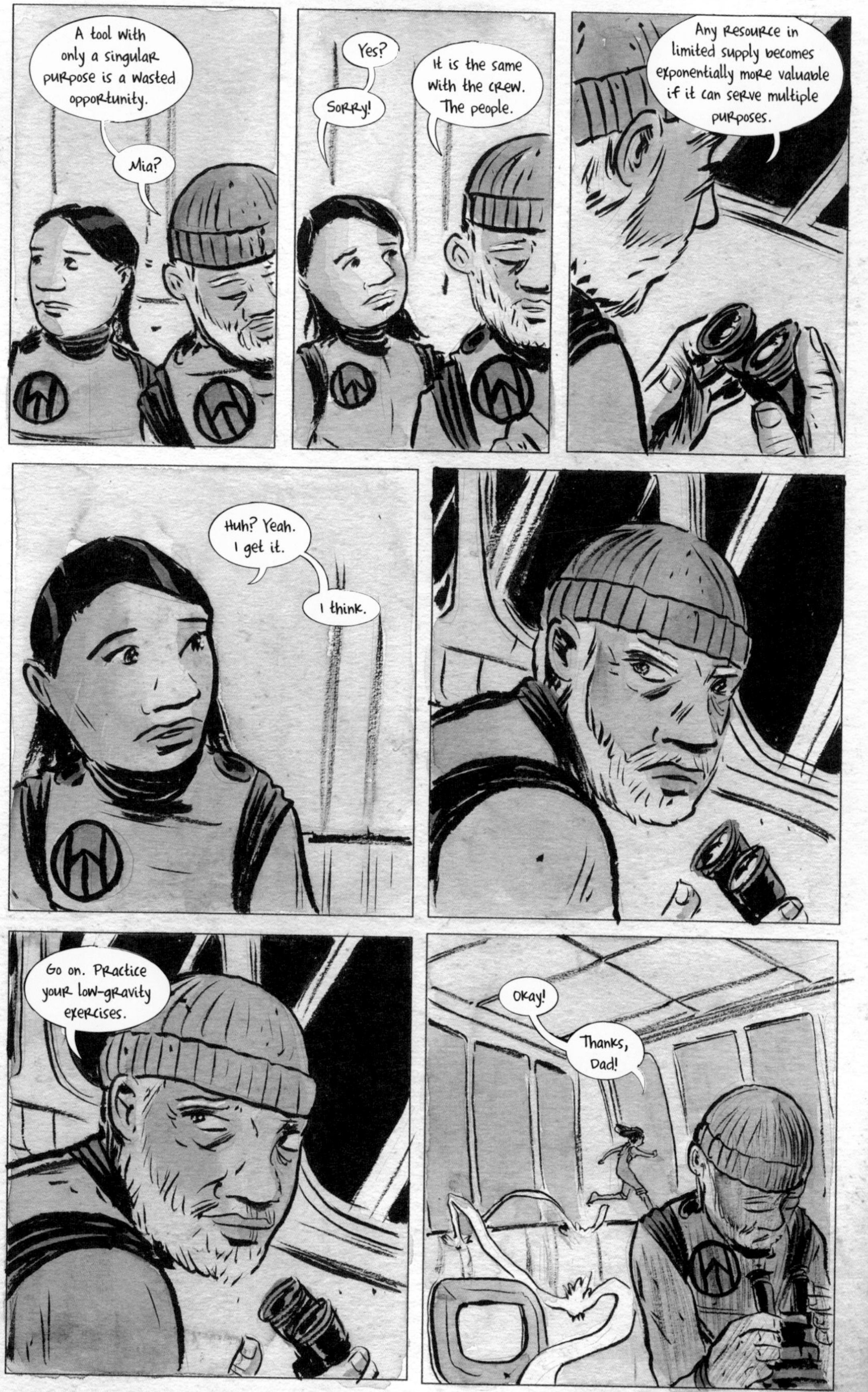
A tool with only a singular purpose is a wasted opportunity.
Mia?
Yes?
Sorry!
It is the same with the crew. The people.
Any resource in limited supply becomes exponentially more valuable if it can serve multiple purposes.
Huh? Yeah. I get it.
I think.
Go on. Practice your low-gravity exercises.
Okay!
Thanks, Dad!

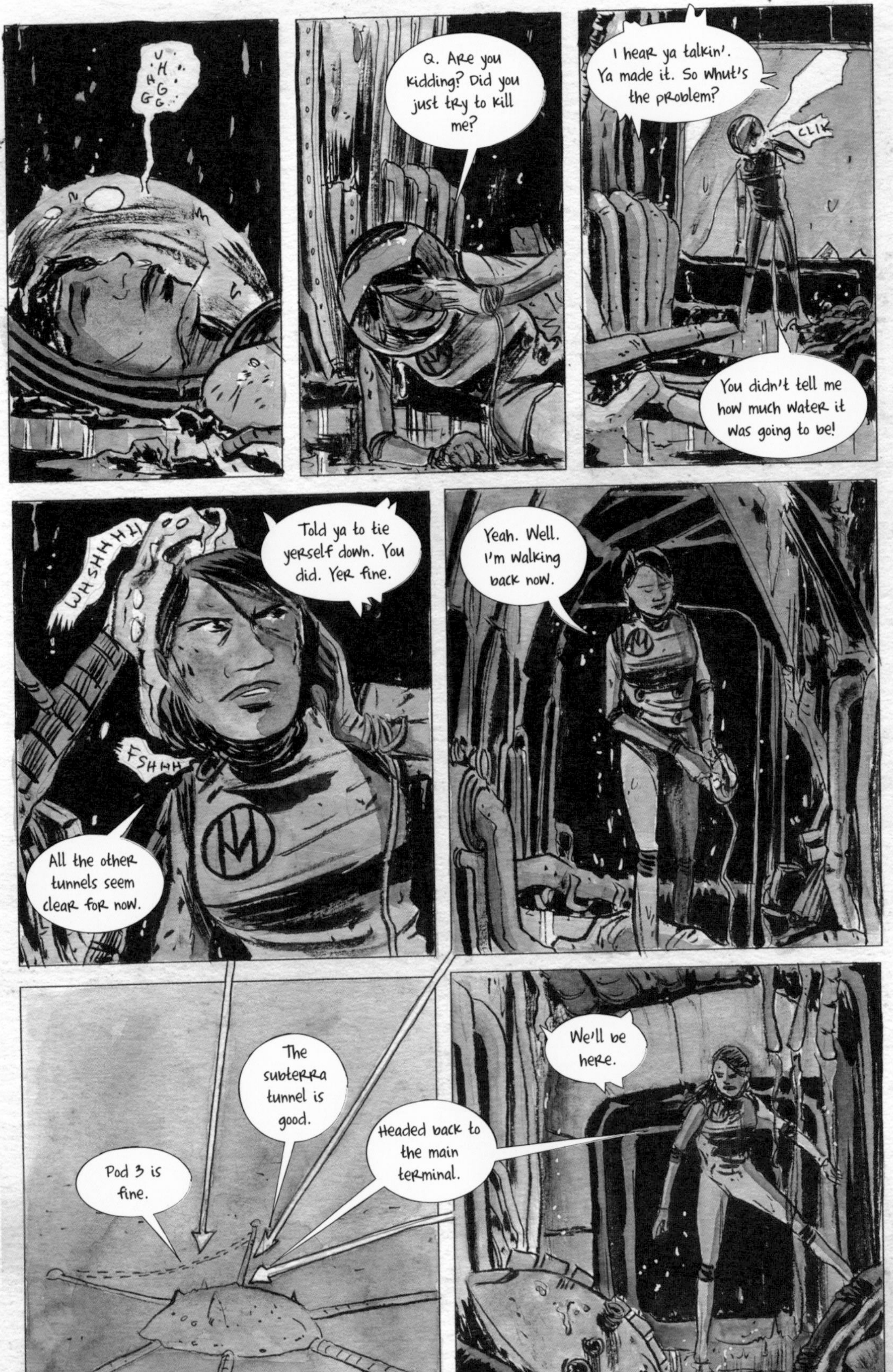
UHHGGGG
Q. Are you kidding? Did you just try to kill me?
I hear ya talkin'. Ya made it. So whut's the problem?
CLIK
You didn't tell me how much water it was going to be!
WHSHHHH
Told ya to tie yerself down. You did. Yer fine.
FSHWH
All the other tunnels seem clear for now.
Yeah. Well. I'm walking back now.
Pod 3 is fine.
The subterra tunnel is good.
Headed back to the main terminal.
We'll be here.

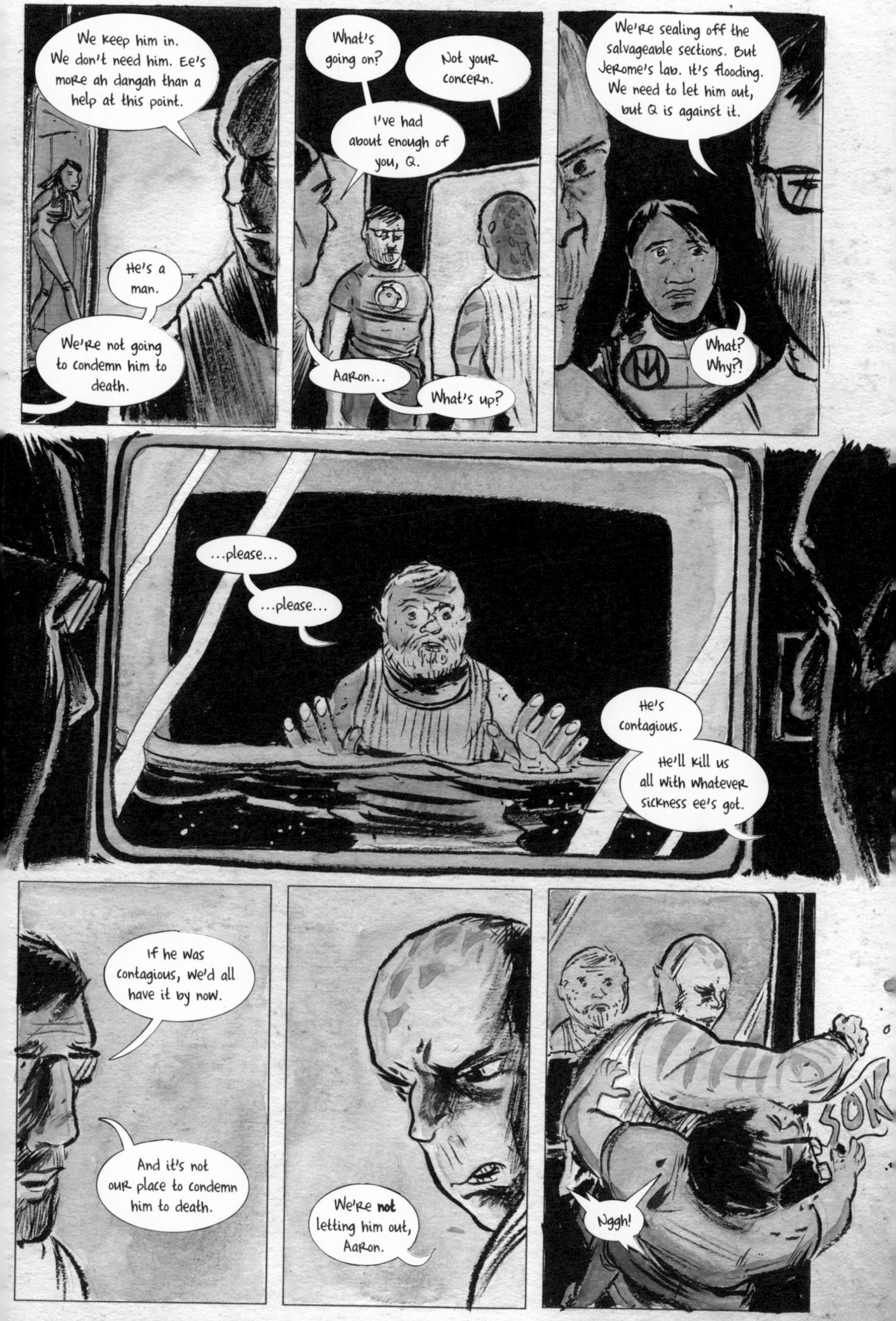
We keep him in. We don't need him. Ee's more ah dangah than a help at this point.
He's a man.
We're not going to condemn him to death.
What's going on?
Not your concern.
I've had about enough of you, Q.
Aaron...
What's up?
We're sealing off the salvageable sections. But Jerome's lab. It's flooding. We need to let him out, but Q is against it.
What? Why?!
...please...
...please...
He's contagious.
He'll kill us all with whatever sickness ee's got.
If he was contagious, we'd all have it by now.
And it's not our place to condemn him to death.
We're **not** letting him out, Aaron.
Nggh!
SOK

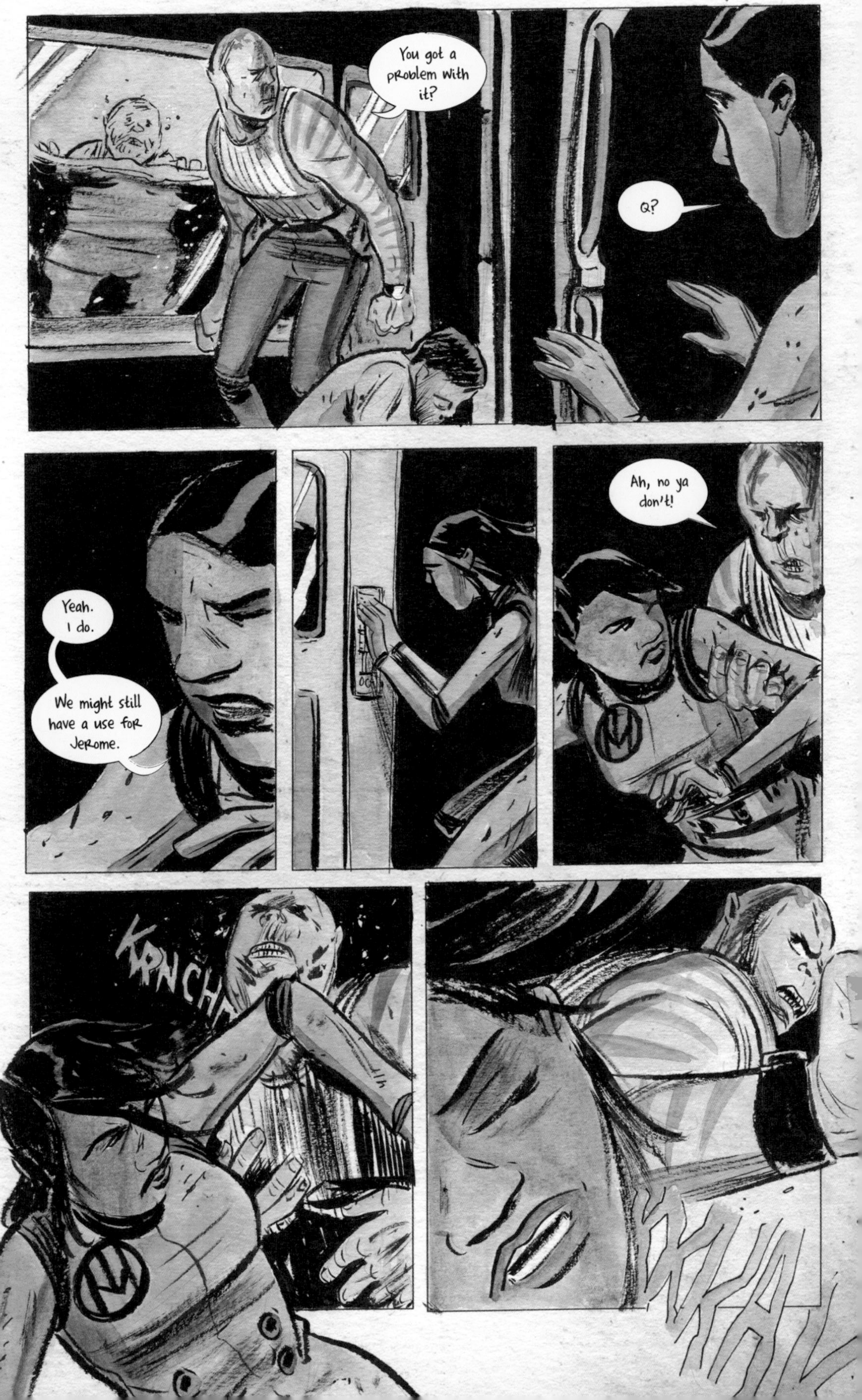
You got a problem with it?
Q?
Yeah. I do.
We might still have a use for Jerome.
Ah, no ya don't!
KRNCH

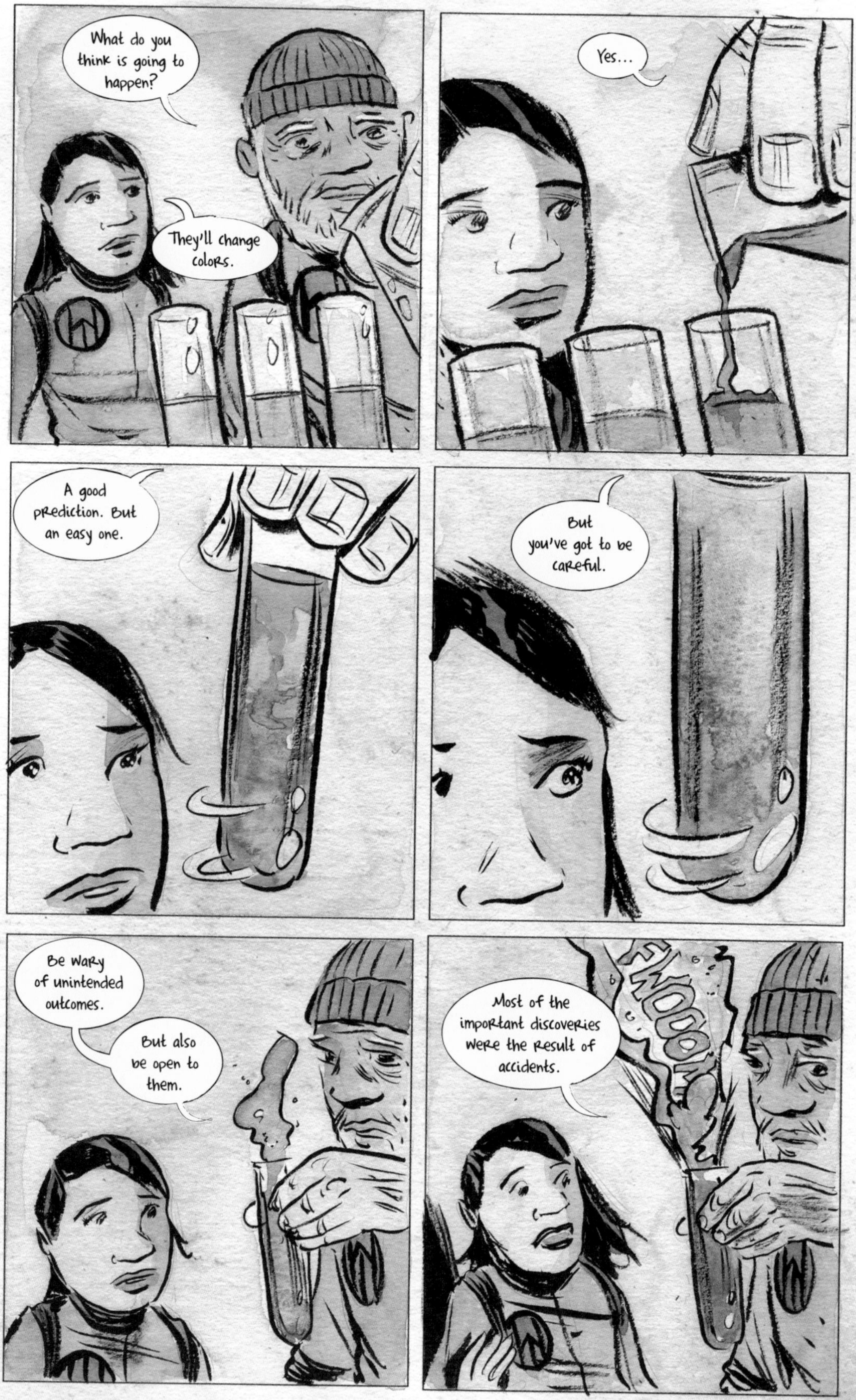
What do you think is going to happen?
They'll change colors.
Yes...
A good prediction. But an easy one.
But you've got to be careful.
Be wary of unintended outcomes.
But also be open to them.
FWOOOM
Most of the important discoveries were the result of accidents.

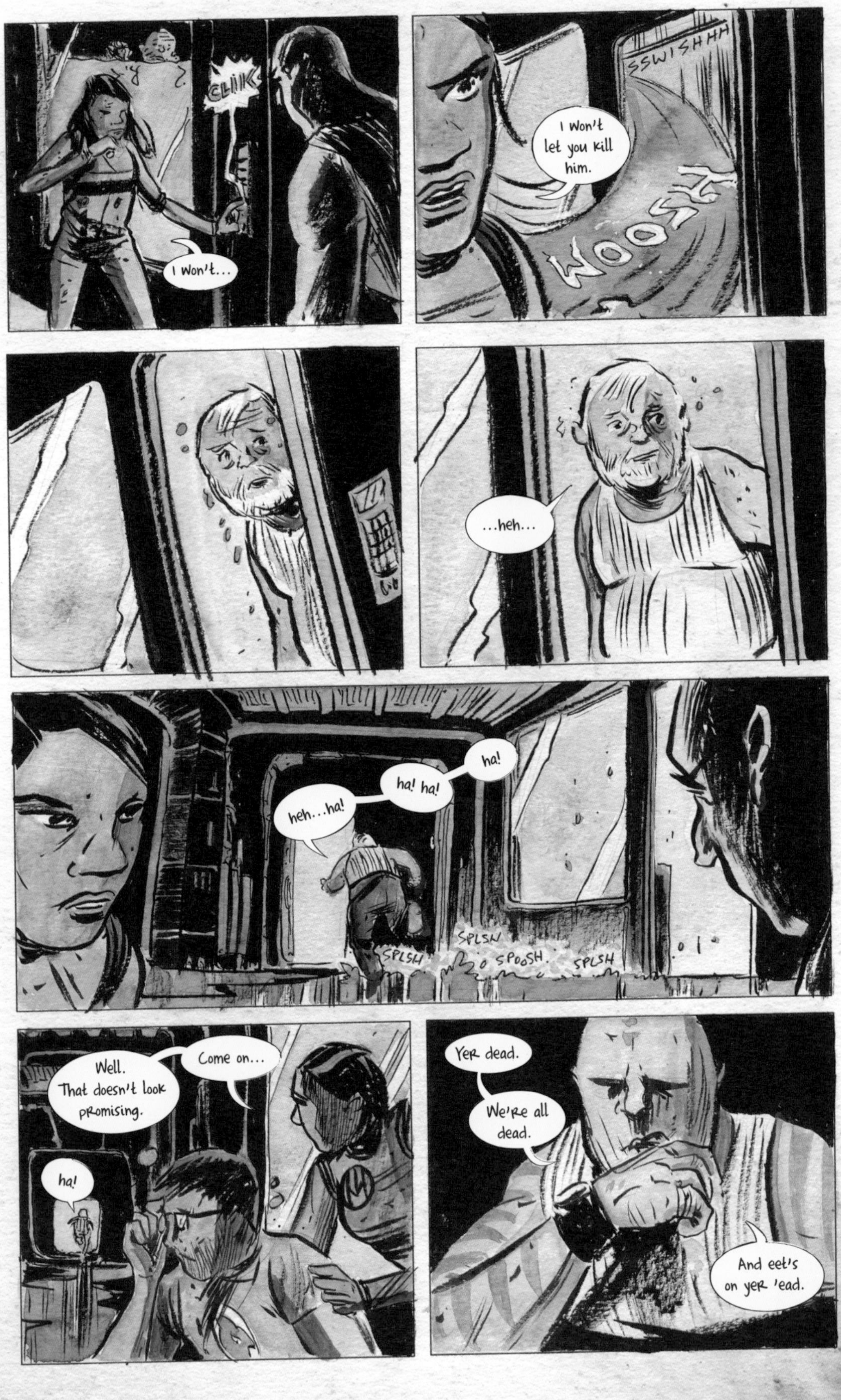
CLIIK
I won't...
SSWISHHH
I won't let you kill him.
WOOSH
...heh...
heh...ha!
ha! ha!
ha!
SPLSH
SPLSH
O SPOOSH
SPLSH
Well. That doesn't look promising.
Come on...
ha!
Yer dead.
We're all dead.
And eet's on yer 'ead.

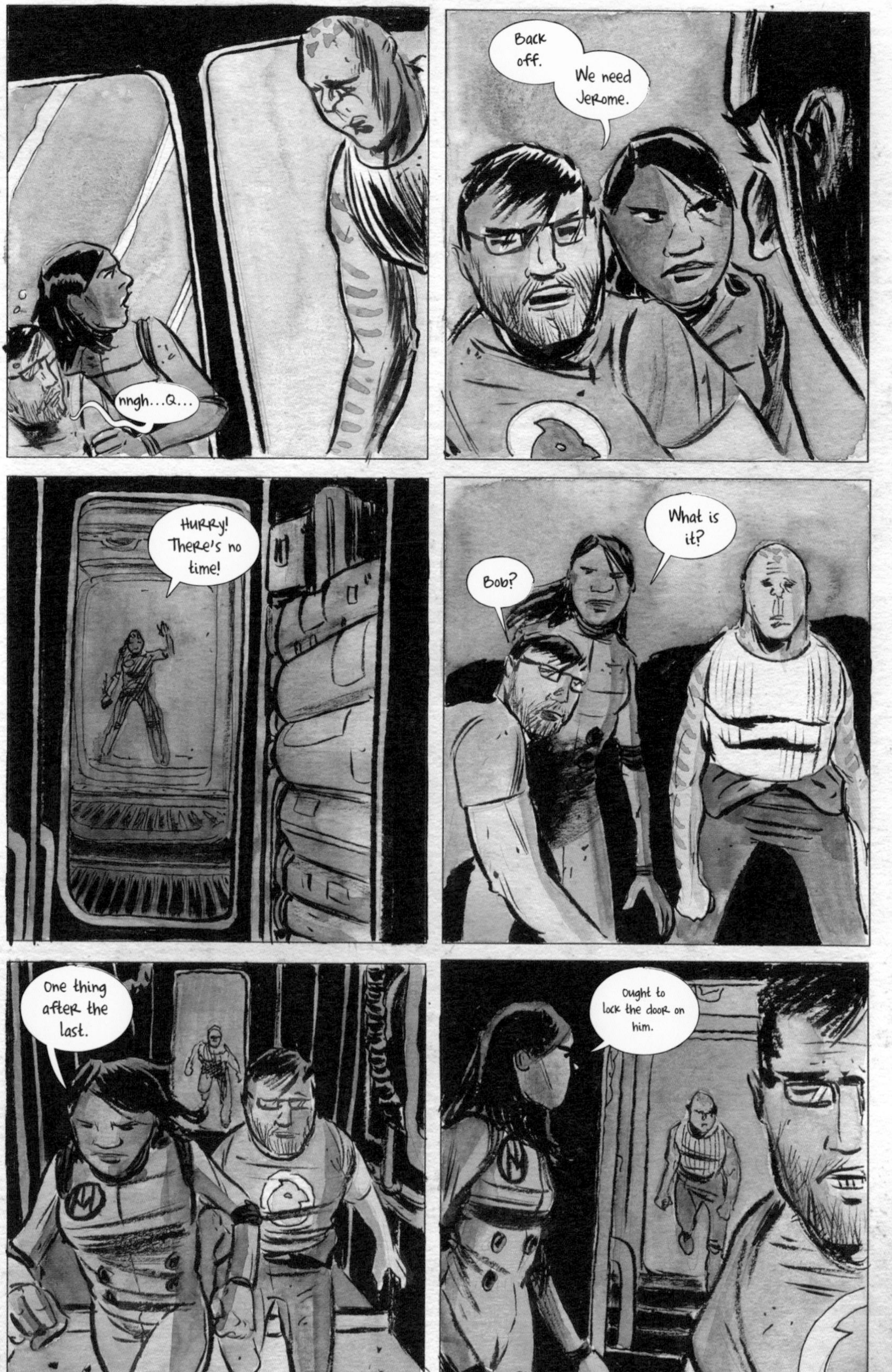
nngh...Q...
Back off.
We need Jerome.
HURRY! There's no time!
What is it?
Bob?
One thing after the last.
Ought to lock the door on him.

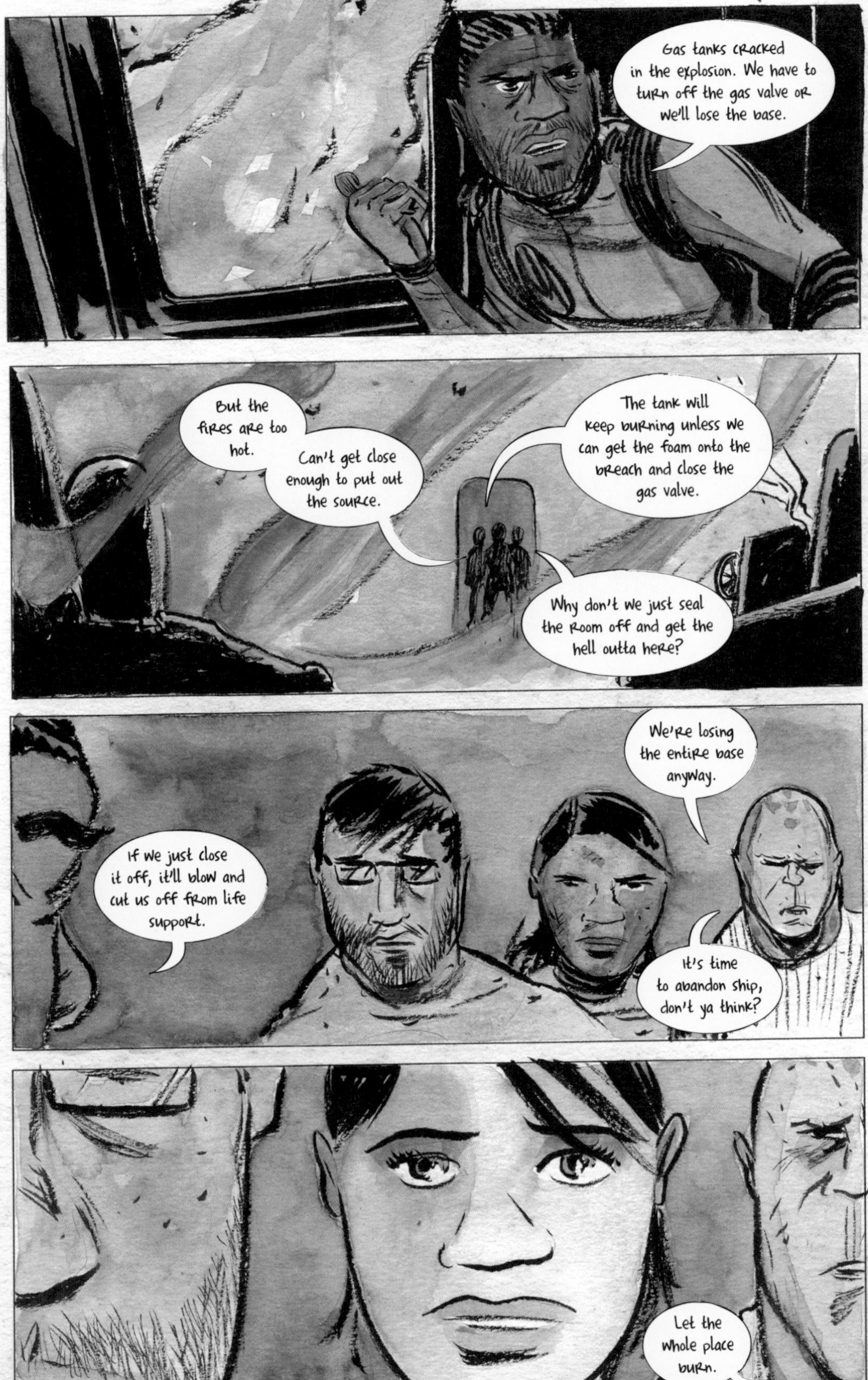
Gas tanks cracked in the explosion. We have to turn off the gas valve or we'll lose the base.
But the fires are too hot.
Can't get close enough to put out the source.
The tank will keep burning unless we can get the foam onto the breach and close the gas valve.
Why don't we just seal the room off and get the hell outta here?
If we just close it off, it'll blow and cut us off from life support.
We're losing the entire base anyway.
It's time to abandon ship, don't ya think?
Let the whole place burn.

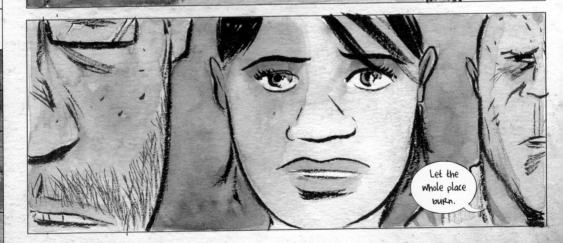

Careful. Hold that there.
Got it?
Okay.
And the final touch.
What's the symbol mean?

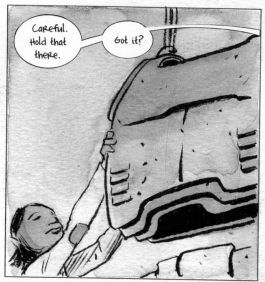

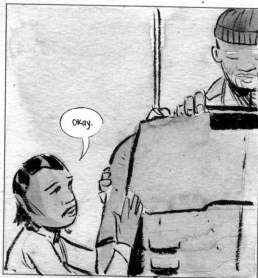

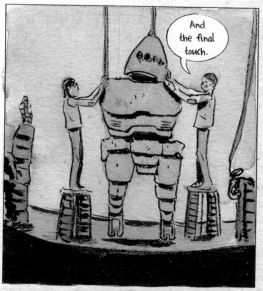

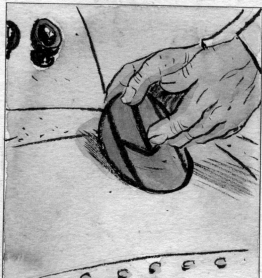

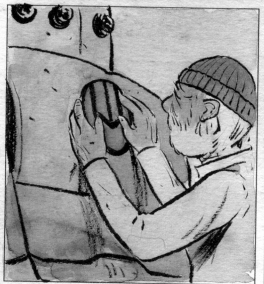

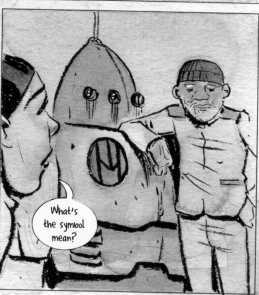

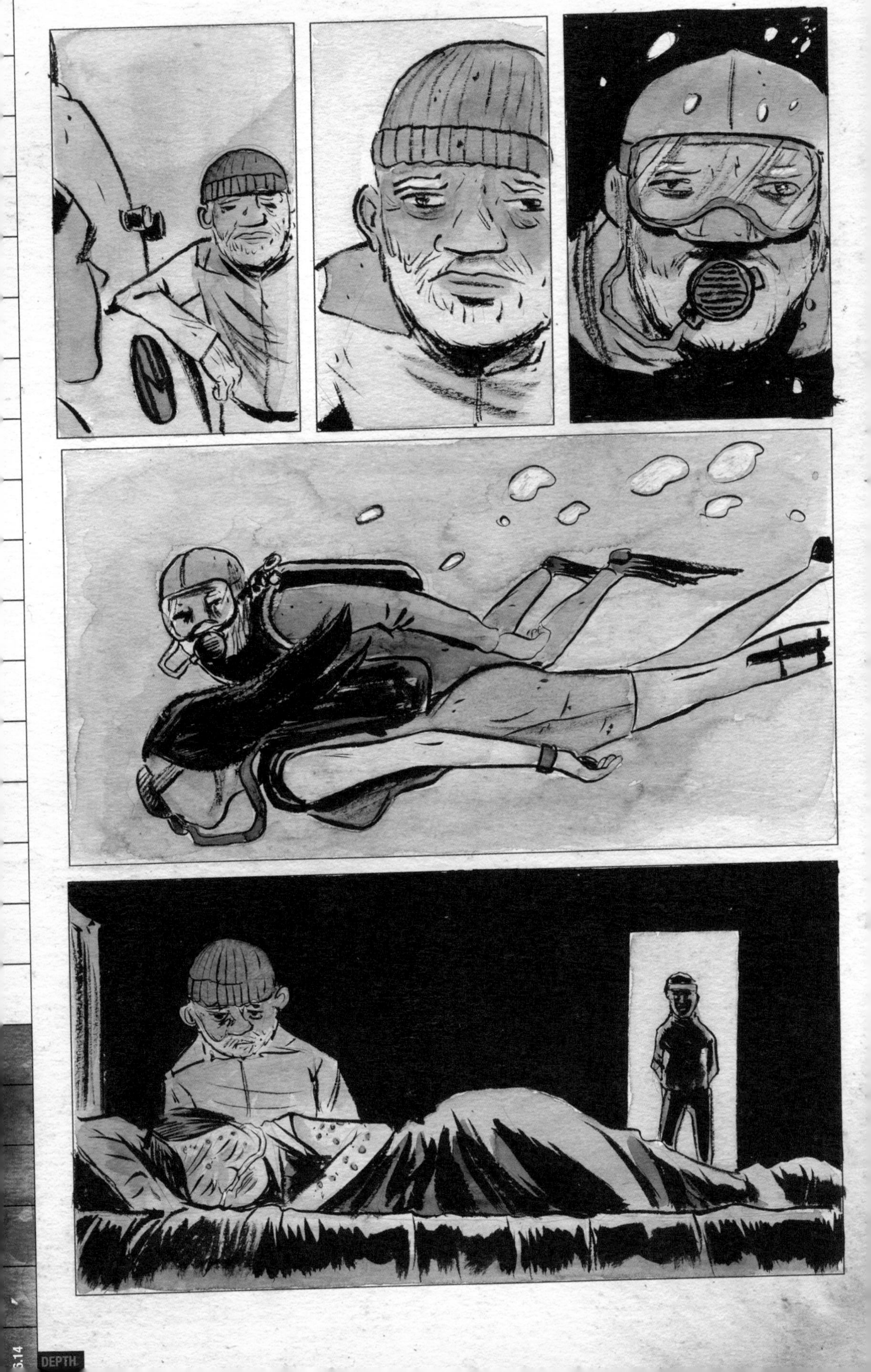

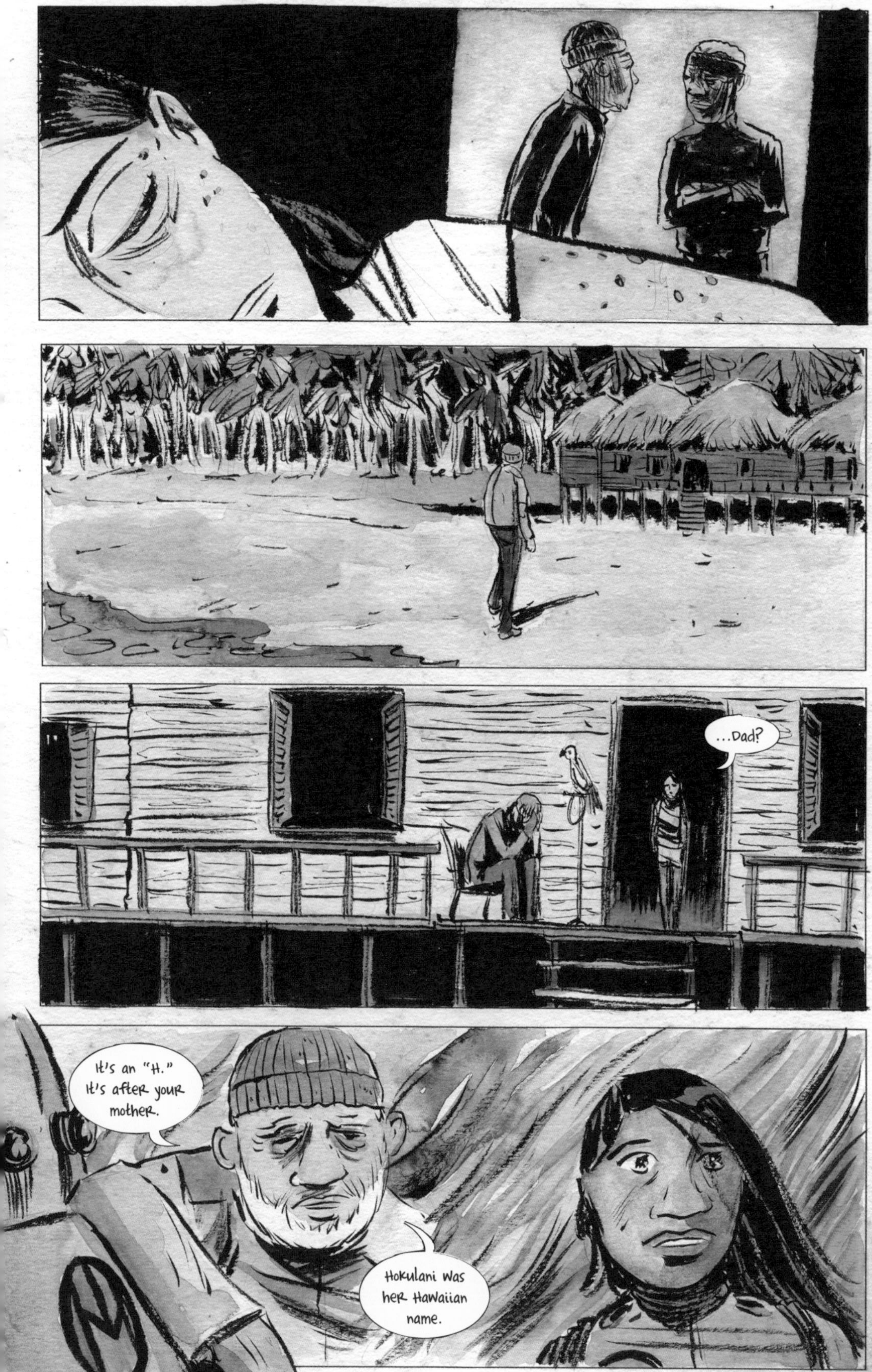

...Dad?
It's an "H." It's after your mother.
Hokulani was her Hawaiian name.

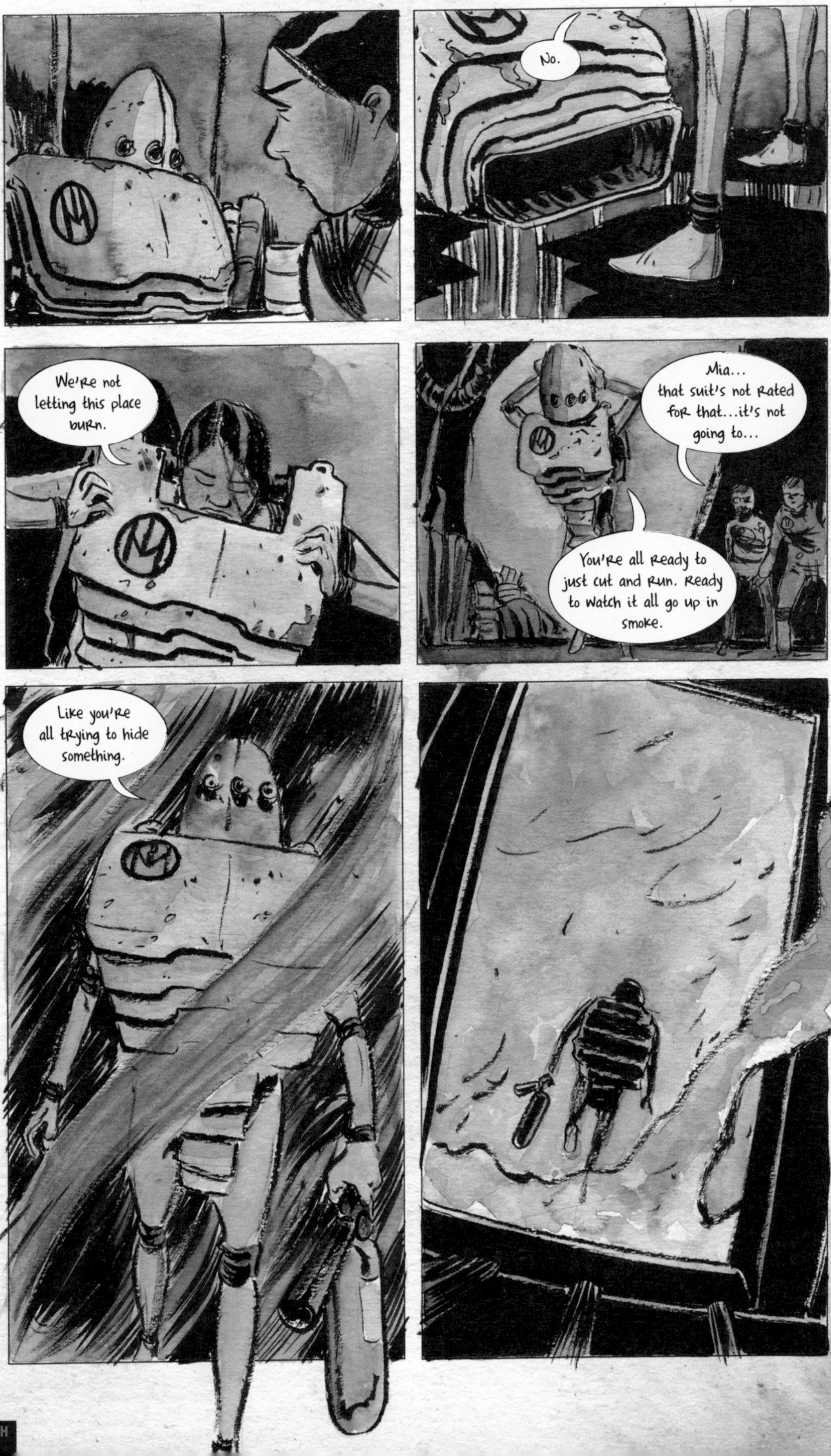
No.
We're not letting this place burn.
Mia... that suit's not rated for that...it's not going to...
You're all ready to just cut and run. Ready to watch it all go up in smoke.
Like you're all trying to hide something.

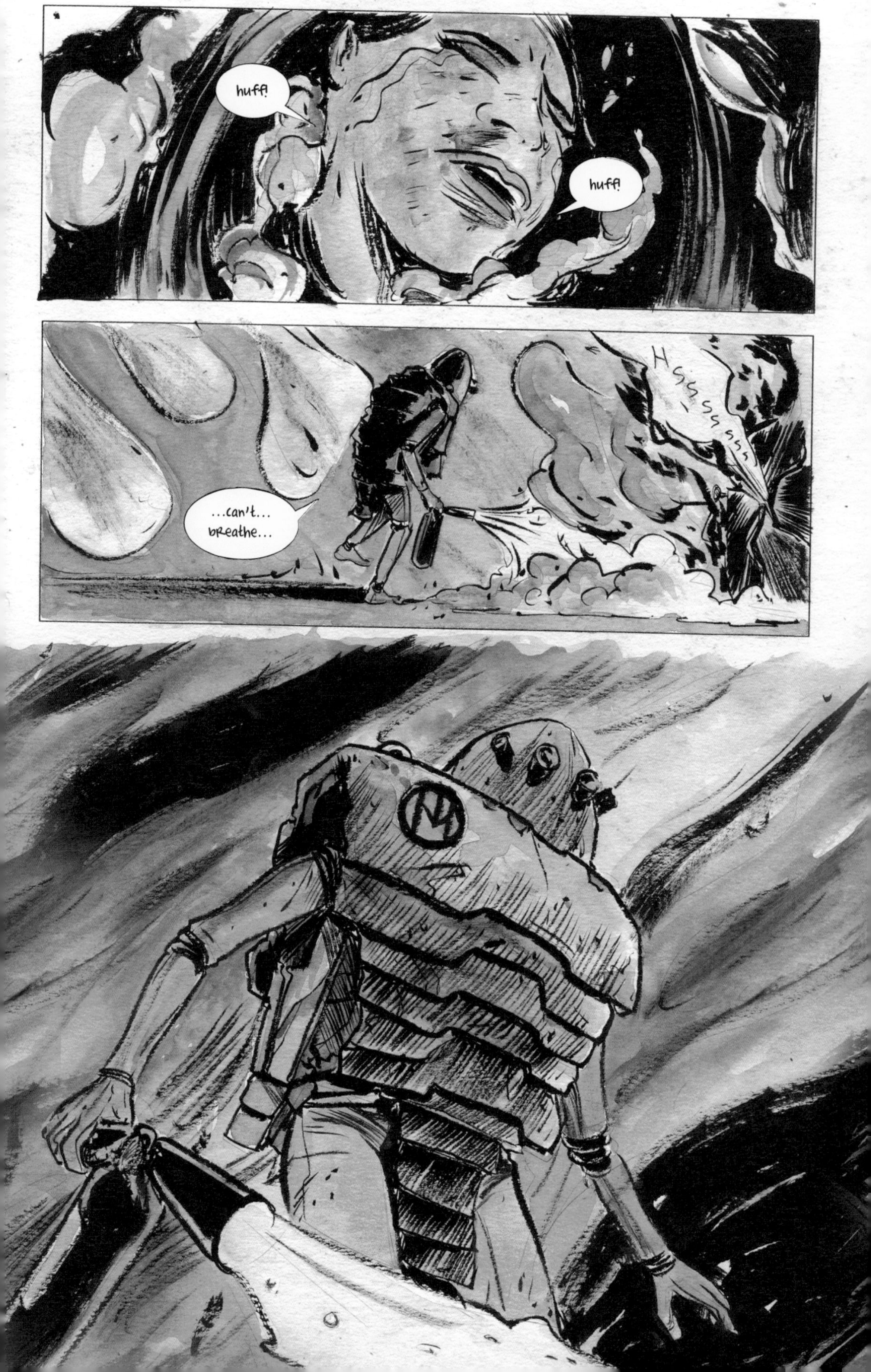
huff!
huff!
...can't... breathe...
Hsssssssss

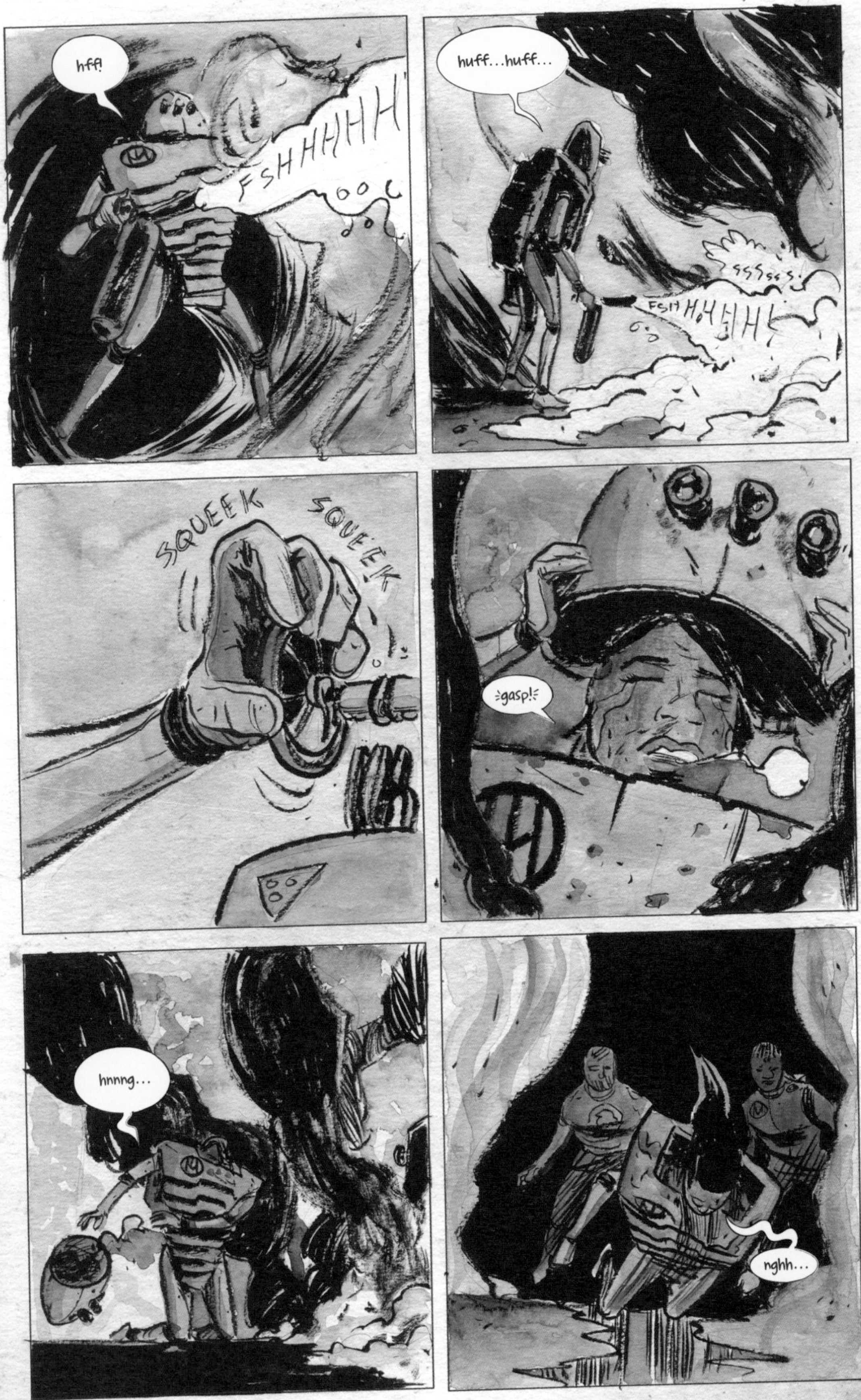
hff!
huff...huff...
SQUEEK
SQUEEK
gasp!
hnnng...
nghh...

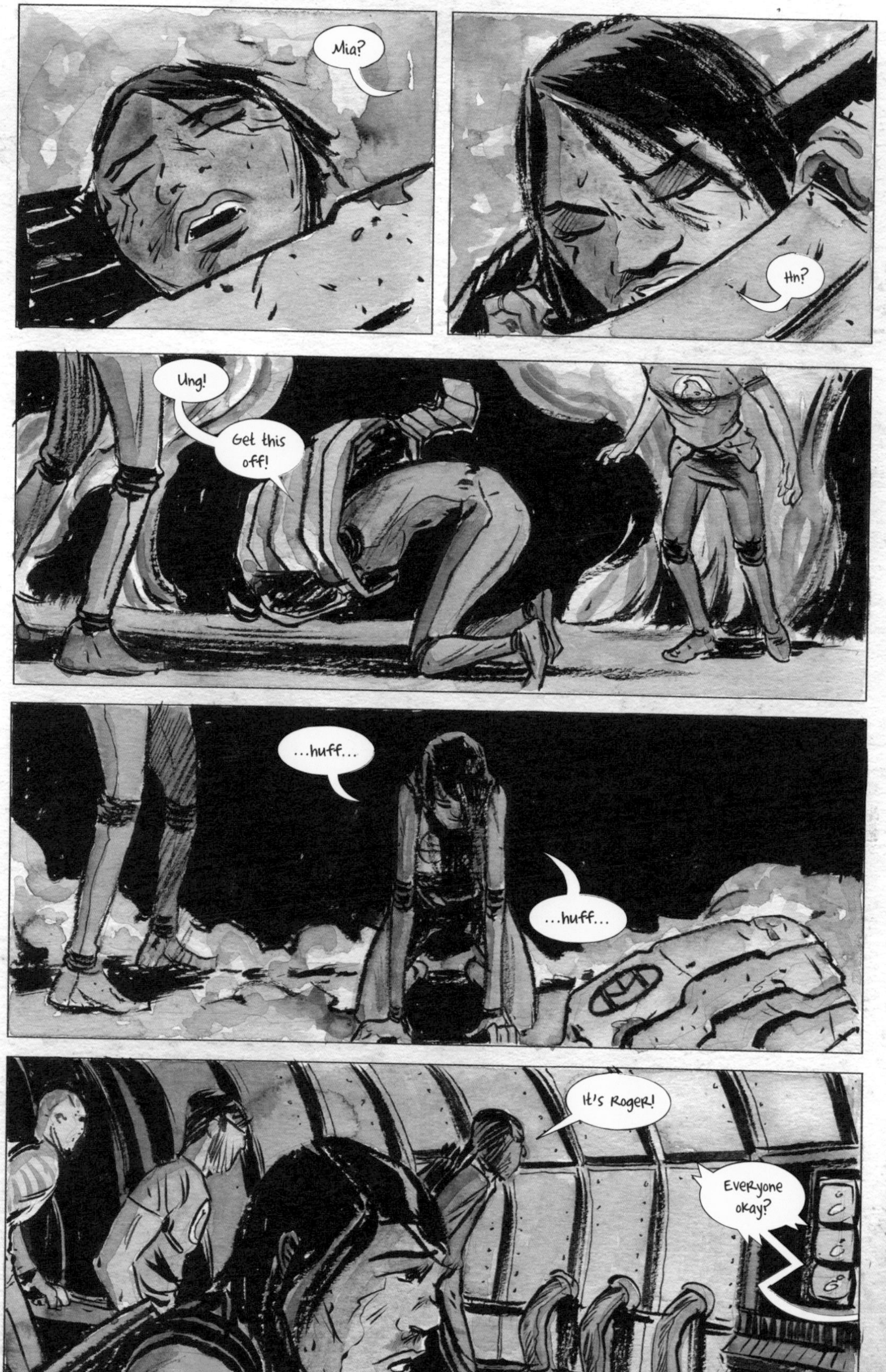
Mia?
Hn?
Ung!
Get this off!
...huff...
...huff...
It's Roger!
Everyone okay?

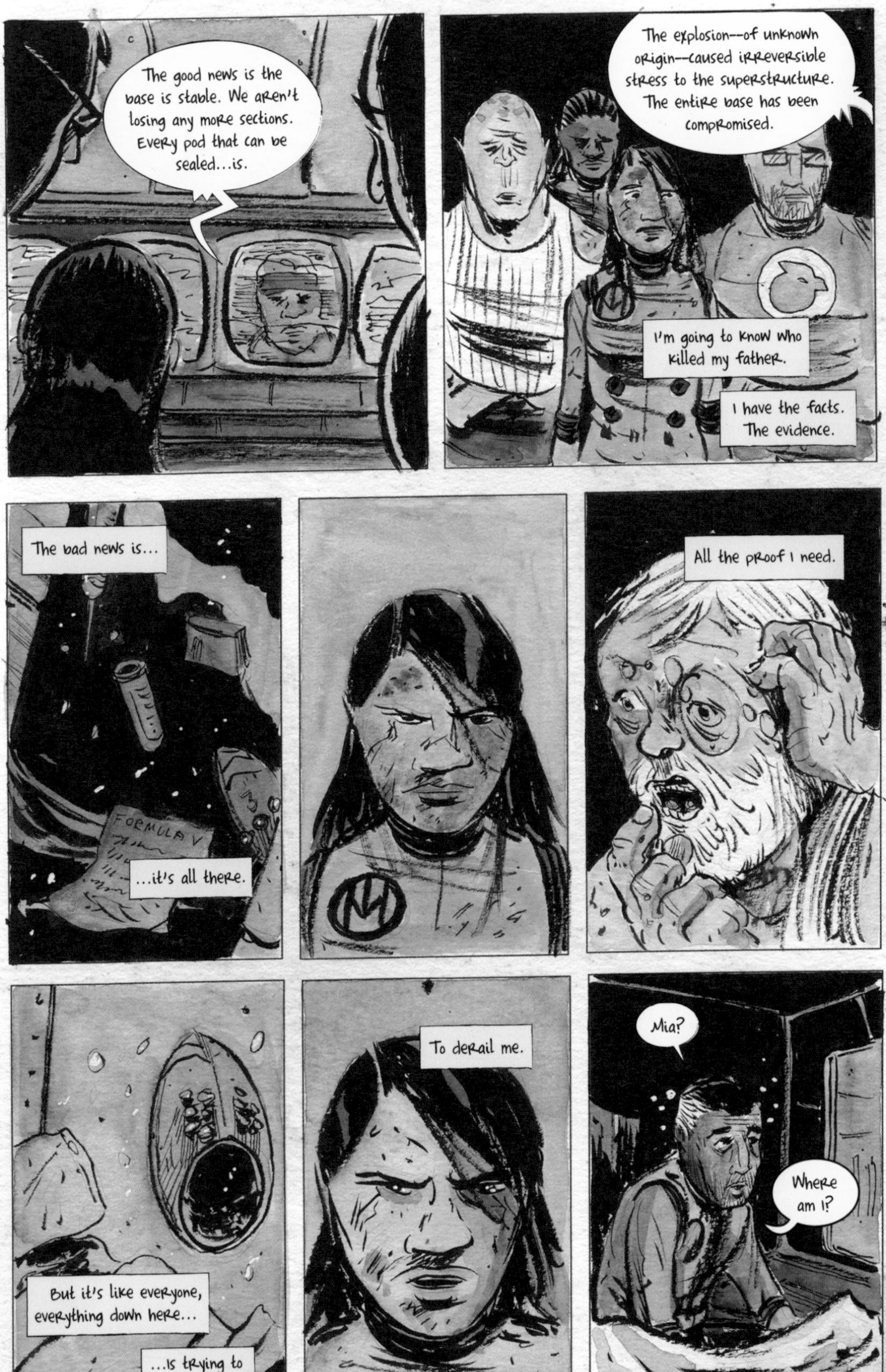
The good news is the base is stable. We aren't losing any more sections. Every pod that can be sealed...is.
The explosion--of unknown origin--caused irreversible stress to the superstructure. The entire base has been compromised.
I'm going to know who killed my father.
I have the facts. The evidence.
The bad news is...
FORMULA V
...it's all there.
All the proof I need.
But it's like everyone, everything down here...
...is trying to distract me.
To derail me.
Mia?
Where am I?

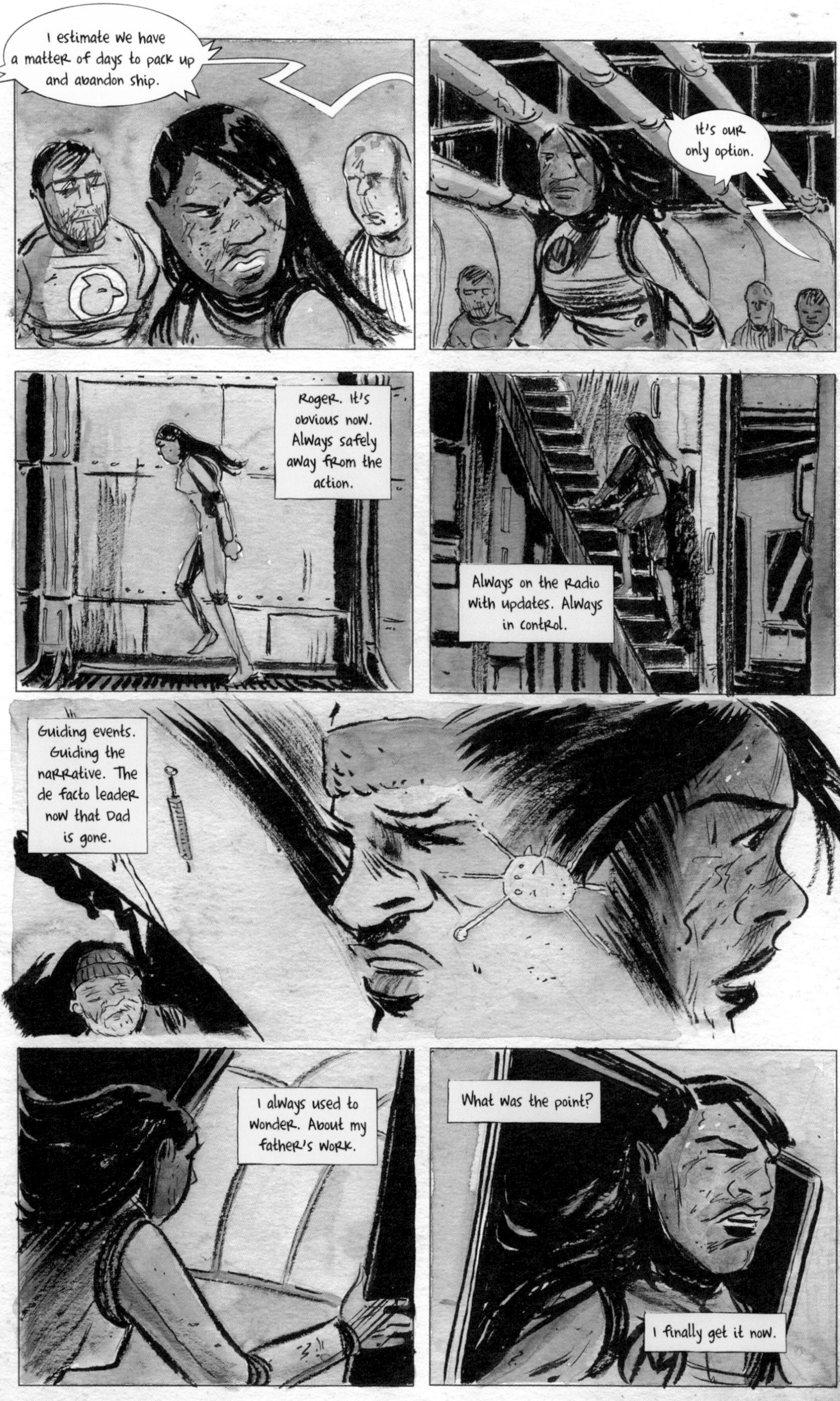
I estimate we have a matter of days to pack up and abandon ship.
It's our only option.
Roger. It's obvious now. Always safely away from the action.
Always on the radio with updates. Always in control.
Guiding events. Guiding the narrative. The de facto leader now that Dad is gone.
I always used to wonder. About my father's work.
What was the point?
I finally get it now.

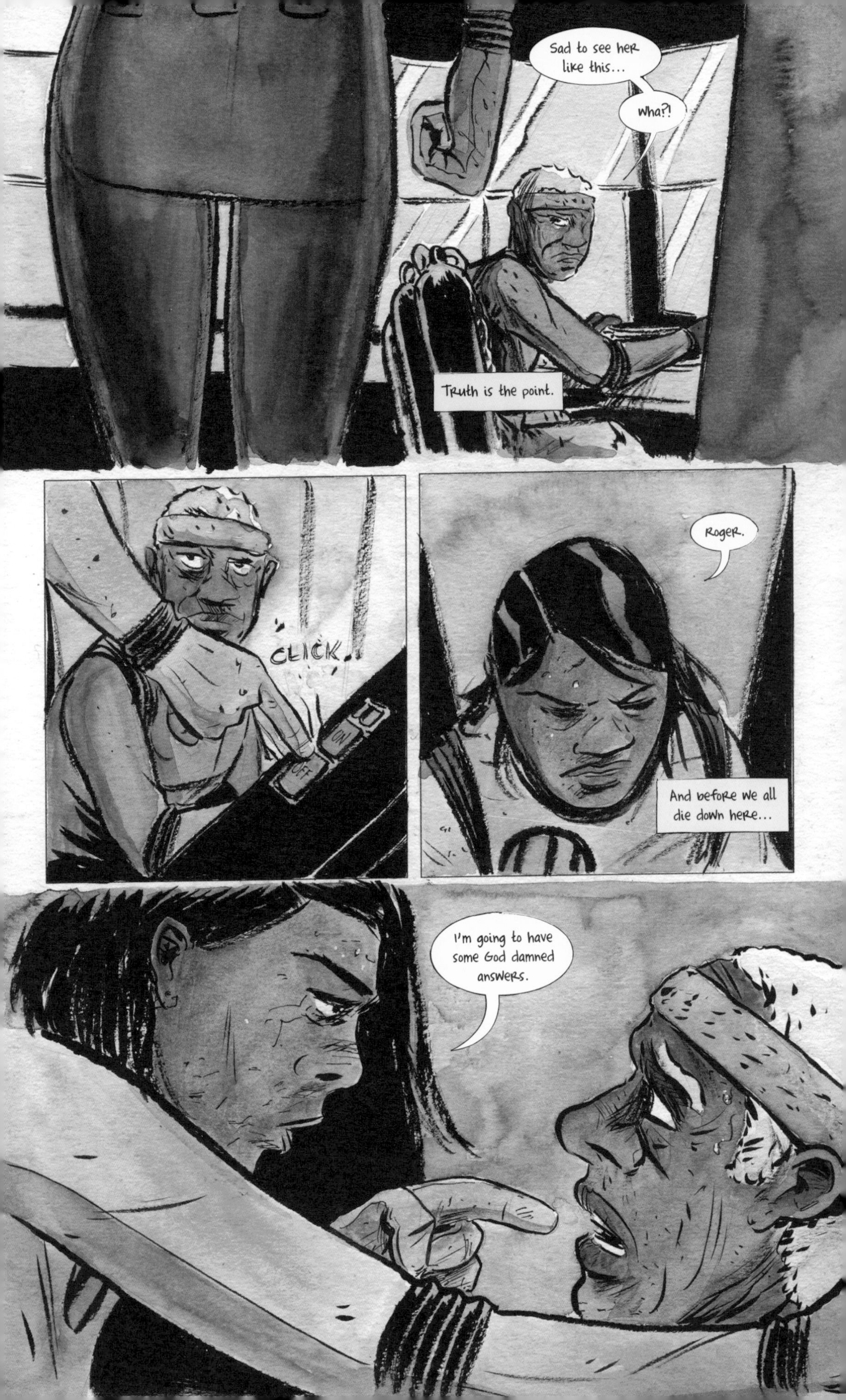
Sad to see her like this...
Wha?!
Truth is the point.
CLICK
ON
OFF
Roger.
And before we all die down here...
I'm going to have some God damned answers.

DEPT.H

Sketchbook
Notes by Matt Kindt

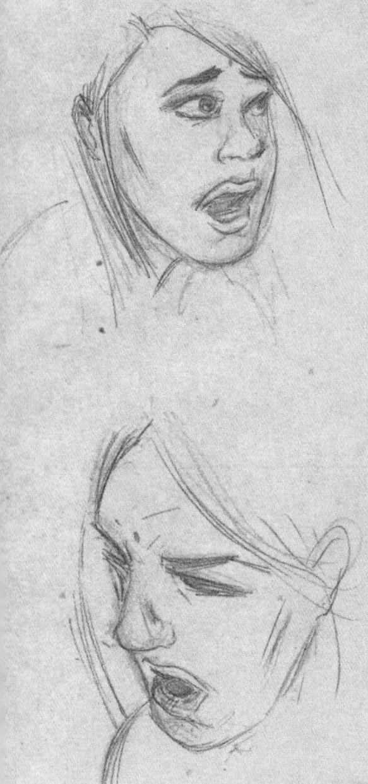

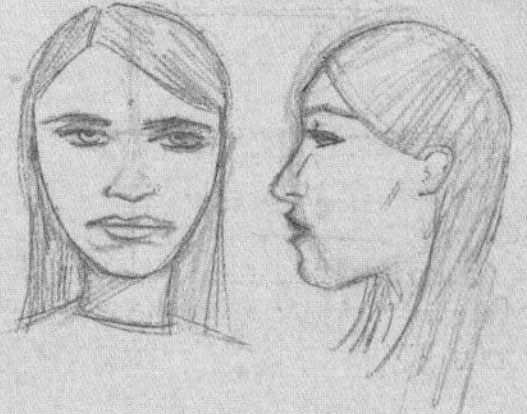

MIA
Preliminary design for Mia and the action suit that all of the characters would end up wearing. I wanted something universal and functional that could work in different colors to indicate rank or experience. And the logo is a straight-up homage to the classic G.I. Joe action logo from my childhood.

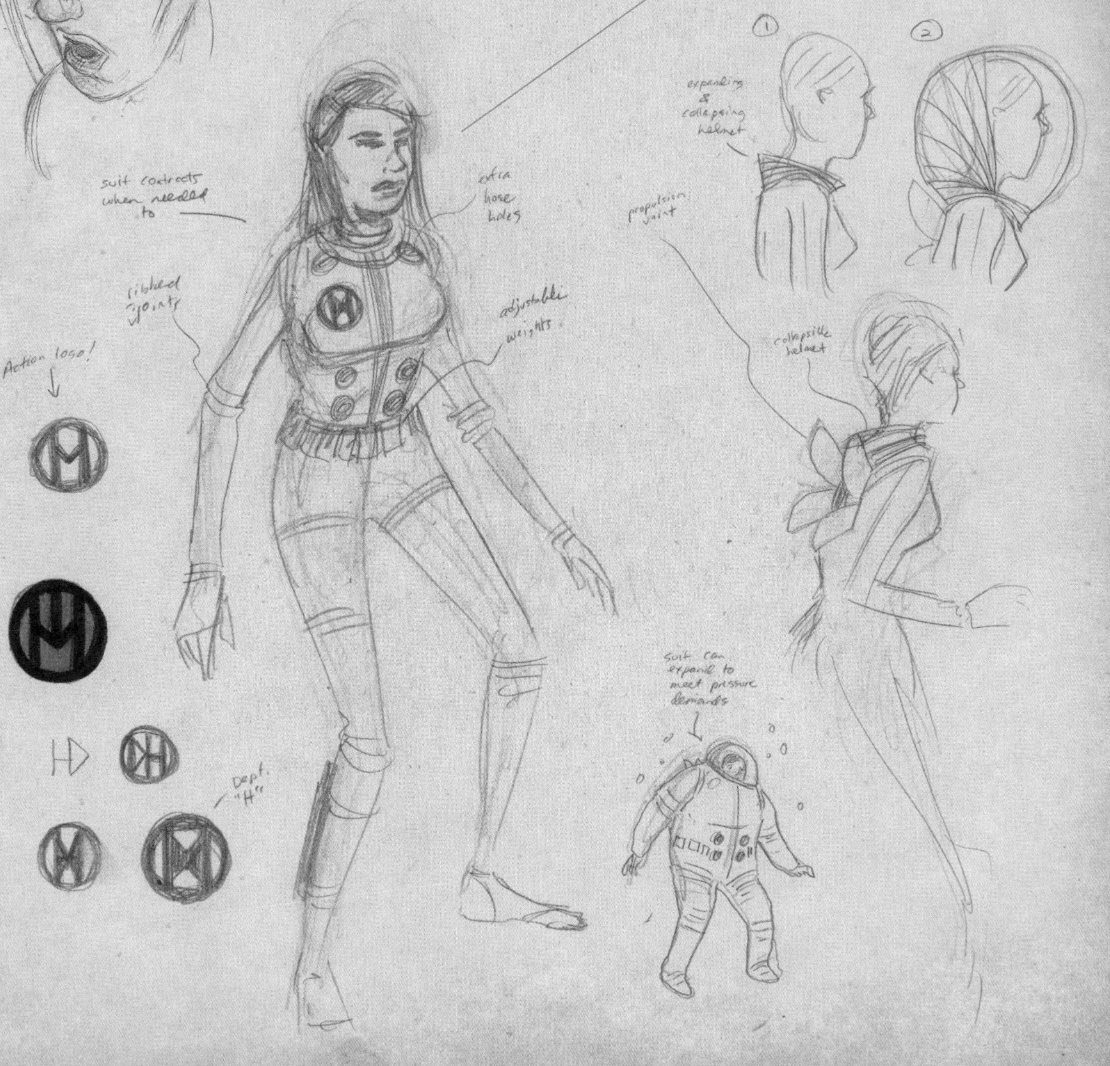

suit contracts when needed to
extra hose holes
ribbed joints
adjustable weights
Action logo!
Dept. "H"
1
2
expanding & collapsing helmet
propulsion unit
collapsible helmet
suit can expand to meet pressure demands

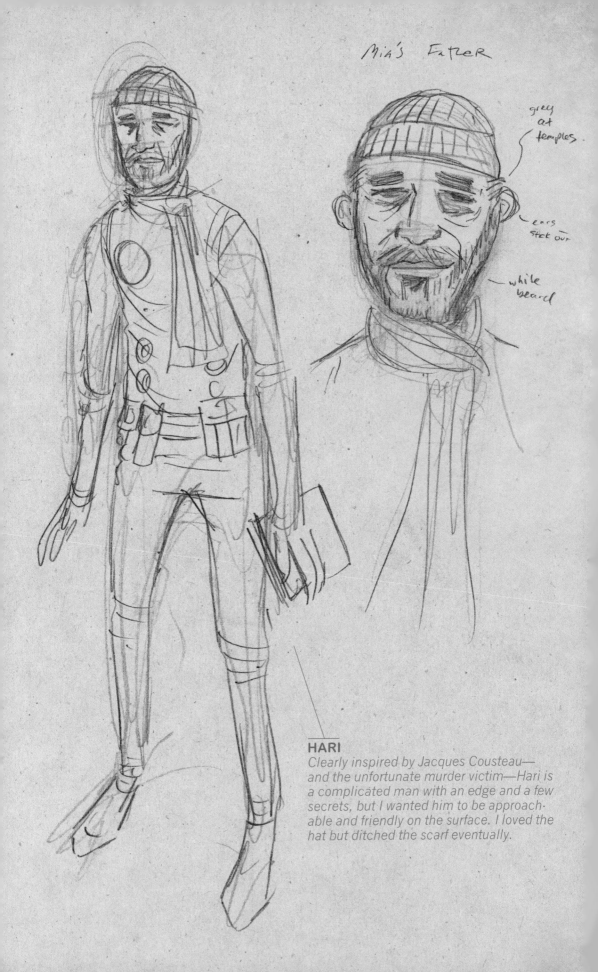

Mia's Father

grey at temples

ears stick out

white beard

HARI

Clearly inspired by Jacques Cousteau—and the unfortunate murder victim—Hari is a complicated man with an edge and a few secrets, but I wanted him to be approachable and friendly on the surface. I loved the hat but ditched the scarf eventually.

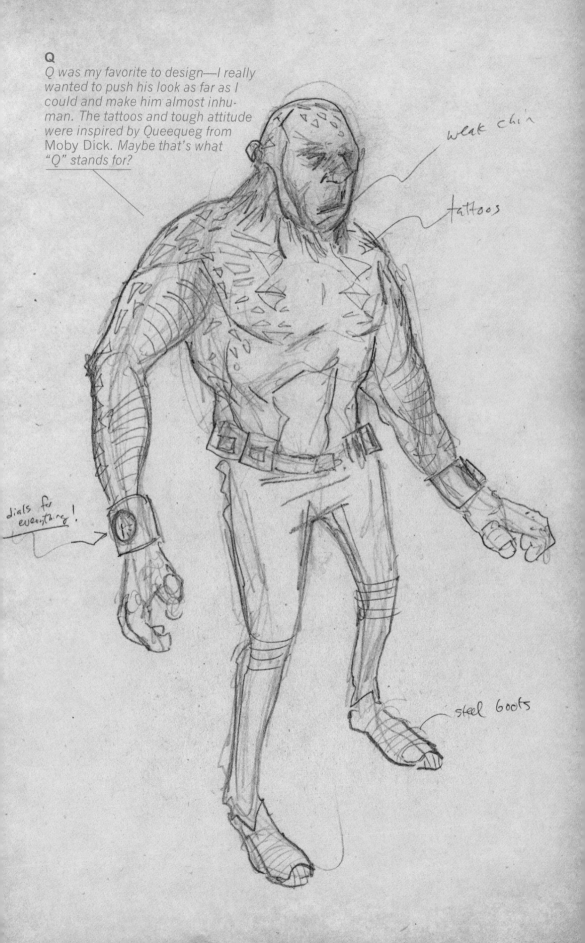

Q

Q was my favorite to design—I really wanted to push his look as far as I could and make him almost inhuman. The tattoos and tough attitude were inspired by Queequeg from Moby Dick. Maybe that's what "Q" stands for?

weak chin

tattoos

dials for everything!

steel boots

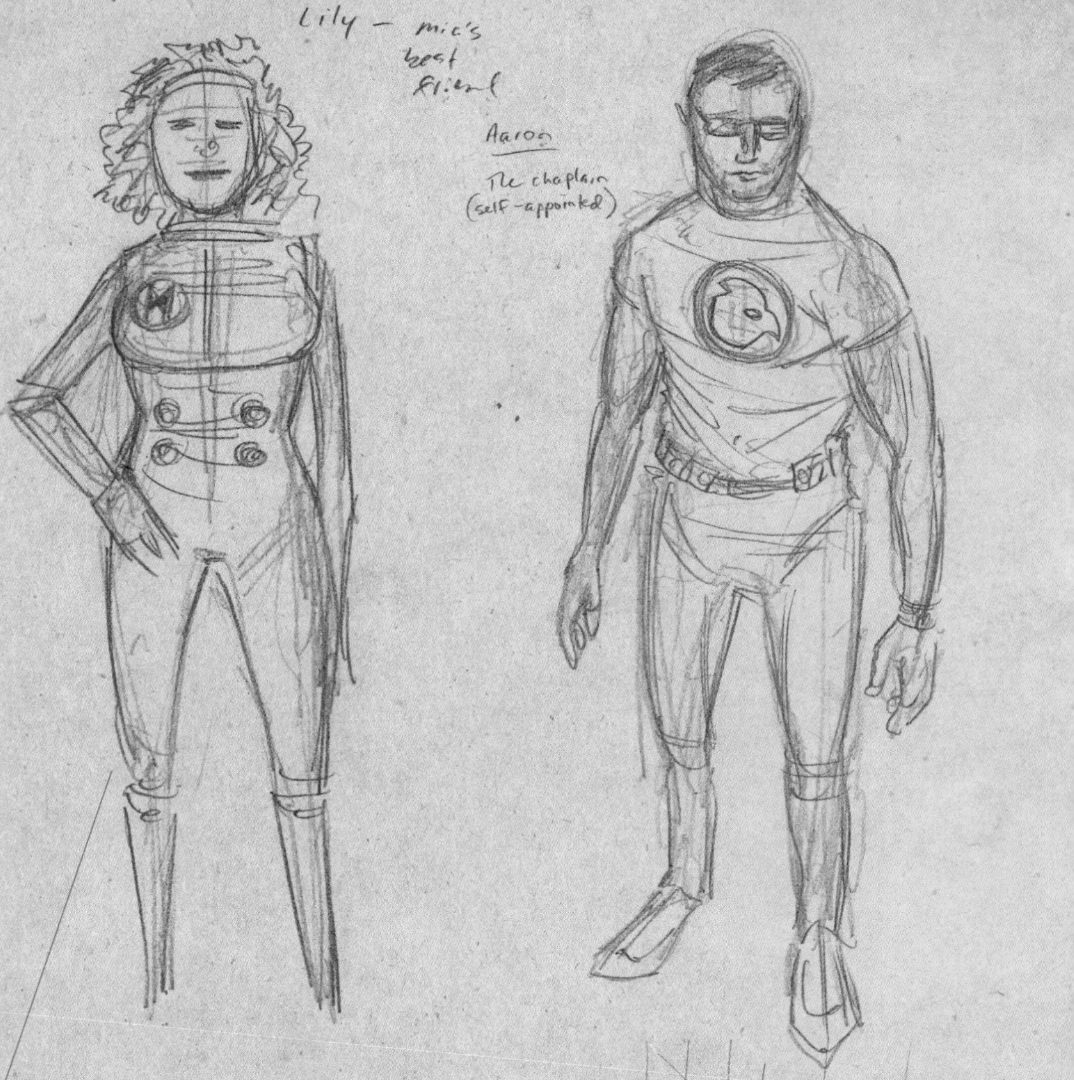
Lily – mic's best friend
Aaron
The chaplain (self-appointed)

LILY

It's impossible for me to pull character names or designs from thin air. Lily is actually named after and modeled on my daughter's friend next door—she's eleven years old now, so I just took a guess at what she'd look like grown up. The real Lily is much nicer than this character.

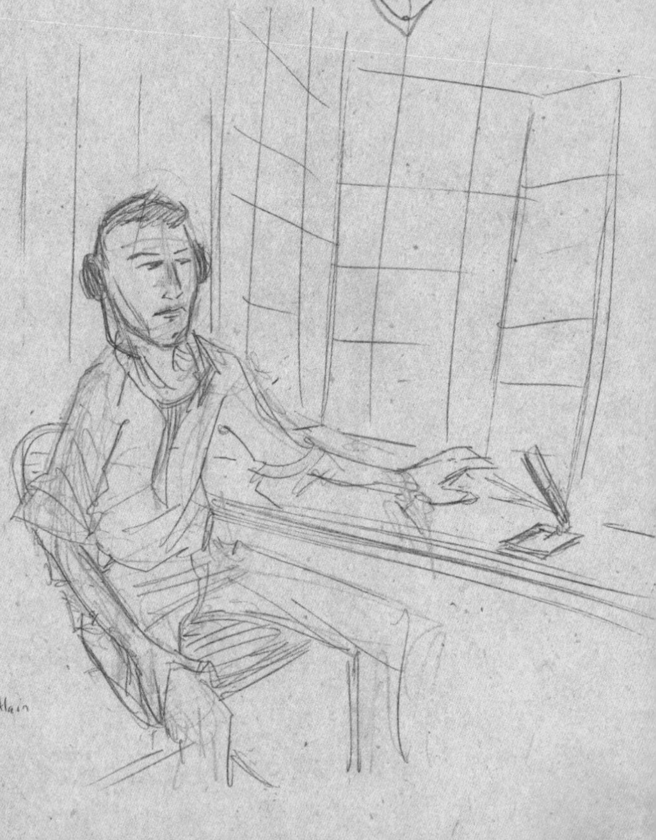
Alain

ALAIN

The man on the surface. Named after my favorite editor in France, Alain David at Futuropolis.

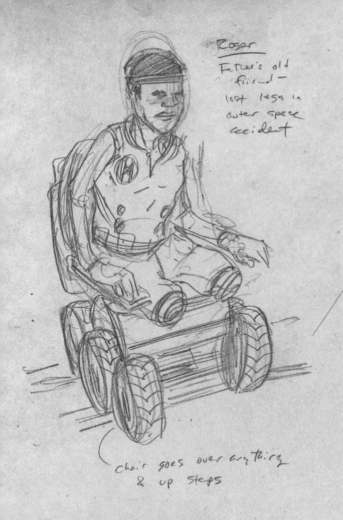

Roger
Father's old
friend —
lost legs in
outer space
accident

chair goes over anything
& up steps

ROGER
I wanted to have a tough character who has some obvious physical hurdles but isn't bothered by them. It's never an issue. Water and confined spaces are great equalizers. Also, headbands are cool.

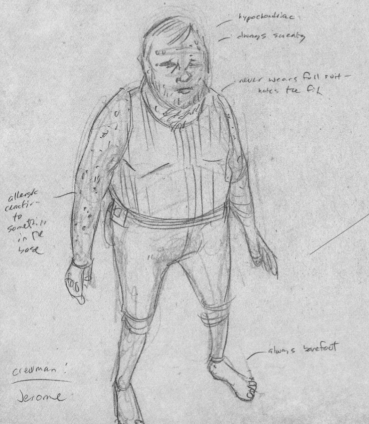

hypochondriac
always sweaty

never wears full suit —
hates the feel

allergic
reaction
to something
in the
food

always barefoot

crewman:
Jerome

JEROME
The science officer gone crazy. Inspired by a friend of mine who is an anesthesiologist. One of the craziest jobs I know—purposefully walking someone to the edge of death and keeping them there. I can't think of a more stressful job.

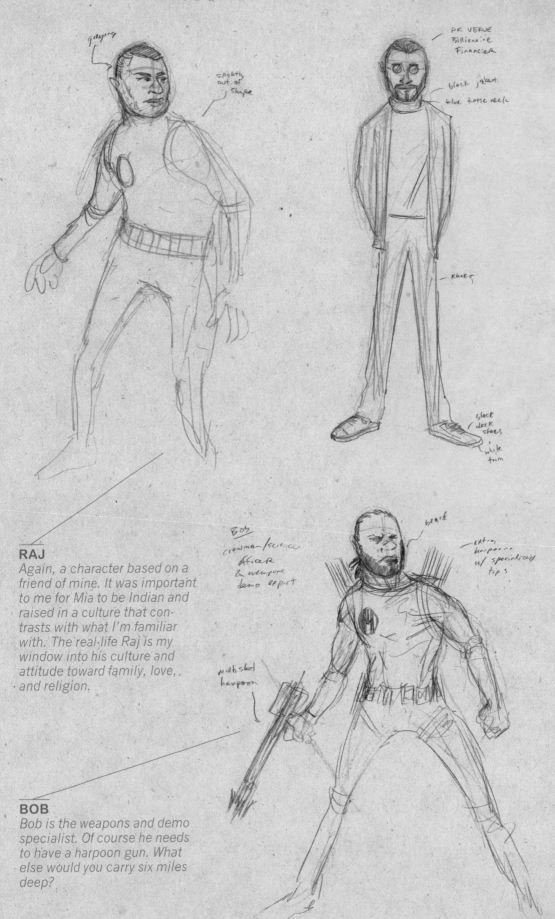

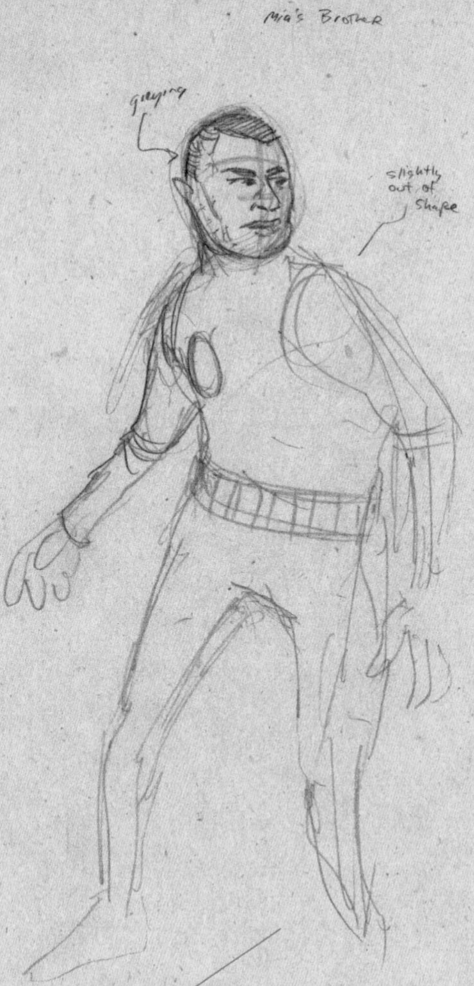
Mia's Brother
greying
slightly out of shape

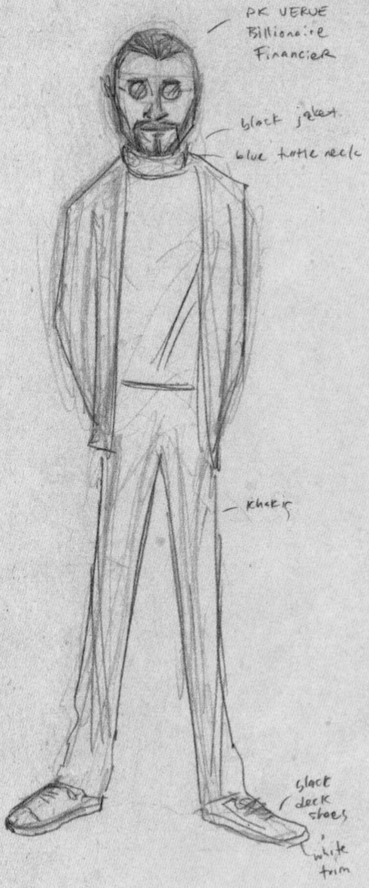
PK VERUE
Billionaire
Financier
black jacket
blue turtle neck
khakis
black deck shoes
white trim

RAJ

Again, a character based on a friend of mine. It was important to me for Mia to be Indian and raised in a culture that contrasts with what I'm familiar with. The real-life Raj is my window into his culture and attitude toward family, love, and religion.

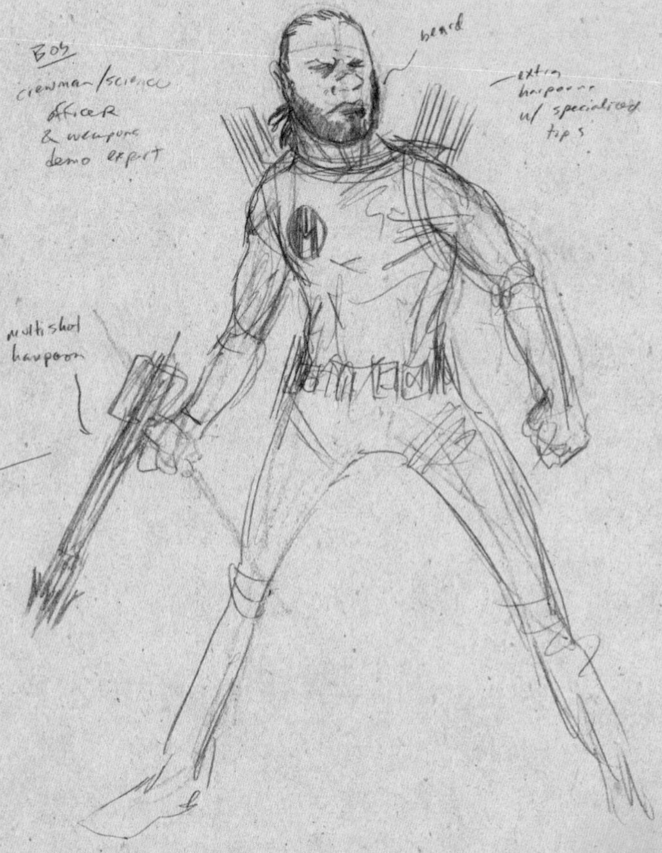
Bob
crewman/science officer
& weapons demo expert
beard
extra harpoons w/ specialized tips
multishot harpoon

BOB

Bob is the weapons and demo specialist. Of course he needs to have a harpoon gun. What else would you carry six miles deep?

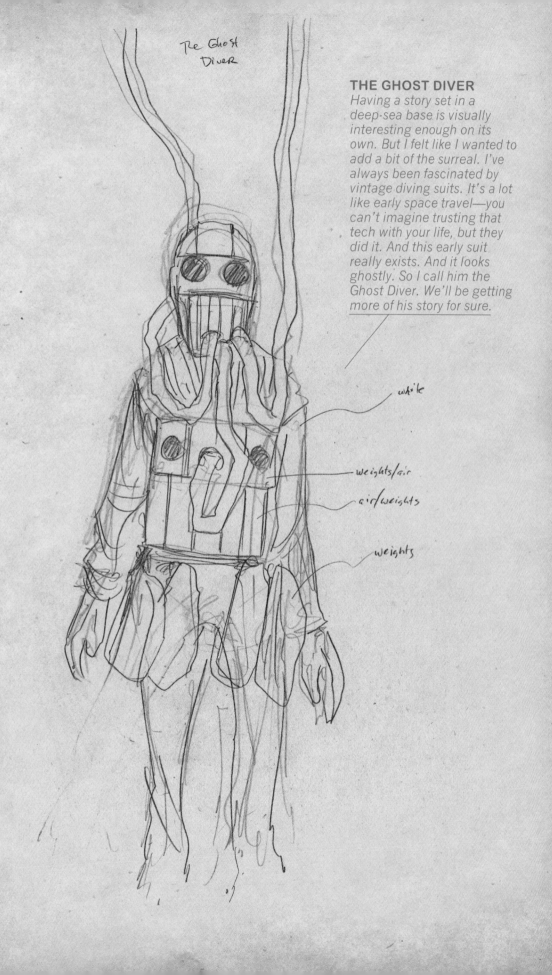

The Ghost
Diver

THE GHOST DIVER
*Having a story set in a
deep-sea base is visually
interesting enough on its
own. But I felt like I wanted to
add a bit of the surreal. I've
always been fascinated by
vintage diving suits. It's a lot
like early space travel—you
can't imagine trusting that
tech with your life, but they
did it. And this early suit
really exists. And it looks
ghostly. So I call him the
Ghost Diver. We'll be getting
more of his story for sure.*

white

weights/air

air/weights

weights

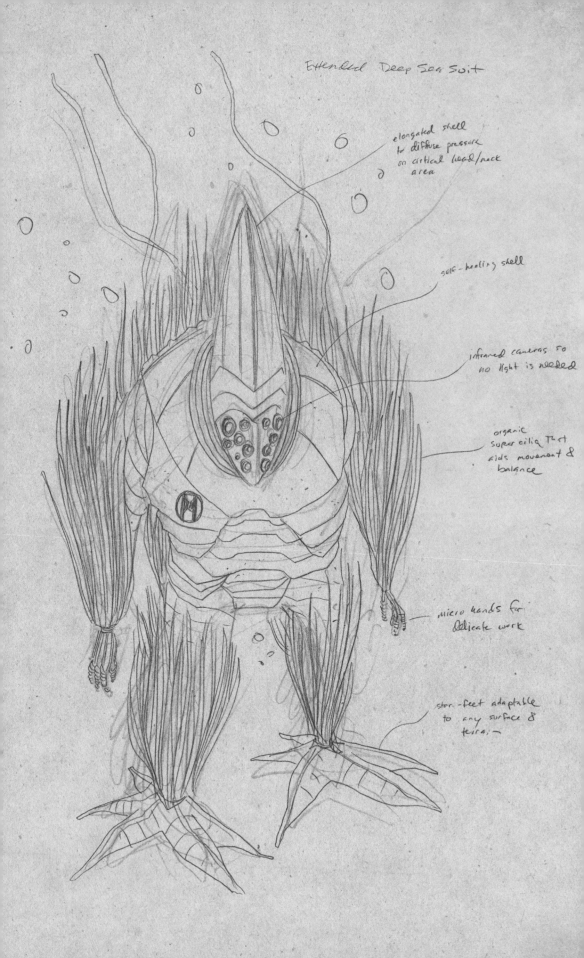

Extended Deep Sea Suit

elongated shell
to diffuse pressure
on critical head/neck
area

self-healing shell

infrared cameras so
no light is needed

organic
super cilia that
aids movement &
balance

micro hands for
delicate work

star-feet adaptable
to any surface &
terrain

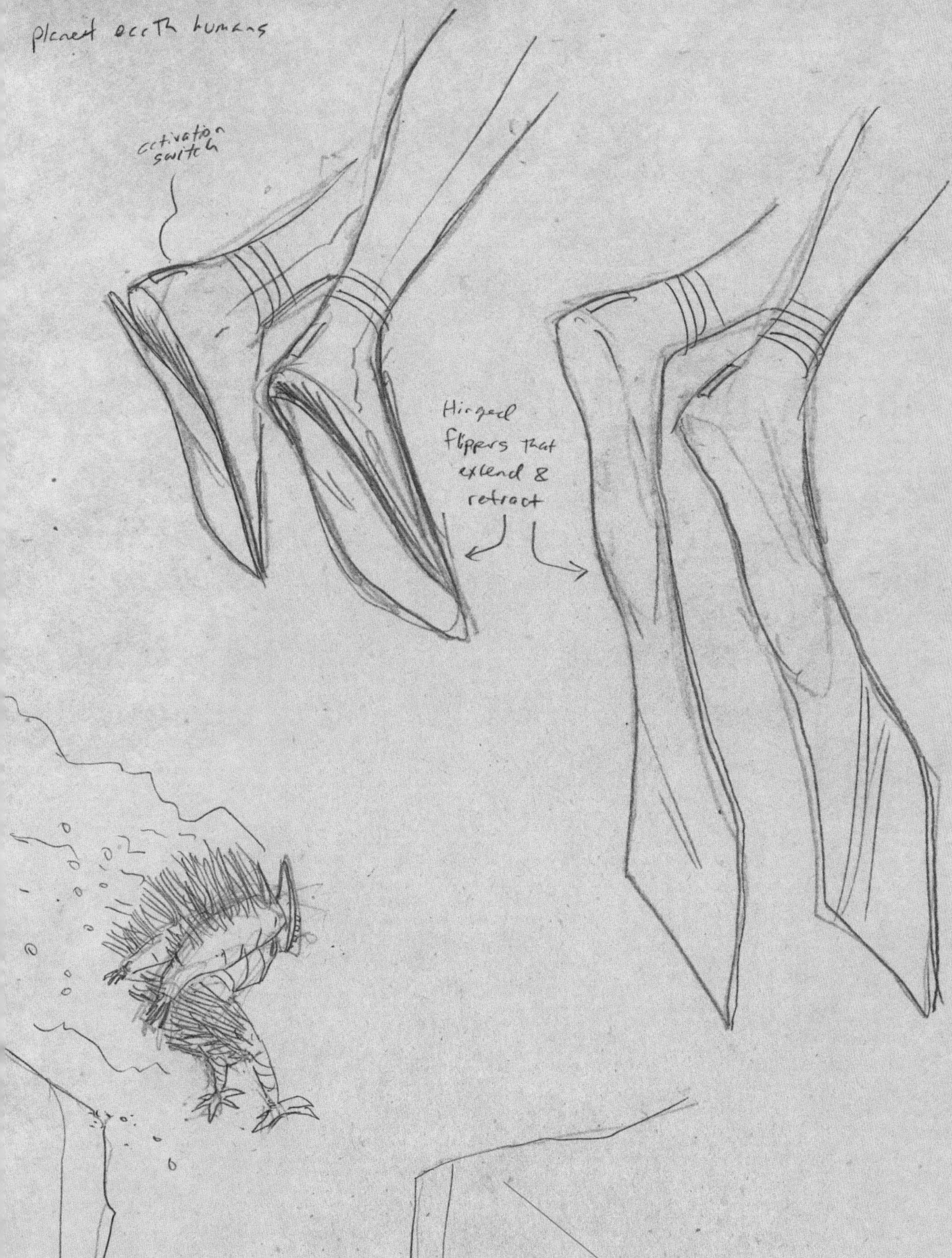

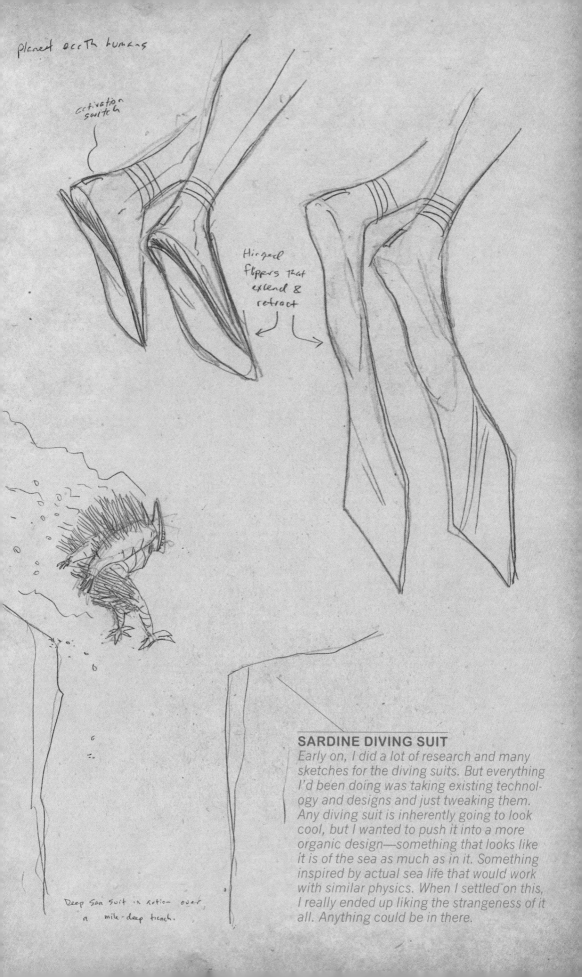

planet earth humans
activation switch
Hinged flippers that extend & retract

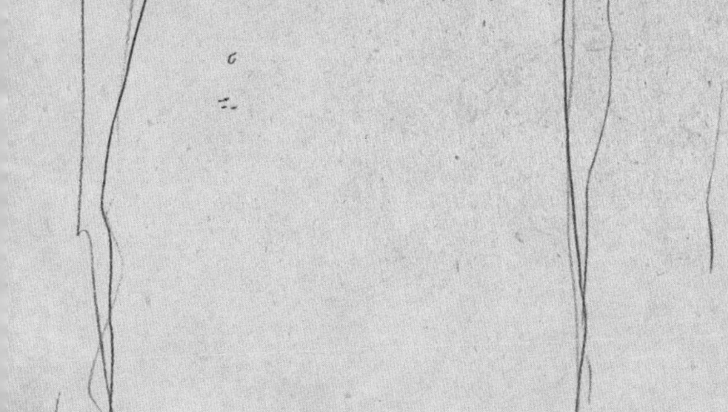

Deep Sea Suit in action over a mile-deep trench.

SARDINE DIVING SUIT

Early on, I did a lot of research and many sketches for the diving suits. But everything I'd been doing was taking existing technology and designs and just tweaking them. Any diving suit is inherently going to look cool, but I wanted to push it into a more organic design—something that looks like it is of the sea as much as in it. Something inspired by actual sea life that would work with similar physics. When I settled on this, I really ended up liking the strangeness of it all. Anything could be in there.

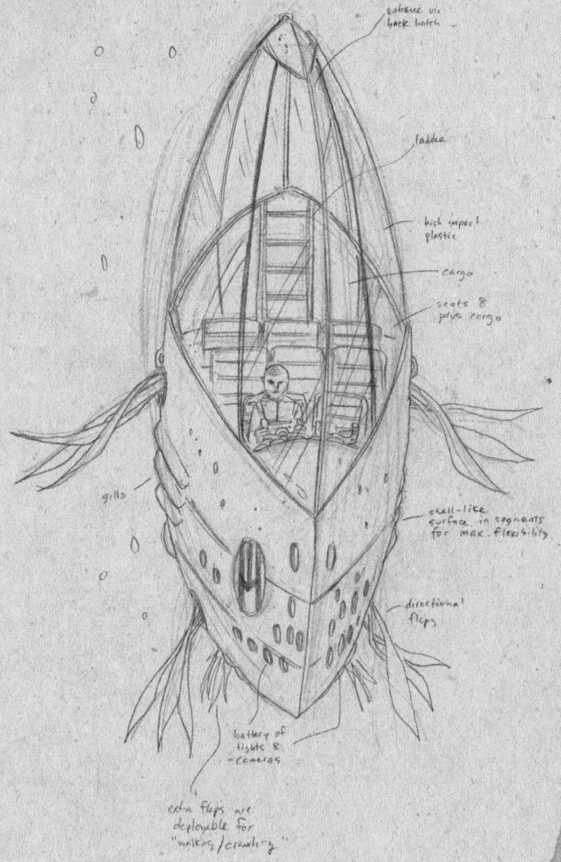
entrance via back hatch
ladder
high impact plastic
cargo
seats 8 plus cargo
gills
shell-like surface in segments for max. flexibility
directional flaps
battery of lights & cameras
extra flaps are deployable for "walking/crawling"

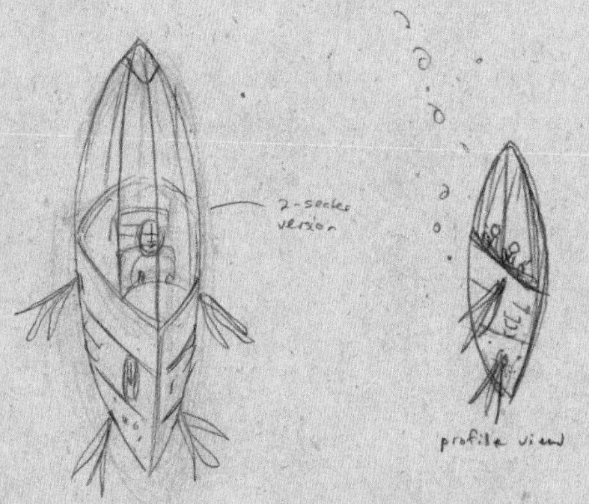
2-seater version
profile view

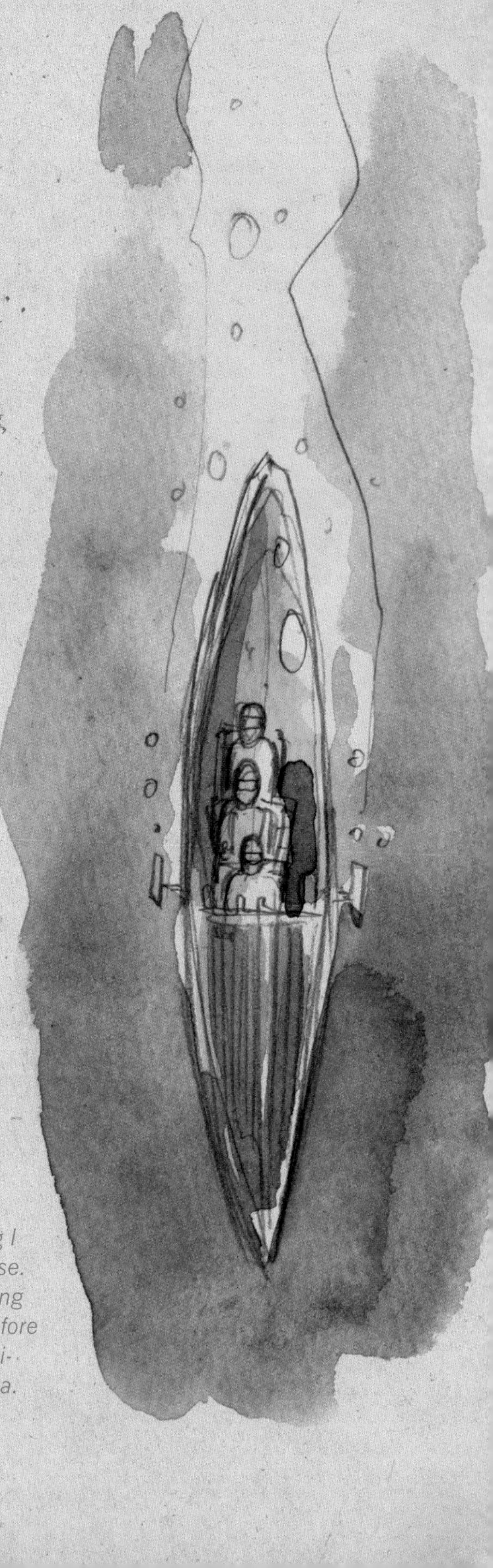

SUBMARINE

The pressure of the deep sea was something I kept trying to get my head around. It's intense. Again, I was trying to come up with something that would contrast with subs we've seen before and also mimic nature. Something thin, vertical, and fish-like seemed like the perfect idea.

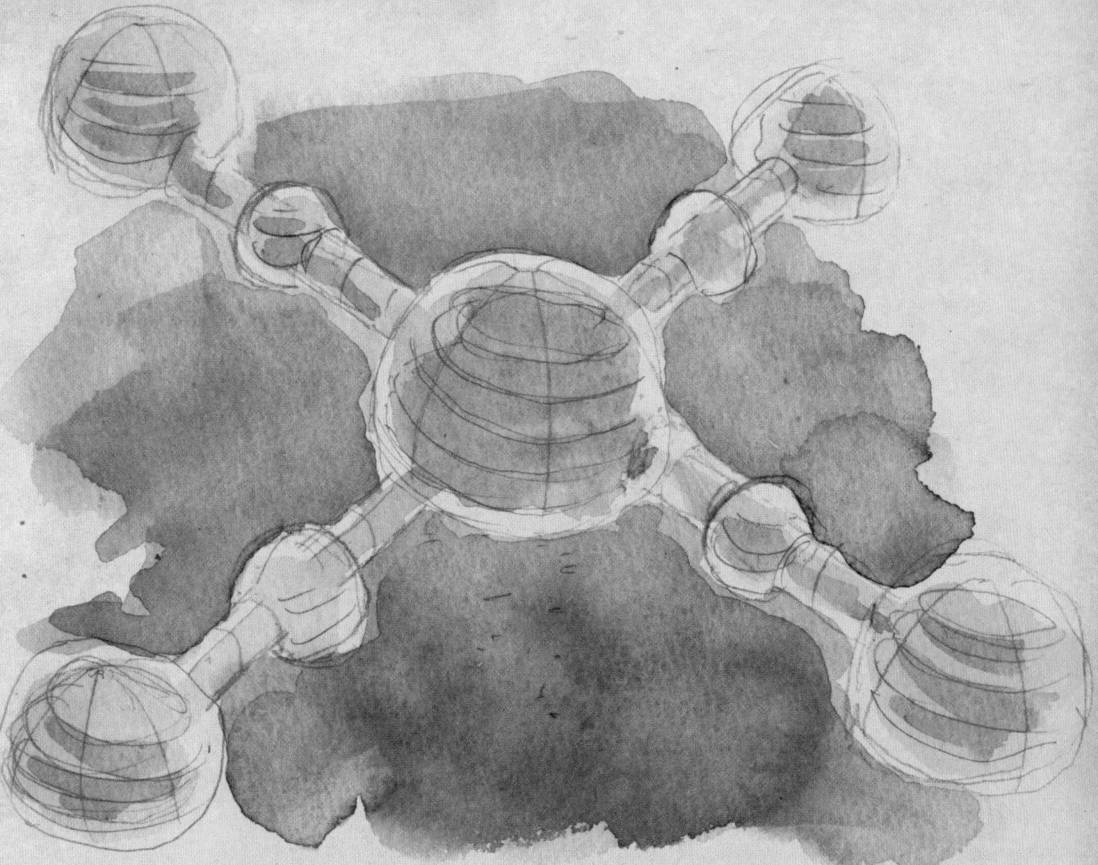

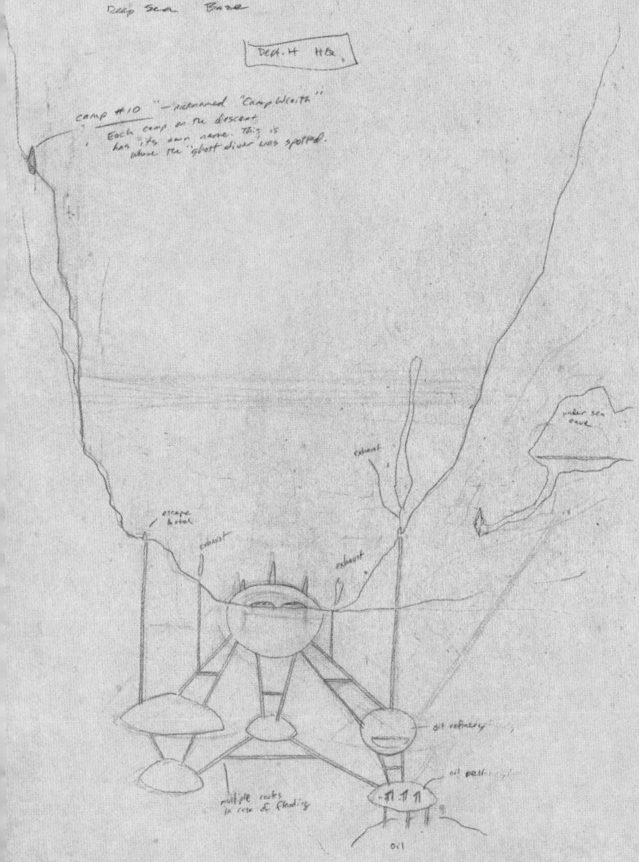
Deep Sea Base
Dept. H HQ
camp #10 "—nicknamed "Camp Wraith"
Each camp on the descent has its own name. This is where the 'ghost diver' was spotted.
under sea cave
exhaust
escape hatch
oil refinery
oil well
multiple rooms in case of flooding
oil

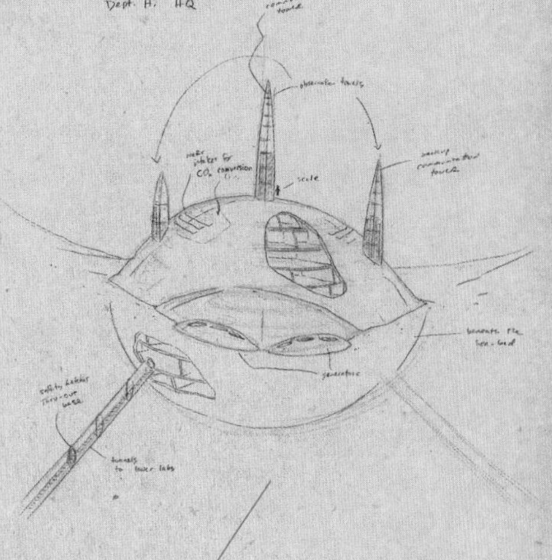
Dept. H HQ
scale

HEADQUARTERS

The scene of the crime. The underwater HQ was critical: it needed to be big enough to allow for different scenes and backgrounds, but also feel claustrophobic. The idea with the HQ is that it's been a work in progress over many years, so it's more of a patchwork. Some of it is old and some of it is new, which gives wide latitude for the visuals I get to draw inside.

CREATURES

Some of the very early concept drawings, from back when I was still trying to figure out how far I was going to push reality in the series. I ended up nixing the alienesque creatures. There are no aliens in this series. Too many films and baggage to go along with that kind of story, and I felt like that would distract from what the story is really about . . . which I won't spell out, but it's *<u>not about aliens.</u>*

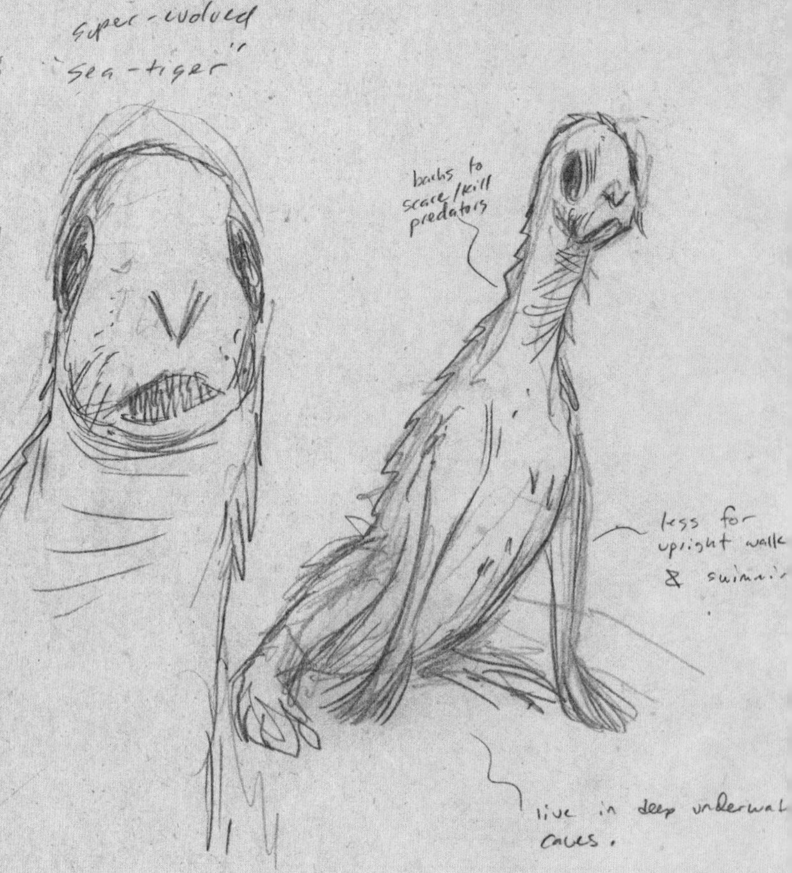

super-evolved
"sea-tiger"
barbs to scare/kill predators
less for upright walk
& swimm
live in deep underwat
caves.

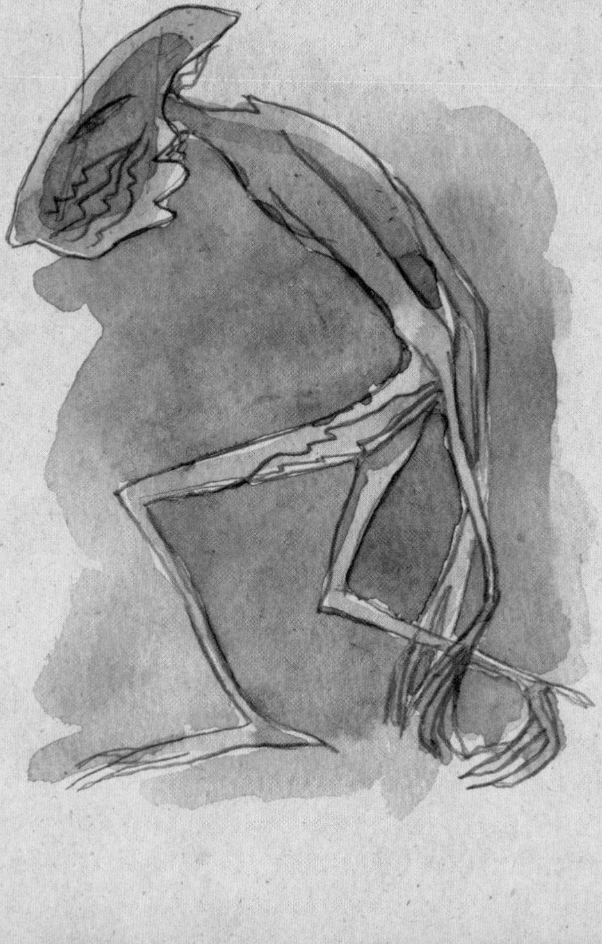

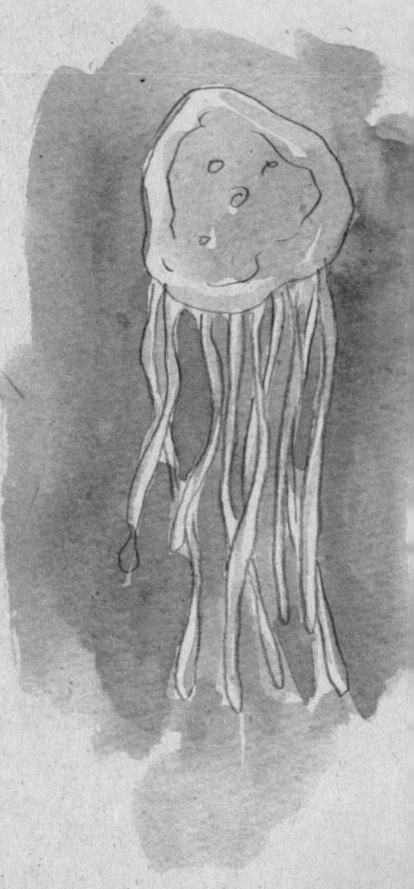

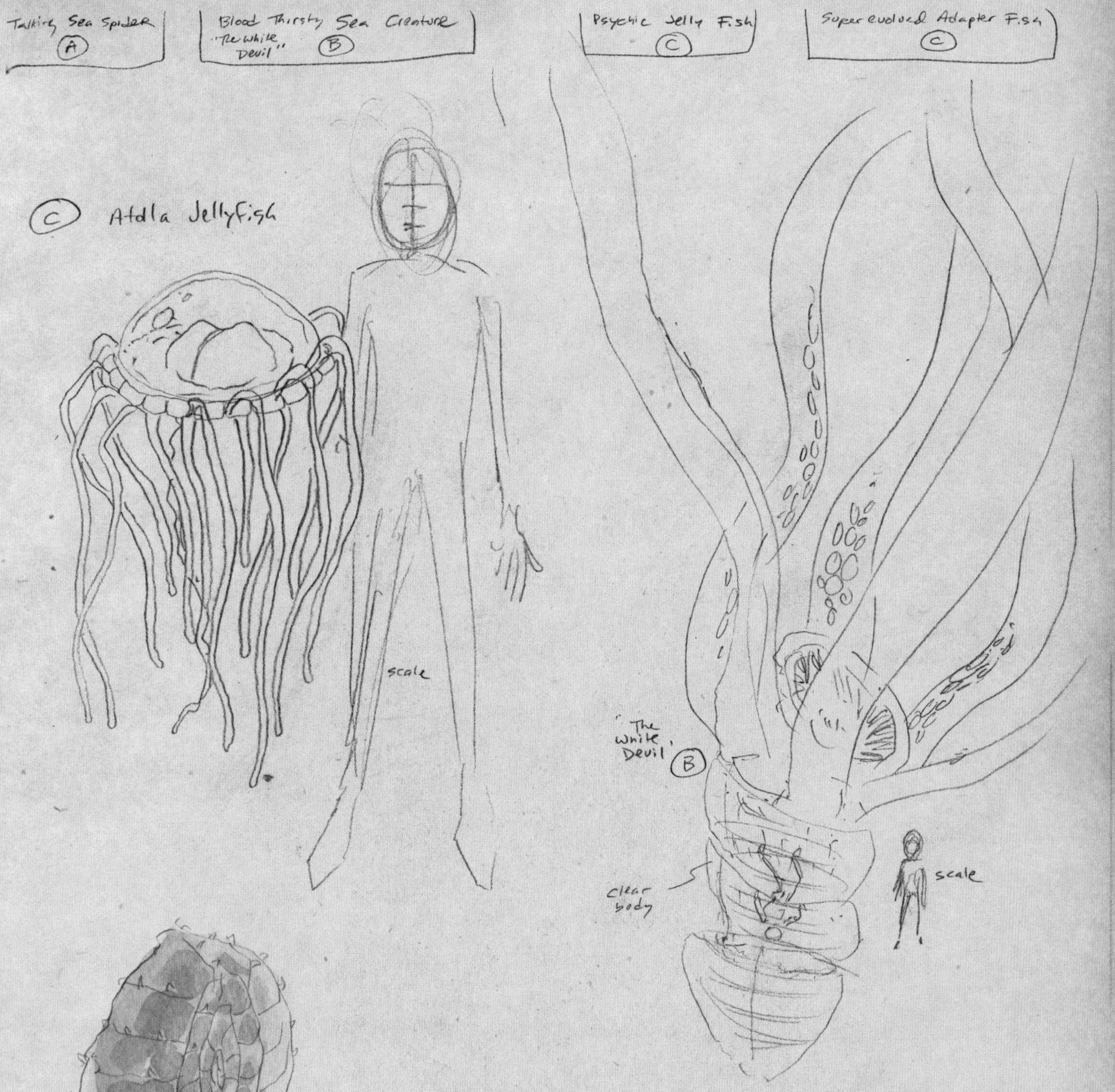
Talking Sea Spider
A
Blood Thirsty Sea Creature
"The White Devil"
B
Psychic Jelly Fish
C
Superevolved Adapter Fish
C
C Atola JellyFish
scale
"The White Devil"
B
clear body
scale

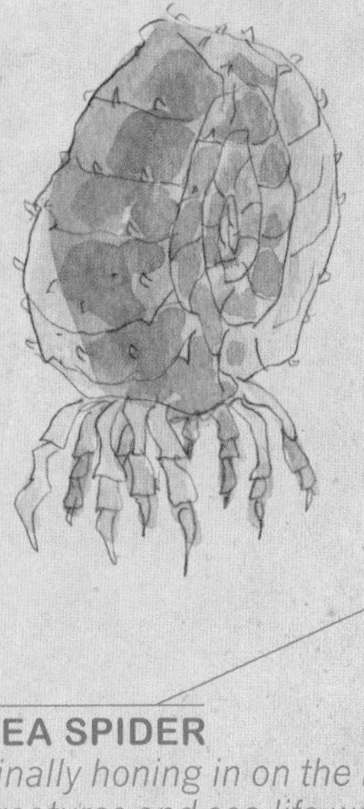

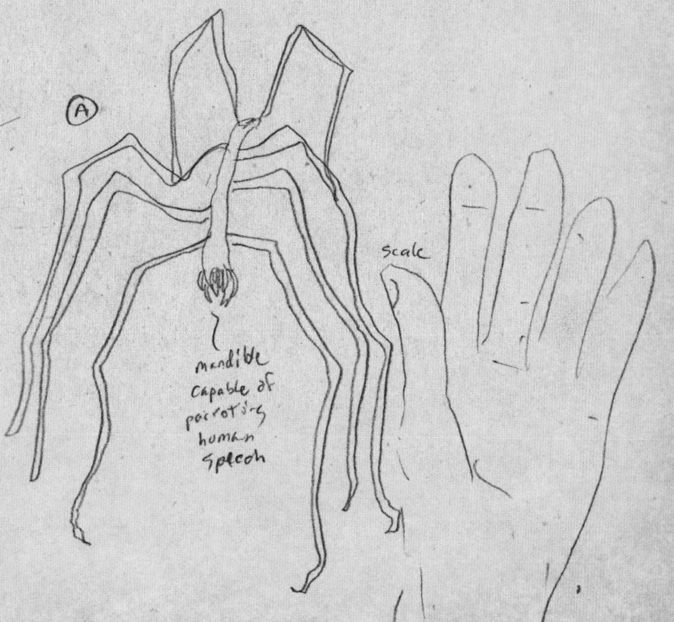
A
scale
mandible capable of parroting human speech

SEA SPIDER

Finally honing in on the kinds of creatures and sea life we will see in the series. The wonder of the unknown and the undiscovered has always been what's intrigued me most about deep-sea exploration. So getting to design what might be possible—what could possibly be found down there—was a lot of fun. Also, in addition to my fear of drowning, I can't stand spiders. So . . . sea spiders!

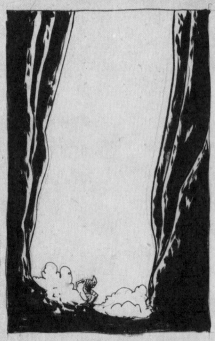

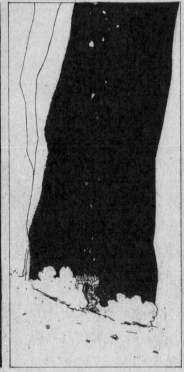

INK TESTS
These are some early ink tests to see how the suit would look, and also studies to figure out how I would approach inking. The inking needs to accommodate Sharlene's watercolors and also provide maximum claustrophobia.

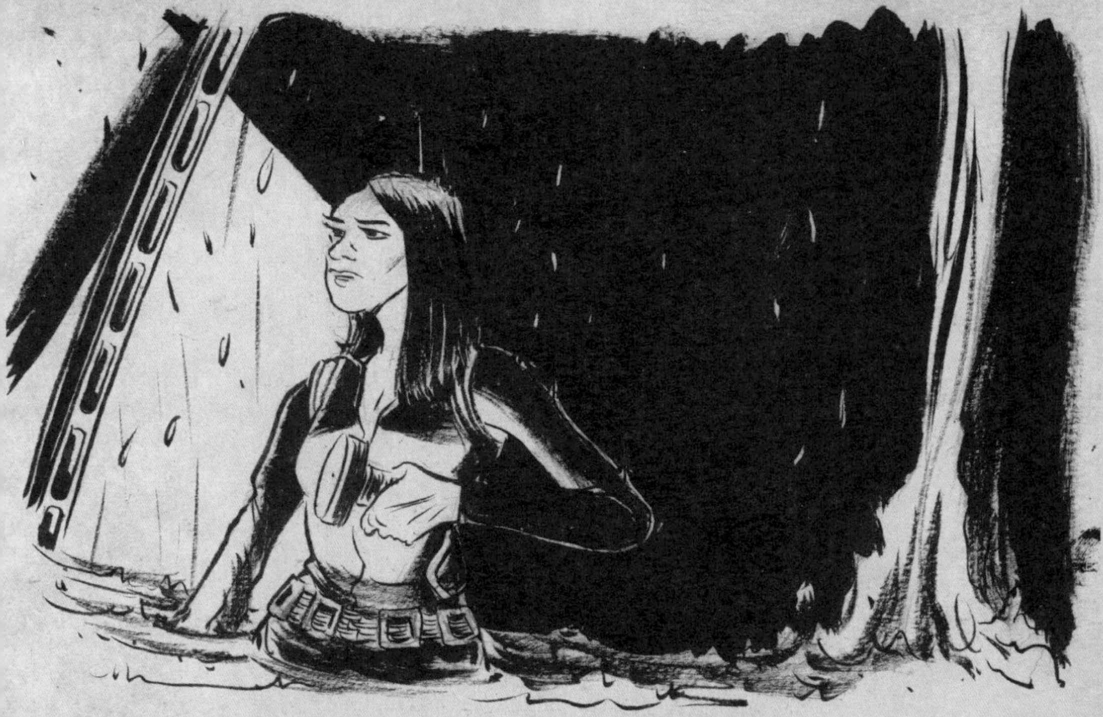

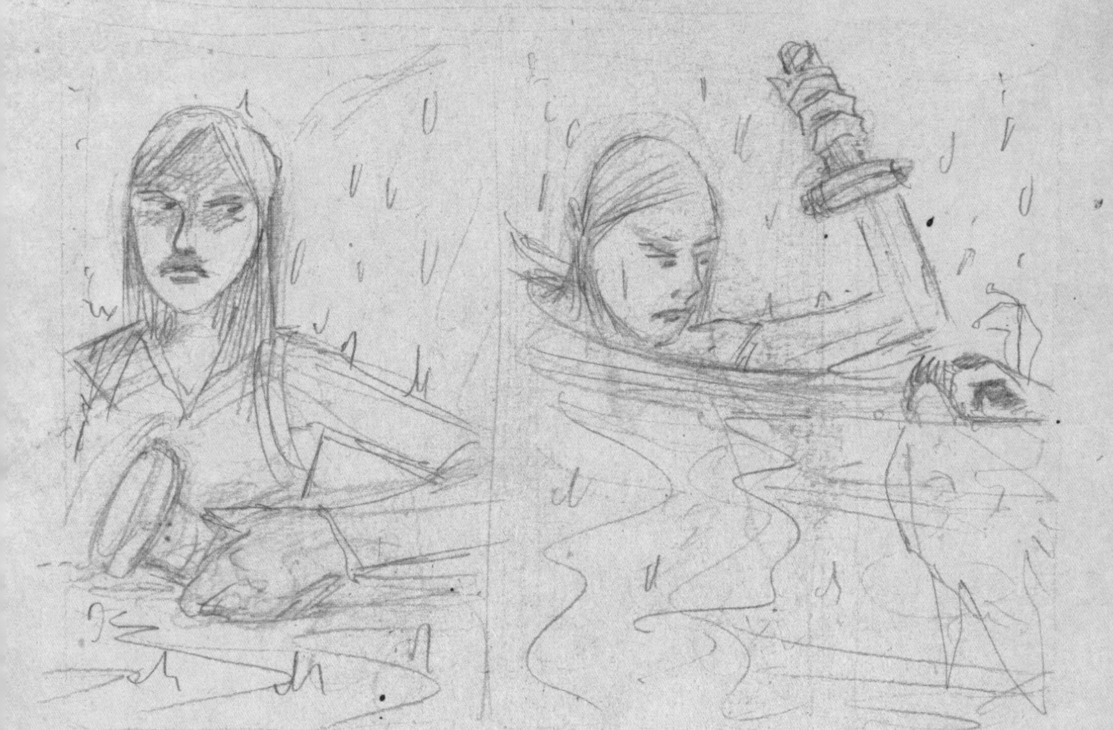

EARLY SKETCHES

I hadn't yet figured out Mia's look. At this point all I knew was she was a woman with longish, dark hair.

STUDY

Another study, trying to figure out the atmosphere, lighting, and space inside the headquarters. And how I was going to treat the tattoos on Q: with ink, Photoshop, or waterproof color ink (which we finally decided on).

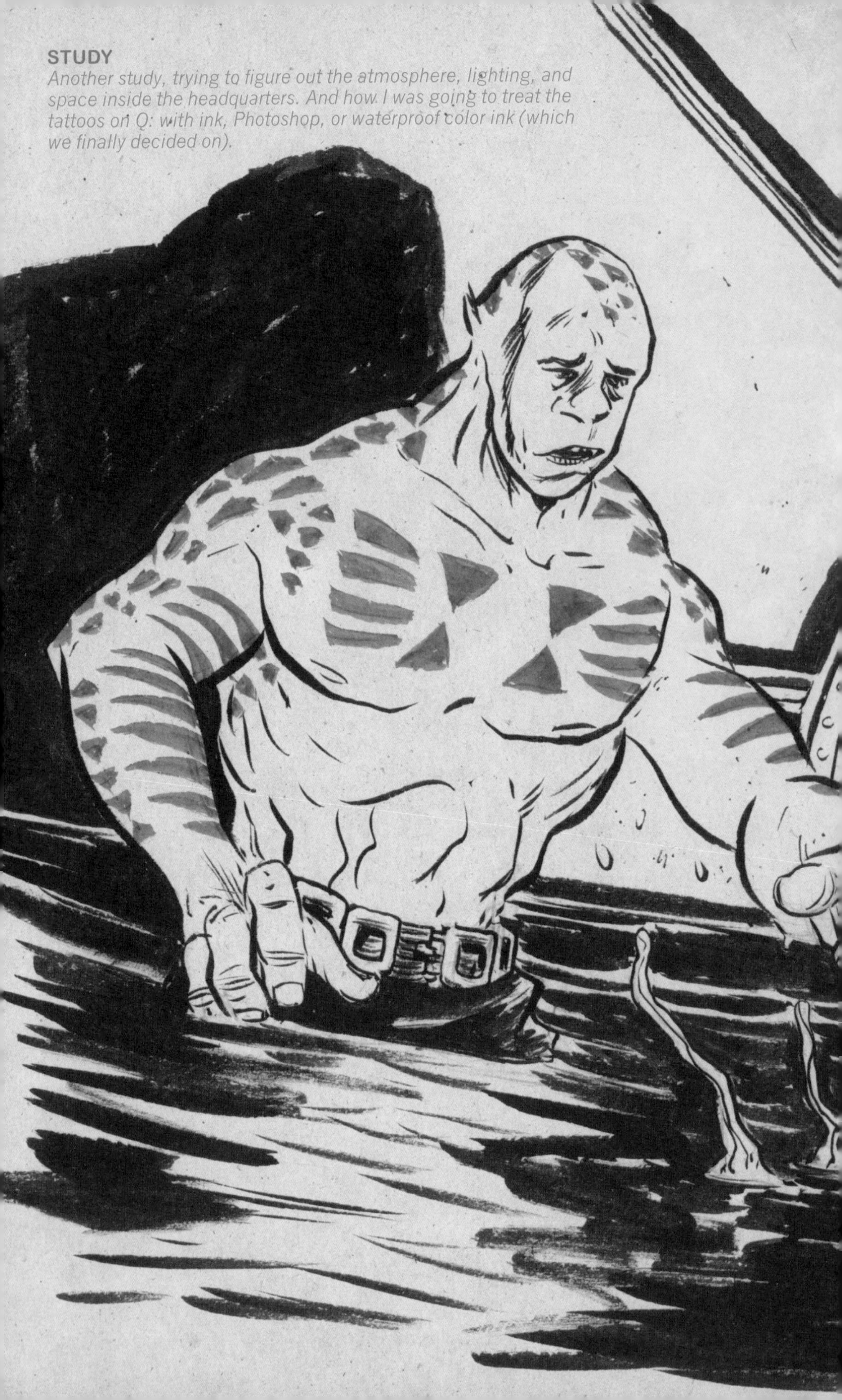

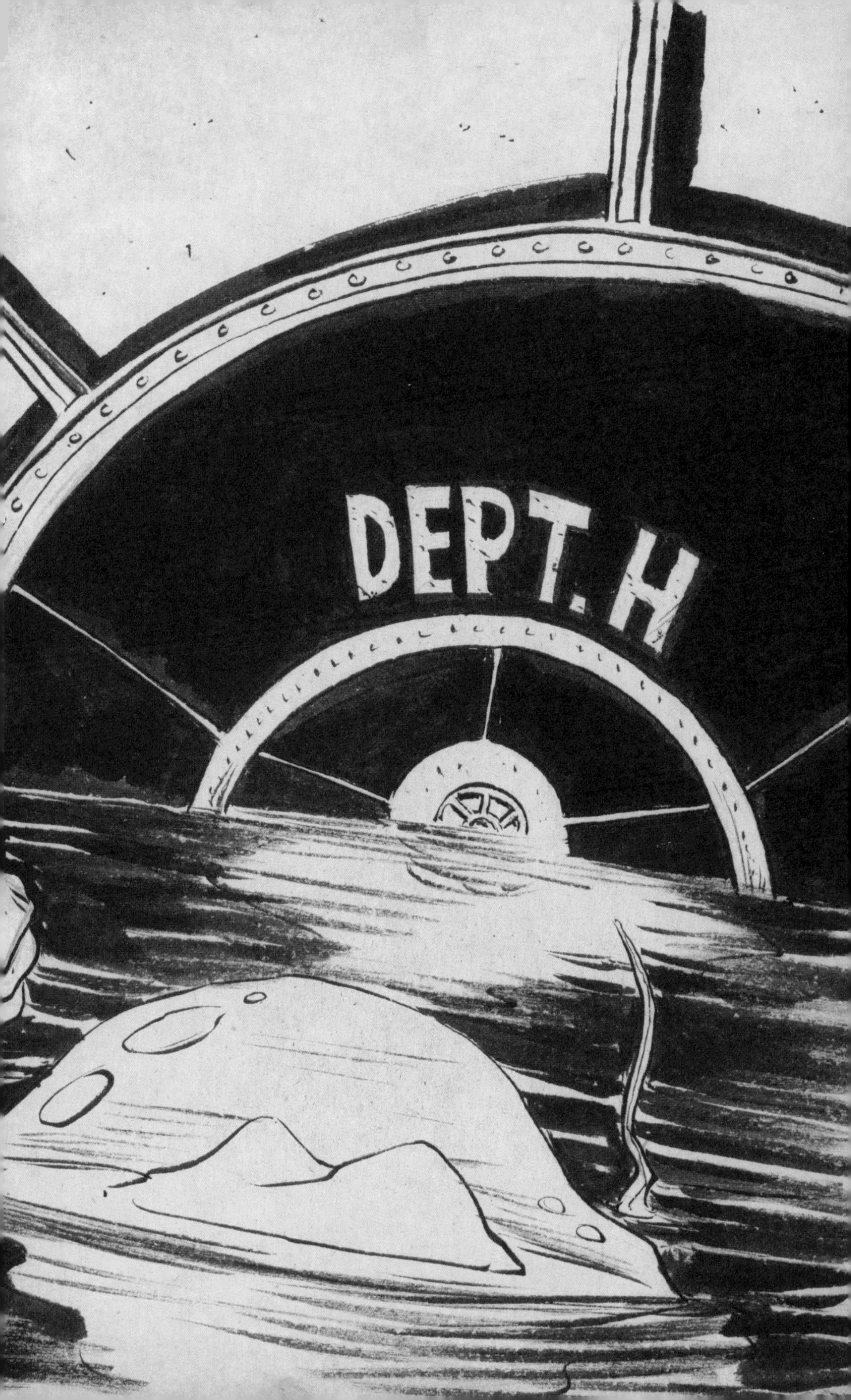
DEPT. H

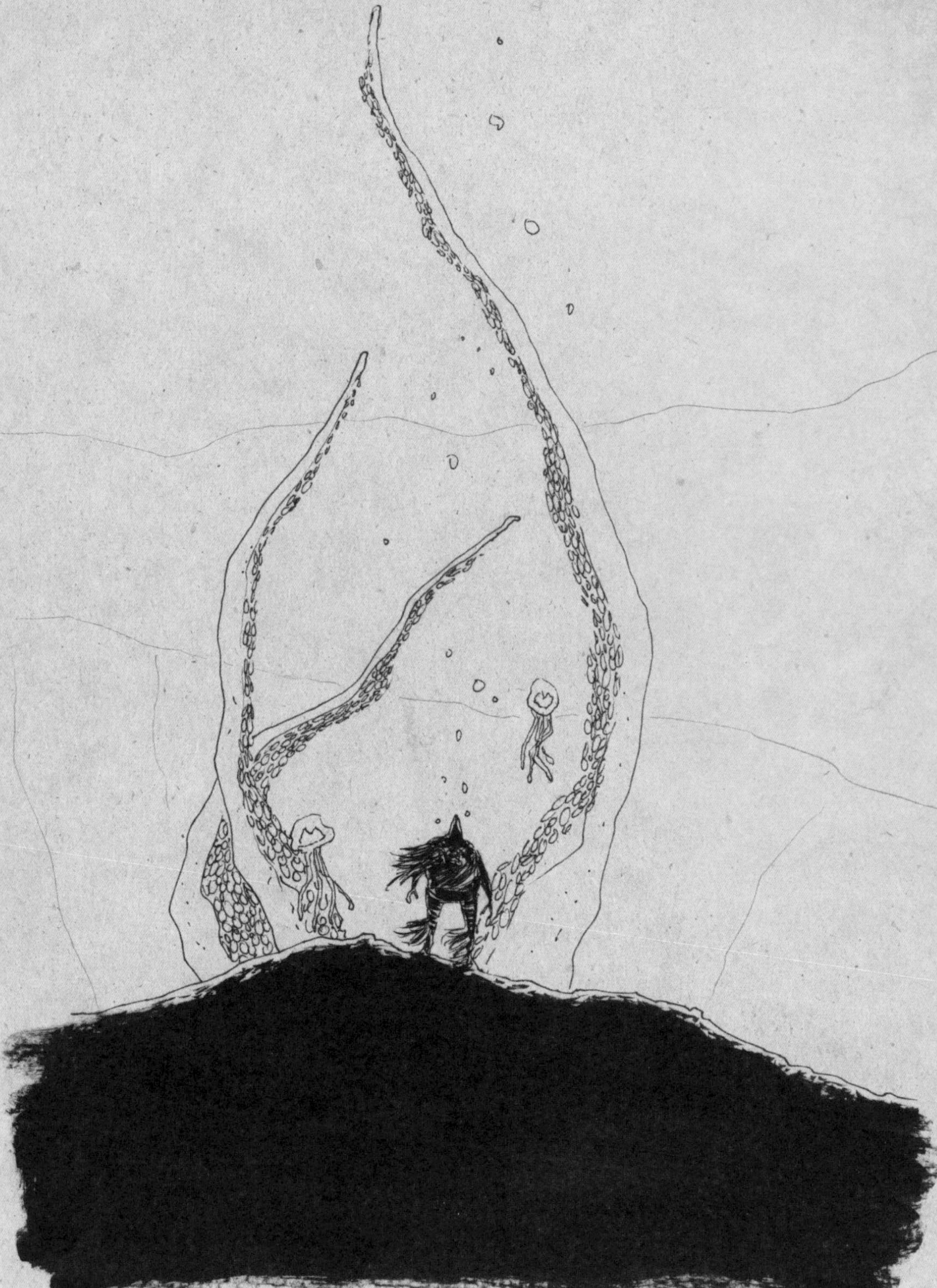

INK TEST
Another study testing inking styles and figuring out a balance between solid blacks and open spaces for watercolor.

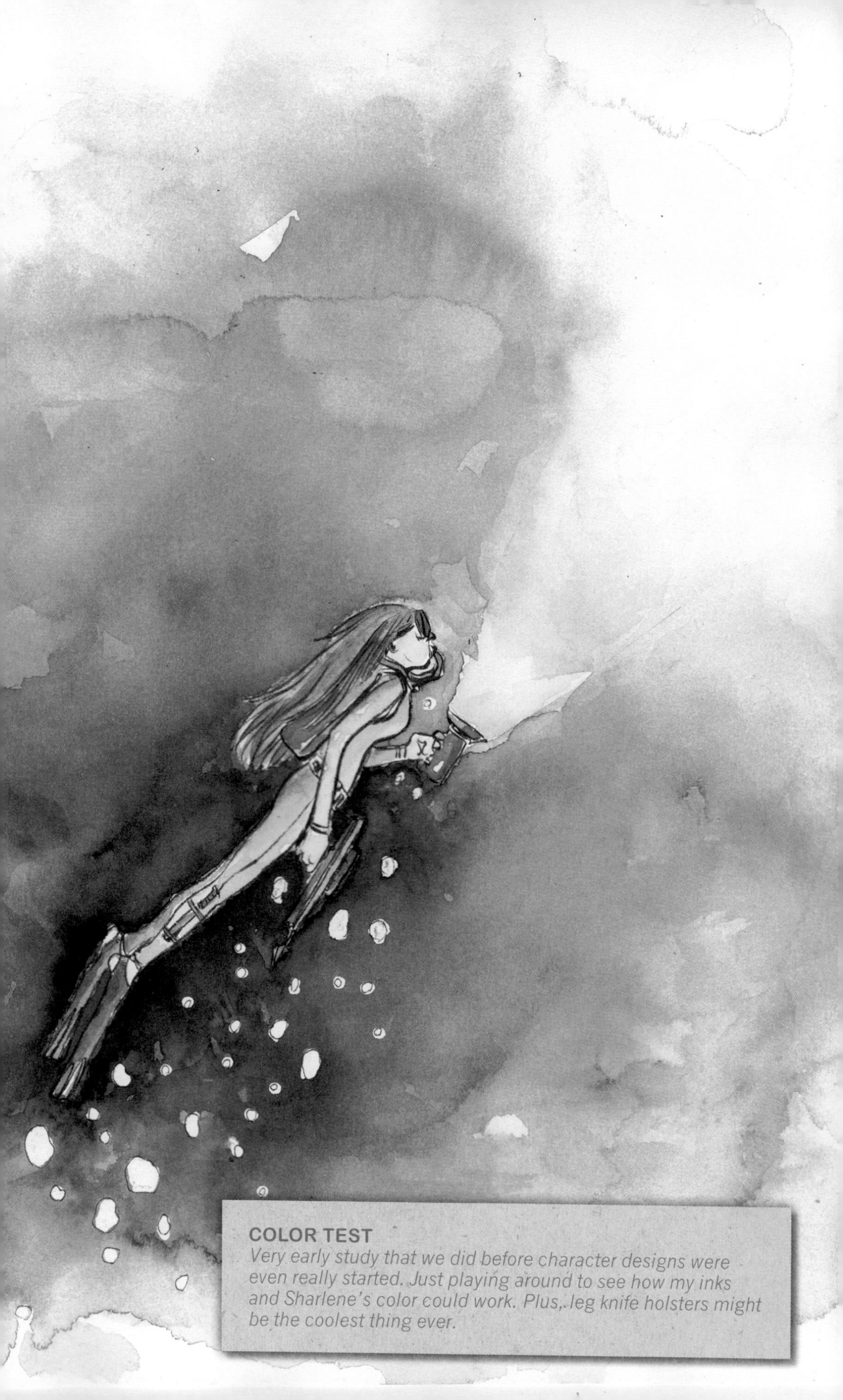

COLOR TEST

Very early study that we did before character designs were even really started. Just playing around to see how my inks and Sharlene's color could work. Plus, leg knife holsters might be the coolest thing ever.

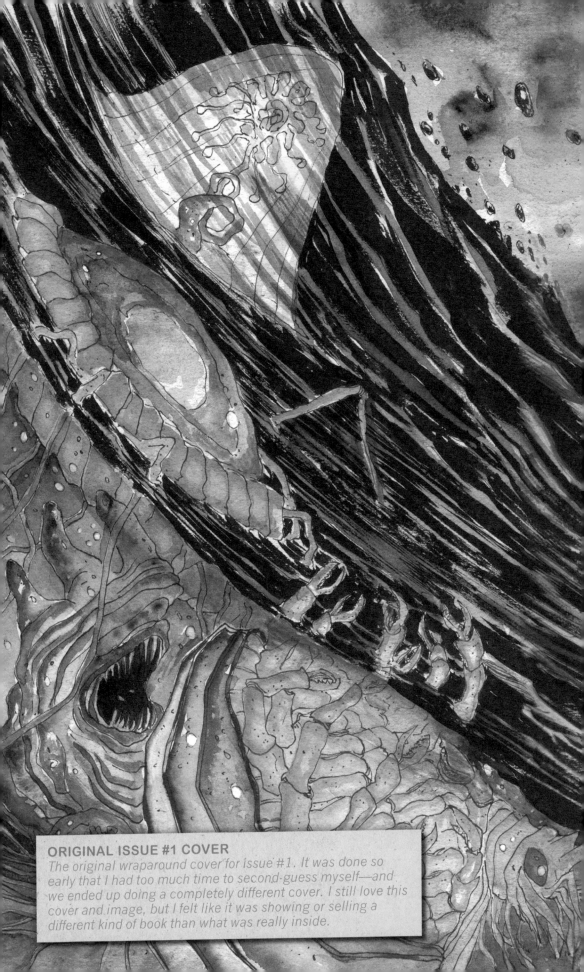

ORIGINAL ISSUE #1 COVER
The original wraparound cover for Issue #1. It was done so early that I had too much time to second-guess myself—and we ended up doing a completely different cover. I still love this cover and image, but I felt like it was showing or selling a different kind of book than what was really inside.

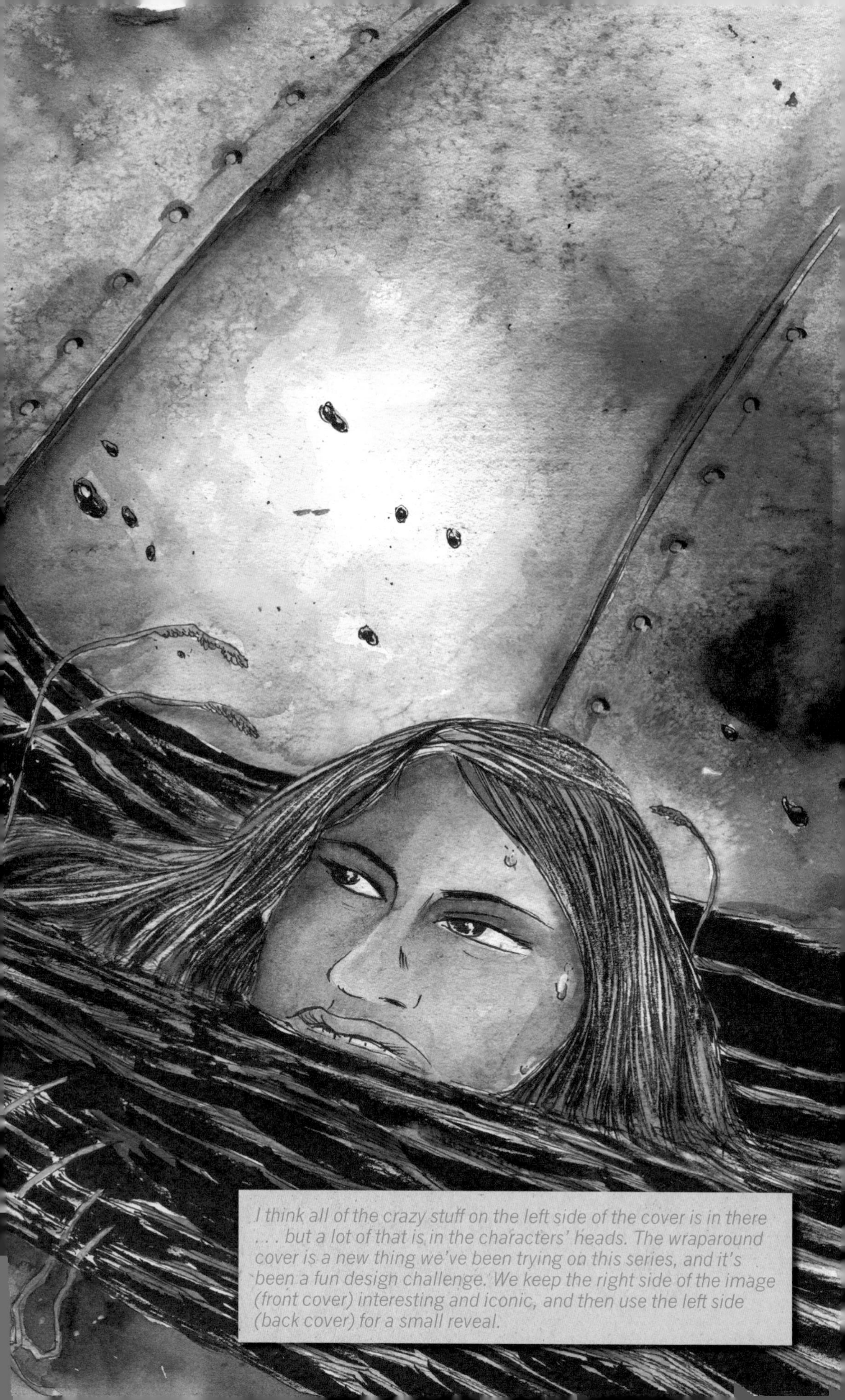

I think all of the crazy stuff on the left side of the cover is in there . . . but a lot of that is in the characters' heads. The wraparound cover is a new thing we've been trying on this series, and it's been a fun design challenge. We keep the right side of the image (front cover) interesting and iconic, and then use the left side (back cover) for a small reveal.

matt kindt

MIND MGMT
VOLUME 1: THE MANAGER
ISBN 978-1-59582-797-5
$19.99
VOLUME 2: THE FUTURIST
ISBN 978-1-61655-198-8
$19.99
VOLUME 3: THE HOME MAKER
ISBN 978-1-61655-390-6
$19.99
VOLUME 4: THE MAGICIAN
ISBN 978-1-61655-391-3
$19.99
VOLUME 5: THE ERASER
ISBN 978-1-61655-696-9
$19.99
VOLUME 6: THE IMMORTALS
ISBN 978-1-61655-798-0
$19.99

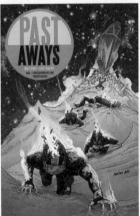

POPPY! AND THE LOST LAGOON
With Brian Hurtt
ISBN 978-1-61655-943-4
$14.99

PAST AWAYS
With Scott Kolins
ISBN 978-1-61655-792-8
$12.99

THE COMPLETE PISTOLWHIP
With Jason Hall
ISBN 978-1-61655-720-1
$27.99

3 STORY: THE SECRET HISTORY OF THE GIANT MAN
ISBN 978-1-59582-356-4
$19.99

2 SISTERS
ISBN 978-1-61655-721-8
$27.99

DEPT. H VOLUME 1: PRESSURE
ISBN 978-1-61655-989-2
$19.99